OTTO RAHN AND THE QUEST FOR THE HOLY GRAIL

The Amazing Life of the Real "Indiana Jones"

Nigel Graddon

Other Books Of Interest:

THE HISTORY OF THE KNIGHTS TEMPLARS
PIRATES & THE LOST TEMPLAR FLEET
GUARDIANS OF THE HOLY GRAIL
THE STONE PUZZLE OF ROSSLYN CHAPEL
THE TEMPLARS LEGACY IN MONTREAL
MARY MAGDALENE: THE ILLUMINATOR
NOSTRADAMUS & THE LOST TEMPLAR LEGACY

OTTO RAHN AND THE QUEST FOR THE HOLY GRAIL

Adventures Unlimited Press

Otto Rahn and the Quest for the Holy Grail

ISBN 13: 978-1-931882-82-8

Published by:
Adventures Unlimited Press
One Adventure Place
Kempton, Illinois 60946 USA
auphq@frontiernet.net

www.adventuresunlimitedpress.com

OTTO RAHN AND THE QUEST FOR THE HOLY GRAIL

The Amazing Life of the Real "Indiana Jones"

"It is a heretic that makes the fire,
Not she which burns in't."

William Shakespeare
The Winters Tale

CONTENTS

IN MEMORIAM

This book is dedicated to the memory of sister and brother, Sophia and Hans Scholl, and to all their brave companions in the White Rose movement who gave their lives in passive resistance against the tyranny of National Socialism.

Otto Rahn in the "cathedral" of Lombrives (Archives Stock)

Acknowledgements

Over the years I have received encouragement from many people in the preparation and writing of this present work. In particular, I would like to thank Gary and Doc Nelson for their unstinting support.

Jonothon Boulter needs a hearty thank you. Jonothon has always believed in the importance of getting the Rahn story out into the English speaking world and his own contribution to the research, epecially on the early days of National Socialism, has been warmly welcomed.

I must thank both the Rennes group and the Saunière Society for the opportunities to write articles and to make presentations on Rahn and associated subjects. These allowed me to advance my understanding of, and insights into, the complex character of Otto Rahn, which contributed in no small measure to the evolution and formulation of this book.

I give special thanks to Peter Boyce and Roy Dart for their continual support over the years. It was Peter who funded the trip to Lake Constance in 1999 for the interview with Frau Gabriele Winckler-Dechend, a close friend of Otto Rahn's and a favourite of Heinrich Himmler, a man she called "Uncle."

In Stuart Russell, our "man on the ground" in Germany, we found a real pal whose help was invaluable in securing contacts and interviews. Moreover, as a first rate historian in his own right Stuart was a rich source on Rahn and his times and for this I was most grateful. I was very sorry to hear recently that Stuart, still in relative middle age, passed away only two or three years ago.

I give warm thanks to Marcus Williamson for his sterling efforts in proofreading earlier drafts and for his common sense insights, which have made the book a better read.

Gabi Veith did a fantastic job in translating source material into English and for that I cannot thank her enough. I am also very grateful for Jan Beutler's help; life would have been so much harder in its absence.

Lastly, and by no means least, I would like to thank Hans-Jürgen Lange for passing me the Rahn baton for an English speaking audience and to his publisher Arun Verlag for their good wishes. I also thank them for permission to reproduce the photographs that illustrated Lange's two books on Rahn.

Sketch portrait of Otto Rahn made in 1937 by Frau Hartmann (née Götz) around the time of her wedding, which Rahn attended. University archive Gießen, by permission of Hans-Jürgen Lange and Arun Verlag.

Preface

Otto Wilhelm Rahn was the young philology graduate who explored the grottoes of the French Pyrenees in the early nineteen thirties in search of the Holy Grail. Rahn was convinced that his researches had provided sufficient clues to pinpoint the Languedoc as the long sought hiding place of the fabulous Treasures of the Temple of Solomon. In his lifetime, Rahn never once indicated that his motivation to undertake this quest was anything other than to satisfy his own hunger to crack a puzzle that had beaten a host of treasure seekers in preceding centuries.

Nevertheless, there remains a considerable suspicion that Otto Rahn was directed in his activities by the highest figures at the helm of the German Reich, notably Heinrich Himmler who spared neither expense nor effort before and during the war in seeking talismans of power by which he could strengthen his position in the Nazi high command. Many believe that Rahn either found something of enormous value in the caves of the Sabarthès or he identified enough clues such that it was a relatively simple task for Himmler's men to later follow the trail and unearth the cache. But the slightly built son of Michelstadt did not make any such claims during his short life.

It has been an immense frustration for me that the major works to date on the life and work of Otto Rahn have, unsurprisingly, been written and published in languages other than English. The principle authors are Hans-Jürgen Lange and Christian Bernadac.

Lange has done an excellent job in locating a great deal of valuable archive material and he has enhanced the biographical value of his work by interviewing a number of Rahn's contemporaries. The result of his labours is that the details of the day-to-day personal and professional lives of Otto Rahn have become much more accessible.

Where Lange is less accommodating, nonetheless, is in offering any insights into the creative and metaphysical wellspring that nourished Rahn's work. It is evident from even a cursory reading of Rahn's written legacy that the Hessian scholar had an immense grasp of European esoteric and romantic history. His works contain innumerable sub-texts which, to be appreciated and interpreted, require the discerning reader to take pick and shovel to the material just as Rahn did in searching for treasures in the Pyrenean grottoes. Consequently, I believe that the real prize is to be gained from exploring the abstract in Rahn's life as distinct from the physical tread of the footprints he left in the caves of the Languedoc, the forests around Muggenbrunn and the streets of Berlin.

Hans-Jürgen Lange is to be praised for his workmanlike and tireless efficiency in laying bare the visible world of Otto Rahn but one searches the bookshelves and libraries of Europe and beyond in vain for anything that delves any deeper.

French author Christian Bernadac does at least attempt to scratch the surface, examining for instance the alleged relationship between Rahn and the mysterious sect known as the Polaires whose members were as equally vigorous as Rahn in excavating the Pyrenean caves in search of ancient secrets. But even so, the reader hopeful of obtaining insights into the vast range of Rahn's learning and any clues as to his real agenda comes away unsatisfied and wanting more.

I am not an academic in the classic sense and so I am not constrained by the paradigms and conventions which, oftentimes, result in biographies long on information but short on passion, insight and an uninhibited freedom to explore all dimensions of experience: rational and irrational. In my philosophy both worlds are equally valid and the synchronicities that make a pathway between them can only be wholly explored if one does not mind taking a pratfall from time to time. The landing may not be soft but oftentimes the tumble reveals a fissure in the hillside leading to genuine and fantastic discoveries.

I know that there are many who will welcome the publication of an English language treatment of Otto Rahn and I can only trust that this present work meets in some small measure their demands and expectations. For those among my readership drawn to this book out of curiosity or by chance, my hope is that they will derive at least some measure of enjoyment from reading of the life and times of one of the most fascinating but least understood personalities of the twentieth century.

In 2004 Hans-Jürgen Lange responded to a letter of mine in which I had sought permission to quote extracts from his works on Rahn and to reproduce the associated photographs. His response took me aback. Lange confessed that he was "really tired by Rahn," especially after the 2003 publication of two new books: Monika Hauf's *Wege zum Heiligen Gral*[1] and Michael Hesemann's *Die Entdeckung des Heiligen Grals*.[2] He did not explain why these particular books had

[1] published Langen/Müller
[2] published Pattloch; Auflage: 1

contributed to his Rahn fatigue but he concluded his email by stating that: "my research is come to an end…the rest is up too you…an English spoken man find something new [*sic*]." I am very grateful for Lange's endorsement.

Moreover, I do honestly believe that in this present work I offer new insights about the life of Otto Rahn in the context of pre-WW2 Germany and of the wider canvas of European realpolitik and esoteric belief.

Introduction

Over the years a tremendous amount of heat has been generated by the quest for meaning into Otto Rahn's life but barely enough light to cast the meanest glow into the Grail caverns he explored. But why?

Otto Rahn's name has become synonomous with the search for one of humankind's most enduring and precious artefacts: the Grail Cup from which Jesus and his disciples shared wine at the Last Supper. But why should this have marked Rahn out in history when he is only one of so many during the Chistian era who have devoted time and resources, some entire lifetimes, to this undertaking?

Rahn's brief life is full of mystery but, despite the holes in the facts, persistent rumours abound that the young explorer and philologist found the Grail treasures in the Languedoc in the early 1930s and gave them to the Nazi cabal. Science fiction? Or one of the most incredible episodes of the twentieth century, perhaps of the Christian era?

Although Rahn is still largely unknown mention of the writer and adventurer has been steadily increasing in recent articles, books and film documentaries examining the common theme of Hitler's search for the Grail. Irrespective of the conclusions reached by these claims, they all stress the enormous lengths to which the Nazi elite strove to secure legendary artefacts such as the Ark of the Covenant, the Spear of Destiny and the Grail chalice. In pursuing these efforts, Angebert[1] claimed that Hitler's cohorts spent more money than invested by the allies in developing the atom bomb, and co-opted the brightest minds to lead the search.

Otto Rahn's star shone the most brightly in that firmament of talent. At the age of twenty seven he made his first exploratory trip to France, already convinced from his researches into medieval texts that the Grail was buried in the grottoes of Lombrives in the French Pyrenees. Students of Rahn's life tend to the view that he was unknown to the Nazi leadership until 1934 when Gabriele Dechend (now Gabriele Winckler-Dechend), surrogate "daughter" to Karl Maria Weisthor (Himmler's "Rasputin"), read Rahn's first published book *Kreuzzug gegen den Gral.*[2] Enthralled, Gabriele immediately informed Weisthor who, in turn, excitedly told Himmler. The approach from on

---

[1] Angebert, Jean-Michel. *The Occult and the Third Reich,* MacGraw-Hill, 1975

[2] Freiburg i/Breisgau: Urban Verlag, 1933

high was quickly made and Rahn's destiny was set in stone. Personally, I am not convinced that the link was made so late. There are elements in the description of Rahn's activities from 1930 onwards that suggest an earlier relationship between the scholar and the high command of the Nationalsozialistische Deutsche Arbeiterpartei (NSDAP). But facts on the surface invariably hide numerous twisting pathways to their arrival and Otto Rahn's contribution to the Nazi cause is steeped in mystery.

The “first division” researchers and authorities on Rahn, principle among them Hans-Jürgen Lange, author of two excellent German language books on Rahn, are unanimous in their belief that Otto Rahn died, in all probability by his own hand, in March 1939. I declare right now that I have a good deal of difficulty in accepting this popular wisdom for inviolable fact due to the large number of conflicting accounts of Rahn’s demise put forward by friends and other contemporary observers. This belief is not universally shared. Nevertheless, I am not especially uncomfortable with this position, being an ardent advocate of the Groucho Marx School of Philosophy whose famous dictum warns that we should be ever wary of joining a club that would accept us as a member.

The question remains: if Otto Rahn was truly the ultimate treasure seeker and succeeded where so many others before him had failed, then why have many more of us not heard of him? However, the paradox is that we do know Rahn, and by this I am referring to tens of millions of movie fans who since 1980 have thrilled to the daring-do exploits of Indiana Jones in three massively successful movies with a fourth instalment, *Indiana Jones and the Kingdom of the Crystal Skull*, in production. But before delving into this fascinating link we need to ask a more fundamental question. How does knowledge of Otto Wilhelm Rahn come to a person and, once encountered, lead us by the tiny light of a caver’s carbide lamp into who knows where?

In my case I have to go back to a time in my early childhood. The details are very hazy. I suppose I must have been around six or seven years of age. I recall one night after I had gone to bed and I was dreaming or imagining a scene that might have derived from a comic book, although how a six year old boy in 1950s suburban Birmingham might have come across a horrific piece of pulp literature is a mystery that will never be solved. In my "dream" I saw men dressed in SS uniform. They were standing around or over what looked like an operating table. I cannot recall if anyone was on the table but if the evil grins upon the men's faces were anything to go by they were enjoying some poor soul's misfortune.

Looking back, I also have the feeling that maybe the SS men were not quite human; that maybe they were humanoid, creatures fashioned from something awful and unworldly, something that had "come in" from a place beyond our experience. I also had the eerie feeling that they knew I was observing them. The dream stamped my imaginings, and every once in a while throughout the growing years I would recall the incident as if it steered me to a pathway to which I was bound. When I read the startling research conclusions of Bruce Rux on the countless instances of aggressive humanoid activities in his brilliant 1999 book *Architects of the Underworld,*[3] I understood for the first time that the experience had perhaps been a sentient insight into real and terrible events.

In the sixties and seventies I read voraciously on every conceivable topic in the religio-philosophic sense: from Sufism to Taoism, from Merlin to McLuhan. I could not get enough of all that rich seam of information for which we have to spend that extra effort to dig out and to assimilate. Perhaps I was appreciating at an early age that what matters in life is the journey, not the arriving. I believe that Otto Rahn lived by the same quixotic principle, understanding that our beginnings and our endings are inevitable; that what takes place in-between distinguishes a life of joy and adventure from one of drudge and boredom.

I had the good fortune in 1977 to meet and talk with Trevor Ravenscroft who was giving a talk to a small group on his book *The Spear of Destiny.*[4] In it Ravenscroft delves into the legend that Adolf Hitler sought, and eventually obtained, the Spear of Longinus for its ancient talismanic powers. I am aware, of course, that Ravenscroft's views have been discredited in some quarters but this is irrelevant in that the startling nature of the author's work moved me beyond passive reading towards an investigative frame of mind. In turn, this gradually encouraged me towards a consideration that I might personally contribute some original thinking to a better understanding of European esoteric history. Within the pages of *The Spear of Destiny* I read for the first time of key Nazi personalities such as Karl Haushofer: the "Wizard of Germany," and Dietrich Eckart, occultist and drug addict, who said in 1923 as he lay dying choked by mustard gas in a Munich street: "Follow Hitler! He will dance, but it is I who has called the tune...Do not mourn for me: I shall have influenced history more than any other German." But no mention of Otto Rahn.

---

[3] Berkeley: Frog Ltd, 1996

[4] London: Neville Spearman, 1974

Three years later a book was published that had an earth shattering effect on its myriad readers worldwide. *The Holy Blood and the Holy Grail*[5] brought to mass public attention the curious story of a Pyrenean parish priest, Bérenger Saunière, and his apparent discovery in the tiny village church of Rennes-le-Château in 1891 of something: riches, documents and/or precious artefacts—no one knows for sure—that brought him wealth, power and influence beyond all understanding. It was in those pages that I first read of Otto Rahn; just a small piece and nothing to get too excited about, but to say the book as a whole transfixed me is an understatement. It wound together so many skeins of my own burgeoning thoughts on European metaphysical history that I knew I had to get off my backside and join in the fun of it all. I will always be grateful to Lincoln, Baigent and Leigh for bringing this seminal work into the public orbit. It is still an absorbing read. Sadly, Richard Leigh passed away in November 2007.

The Holy Blood and the Holy Grail sowed a seed and a few years later a friend recommended I obtain the books of Colonel Howard A. Buechner, in particular *The Emerald Cup-Ark of Gold: the Quest of SS Lt Otto Rahn of the Third Reich.*[6] Buechner was an M.D. in the American forces in WW2 and his 157th Infantry Regiment liberated Dachau in May 1945. He was the first American physician to enter that infamous prison. Although Buechner's work is heavy with unsubstantiated speculations he does deserve our gratitude for highlighting aspects of the Third Reich's largely unobserved quest for history's fabulous artefacts that would otherwise have remained buried. Buechner's account of Otto Rahn's quest for the Holy Cup strengthened my growing interest and I knew I had found the research subject to which I would dedicate my time and personal resources.

Briefly, Otto Rahn was born in 1904 in Michelstadt; obtained his baccalaureat in 1924; enrolled in law studies he did not complete; embarked on a Ph.D. in Philology he did not finish; then set off to Geneva on a study tour in 1929, returning briefly to Germany to a life of poverty. He then moved quickly to France where, according to twentieth century mythology, Rahn found the legendary Grail Treasure of Eschenbach's *Parsifal*, which he promptly handed over to Heinrich Himmler who, to save his own position in the Nazi heirarchy, pressed his subordinate into suicide in 1939.

Given this thumbnail sketch, we have in our mind's eye an ill-

---

[5] Baigent, Michael; Leigh, Richard; Lincoln, Henry. *The Holy Blood and the Holy Grai*l. United Kingdom: Random House, 1982

[6] Illinois: Thunderbird Press, 1991

disciplined, ne'er-do-well who handed the world's foremost historical prize to the sons of Satan, and who hardly had time to rue his treachery before departing this world in self-inflicted ignominy. In short, there is no reason why the popularly perceived particulars of Otto Rahn's life should encourage us to picture him as a modern day Knight: a dupe is the kindest description, an unprincipled Nazi bounty hunter the cruellest but most probable.

The latter persona was seemingly what the research team behind the development of the early Indiana Jones movie stories had in mind. In naming the character of the story's unprincipled archaeologist, the writers made a telling construct: René=Rahn, Belloq=Abello, the Celtic derivation for Apollo, the Lightbringer, by which epithet Rahn was known in admiring circles during his latter years. As if to cement the reference to Rahn and his particular circumstance in the Nazi fold, the coathanger-wielding psychopath Toht was modelled on Himmler, Rahn's boss between 1936 and March 1939.

Joan Baran and Tracy Atkinson, preparing their documentary *Nazis: the Occult Conspiracy* (broadcast on the Discovery Channel in 1998), interviewed the film's researcher. She confirmed that her background reading had revolved around a number of the books available at the time on similar themes and that from these core ideas the story line for one of the all-time favourite action movies was developed. However, Baran and Atkinson were at least eight years after the event in asking these enticing questions.

In March 1990 Starlog Magazine ran an article by California-based journalist Robert Dassanowsky-Harris titled "*The Real Indiana Jones*." Dassanowsky-Harris digs much deeper than the Discovery Channel researchers into a Rahn provenance for the character of Indiana Jones. He is unequivocal in concluding that the true historical source for Jones is Otto Rahn. In an excellently researched piece Dassanowsky-Harris maps the character and activities of the Indiana Jones character, especially as portrayed in the *Raiders* and *Crusade* episodes, to key historical themes, legends and individuals. The crux of the article is Dassanowsky-Harris' express supposition that Spielberg and Lucas put the elements of these films together to reflect the complete picture of Otto Rahn's 1930s search for the Grail in the South of France. In a nod to the Rahn-René Belloq assumption Dassanowsky-Harris remarks that Hitler's funding of the researches can encourage one to link Otto Rahn with the personality of Belloq. Nevertheless, the overall tenor of his article portrays Rahn as an earnest, well-intentioned explorer.

Moreover, when we examine in Chapter 4 the activities of a curious Rosicrucian French-based sect, the Polaires, we will see that Otto Rahn was wrongly associated by the press with the group's excavations in the Montségur area for traces of Christian Rosenkreutz' travels in the Languedoc. Without possession of the complete facts, a film researcher might easily make a simple error of interpolation and assign Rahn's activities with the same kind of shadowy Belloq-style motives that drove the covert searches undertaken by the Polaires group, which included dynamite crazy members whom Rahn loathed.

Starlog Magazine, #152, March 1990

I welcome Dassanowsky-Harris' astute observations. In the pages of this book I seek to demonstrate that the on-the-surface depiction in *Raiders of the Lost Ark* of Rahn as the evil Belloq is an unjust characterisation and that, in truth, if there ever was a legitimate real life persona for Indiana Jones it is philologist, historian, writer and Grailhunter—Otto Rahn.

But I am running ahead of myself. Having read all the material on Rahn's life and work and having interviewed Gabriele Winckler-Dechend who knew him closely, I am left with the strong impression that Otto Rahn's journey through life was not a happy one; that for all his academic brilliance he allowed himself to be played as a pawn by powerful men deep in the black heart of the Third Reich. But who is to say that that was not a mask deliberately fashioned by Rahn to protect himself (and perhaps others) during a time of unprecedented cruelty and chaos?

Gradually, I have come to believe that Otto Rahn possessed certain qualities that allowed him to conceal his true nature from the madmen who sought to enslave the free world. Information deriving from American sources appears to indicate that Rahn was not what he seemed. If this supposition can be borne out by further enquiry and research then we must radically re-evaluate his place in twentieth century history. Subsequently, we might ask ourselves if Otto Rahn, incredibly, was one of a small band of "Grail Knights" who, at terrible risk to themselves, strove to counter Adolf Hitler's quest to open literally a doorway from this world to another; some say to "Hell" itself.

Each of us, in our own way, is familiar with the Grail Quest. Even if our personal interests and reading habits have never brought us to the medieval Grail romances such as those of Chrétien de Troye, Wolfram von Eschenbach or Mallory each of us, I suggest, is searching for something unavailable in the physical world. The compelling urge to seek the intangible is a powerful and ageless paradigm of human expression. This immutable trait cemented deep within the human spirit reflects, I believe, the innate desire to commune consciously with that immortal part of ourselves embedded in the heart of our being.

Contrary to the knights of old with limitless time on their hands and no domestic responsibilities, very few of us have the opportunity to abandon hearth and home to vanquish all manner of foe and claim a bright, shiny cup from a fair damsel's hand as reward. Simply by living our lives day to day, working and dealing with the never-ending minutiae that fill our waking hours, we proceed a little further on our private, personal and special journey. This is our critical path. It is not the arriving that matters so much as the quality of the adventures we have in between. There are no absolutes and so it follows that we can never arrive anywhere that is not relative to another path or staging post on the way to a new destination. Quest adventure is lived, learned and enjoyed by moving *through* our life experiences rather than by a process of accumulating increased status or material trappings. The latter can be very welcome but is merely a rewarding by-product of the quality of our overall journey. Otto Rahn was always on the move: physically, mentally, emotionally and philosophically. His is a truly fascinating journey. No one knows for certain what prizes he unearthed, but he is increasingly drawing attention because we only need a hint of a successful treasure hunt, especially in the midst of uncertain times, and we are hooked to the last gasp of the tale.

So let us look down the time tunnel upon the life of Otto Rahn. Did he tilt at windmills or did his troubadour's song awaken the sleeping millers, the seven dwarves of Laurin, to show the young German the pathway to worlds of mystery and enchantment? Did he seek and find the Grail talisman knowing that it alone had the power to protect the integrity of the veil between this world and its demonic assailants?

Was Otto Rahn a key protector of twentieth century freedoms? Or am I seduced by a romanticist veil drawn over a stark and inescapable truth: that Otto Rahn was an SS guru, an inspiration to Hitler and his cronies to perform the devil's deeds on a hitherto unsurpassed scale?

In *OTTO RAHN AND THE QUEST FOR THE HOLY GRAIL: The Amazing Life of the Real "Indiana Jones"* we will from time to time review truly bizarre statements and hypotheses, which have been offered by various writers, theorists and modern day mystics about the covert Nazi agenda and Rahn's position, as willing actor or reluctant sage, within it. Much of this opinion takes us into the worlds of the weird and the supernatural: occultism, Tibetan mysticism, time travel and interdimensional non-human entities among them. These are the realms in which, at least in part, Otto Rahn's work is more closely associated and understood. We do not have to agree with any of it. Much of it, frankly, is mind-bendingly unbelievable, even downright scatty. Nevertheless, we will need an open mind. In the words of Maupassant: "*Qui Sait?*"

We owe it to history to be as neutral observers and to see beyond the sensational to the wider construct of 20th metaphysical history. Above all, we need to acknowledge and appreciate the undeniable premier position in which Otto Rahn held centre stage as writer, Grailseeker and mystic in a time of unparalleled cruelty and aggression.

PART ONE

LIFE

Chapter ONE

Treasure and Legend

The Cathar fortress on the Pog of Montségur

In his book *Otto Rahn: Leben und Werk*[1] Hans-Jürgen Lange draws an interesting parallel. He describes the small castle of Waldeck situated in the Hunsrueck forest between the Rhine and Mosel rivers. Inside the castle walls sits a round stone bench. What makes it unique is that it is constructed from stones hauled by hand from the ruins of Montségur, the Cathar mountain citadel described by Rahn as the Golgotha of Occitania. This ritual, originated by Nerother vicar Martin Kuhn, has been practised since 1964. It is a gesture of reconciliation for the slaughter of more than two hundred Cathar brethren, devil-worshippers in the eyes of the Catholic Church.

In March 1244 papal inquisitors dragged the martyrs from Montségur's Pog (summit) and sacrificed them in one huge pyre. The bench at Waldeck, Lange suggests, represents an allegory of Otto

[1] Engerda: Arun Verlag, 1995

Rahn's literary work. The fate of the Cathars held a fascination that gripped Rahn throughout his brief but enigmatic life. Gabriele Winckler-Dechend, a friend of Rahn's from 1935 to 1939, told me at her home at Lake Constance in 1999 that Otto Rahn believed firmly that he was no less a Cathar in thought, word and action in his own lifetime than those who suffered in the papal genocide pogroms in the Middle Ages.

In his twentieth century incarnation, Rahn travelled long distances to find out more about the Pure Ones branded by Pope Innocent as heretics. In his creative quest Rahn, too, tried to build a lasting monument to the eternal truths that he sincerely believed the Cathar faith emphasised most powerfully. He believed that the Cathars were the forerunners to the Lutheran Reformation, accepting the belief held by many that the Cathars were the protectors of the Holy Grail, and that their temple at Montségur was the Grail Castle described by medieval authors. But it was in the pages of Wolfram von Eschenbach's *Parsifal* that Otto Rahn believed he had found the cypher identifying the true seat of the Grail: Montségur. This vision of Rahn's is the centrepiece of his life's work. All else is peripheral.

Before going any further it is helpful that we should have a deeper appreciation of the history of Montségur and its context as the site of the most infamous slaughter of gnostic Christians during the Albigensian Crusade. Many readers drawn to this book and its subject matter will in some degree be familiar with Montségur and its importance in the history of so-called heresy in the Languedoc. However, the critical role that Montségur played, both in providing a bastion for the Cathar faithful and as the place from which many believe the Grail treasure was delivered to subterranean safety, requires a reminder of its unique standing and the terrible events that took place there in the spring of 1244.

Montségur, the Mount Tabor of the Cathar of Aquitaine, was the Catharist Church's open and official headquarters in Languedoc. Known in medieval times as a 'vessel of stone' (much in the same way that Rosslyn Chapel in Scotland, to which we will return, is today called a Grail in Stone), Montségur is a gigantic rounded outcrop a little over one thousand metres in height, shaped like a sugar-loaf and inaccessible save on its west flank. In remote times Montségur was a sanctuary dedicated to to Belissena, the Celtic appellation for the Goddess Astarte.

The rock lies on the northern slopes of the Pyrenees, dwarfed by surrounding peaks up to three thousand metres high and flanked on three sides by deep valleys. The rock faces are everywhere dotted with fragrant box bushes. Montségur's architecture displays technical and mathematical knowledge extremely rare for medieval Western Europe: the orientation of the walls is designed to catch the light in relation to the rising sun. The fortress had two main gates. The entrance was known as the Great Gate and its size and character ran counter to all medieval rules of architecture. The upper chamber of the keep was fifty metres square, the pentagonal courtyard six hundred metres square.

The Cathar perfecti (*bons hommes*) lived in huts below the walls. Knights and their families made pilgrimages and received blessings from the perfecti. The site was on land belonging to Guy de Lévis, the 'Marshall of the Faith' and the new suzerain of Mirepoix. It had been part of the inheritance of Esclarmonde, the sister of Raymond-Roger Trencavel of Foix. Esclarmonde was made a Perfecta in 1206 and legend has it that she was the keeper of the Cathar Manisola or Mani—the Grâl. Rahn wrote that the Mani was an emerald, called also by the Cathars the Stone of Wisdom and the Stone of Chastity.

In 1244 Montségur was held in trust by the seigneur Raymond de Perella, vassal to the Counts of Foix. Perella and his brother-in-law Pierre-Roger of Mirepoix were the most active resistance leaders during the time when the Catholic pogroms were reaching their peak of brutality towards the middle of the thirteenth century.

Cathar deacons and recluses occupied the narrow strip along the stony face of the mountain between the fortress wall and the temporary defences thrown up around the small shelving slope encompassing it. The broad stone-built edifice was ringed about with a collection of little wooden huts to a depth of several metres.

A sizeable Catharist colony had built up since the Crusade and was visited by merchants. The Cathar leaders were Guilhabert de Castres (Bishop of Toulouse from 1223), Bernard de Simorre, Sicard Cellerier (Bishop of Albi), Bertrand Marty (Guilhabert's successor), Raymond Aiguilher and Jean Cambiaire. Principal safe houses were provided at the chateaux of the Lords of Niorts, Lanta Jourda (Lord of Calhavel), and by the nobility of Fanjeaux, Laruac and Miramont, and in the Boroughs of Sorèze, Avignonet and Saint-Felix.

Guilhabert asked for Perella's permision in 1232 to turn Montségur into the official asylum of the Catharist Church. Seigneurs of the Counts of Foix organised armed resistance. The noblemen's domains straddled the Pyrenees on the French side in Languedoc, including the Ariège Valley; in Spain was the Viscountcy of Castelbon. Knights loyal to the Cathars were called Faidits. They brought spears, crossbows, arrows and armour to Montségur. This is why Montségur was at the very heart and centre of resistance in Languedoc.

In 1233 the Catholic Church started referring to Montségur as the Synagogue of Satan. Olivier de Termes had several strong fortresses in the Corbières, which were used as arms depots and assembly points. In the mountains of the Corbières the Sault district and Cerdagne Valley were centres for the planned uprising of the seigneurs.

At the request of the Pope, in 1235 Raymond VII of Toulouse dispatched three Knights to take formal posession of Montségur. These knights were admitted, did obeisance (*adoratio*) before Guilhabert de Castres and went back to Toulouse. Afterwards Raymond sent his bailiff, Mancipe de Gaillac. He also 'adored' the *bons hommes* and then went home. Mancipe was then sent back a second time, together with men-at-arms. They seized Jean Cambiaire and three perfecti for burning in Toulouse. In 1242 it was Montségur that despatched the small band of men accused of assassinating the inquisitors at Avignonet. Reprisals were swift.

In May 1243 Hugues des Arcis, at the head of an army of French knights and men-at-arms, pitched camp below Montségur on the Col du Tremblement, so depriving the besieged of the easiest way down into the valley. Arcis was expecting a further ten thousand reinforcements, mostly conscript auxiliary footsoldiers unwilling to fight fellow countrymen.

There were five to six hundred persons in the fortress in 1244: the garrison of one hundred and fifty or so knights and men-at-arms, their families and around two hundred and twenty Cathars. The French army's plan was to sever all communications and let the hot summer dry up the defenders' cisterns.

Summer passed, rain came. Abundant gifts from *credentes,* members of the Cathar underground cell of supporters, provided food. During the siege a group of Basque soldiers was guided one night up the sheer rock face. They set up a rock-throwing catapult very close to the fortress. On 1st March the crusading army managed to take up positions on the slopes of the Pog. The Knight Del Congost managed to spend three months beneath the fortress while the siege was going on. The phrase *infra castrum* appears in testimony but there is no evidence of any underground passageways.

Hugues des Arcis signed on a team of Basque mercenaries in October 1243. They got a foothold on a narrow ledge at the eastern face, eighty metres downhill from the fortress. The Cathar supporters brought in Bertrand de la Baccalaria, an engineer, from Capdenac. He broke through the blockade, reached the fortress and had another machine mounted in the eastern barbican that could return the Bishop of Albi's stone-gun's fire. Meanwhile the perfecti in the fortress invited knights and certain men-at-arms in to receive gifts. The nature of these gifts is not recorded.

At one point in the seige Imbert de Salas had a personal interview with Hugues des Arcis. Pierre Roger de Mirepoix criticised him for it and had his armour taken from him. This is suggestive of an act of betrayal.

Shortly after Christmas the attackers succeeded in rushing the barbican and installed a siege gun. They stormed the eastern barbican by following a trail cut from the rock face. This was a secret route from the Gorge of Luzset that was betrayed by local shepherds. After the capture of the eastern barbican Matheus and Peter Bonnet left the fortress with gold and silver bullion and 'pecuniam infinitam.' These two men had a secret understanding with sentries who were from Camon-sur-l'Hers in the fief of Mirepoix. The treasure was cached in the woods on the Sabarthès Mountains until a safer place was found. Many believe that Otto Rahn, seven hundred years later, found evidence to indicate its location.

Bertrand de la Baccalaria set up another machine. Matheus

returned to the fortress at the end of January with two crossbowmen, a meagre reinforcement but better than nothing. Only very dexterous and brave men could have risked the climb up the Porteil chimney and so they must have been extremely devoted to the Cathar cause. This same Matheus then went down a second time to seek reinforcements but came back with just one man.

The men-at-arms smuggled in by Matheus brought a message from Isarn de Fanjeaux to Pierre Roger de Mirepoix. The Count of Toulouse wanted to know if Montségur could last until Easter, by which time the Count had hoped to levy an army to raise the siege. The Count had no real chance of doing this but did have good reason to ask the men to hold on because Matheus had persuaded two local seigneurs, Bernard d'Alion and Arnold d'Uson, to contact an Aragonese mercenary captain called Corbario. He promised the captain fifty *livres melgoriennes* if he would bring twenty five men-at-arms to Montségur. Had these elite men arrived the siege engines would have likely been burned but they failed to break through the besiegers' cordon.

The fortress held all through February, the stone-gun keeping up a constant barrage on the besiegers day and night. Inside the fortress the shortage of food was making life unbearable. Pierre-Roger de Mirepoix counselled with Bishop Bertrand and Raymond de Perella and decided to attempt a night sortie with the object of retaking the barbican and setting the siege engine alight. The sortie failed. The Crusaders gained more footing into the fortress forecourt. The knights' wives hurriedly asked for the *convenensa* (the initiation ceremony for a *credens*—a believer). The morning after the failed sortie the fortress leaders decided to surrender.

A footpath to the Pog of Montségur

Negotiations began on 1st March. Discussions were very short as even the Crusaders were exhausted. The conditions were: i) the garrison to remain in the fortress for fifteen days and give up all hostages; ii) they would receive pardons for all past crimes, including the Avignon affair; iii) the men-at-arms to retire with their arms and baggage but would have to report to the Inquisition and confess their errors; iv) all other persons in fortress would be freed with light penances provided they recanted their heresy and made confession to Inquisitors, those who did not to be burned; v) the fortress of Montségur was to pass into the hands of the Church and the French Crown.

On 14th March a festival of sorts was celebrated. It seems as if the two-week truce was engineered so that the Cathars would have time to hold the festival and that the escape of four *parfaits* on the night of 16th March was linked with the events of the festival. Also during the truce at least six non-Cathar women and fifteen fighting volunteers received the Consolamentum and so committed themselves to certain death.

During the night of the 16th Pierre-Roger dangled ropes down the west face of the rock and let down four people, stories handed down naming them as: Amiel Aicart, Hugo, Poitevin and Alforo. None of these four or the treasure in their care, the Oriflamme (Grâl or Mani) of the Cathar faith and, it is rumoured, the Ark of the Covenant and the Grail Cup, fell into the hands of the authorities. The four knights are said to have handed the Mani to a Son of Belissena (Son of the Moon), Pons-Arnaud de Castella Verdunam, who in turn hastened it to its place of concealment in the caverns of Ornolac in the Sabarthès.

At daybreak more than two hundred *haeretici* were fettered and brutally dragged down the mountain. The pyre on which they were burned en masse was made of huge mounds of faggots, straw and pitch. The clergy chanted their psalm and the executioners shouted as they set fire to the palisade at each of its four corners.

The actual place of the burning, the Camp des Crémats (the field of fires), is not believed to be at the foot of Montségur. No one knows exactly where it took place but the ancient chronicles refute some of the popular misconceptions. Some speak of the flat area of ground visible from the mountain, slightly set back from and to the right of the village.

The Dominicans sought to make life difficult for those on the run to keep hidden in the region's dense undergrowth and drafted in Bernard l'Espinasser (the thorn-cutter) to burn all the gorse and brambles in the Montségur area. Bernard soon came to a sticky end and local legend has it that he was hanged by the Moon. If there is any truth to this curious account the "Moon' is most likely a contraction of the phrase "Sons of the Moon," the name by which the vassals of the counts of Foix were known. These knights carried shields depicting the moon, a fish and a tower. They claimed to be descended from Belissena, the Celtic Iberian Astarte.

Throughout history there have been accounts of those meeting a grim fate because they sought to subvert the symbology of the Grail. In *Indiana Jones and the Last Crusade* the enemies of the Grail meet their demise in the Canyon of the Crescent Moon, a pointed, if perhaps unconscious, reference to the Seigneurs de Belisse and their role as the Pyrenean guardians of the Grail tradition.

Six hundred years later Otto Rahn revived the history. For him the intervening centuries were no more than a fleeting moment. All was vivid, bloody and fresh. Rahn wrote about it with such passion and indignation that it was as if he had fashioned a window across time that afforded him a ringside view of those terrible events.

It is clear from even a superficial reading that Rahn's literary creations are very much a mixture of mythological reflection, the pathology of Christian mass murder and autobiographical memories of a twentieth century Don Quixote. But is it just to compare Rahn to the Spanish adventurer who, although he seemingly walked a tightrope between illumination and madness, was at heart the greatest Knight of them all? We will return to the clues peppered in Cervantes' masterwork when we review Rahn's connections, albeit lateral links, with Rennes-le-Château and other prominent European mystical energy centres. Dare we afford Otto Rahn the same measure of courage and dignity as our grandee from La Mancha or will our exposition of Rahn's life reveal a somewhat different stripe of character?

Until the publication of Lange's two books on Otto Rahn the only available sources of biographical information were references in Rahn's book *Luzifers Hofgesind: Eine Reise zu den guten Geistern Europas* (*Lucifer's Court: a Journey to Europe's Good Spirits*),[2] snippets from his SS file, and testimony from his Swiss friend Paul-Alexis Ladame (1900-1991). Ladame, descended from a Cathar family (originally named la Dama), was a professor at the Faculty of Economics and Social Sciences, University of Geneva, who knew Rahn in the period 1929-1936. These recollections are published in Ladame's forward to the 1974 French edition of *Luzifers Hofgesind* and in his correspondence with Christian Bernadac. We should not be too eager to accept Ladame's recollections at first hand. Let one bear in mind that for more than thirty years Ladame was a lecturer in politics specialising in information *and* disinformation.

Jean-Michel Angebert, pseudonym for writers Jean-Michel Bertrand and Jean Angelini, maintains in *The Occult and the Third Reich* that Otto Rahn, a brilliant young historian and philologist, was a member of the ultra powerful Society of the Seekers of the Grail, a sub-

---

[2] Leipzig: Schwarzhaupter Verlag, 1937

clique of the Bavarian Illuminati, having been inducted into the order by Alfred Rosenberg, the chief ideological guru of the NSDAP. Rosenberg is said to have given Rahn the mission to explore Montségur and its environs in 1931. This mission was in many ways a continuation of the German fascination for exploring the Ariège, which by Rahn's day had been going on for centuries. There is no evidence that Rosenberg ordered Rahn to France.

The writer Saint-Loup examined Rosenberg's records after the war and read that Rahn killed himself in a mountaintop (Cathar Endura) ceremony with a dose of cyanide on top of Mount Kufstein in 1939 for politico-mystical reasons. This is not proven.

Colonel Howard Buechner states that Reichsführer SS Heinrich Himmler stands out as a significant figure in the Nazi-Grail mystery; that were it not for his determination the Treasure of Solomon would still be sleeping peacefully in a cave in the Languedoc. This, of course, pre-supposes that the Nazis did find something of inestimable value in the Pyrenees. Buechner says it was Rahn's task to excavate the Sabarthès and steal for Germany Solomon's Treasure: a fabulous cache comprising the Tablets of Moses, the Ark of the Covenant, the Sword and Harp of David, the Sacred Candelabra and the Golden Urn of Manna, in addition to other insignificant items of value such as the Grail Cup and the Holy Lance.

Ancient legend posits that Lucifer was the first Son of God and that Jesus was the second. The first son fell from Grace and Lucifer, on tumbling from Heaven, lost his crown's diadem, which, esoteric mythology will have us believe, symbolises his third eye and which conveniently landed on top of Montségur's Pog. According to the legend its centrepiece was found centuries later by a Pyrenean shepherd, who had it wrought into a vase or vessel with one hundred and forty four thousand facets. These facets represented the first converts to Christianity, each soul becoming an angel and replacing one by one Lucifer and his deposed followers. The Emerald Cup became the Cup of God and later the Cup of Jesus, signifying the power of God and his second Son over the power of darkness.

During Rahn's explorations in and around Montségur a ninety-year old shepherd told him that in 1244 the armies of Lucifer wanted to seize the Holy Grail from the mountain and reset it into the diadem of their Prince.

Evidently, Rahn acknowledged the existence of more than one "Grail" artefact. He believed that the original Grail was an emerald—the Cathar's Stone of Wisdom—with one hundred and forty four facets.

He also held that a "second" Grail existed, consisting of stone tablets of Aryan origin and inscribed in an indecipherable language with the wisdom of the ages or the ultimate truth. Wolfram von Eschenbach wrote in *Parsifal*:

Guyot, the master of high renown,
Found, in confused pagan writing,
The legend which reaches back to the prime source of
(All) legends.

Also:

On an emerald green achmardi
She bore the perfection of Paradise
It was the object called the Grail.

Rahn saw in Parzifal that Eschenbach's heroes were modelled after real Middle-Ages personalities. Parzifal was le Vicomte de Carcassonne Trencavel, one of the foremost and heroic victims of the Crusade. Répanse de Schoye was Esclarmonde de Foix. The mother of Trencavel Adelaide de Toulouse made a perfect Herzeloyde. The hermit Trevrizent was the Cathar Bishop Guilhabert de Castres. The King Anfortas was Raimon-Roger de Foix. Montségur was Montsalvage.

In his Starlog article Dassanowsky-Harris similarly maps Eschenbach's characters, identifying Indie's father, Dr. Henry Jones, as the wounded Grail King Anfortas; Indiana Jones as the Grail Knight Parzifal; and Nazi archaeologist/art historian Dr. Elsa Schneider as Cundrie, messenger of the Grail, who curses Parzifal for losing his honour. Scheidner is symbolic of the feminine aspect of those who misuse the Grail whereas René Belloq fulfils the role of the archetypal male antagonist towards the Grail heritage.

Moreover, in Eschenbach's work Montsalvage is protected by a Fountain "Salvage" in which Rahn believed he recognised the intermittent fountain of Fontestorbes, a few kilometres from the Pog, Montségur's promontory. Also, the forest around Montsalvage is called the "Briciljan" and close by Montségur is Priscilien Wood. These factors helped to convince Rahn that the Fortress Castle of Montségur was the Temple of the Grail.

Rahn associates the Cathar Church with the Church of the Grail and with the mystical group Fidèles d'Amour of Dante.[3] He believed that after their enforced dissolution the Templars found refuge in the Pyrenean caverns. Rahn wrote of the many indications that the white

---

[3] Evola, Julius. *Le Mystère du Graal et l'idée Impériale Gibeline*. Paris: Editions Traditionelles, 1984

tunic with the octagonal red cross of the Templars was to be found with the black cassocks with yellow cross of the Cathars in the dark grottos of Sabarthès.

For Rahn, the Light came not from the east but from the north. He travelled around the ancient and sacred places of Europe. These included the Forest of Teutonburg, scene of Arminius' victory over the Roman legions of Varus; Externsteine, site of Irminsul, sacred symbol of the Saxons; Thingveillir, place of assembly of the ancient Icelanders; and Reykholt, birthplace of Snorri Sturlusson, the Nordic Homer and author of the Edda.

The etymology of the word Grail was said by French mystic-philosopher René Guénon to derive from: Grail=Gor=precious stone and Al=stylus, combined giving precious engraved stone. This Grail reveals the Book of the Key or the final secret. The stones were engraved by a race of pre-Flood, Aryan supermen, residents of Hyperborea (Thule, White Island), perhaps linked geographically with Iceland or Labrador.

The Nazis believed that the Grail was the Sacred Book of the Aryans. If they could get their hands on the records of the secret genesis of the world, it would be used to justify their extreme political theories. Opinion therefore has it that Rahn was sent by the Nazi leadership to find the Grail stone mentioned by Wolfram von Eschenbach in *Parsifal*. The thing found, it would revivify the ancient Germanic myths that would be promulgated to the masses via Hitler, the mystical communicator. It would re-awaken all the German deities and repackage the Cathar solar cult as the swastika of the Third Reich. Angebert says that, in effect, Rahn embarked on the Ninth Crusade.

Rahn wrote to Weisthor in September 1935 telling him excitedly of a place he was visiting in his search for the Grail and asking for complete secrecy except for Himmler.

In 69 A.D. Titus Flavius, the son of Emperor Vespasian, led a campaign against the Jews who were in revolt against the Romans. In September of 70 A.D. Flavius took Jerusalem and plundered the temple, supposedly sezing the silver trumpets, the Ark of the Covenant, the golden table of the shewbread and the great seven branched candlestick. The triumphal arch of Titus in Rome clearly shows this object being carried from the Temple from where it was taken to the Temple of Peace in the forum of Vespasian.

One version of what afterwards happened to the treasure, a theory to which Rahn evidently subscribed, is that it was seized by Alaric the Visigoth king when he sacked Rome in 410 A.D. Alaric died very shortly after this event and his successor, Ataulphus, led the Visigoths to Southern Gaul and to Spain where they settled. It was well known that they possessed considerable booty from their sacking. This treasure was kept in two parts: one at Toulouse and the other at Carcassonne. Arab tradition does record that a part of the looted treasure included the Grail (called the Case or Table of Solomon) and that the Visigoths concealed it in a Sabarthès grotto.

Similarly, Spanish ballads speak of a skeleton key (a *dietrich*) hidden in the enchanted cave of Hercules in the Pyrenees, which resolves the mystery of the Grail. Other similar legends refer to Solomon's jewel-case being hidden in Hercules' magical grotto at Ornolac and, specifically, in the "Cathedral" of Lombrives, the very same grotto described by Eschenbach on the strength of the information provided to him by Master Guyot. Lenau's poem *les Albigeois*[4] describes the theme:

There is, in the forest, a deep grotto and still;
No ray of light reaches it, no breeze touches it.
Wild animals, grown old, feeble, fall into it
To die there undisturbed in the darkness.

The Visigoths were routed by the Arabs at the Battle of Jerez de la Frontera in 711 A.D. At that time the Visigoths were still reputed to be the keepers of Solomon's treasure. The treasure fell at Toledo but was said not to have included the Grail.

When the Grail had been safely removed from Montségur by the four companions a beacon was lit on the neighbouring mountain of Biaorta. Rahn believed that the carefully chosen Sabarthès cavern had to be extremely deep or else the cache would have been uncovered when the Dominican Inquisitors used sniffer dogs to root out sympathisers when Montségur fell. (The rock of Montségur was once said to have been pierced by hundreds of deep cells like a beehive, and that a stairway of some three thousand steps led to a hidden exit on the banks of the River Hers.)

The Cathedral of Lombrives, its huge walls clad in brilliant rock crystal, was two hundred and sixty feet in height and in the distant past had been used as a temple consecrated to the Iberian god Ilhomber (Hercules), god of the Sun. Rahn told how he walked, deeply moved, through the crystal halls and marble crypts of the Cathedral, his hands putting aside the bones of fallen Pure Ones and Faidit knights.

In another grotto, Fontanet, leading off from the first, Rahn

---

[4] Lenau was the *nom de plume* of Hungarian poet, Nikolas Niembsch Edler von Stehlenau, 1802-1850

points out a stalagmite called "the altar." Returning to Eschenbach's tale, Parsifal is led into a cavern by Trevrizent to initiate him into the mystery of the Grail:

To a grotto his host led him,
Where hardly a breath of wind ever came
There, was a robe: his host
Put it on him and then led him
Into a nearby cell.

Eschenbach must have been remarkably well informed as to the whereabouts of the Grail because on the strength of information provided to him by the Master Guyot he writes:

Eraclius or Hercules,
Then the Greek Alexander,
For they are all familiar with
The stones...

And:

There stood, also, according to the custom of the time,
The altar. Exposed thereon
Was the jewelcase.

With these facts brought into light the presence of the Grail in the Pyrenees seemed to be unarguable fact. Angebert believes that this was certainly the case among Hitler's circle otherwise the Nazi high command would not have attributed such outstanding importance to Rahn's mission. Nevertheless, as the authors observe, it is unlikely that a foreigner would have been able to spirit away a cache of fabulous treasure from under the noses of the local people, and so one can virtually rule out the possibility that Otto Rahn made off with the Grail during the trips he made to the Pyrenees in the thirties. However, rumours persist that Rahn *did* find something of fabulous historical provenance but left it behind in its place of concealment.

Perhaps Himmler was not completely convinced that Otto Rahn had accurately pinpointed Solomon's treasures. Monks today can still recall Himmler's visit in 1940 to the monastery on Montserrat,[5] one of the suggested sites for the Grail Temple and, according to present day researchers, a key power centre at the heart of the “Reshel” energy grid system installed, so the story goes, several thousand years ago by the Hebridean priests of Ruta, referred to in Psalms 188: 19-23 as the "Chief Head Stone." The Reshel grid and its present-day purpose has become a key component in my researches on Rahn and the extraordinary time period in which he lived. We will return to the topic.

---

[5] Brissaud, André. *Hitler et l'ordre noir*. Librairie Académique Perrin, 1969, P. 276

In *Die Entdeckung des Grals (The Discovery of the Grail)*[6] the Fiebag brothers wrote that a group of people around Himmler in the last days of the war were considering an expedition to find the Grail in the Pyrenees. Otto Skorzeny, "Hitler's Commando," (also labelled by American forces as the "most dangerous man in Europe" after learning of his plan to assassinate Eisenhower), was mooted as the expedition's group leader. Skorzeny makes no mention of such a mission in his memoirs. On the contrary, Skorzeny had little time for Himmler who used to irritate the huge Austrian by scolding him openly during meetings.

Nevertheless in 1943 a group of German geologists, historians and ethnologists camped on Montségur's summit and made searches in the vicinity of the Gorge de la Frau (the Gorge of Fear). They were encouraged by the contents of papers Otto Rahn had supposedly left behind eleven years before in which he had given details of his study of the sacred geometry of Montségur, its sunrise orientations and their relationship with other sacred power places, and its secret underground passages. The excavation lasted until November 1943 and resumed in the spring of 1944.[7] It is theorised by Angebert that the excavation was successful and that the runic tablets were discovered, not in the grottoes of Sabarthès where Rahn had been searching but near the crest of La Peyre. It has been claimed that just before something was found Reichsminister Rosenberg visited the "forbidden zone" around Montségur, an area whose size is known from warning notices posted around forbidding camping within five hundred metres of the mountain.

On March 16th 1944, Montségur residents gathered on the Pog to commemorate the seventh hundredth anniversary of the mass burning of the Cathar faithful. Eyewitnesses (including a grocer, an engineer and a parish clerk) stated that as noon was approaching a German Fieseler Storch arrived overhead and put on an impressive aerial display for the pilgrims in the castle. In the form of a sky-writing trail the plane carved an enormous Celtic cross before flying off towards Toulouse. The onlookers bared their heads in respect. It was thought that Rosenberg was aboard but Saint-Loup discovered that he was in Toulouse at the time and so the identity of the prominent Nazi said to have been aboard the craft is a mystery. Others believe that Otto Rahn was aboard to herald the successful outcome of his Herculean labours

---

[6] Munich: Goldmann/Bertelsmann, 1989

[7] Cited by Michel Bertrand, author of *le Soleil des Cathares* (1982), edition Atlas, and with Jean Angelini, under the name of Jean-Michel Angebert of the work *Hitler and the Cathar Tradition*

several years earlier.

On 2nd May 1945 an SS Company delivered a convoy to Zillertal Mountain Pass where a select group of officers took possession of a number of heavy lead-lined boxes.[8] In a torchlit ceremony the officers transported the boxes to Schleigeiss Glacier at the foot of the nine thousand feet high Hochfeiler Mountain and buried them in a ledge of snow at the edge of a precipice. This ritual finds echo in the penultimate scene in *Raiders of the Lost Ark* where the Nazis disembark the Ark of the Covenant from the submarine and carry it in solemn procession into the island's interior for the grand, but ultimately apocalyptic, opening ceremony.

Subsequent to the Zillertal Pass concealment, many seekers over the years were drawn to the Schleigeiss Glacier, pulled by the promises and rumours of treasure. All were found dreadfully mutilated or decapitated, among them: Franz Gottliech mutilated, Emmanuel Werba beheaded in 1952.

The Austrian mountain Schloss in *Indiana Jones and the Last Crusade*, where Indiana retrieves his father's Grail Diary, pays compliment to the place of concealment of whatever had been excavated during or subsequent to Otto Rahn's Pyrenean searches.

Arfst Wagner, anthroposophist and co-producer of the Flensburger journals, sought information on Otto Rahn via the Internet during 1997/98. A message left behind in his mailbox from an unknown respondent said: "*I have reason to believe that many artefacts, including some found by Otto Rahn, were shipped to the U.S. in 1938...I think the Grail you may be looking for is a superconducting stone that Hitler shipped to the L.A. area.*"

The correspondences between this enigmatic passage and the storyline of *Raiders of the Lost Ark* are startling. Many will recall the film's final scene where the wooden crate containing the Ark, heroically captured from the Nazis by Indiana Jones and brought to the U.S.A. in a submarine, is wheeled into a vast anonymous military depository. It has even been suggested that movies of this kind are made at the suggestion of Government security services as a means of imparting official truths on alternative and esoteric topics in a universally acceptable manner.

In Chapter 31 we will read a short story about U-Boat 33 and its fictional basis in the alleged but tantalising connection between a very much alive "post mortem" Otto Rahn and British security representatives in MI6.

The troubadours wrote: *Al cap des set cen ans verdegeo el*

---

[8] Buechner ibid

laurel (at the end of seven hundred years, the laurel will be green once more). Did Otto Rahn green the laurel or, like the playing card courtiers in Alice in Wonderland, did he paint the white roses red either to hide the Grail from Hitler or simply because, despite his claims, he really knew nothing and worked a brilliant deception to save his skin?

Chapter TWO

1904-1930
Relative calm

What may we see in Otto Rahn's early years that might signpost a future career as a Grailseeker without equal, a twentieth century Argonaut no less brave and adventurous than Jason? On the face of it, we find precious little. Personal details of Rahn's childhood, indeed of most parts of his life, are conspicuous by their scarcity. This fact alone might suggest to the suspicious enquirer an attempt to deflect attention away from family intimacies and to provide a degree of shielding. When we examine the possibilities that indicate the nature of Rahn's true agenda in life we may understand better why such a shroud would have been necessary.

In *Luzifers Hofgesind* Rahn mentions the occasion of his return at the age of twenty seven to Bingen am Rhein on the eve of his tour of Europe's Apollonian strongholds. His childhood house was no longer standing and the fields in which he had ran and played were no more. Curiously, the sole links with the past were the vines that were still growing where the bottom of the family garden used to be. This link to Rahn's boyhood past was an object in nature. Throughout Rahn's researches and writings we see an unbroken allusion to nature as exemplifying all that was good and constant during the Age of Chivalry, the Troubadours and L'Amour Courtois.

In Rahn's eyes the Cathars had planted a rich vine of Gnostic lore that the diligent seeker might harvest down through the ensuing centuries. More significantly, the vine has long been a favoured device that mystics and seers have used to symbolise an unbroken lineage or ancient alchemic tradition. In depicting this image, was Rahn indicating to those who could read between the lines that he was a representative of a metaphysical ancestry? We will return often to this intriguing question.

According to the resumé that Rahn wrote for his SS entry dossier, Otto Wilhelm Rahn was born at four o'clock in the afternoon of Thursday 18th February 1904 in Michelstadt, Odenwald, first child of Karl and Clara (née Hamburg). The boy's upbringing was stamped by his Protestant parents' religious attitudes, his father's vocation as a civil servant (bailiff), and by the dominant personality of his mother.

Michelstadt is the Odenwalt: the forests of Odhinn-Alfadir, the grand god of the North. It is here that the hero Siegfried, immortalised by Wagner, the killer of dragons in the Nibelung Saga, would be assassinated. Michel is the Christianised pagan Siegfried, hence the derivation of the name Michelstadt, the town of Michel the dragon slayer. Rahn said: "I am therefore come from a world in the orbit of the Grail. Parzifal, Siegfried and Odhinn-Wotan were my Godfathers."[1]

Otto's mother introduced her son to the Grail romances and to the stories of Parzival, Siegfried and other heroes of literature. Rahn's birthplace at Michelstadt was near Marburg on the Lahn River, between the Rhineland and Thüringen. The present day Römer-Rahn family resides near Wildenberg at Amorbach, twenty kilometres east of Michelstadt, the site of the grail castle in the Odenwald and a place of particular importance to Otto Rahn because it was here that Wolfram von Eschenbach wrote part of *Parzifal*. This whole area was

---

[1] *Luzifers Hofgesind*

impregnated in European legend. Rahn wrote: "my ancestors were pagans and my grandparents were heretics."[2] Marburg is the ancient seat of the notorious Inquisitor, Konrad, and was at the centre of repression of heresy. The odour of the butchers was no less a stench in Marburg than in the South of France. Otto Rahn believed that a number of his ancestors had been slain by Konrad and his fellow Inquisitors although he never specified the reasons for his conviction.

1910 Rahn entered junior school, firstly at Bingen am Rhein, and then at Gießen where, in 1924, he obtained his Reifeprüfung (Baccalauréat). Rahn tells us that his religious tutor at Gießen, Baron von Gall, excited his imagination in telling the story of the mysterious Cathars, the heretical sect in the eyes of the Catholic Church, who believed that the material world is the work of Rex Mundi.

Latter day researchers have challenged this account. Rahn always presented his Grail quest as if it had been his lifelong task to find out about the Cathars and their sufferings. However, Hans-Jürgen Lange believes that Rahn hit on the theme completely by accident through his close friendship (and homosexual relationship) with Albert Heinrich Rausch (1882-1949). In Lange's view, during the course of the many visits Rahn paid Rausch in Paris he was introduced to members of the literary intelligentsia who inspired him to take up the Cathar histories as a topic for investigation. Maybe, none can now say. The important factor is that, for whatever motivation, Rahn embarked on his journey to find the Grail treasures. For my own part, I can see no pressing reason why we should not at least be prepared to meet Rahn half way in accepting his own story. More likely it was a combination of both aspects: an early interest arising from an enthusiastic and inspirational teacher, later given increased shape and urgency by the Paris intellectual milieu and its diverse characters.

The Cathars believed in Christ, read the New Testament, and

---

[2] Ibid

placed particular reference to Saint John on whom they founded their beliefs. As we have seen they went much further, stating that they were the sole representatives of the one true Christian faith. One can only imagine how this Cathar dogma must have rankled within the higher reaches of the Catholic Church.

In the Cathars' view the Creator of the Old Testament was the architect of Evil. Consequently, when the Roman Church identifies Him with the Christian God of the Gospels it is in complete contradiction to the tenets of the Cathar faith. Theirs was a dualist belief deriving from 11th century Bogomilism whose principle tenet was that only God can create Good; He cannot have wished to create Evil, even as a test for Man's redemptive powers. The Cathars regarded the physical world, therefore, as a manifestation of Evil, which is not a God but a lower principle incorporating the illusory dimensions of time and matter. To this end, Evil imprisons a small part of life (the soul) in a material wrapping (the body), and invents Time (limit, duration): the essential ingredients of corruption and destruction. Man, thus, stands at the crossroad of eternal life and corruption. He is torn between his spirituality, the divine part of himself, and material temptations, which draw him towards Evil. For the Cathar, salvation necessitated freeing oneself from the world of Evil and reaching the Kingdom of Good in full awareness. The Cathar's Manichean, Light versus Dark philosophy is, of course, the dominant theme that underscores the Indiana Jones stories.

What I find most telling is that in Rahn's published works there is so little mention of the Great War in terms of the profound impact it must have had on the home and personal life of a sensitive boy between ten and fourteen years of age. In *Luzifers Hofgesind* Rahn affectionately describes the Protestant church of Saint John in Gießen where he made his first communion. In his youth the church was a relatively new temple of worship; Otto's father had seen it built as a boy. Otto used to enter the church when it was empty and pass along the deserted nave on tiptoe. His footfalls would resonate, he said, like haunting phantoms.

Rahn informs his readers that he would never forget the time during the Great War when he and some schoolmates entered the church and made their way up the spiral staircase leading to the imposing organ, passing by a large and splendid clock, pushing on up to the four balconies of the bell tower. In the distance the friends heard the rumbling of thunder, slightly muffled. It was the sound of a battle raging on the western front in defence of the distant valleys. In reminiscing about those times, Otto also recalled other distasteful memories such as the shortages brought about by war. He would gather beechnuts near Buseck to make cooking oil, and nettles to help prepare cloth. Once a week he would go to a miller's house near Wetzlar to find flour and milk for his sickly younger brother, Karl. In Gießen Otto would hear night and day the footsteps of prisoners of war, mostly Russian and French soldiers. He saw the uninterrupted flow of Germany's troops, returning from the front to their garrison. Rahn also pictures a more recent scene where, as a naïve and unworldly student, he got drunk at the castle at Gleiberg.

Rahn confided in Tarascon poet, Jean-Baptiste Fauré-Lacaussade, that he had never shone at school because he was apt to prolong his nighttime dreams in class. That Rahn's dreamsight was keen is evidenced by a teenage obsession when he meditated on the protective role of the rose-thorn for a year. The rose has long been a symbol of eternal life and Rahn did believe that we live many lifetimes; that the last has to have a frugal, primitive quality, returning for this final earth experience to the essence of the first men. Rahn was to pursue this study further in his graceful exposition of the Middle Earth legend of the Garden of Roses.[3]

After attaining his High School diploma, Rahn dutifully obeyed his father's wishes and enrolled in law studies at Freiburg and at Heidelberg. He interrupted his studies between 1925 and 1928 to make a living to supplement his family's scarce income. In Heidelberg Rahn worked at an assortment of jobs, including publishing, so that he could quickly return to his studies.

Rahn enjoyed exchanging correspondence with his friends and associates and a study of these from 1928 onwards makes for fascinating reading. This is especially true in respect to Rahn's correspondence with Albert Rausch. We are indebted to Hans-Jürgen

---

[3] Bernadac, Christian. *Le Mystère Otto Rahn (le Graal et Montségur Du Catharisme au Nazisme)*. Paris: Editions France-Empire, 1978

Lange for unearthing these exchanges.[4]

More than twenty years older then Rahn, Rausch, a 1933 Georg Büchner prizewinner, wrote under the pseudonym Henry Benrath. In 1933 Rausch wrote an introduction for the book *Kreuz und Gral* (Cross and Grail), which appeared later that year in the Swiss daily newpaper *Basler Nachrichten.* He was openly homosexual, living in Paris from 1929 onwards, and worked occasionally as a press officer for the International Red Cross. The postcards and letters exchanged between the two friends are important because their intimacy allows the observer to peer closely into Rahn's life and times between 1927 and 1935.

Ascension Day 1919

We learn that in January 1928 Rahn had left the family home and was living in Berlin. He was planning in February to travel into the Rhineland and was meanwhile spending his time enjoying silence and solitude, devoting his evenings to reading, writing and improving his education. He had received a film script from Lux-Europa-Filmgesellschaft. He knew one of the company bosses very well and this important contact had set everything in motion and was guiding Rahn through the script and technical processes. As a result, Rahn was feeling very pleased that this creative opportunity provided just the right counterpoint in the run up to his forthcoming Rhineland travels.

---

[4] Lange, Hans-Jürgen. *Otto Rahn und die suche nach dem Gral*. Engerda: Arun Verlag, 1999

This is one of the very first references to Rahn's connections with the early German film industry and perhaps goes some way to explaining why in 1997 an American friend of mine researching Otto Rahn received a letter from an elderly Englishman named Cecil H. Williamson (1909-1999), sent apparently at the suggestion of a then serving but unidentified British security source. Williamson was an operative in MI6's occult bureau during WW2. We will explore this critical link with Otto Rahn in Chapter 14.

By November 1928 Rahn had returned to Lorsch to live with his parents and intended to stay there for the next two semesters, driving daily to Heidelberg for his doctorate studies in Philology. In a letter to Rausch around this time Rahn makes what is possibly the first mention in writing of the new love in his life: "one also takes care of the heart. 19 years old, beautiful, even very beautiful, and from Geneva."[5]

This is an unguarded and startling reference to Raymond Perrier, a man five years Otto's junior who would remain lover and companion to Rahn for the next ten years. A year earlier Rahn had made mention in correspondence that he had made a gift of Rausch's sonnets to a "friend," in all probability a reference to Raymond.

June 1920

In November 1928 Raymond was staying as a houseguest with Rahn's parents to learn the German language. Perrier's uncle, Brett Perrier, was Geneva's Honorary-Chancellor of the Republic and this high office indicated the family's prosperous upper-middle class

[5] Ibid

background. On the face of it, Rahn had few inhibitions about declaring his sexual feelings and desires in correspondence. This naïve and garrulous tendency would land Rahn into deep trouble in the coming years. Perrier died at Nyon in 1998.

Rahn embarked on his doctorate, specialising in the literary history of the language and romances of meridional France. His professor was named Gundolf (pseudonym for Friedrich Gundelfinger, a Jewish member of the literary circle around the poet Stefan George) who had also taught (and similarly inspired) Joseph Goebbels in the summer of 1920. Rahn's thesis was titled "*to the Research of Master Kyot of Wolfram von Eschenbach*," dedicated in 1929 to the author of Parzifal, to Wagner, and to the troubadours.

Typically, Rahn did not finish his studies and after two terms at Heidelberg he decided to embark upon a study tour in Switzerland. In November 1929, after eight months in Heidelberg and two months at Raymond's parents' house in Nyon near Geneva, the two friends had moved to Berlin, sharing accommodation in Martin Luther Street. If the unguarded tone of Rahn's correspondence with Rausch is anything to go by then the nature of the relationship between them must have been fairly obvious, especially to Raymond's parents. If the pair stayed in the family house for a full two months then Raymond's folks were either extremely liberal, alarmingly naïve or under pressure to turn a blind eye.

Otto remarks that he is impressed and excited that Raymond is burning to learn; but to learn what? We are not told. He insists that Rausch will be light with joy on meeting Perrier who is so beautiful and so loyal in friendship. Rahn is ecstatic that Raymond and he have lived together for a year and that their love is stronger than ever. This is strong stuff. Did Rahn ever stop to consider that even his close friend Albert might not keep these declarations confidential? Considering the nature of these blatant outpourings, it is no wonder why Rahn's mother burned all her son's correspondence some years after the war. But Raymond was just as loose-tongued as his elder friend, writing at this time to Rausch: "Friend of my friend, I do not yet know you. Your books are locked to me because I do not yet think of reading them. You, however, are already dear to me. The time of my love with Otto is the happiest in my short life; he always says to me that we would not have our friendship were it not for your influence and your guidance, which has illuminated him so much. It is by this added strength that he is able to give me what I have missed, and I thank you for it. From my whole heart."[6]

The study tour was put on hold while Rahn stayed in Berlin and scratched a living. It was at this time that Rahn met Paul Ladame and the pair became close friends. Ladame described Rahn at this first meeting as of medium height, rather pale and sickly looking, with no taste for energetic activities and a mania for perfect punctuality. Based on the combined recollections and testimony of those who knew him Rahn can further be described as a completely 'un-bourgeois' person with a very unsettled nature, always on the move, never staying in one place for very long. He was naïve and trusting to a fault but had a tendency to occasional boastfulness. Rahn was extrovert, sociable and charming, always looking to make new contacts because new connections might lead to paid work to cover his living costs, affording him the means and freedom to write newspaper articles and radio scripts.

Rahn working on *Kreuzzeg gegen den Gral* at Villa Bernadac, Ussat-les-Bains

Rahn told Ladame of his hopes of becoming a literary critic but the effects of the economic crisis began to make themselves felt throughout Germany, forcing both men, like millions of others, to take temporary jobs. To survive, Otto Rahn took a stream of jobs, including cinema attendant, salesman, packer, proof-reader, translator, film-extra and screenwriter for the budding talking picture industry, but most often he was unemployed. At one time, Ladame recounts, Rahn even considered applying for a job as a shoemaker's runner after seeing the position advertised in a shop-window poster ("must provide own bicycle"). Ladame had a small supporting role in the film *Dreigroschenoper* and, like Rahn, was an extra in *Vier von der Infantrie*. The friends jointly wrote a screenplay for Drehbuch von Klabund's[7] marriage comedy *XYZ* but they were unable to attract any financial backing.

By August 1930 Rahn had had his fill of Berlin and was living once more in Nyon. Raymond and he were preparing for their mid-month move to Paris, which was an opportune move for them both.

[6] Ibid

[7] Klabund was the pseudonym of Alfred Henschke, 1890-1928

Rahn had been working as a screenwriter since the start of the year on a project, possibly linked with *XYZ*, which was a joint venture between a German and a French film company that had been brought about because of his excellent Parisian contacts. Rahn was hoping to have an acting part in this film.

December saw Rahn living in Rue Croix d'Or, Geneva, working as a language teacher in a Catholic school and as a translator. He had quickly become acquainted with the school headmaster, a Mr Bernard, whom Rahn now counted as a "dear friend." However, his ability to make new best friends at the drop of a hat had not dampened his ardour for Raymond, remarking to Rausch that his friendship with Perrier was unchanged and that it brought him peace and good fortune. His appetite for companionship was clearly unquenchable. Rahn's friendships, mixed with agreeable diversions for literary and cinematic works, brought him contentment. He might have treasured it more had he the foresight to visualise the perils of the coming years.

During his time in Geneva Rahn studied Calvin, Rousseau and Voltaire. He was particularly keen during this period on the music of Debussy, especially *Pelléas et Mélisande*. Rahn told Fauré-Lacaussade that he had bad memories of Geneva where he had been poorly accommodated and ill nourished, and had to manage a month on a wage barely sufficient for a week.

In his room there was no running water or electrical power and in these conditions he set about writing several articles, starting with the main Inquisitor of his country, Konrad of Marburg, the heretic-hunter and confessor of the Countess of Thuringia. Despite these inconveniences Rahn threw himself into his work, typing the Konrad article again and again to make copies for more than fifty newspapers and journals. Only one agency expressed an interest in seeing new works. Before he departed from Switzerland to Paris Rahn drove to Germany for a meeting with the agency but the outcome is unknown.

Fauré-Lacaussade met Rahn after his return from Geneva and was struck by the young German's sickly appearance. His jaw was clenched tight and his pallour was so white his cheeks were transparent.

Rahn was clearly under tremendous stress, no doubt due in part to the relentless need shared by so many of his countrymen to keep body and soul together in the face of spiralling recession and economic collapse. But maybe there were other factors arising from more sinister sources that contributed to Rahn's emotional malaise even before he entered France to begin his Grail quest.

Considering Rahn's intellectual gifts, the subject choices he had made during his university years for his doctorate and the identity of his professor at Heidelberg, it would not be surprising if all these factors marked him out among the Nazi cabal. Here was a young man of brilliant intellect ideally equipped to help fulfil their goal to re-establish the old legends along their path towards assuming occult and messianic power over the free world. In weighing up these factors, it is more than possible that by the mid-1920s Rahn had already been suborned by powerful figures such as Himmler to play a not insignificant part in advancing that terrible agenda.

Biographical material on Otto Rahn's first twenty four years is scant. His childhood was unremarkable but he was encouraged by his parents, his mother in particular, to delve into the rich seam of legend that wove through the Odenwald like a running dragon. Consequently, the circumstances of his upbringing instilled in the young boy a passion for the region's heretical histories and to learn and discover much more in the coming years.

Like most youngsters, Otto's imagination was highly receptive and he soaked up the histories ardently. His vivid elucidation of these in his later writings suggest that Rahn could step into them as easily as if they were being playing out in the meadow beyond his study. All of the elements of his upbringing melded together to create a mental tableau on which was laid a superabundance of imagery undimmed by the passage of time. He believed that his own forbears had been fed to the Inquisitors' flames. The mental and emotional paradigms shaped by these actions were further developed by Baron von Gall's inspirational lessons during Rahn's high school years.

Chapter THREE

France 1931-1933

At the beginning of 1931 Rahn had quit Geneva and was resident in Paris in Rue de Lille. Ever restless, Rahn packed his bags six weeks later, returned to Switzerland and took lodgings with a Mme Gaudenzi in the Rue du Perron, Geneva. Straightaway he penned a note to Rausch, remarking that he had serious intentions to establish a publishing house by April.

Entrepreneurship was a new venture for Rahn and he was evidently excited by the prospect. The new company would publish French and German literature, both in the form of original material and in translations. Startup funding was available and the business was likely to be established somewhere other than in Geneva because Rahn had been having trouble extending his Swiss residency and work permit. He and the un-named friend helping him with the venture (quite likely Raymond Perrier) were busy organising the distribution process and fervently hoping for an appropriate first publication that would have the widest appeal. Rahn thought it was premature, however, to sing the project's praises before they had got it off the ground; very wise, it all came to nothing.

Curiously, Rahn mentioned to Rausch that his ambitious plan ran contrary to advice from a friendly advocate that he should present an anonymous face to society. At this time Rahn was largely unknown in literary or commercial circles and so it is unclear as to why he should have received counsel to keep his head down in business affairs. Could it have been Rahn's increasingly brazen gay lifestyle that threatened to draw unwelcome attention if he stepped into the public eye? Or was there, as I have already suggested, an evolving master-servant relationship between Rahn and the NSDAP, which demanded a high degree of care and circumspection? Why this project came to nought is not clear but Rahn was hopeless with money and, as we shall see, was not ill-disposed to borrowing funds when it suited him and neglecting to repay his debts. Business acumen was not a strong component in his inventory of personal talents.

In between times Rahn was trying to keep fit by skiing every

Sunday with Raymond. Rahn was not a practised skier and Raymond was teaching him the basics, using a training routine that did not leave his elder friend too tired in the evening.

Later in 1931 Otto Rahn departed Switzerland a second time and made his way to the southern French Pyrenees, after having stayed a while in Paris, Provence, Switzerland, Spanish Catalonia and in Italy. Correspondence does not enlighten us as to why Rahn made these trips. There are no tell-tale signs that Rahn had experienced a "*eureka*" moment and was hot on the trail of fabulous treasures. Up to this point Rahn seemed destined to try to make a life in the film business. Therefore, in the absence of any declarations from Rahn to the contrary any travelling that he undertook in these times cannot be regarded as anything more than casual tourism as distinct from the single minded activities of a dedicated treasure seeker.

The Cathar Dove

Christian Bernadac claims in *Le Mystère Otto Rahn: Du Catharisme au Nazism*[1] that Rahn was first seen in the Languedoc region in July 1930 but this is not corroborated. Rahn was fluent in both French and in the ancient Occitan language of the region. Ironically, Rahn spoke French so well that on his return to Germany in 1933 he was a little rusty in his own language.

According to record, Rahn arrived in the Languedoc in November 1931 telling locals he was a journalist. He stayed initially at the home of Mlle Bernadac, Christian's grandmother, and then moved on to hotels Cousture, Charmilles and the Hôtel-Restaurant des Marronniers.

In Paris, in all probability via introductions from Albert Rausch, Rahn became acquainted with a circle of literary figures and scholars, including Maurice Magré from Toulouse: poet, novelist, and author of *Pourquoi Je Suis Boudhiste* published in 1928. Magré wrote in *Magiciens et Illuminés* that the Cathars were the Buddhists of the Occident. His theory was that the Hindu doctrines on transmigration of

[1] ibid

the soul and of Nirvana had been imported into meridional France by a Tibetan sage.

Otto Rahn had sympathy with some of these ideas but in *Kreuzzug gegen den Gral* he poured cold water on Magré's Tibetan proposition for want of supporting evidence. Nevertheless, Rahn did regard Catharism as containing other influential philosophic elements including Druidism, Priscillianism and Hellenic thought, permeated throughout by the rich influences of Spanish and Persian Islam. Rahn's belief was that Catharism had been a ferment of evolutionary thought at a time when the Middle-Ages were marked by wholesale spiritual vacuity.

Paul Ladame's testimony also refutes Hans-Jürgen Lange's opinion that Rahn only picked up an interest in the Cathars as a result of meeting Magré and his circle. According to Ladame, Rahn was already engaged in research at the Bibliothèque Nationale in Paris when Magré encouraged Otto Rahn to continue his studies in the field. Ladame reports on a breakfast meeting at La Closerie des Lilas Café where Magré expressed the opinion that the mysterious Nicetas, the Bogomil deacon who chaired the Cathar Council of Saint-Félix-Lauragais in 1167, left a written document of his teachings before returning to the Orient and disappearing from this world. This manuscript, Magré suggested, would have been stored with the Cathar treasure in the Chateau of Montségur and in 1931 resided in the grotto of Ornolac. Encouraged by these ideas, Rahn prepared to explore the Montségur area for himself.

Magré introduced Rahn to a number of his Occitan friends, including the elderly Comtesse Miryanne de Pujol-Murat with whom Rahn enjoyed a deep platonic friendship and Arthur Caussou (known to most as M. Rives). Rahn held the old Ariègois fellow in great esteem and it was Caussou who told Rahn of the legend of Esclarmonde de Foix (Esclarmonde means 'light of crystal'). According to the legend, on the evening of the fall of Montségur Esclarmonde was given custody of the Grail that had been guarded by Cathar Parfaits. The handover complete, Esclarmonde transformed herself into a dove and flew off towards the East. It was Arthur Caussou and Pujol-Murat together that were the principle influences on Rahn's growing belief that the chateau of Montségur was none other than the legendary Grail castle.

Countess Pujol-Murat was a spiritualist with connections with the Polaires and an interest in Hanns Hörbiger's glacial cosmology theories. She believed that she was the direct descendant of Esclarmonde de Foix and that she was in contact with the Perfecta's departed spirit. She also believed she was descended from Hugues de Payen, one of the nine founders of the Knights Templar.

The Countess wanted Rahn especially to appreciate the point she emphasised to him that Inigo de Loyola, founder of the Society of Jesus, conceived his spiritual exercises and his cult of the Sacred Heart of Jesus at Montserrat. She believed this was an attempt by Loyola and the Jesuits to falsely associate the Catholic Church with the Grail Cult and hijack the tradition. She told Rahn that the Jesuits were masters of lies. Rahn was deeply interested in the Jesuits, sometimes to the point of obsession, because he writes about them at length in *Luzifers Hofgesind*. He wrote that the Basque nobleman, Loyola, was dead set against the spirit of the Court of Lucifer.

The Countess supported Rahn's investigations in Ornolac and put at his disposal her car and driver, the German Joseph Widegger, making it appear as if Rahn had his own servant. Widegger was Rahn's junior by four years and his winter clothing consisted of a loud golfing outfit complete with chevrons and a half-belt jacket. True to type, Rahn borrowed money from Widegger and failed to repay him. The Countess died in 1935.

Magré particularly wanted to introduce Rahn to Antonin Gadal, premier historian of the Syndicat d'Initiative of Ussat-Ornolac. A close master-pupil friendship developed between Gadal and Rahn. The young German would speak of his mentor as "Trevrizent whom I never expected to discover."[2] Gadal's medieval hero was Galahad, in French Galaad, and he was proud that his surname was an anagram for the Grail Knight. According to many observers, the theories in Rahn's Crusade came directly from Gadal who published nothing himself. Many people resented Rahn for what they saw as his cursory acknowledgement of Gadal and passing off his mentor's work as his own. Gadal believed that Catharism derived from a gnostic form of Christianity—'Johannic'—that originated in Alexandria in the early centuries after Christ and was brought to Spain by Mark of Memphis around the year A.D. 300. It gradually spread across the Pyrenees to the Languedoc where it flourished. 'Bogomil' missionaries arrived in the area around the year 1000, found this established gnostic religion, and the fusion of the two gave rise to Catharism. 'Johannic Christianity' was based on the teachings of Saint John the Evangelist and it was believed that the Cathars possessed the original version of John's Gospel.

When Rahn came to stay at Louise Bernadac's tiny family *pension* in Ussat-les-Bains in November 1931 he signed the register as

---

[2] Rahn, Otto. *Kreuzzeg gegen den Gral.* Freiburg i/Breisgau: Urban Verlag, 1933

"coming from Geneva." According to Christian Bernadac, however, Rahn had spent the preceding months visiting a number of towns and villages in the region, among them Foix, Palmiers, Mirepoix, Lavalenet and, if claims can be substantiated, Rennes-le-Château.

Inside the Sabarthès grottoes

Rahn concentrated his studies on the Visigoths whose capital was Toulouse, the troubadours and the Albigensian heretics. He focused his excursions in the grottos and caverns of Ussat-les-Bains, Lordat, Montségur, Niaux, Vicdessos and Bédeilhac. Rahn also explored the grottoes of the Sabarthès area, notably Ornolac and the massive cavern of Lombrives. Here was a huge chamber called by locals "the Cathedral." There was a stalagmite called "The Tomb of Hercules" and another called the "Altar." These names were those used by Eschenbach. Rahn also discovered that the chambers in the Sabarthès were covered with Templar symbols, side by side with Cathar emblems. There was also a carving of a bleeding lance. This greatly excited the Nazi leaders.

Otto Rahn also fell in with a band of boisterous Pyrenean poets, the Seigneurs de Belisse, a group whose medieval origins were discussed earlier. Rahn's companions of this order included Palanqui, Meslin, Manpome and Deodat Roché, a magistrate and supporter of anthroposophist Rudolf Steiner. Together these men lauded the grandeur and myths of the Ariège and the existence of the Pyrenean Grail. Roché and Rahn often held long conversations on the old histories. Seeing that Roché was an avowed opponent of Nazism, it is hard to envisage why he would have wanted to spend the time of day with the young German scholar if he held any suspicions that Rahn was an advocate or supporter of Hitler's creed.

None of the youngsters in the region were interested in the myths and legends and it was Rahn who got the discussions going on hidden treasure and their proud past. The locals called him a "seducer doubled with believer, an eternal adolescent with a superhuman passion for the Grail and the Hermetic Tradition."[3]

According to Fauré-Lacaussade, Rahn had a "great but disorderly intelligence" and was sometimes too much of a dreamer to make a good student but would pursue obsessively any subject that excited his imagination. Fauré-Lacaussade also recalled that Rahn said little about his childhood and youth. Rahn told the poet that his Cathar research would show that "certain people have the same origin...today the members of the same family are dispersed in several nations. These families must be re-united."[4] Rahn added that he really did not know what he was searching for and pumped Fauré-Lacaussade for information on the properties and possessions of the Counts of Foix at Tarascon: their castles, cemeteries and churches. Paul Ladame states that it was Rahn's love of Wagner that led him to study the work of Wolfram von Eschenbach, which in turn drew him into a study of the Minnesingers and the Troubadours.

All of a sudden in September 1932 things seemed to start hotting up on Otto Rahn's treasure trail. Rahn met with his old friend Ladame back in Paris. He was convinced that he had made one of the most important historical discoveries and that he would become rich and famous through the forthcoming publication of *Kreuzzug gegen den Gral*, which he felt certain would be translated into many languages and be the subject of high literary appreciation the world over.

Rahn urged Ladame to accompany him to the Sabarthès, specifically to the caves around Ornolac, stressing a number of reasons, chiefly because French was Ladame's mother tongue and also because he could serve as Rahn's porter, painter and draughtsman. Ladame had had extensive experience in speleology and in the use of mine lamps and theodolites, having assisted his brother, a mining engineer and geologist, in preparing for his doctorate.

Ladame learned about Rahn's aims: to discover the secret of the Grail that he believed would unify Europe. He agreed to help but when he arrived in the Ariège Rahn was tense and in a terrible rush. Rahn

---

[3] Bernadac

[4] Ibid

drove Ladame the next morning to the Cathar grottos. He tried to convince Ladame of the seriousness of his work.

Notably, these were the first and last references ever reported as having been made by Rahn about his professed "important historical discoveries" and his quest to discover the "secret of the Grail," which, remarkably, would bring together the pieces of a fragmented Europe. If there were any elements of truth in these claims then silence fell on them with lightning speed.

Why might Rahn have made concrete declarations of success in the Grailhunting business if he was not intent on repeating them or, more to the point, in producing the goods for the world to see and thereby earning lasting popular acclaim? There are a number of possible scenarios.

Firstly, Rahn was correct in his statements to Ladame that he had located the motherlode of Judeo-Christian treasures but he had spoken out of turn and was forbidden to speak further by persons who might profit by such phenomenal discoveries. We do not have to search far to identify those who might have been close by in those days and to whose bidding Rahn may have been in tow. We examine these characters below.

Secondly, he made the announcements in the knowledge that he was making false claims but felt obliged to do so to pacify the expectations of others, quite probably the same persons who populated his motley entourage on his Pyrenean excursions and who, in turn, were undoubtedly acting on behalf of one or more members of the Nazi hierarchy, Himmler principally.

Thirdly, Rahn might have genuinely believed he had struck gold and located the Treasures of the Temple of Solomon but, on delving deeper into the grottoes with Ladame's help, simply discovered he was wrong and made no further mention of them to save face.

Lastly, but not least, further investigation could have indicated to Rahn that no actual artefacts, after all, were visibly evident but that sufficient compelling evidence was subsequently identified to make a very convincing case that physical discovery was simply a matter of time and patience. This scenario would support the allocation of resources to the type of mission described by Angebert as having been undertaken in the spring of 1944 for the successful retrieval of runic tablets based on information purportedly left behind by Rahn.

Whatever the true circumstances of Rahn's predicament at that time efforts continued apace to excavate the Sabarthès caverns and Rahn was very much part of the team.

Paul Bernadac, grandfather of Christian Bernadac, was an enthusiastic potholer with an interest in local history. He joined Rahn, Ladame and others on several excursions in 1932, serving as driver and quartermaster. He would always include in the provisions a flask of absinthe, a brew the Swiss called "La Fée Verte" (the Green Fairy). They would imbibe it on a lump of sugar taking sips of cold water to melt the sugar on their tongues. Deodat Roché would often join the group. Paul Bernadac recalled Rahn being roughed up by Joseph Mandement, President of the Syndicat d'Initiative de Tarascon-sur-Ariège, when he caught Rahn faking Cathar engravings. Rahn's defence was that ancient cave drawings, fading over the centuries, needed to have their time-eroded lines sharpened up with a few chalk strokes to make them photograph better.

A Bordeaux engineer named Arnaud was also treasure hunting in the vicinity and was apparently financed in his search by the French Theosophical Society. He was equipped with dynamite and divining rods. Arnaud had agreed a contract with the village commune that owned the chateau, which promised he would give to them half of any treasure he found. He believed this treasure to be gold and silver. Arnaud also told Rahn that he expected to find the real gospel of John the Evangelist, which contained the true teachings of Jesus, having been in the care and custody of the Cathars. When Rahn asked Arnaud how he could be so specific with his information the engineer told him he could not elaborate because he was part of a society that required silence from its members on these subjects. Arnaud also told Rahn that he knew where Esclarmonde de Foix was buried.

Rahn mistrusted Arnaud intensely. Interestingly, Rahn says in *Luzifers Hofgesind* that the engineer would never find the treasure, which was hidden in the forest of Thabor, guarded by vipers, the entrance blocked by an enormous stone. How could Rahn have been so confident that Arnaud would come away empty handed unless he knew the artefacts' precise location or, more intriguingly, that they had already been retrieved, either by himself or by others close to him?

At this time there was a widespread belief among the Languedocian aristocracry that, unlike the peasantry, they were descended from Nordic or German blood and saw themselves as cousins of the Germans. René Nelli believes that when they read Rahn's work the Nazis saw the potential of exploiting this belief. Ferdinand Niel was one of the last Aquitainians to recall Rahn: "his clothes were as tattered as mine…I read his book (the French version: *Croisade Contre le Graal*) as one should read it, as a novel, but he showed me that the importance of Montségur could go far beyond local or regional interest…I concluded: Montsalvage, the Grail Castle, did really exist…the Grail castle is Montségur and none other."[5]

There is a mystery concerning Rahn's finances. During his initial stay in France it was known that he had little money but in May 1932 Rahn tried his hand at being a businessman and bought for fifteen thousand francs a three-year lease on the Hôtel-Restaurant des Marronniers in Ussat-les-Bains. Among the guests he was said to have invited there were Josephine Baker and Marlene Dietrich. His parents also visited from Hessisch-Lorsch.

The hotel was said to have had a bohemian flavour, playing Negro music. Rahn did strike up a particular friendship with a Senegalese barman named Habdu who subsequently became Rahn's manservant and bodyguard. Author Ruediger Suenner believes that Rahn and Habdu might have been lovers. The Hôtel-Restaurant des Marronniers burned down in mysterious circumstances more than twenty years ago.

Where did Rahn obtain the funds for the hotel lease purchase and why did he encumber himself with this responsibility when Gadal and Comtesse Pujol-Murat ostensibly provided largely for his needs in France?

Arnaud d'Apremont writes of excursions into the surrounding areas where Rahn is accompanied by a number of unsavoury characters, sorties whose goal seemed incompatible with serious and scholarly archaeological research. Rahn's sudden enrichment, coupled with his associations with shifty looking strangers, was proof for many that he was in the pay of the German security services. I have already suggested that Rahn's sudden but untypical attack of reticence following his bold claims of success to Paul Ladame may have been imposed upon him by members of his travelling clan.

The group's chief "unsavoury" character was Nat Wolff, a portly man of similar height to Rahn but of larger build and who wore his hair

[5] Niel, Ferdinand. *Montségur, temple et forteresse des cathares d'Occitaine*, pp 11-12

in the severe razored Prussian style. Like Widdeger, Wolff also wore loud clothing. Wolff said he was an American from Rochester, New York; he had lived in Marrakesh but everyone at Ussat-les-Bains called him Karl and he had only a vague grasp of the English language. He said he was in charge of a photographic mission for tourists on behalf of the American consulate in Paris. However, his letters came from Berlin-Charlottenburg and from Munich. Wolff returned several times to Ussat-les-Bains, always accompanied by others and they would roam night and day in the grottoes. Among his companions were Salvador Barcos Escude, a travelling salesman, and artist Alain Albert Haustrate.

During the winter of 1931 this mixed bag of companions travelled with Rahn on a trip to Carcassonne, Port-Vendres, Cerbère, Marseilles and Puigcerdà. While traversing Le Val de L'Incant (the Enchanted Valley) Rahn was obliged to kill a viper he had trodden on. These visits are described in detail in *Luzifers Hofgesind.*

Rahn with friend

Years later in 1938, while on a short trip to the Ariège, Wolff let his cover slip and was discovered by the French authorities to be travelling on two passports (giving different birth dates) and using the aliases Kurt Hermann and Hermann Kubt. He was suspected of being a German agent, eventually being the subject of an expulsion order by the Minister of the Interior.

Christian Bernadac thinks this person could have been the high-ranking Nazi Karl Wolff (1900-1984). Authors have depicted Karl Wolff as one of the original members of the SS on its formation in 1926, saying that he was given the task of cultivating individuals and groups that were sympathetic to the Nazis, initially in Germany and later abroad. Wolff is said to have been engaged in this work until 1933 whence he returned to Germany as Himmler's personal assistant.

According to records, these assertions cannot be true. Wolff did not join the NSDAP until 7th October 1931. At that time the upper-middle class Hessian was owner-manager of a small business—the Karl Wolff-von Römbold Advertising Company, which he had been running for several years and which was struggling to survive. Nevertheless, Wolff, the son of a district court judge, had served with distinction in the Great War, serving in the Bodyguard Infantry Regiment 115 of the Grand Duke of Hess (Queen Victoria's grandson), winning the Iron Cross by the age of eighteen.

Impressed with the rising fortunes of Hitler's Nazi Party and eager to renew his commitment to the Fatherland, Wolff joined the "brown battalions" of the NSDAP. Simultaneously, Wolff signed an SS Acceptance and Commitment Certificate, which initiated a form of basic, unpaid SS membership. It was not until June 1933 that Wolff became a fully-fledged salaried member of the Black Corps, having sold his advertising business to one of his SS comrades. Even then, Wolff's position was that of a lowly adjutant to Himmler and the Reichsführer SS had plenty more of those, including his chief letter writer Haupsturnbannführer Suchsland who in autumn 1933 was deputed to work for Colonel Weisthor.

Although it is fact that Wolff subsequently became a great favourite of Himmler (who called him Wolffchen—"Wolffie") and enjoyed a very rapid rise in seniority, receiving three promotions in just seven months, all this took place two and a half years after Otto Rahn had begun his Languedoc explorations.

On the other hand, there is no certain way to establish if Wolff did indeed have a hidden working relationship with Himmler from an earlier time than history records. Wolff's liaison and organising expertise, which so appealed to Himmler, could have been an enticing package of skills, ideal for a role in the South of France as a covert overseer of Otto Rahn's efforts to locate the Grail cache (in line with the unproven hypothesis that Rahn was directed to mount the investigations on Himmler's behalf). As the man in charge at his advertising company premises in Munich's upper class suburb of Bogenhausen, Wolff could presumably have taken as much time away from his desk as he wished. Ironically, in this scenario it could have beeen Wolff's prolonged absences from a day-to-day, hands-on chief executive role in 1931 that exacerbated his company's worsening financial position. And who can say if Wolff's dizzy ascent to high office was not at least, in part, Himmler's grateful reward for successful management in undertaking the task of secret controller to Otto Rahn during his Grail investigations?

As for the description of Nat Wolff as "portly", the Munich

daily *Süddeutschen Zeitung*, reporting on proceedings when Karl Wolff was brought to trial by the Munich authorities for war crimes in 1963, did describe Wolff as "corpulent."

Isabelle Sandy told Bernadac that Rahn had 'protectors' in the area but refused point-blank to name them except to say that one of them was Antoinette Rives. Sandy said that Rahn was an admirer of Hitler but that he did not regard war, especially with France, as inevitable, and that he hoped his work would lay the foundation of a Franco-German alliance. This was a curious thing to say and one wonders how the unearthing of treasure trove, no matter how valuable or prestigious, could have influenced high level European politics in the way Rahn appeared to wish for.

In 1934 Rahn would confide in a letter to Gadal that the sole factor that denied him any real enjoyment of his Pyrenean adventures was the presence of Nat Wolff. Stressing his own tolerant nature, Rahn deplored Wolff's personality flaws brought about by his mixed "Jewish and American origins," observing that Wolff stood in direct contrast to Gadal's heroic ancestors: meaning the Cathar brethren and the Grail Knights of old who were rewarded for their idealism with immolation at the stake. "Portly" Wolff, Rahn observed bitterly, was incapable of sacrificing a single meal to a starving person let alone give up his life for his beliefs. These are strong sentiments. If "Nat" Wolff was as insignificant a figure as he tooks pain to portray, just one among a bunch of hangers-on deferring to Otto Rahn's group leader expertise, one wonders why Rahn was so rattled unless Wolff was, after all, much more than he seemed.

We will put General Karl Wolff under the microscope in Part 2 AFTER LIFE in the context of examining the actors responsible for post-World War II Nazi survival policy and Rahn's close relationship to those engaged in it.

It has been also suggested that while in France Rahn was in the secret service of Otto Abetz, head of the Dienststelle (Office) Ribbentrop from 1933, and engaging in espionage to influence French politics while posing as journalist and hotelier. Considering that facts, I am prepared to consider that this theory might be more than idle speculation. Otto Abetz played his own unique role in the Nazi movement, especially in his contribution to the efforts to find a third way between National Socialism and Communism, actions that directly contributed to the rise and development of post-war international fascism. Abetz will similarly be placed in the interrogator's chair in Part 2 and asked to provide a full account of his actions in developing the

Fascist International movement that would take shape after the end of the war.

Within five months of Rahn entering the hotel business his finances were once more in a complete mess. It was as if the venture had served a purpose, now fulfilled, and the guise could fall away. Rahn decided it was time to make tracks.

In the same month that Rahn had told Paul Ladame about his big discovery in the caves at Ornolac he left the Languedoc, leaving various unpaid bills. He travelled north to Saint-Germain-en-Laye near Paris. In October a petition for bankruptcy was made by Antoine Arques, owner of Hôtel-Restaurant des Marronniers, and on the 6th the Commercial Court in Foix declared Rahn bankrupt. Because Rahn had left Ussat-les-Bains several weeks earlier a warrant was served against him. He had run headfirst into trouble because in addition to his financial fiasco, Rahn was accused both of being a German spy and of being the leader of an international secret society whose headquarters was the Hôtel-Restaurant des Marronniers. This latter accusation is most startling. Although there is no proof that Rahn was linked at during his life with any such clandestine society this was not the last occasion when third parties would impute him with membership, even leadership, of a secret, influential order.

While Rahn was under siege from his Ariègois creditors he wrote from Paris to Antonin Gadal in November, telling his mentor that he had received the finalised contracts for the German, English and American issues of his first book: *Kreuzzug Gegen den Gral,* translating into English as *Crusade against the Grail: the Romantic Culturé in Creation and in Death.*

The first German issue was to be a luxurious one for which Rahn was to be paid twenty four thousand francs. Before going to the printers the book would be serialised in either the *Vossichen Zeitung* or the *Frankfurter Zeitung* newspapers. Rahn was ecstatic that he was expecting to receive one hundred thousand francs for his masterwork but his letters emphasise just how hard he had had to toil to attract such rewards. He complained of his liver problems (possibly self-inflicted—Rahn found alcohol hard to resist) and of his endless hunger. He says that a Madame Pons saved him but we know nothing about this handy benefactor.

Around this time, Rahn informed Gadal, somebody wrote an anonymous letter to his parents. That its content was derogatory towards the young writer was evidenced by the annoyance of his father who tried to persuade his son to come home and not to return to France.

Otto Rahn told Gadal that he was grateful about the kind words that his friend had spread among the Montségur community in an effort to restore more hospitable attitudes about Rahn's brief but controversial stay in the Languedoc.

Gabriele Winckler confirmed to me in our interview that Rahn was hated by the majority of the locals in and around Montségur because of his supposed heritical views; so much so that he was attacked by farming flails, actions which compelled him to hire the services of a bodyguard, the trusty Habdu from Hôtel-Restaurant des Marronniers.

Remarkably, Frau Winckler tells the extraordinary story of the day when the elderly, local vicar at Montségur came to Rahn, fell on his knees and asked the young German if he could comfort him because he knew his last days had arrived. Rahn turned on the clergyman, putting it to him that he, the vicar, was preaching every Sunday to people, telling them about what happens after death, and that surely he had every qualification to be be able to answer his own question? But for some reason the priest persisted, claiming that Rahn (the "heretic") probably knew more than he.

"What would I have done without you?" Rahn exclaimed in a letter sent to Gadal in November from Saint-Germain-en-Laye. "I have socks with holes which I wash every other day and only one shirt. My coat and my shoes were stolen. But the misery will come to an end, thank God!"[6] Rahn certainly wrote with a strong sense of self-pity. Days later he was complaining about his rights and his parlous finances. "I won't stay silent any longer. I haven't forgotten about those. But where are my rights? Is there anybody who would take a saw from a carpenter? Does anybody take his shirts, his shoes? One should take back the order that I must leave the country and return my shoes! Poor Mr Gadal, I only think of our friendship, our aim, our work. Just imagine, my German publisher would like to accompany me to see you after my book is published, after my debts are paid."[7] It was always "after" Rahn's debts were paid.

Rahn was happy that the first publishing instalment had arrived so that he could pay his room bill. He was expecting a second sum to arrive from England in connection with the proposed British edition. He mentioned to Gadal that he would travel to Berlin to ask his government, the newspapers and the association of German authors for help. How he expected them to solve his problems Rahn does not make

---

[6] letter to Antonin Gadal, 11.20.1932, Saint-Germain-en-Laye, Paris
[7] letter to Antonin Gadal, 11.24.1932, Saint-Germain-en-Laye, Paris

clear. He obviously felt as if the world owed him recompense for injustices he had suffered while in France. What might have shaped his thoughts to these beliefs is uncertain. It is possible, of course, that he presented a hard done by image to deflect attention from a willing relationship with Himmler and his circle.

Another scenario encourages one to consider whether Rahn's stay in France had been a directive from on high rather than by freedom of choice. If Rahn had been ordered there, for instance, by senior Nazi dignitaries and insult was added to injury because of a hostile reception by locals, Rahn would have felt a natural indignation that demanded both recognition and a solution. However, this is supposition. There is actually no hard and fast evidence that Rahn was making his Pyrenean explorations for anyone other than himself and to develop his ambitious theories about the hidden messages in von Eschenbach's *Parsifal*.

Rahn told Gadal that he would not, of course, have suffered from all the attacks had he chosen not to live at Ussat-les-Bains. Curiously, Rahn goes on to say that were it not for these attacks he would not have understood the suffering of the Cathars; that it had to be this way. He saw it as a balancing circumstance to offset his easy life in the past. He had to endure strong feelings to appreciate the passions and beliefs of the Pure Ones. He wondered if his publisher, an old and experienced gentleman, could have possibly understood the power and significance of the Cathar 'Consolamentum' unless he, Otto Rahn, had understood it first hand by virtue of the violent reception he had received from the Ussat-les-Bains villagers.

It appears that Rahn *was* able to convey some of the power of which he spoke to his publisher who, aghast at what he saw happening in Germany, was about to close up his business and move to England. After meeting with Otto Rahn and hearing the writer describe the content and philosophies in *Kreuzzug Gegen den Gral*, the old man decided to stay put. He later wrote to Rahn saying: "I did never look forward to a book as I do to yours. Thousands of Germans paid for it in impatience. You have got a huge task to fulfil. You have to explain what humanity has lost for seven centuries. You have to comfort our fellows and show them the path because they are going in the wrong direction."[8] Rahn was beginning to weave his spell.

The espionage hysteria forced Rahn to return under the cover of darkness to Ussat-les-Bains in late December 1932 to answer the warrant. Rahn was obliged to meet with a Mr Perie and the local Justice of the Peace to have his passport authenticated. Police officials

---

[8] ibid

informed him that Ussat-les-Bains was currently his official residence in France and, consequently, no force on earth could hinder the Ornolac judge in determining what he felt had to be done in Rahn's case. The experience with the judge was a salutary one. Rahn wrote to Gadal from Foix on 22nd December complaining that the judge wanted him to make an immediate contribution towards his debts, failing which he would be prosecuted. Rahn tried to offer his recently negotiated book contract as collateral, a suggestion that was turned down flat. Rahn then tried to offer the proceeds from an article that was about to be published. The judge laughed, saying that: "only liquidity counts."

Rahn was even more upset that the red tape had prevented him meeting with Gadal to discuss the Greek myths and the Apollo cult in Delphi. He retrieved his passport from official custody but how he pulled this off is uncertain. However, it is likely that an expulsion order was served on him. Never again would there be any unequivocal evidence that Rahn returned to the places of his investigations. Rahn quit France soon after this debacle.

What can we deduce from Rahn's activities in France to establish his credentials: Grail Knight or black adept? On the face of it we see a picture of a man more aligned with shadowy and unsavoury forces than with the heroic ideals of the Cathar Pure Ones in whom he expressed such admiration. Rahn tagged along with an eclectic bunch that would not have looked out of place in a travelling circus but whose members may conceivably have included Karl Wolff, Himmler's Chief of Staff and later head of the SS in Italy, whose job would have been to keep Rahn on a very short leash. Rahn borrowed money left, right and centre, which he never repaid. Most crucially, Rahn incurred the wrath of the villagers in and around Montségur to such a degree that, according to Frau Winckler's testimony, they attacked him with pitchforks and flails. What he did to encourage such anger is not recorded but clearly he did not wholly present an image of the blue-eyed golden boy in France that some texts describe. It may have been the case that he did not commit any specific actions that solicited violent opinions, although we have Christian Bernadac's account of Joseph Mandement's physical attack on Rahn for faking cave drawings. The simple fact remains that Germans in France at this time were simply not trusted. They were regarded with outright suspicion and Rahn especially evoked this emotion by virtue of his ragbag travel mates.

But the jury has not yet retired to consider its verdict. It is very early days in our review of this enigmatic man. As we have observed, legends do not grow without good reason. There is something deep within that is titillated by the activities of seekers like Otto Rahn. In his particular case we are moved to unearth the cache, albeit that it may turn out to be an unremarkable cup in a long-forgotten subterranean resting place. At the end of *Indiana Jones and the Last Crusade*, in which the Grail chalice is found to be a nondescript wooden cup, Indie asks his father, played by Sean Connery: "Why have you spent your life looking for the Grail?" His father's simple answer is: "Illumination."

We ask for neither more nor less in our quest to unearth the true agenda of Otto Rahn.

Chapter FOUR

The Polaires

Before we review Otto Rahn's life on his return to Germany in the spring of 1933 we should firstly examine his links with a curious but influential metaphysical sect, *La Fraternité des Polaires,* which nailed its colours to Theosophy and to the nineteenth century supporters of the mythical subterranean realms of Agartha and Shamballah. We will return to these legendary worlds. For the present, this snapshot review will begin to offer us an insight into Otto Rahn's sympathies with the key Western mystical schools of thought, in particular with Illuminist and Rosicrucian philosophies. It will encourage us to link Rahn more transparently with the German occult establishment as exemplified by the influential Vril and Thule Societies. Our review may persuade us to consider that far from being a young man on the fringes of occult-mystical circles, Otto Rahn was a key personality who, unobserved, wielded considerable influence among the courageous movements opposed to Hitler's policies.

In the 6th March 1932 edition of *La Dépêche* an argument arose about the activities of a group of Polaires, a society especially active in France and England. The article questioned the nature of the activities of a German the journalist named as Monsieur Rams, changing the name in a follow-up piece the following day to Rahu. At the same time as Otto Rahn was engaged in his exploration activities, Polaires members were similarly excavating in the caves of Ussat-les-Bains and Ornolac. Rahn was said to be the leader of this group and suspicions were raised because of his nationality, there being much anti-German feeling at this time by rural folk whose memories of the Great War had scarcely diminished. Antonin Gadal wrote to a newspaper in Rahn's defence, saying that his visit had nothing to do with the Polaires. Rahn himself subsequently wrote to the paper, correcting the spelling of his name and stressing that he had never heard of the Polaires before coming to the Ariège. He was a simply a writer interested in the Cathars. Rahn's riposte emphasised that neither his friends nor he were occultists or spiritualists. Do we believe him?

The Polaires originated in 1908 when twelve-year old Mario Fille met a hermit named Father Julian in the hills near Rome. The hermit gave a number of old parchments to Mario containing the *Oracle of Astral Energy*. However, the steps in the process were long-winded and wrapped in a complex system of word and number manipulations.

The complexities forced Mario to put the Oracle to one side and he only returned to the parchments twelve years later when he used them to help with some personal difficulties. The instructions consisted in phrasing a question in Italian. The querent would then add his name and his mother's maiden name, somehow translate them into numbers and, finally, carry out a mathematical procedure. This long and unwieldy process produced a final set of numbers, which the querent translated into letters to provide an answer. In practice, the Oracle always answered reliably with credible responses but, oddly, its answers were as likely to be expressed in French or German as in Italian. True to the wishes of Father Julian, Mario alone possessed the key to decoding the Oracle.

The Oracle was said not to be a form of divination in the conventional sense but, extraordinarily, to be an actual channel with the purported Rosicrucian initiate centre of Asia Mysteriosa in the Himalayas. This channel was directed by the "The Supreme Sages" or the "Little Lights of the Orient" who live in Agartha. These at first included Father Julian but after his death on 8th April 1930 the baton passed to a "Chevalier Rose-Croix." The Knight in question was never named but it was surmised that he was the guiding light of the neo-Theosophists: the "Master Racoczy," otherwise variously known as Roger Bacon, Francis Bacon and the Comte de Saint-Germain. This facet alone of the Polaires account is very interesting in the Rahn context because of the strong link it reveals between the philosophical inspiration behind the Oracle and the source of Rahn's own esoteric beliefs explored in Part 3 MEANING.

Together with his boyhood friend and fellow musician, Cesare Accomani, Fille moved to Paris where the Oracle was shown to a group of journalists and writers. Some were sufficiently moved to publicise it and to contribute to Accomani's 1929 book *Asia Mysteriosa,* published under the pseudonym "Zam Bhotiva."

One of the Oracle's supporters in France was Maurice Magré who, we have seeen, was a major influence on Rahn's research work in France; perhaps, taking Hans-Jürgen Lange's views into account, even directly sewing the seed that Rahn should focus upon the Cathar-Grail legends. The Toulousian poet firmly linked the Oracle's origins to H.P Blavatsky's Theosophy when he wrote that "the existence of this brotherhood, variously known as 'Agarttha' and as the 'Great White

Lodge,' is what it has always been, but unproven by those 'material evidences' of which the Western mind is so fond."[1] He added that: "the revelations of Saint-Yves d'Alveydre in *La Mission de l'Inde,* despite their apparent improbability, must contain part of the truth."[2]

Magré was an undoubted admirer of Otto Rahn but his appreciation for the much younger man was short-lived, subsequently having a dig at Rahn in *La Clé des Choses Cachées* saying that "...his *(Kreuzzug gegen den Gral*) book, while written with love, carries an abundance of documentation." Magré ended up suspecting that Rahn was a spy, convinced that the nationalist political events of the early thirties were bound to exert an influence such that even a passionate scholar and adventurer like Rahn could not resist. Perhaps the truth is that Magré, quite simply, was jealous of Otto Rahn's enthusiasm and academic rigour. Magré would doubtless, too, have been still smarting about Rahn's published dismissal of his Tibet-Cathar theory. Magré later severed his connections with the Polaires after an internal squabble. Interestingly, Magré was one of the insipirational figures behind the establishment of the late nineteenth century occult Paris salons of Joséphin Péladan and J.K. Huysmanns. We will recall this when examining the links between Rahn and the European occult underground, which grew into full bloom in the late nineteenth century.

Another supporter of *Asia Mysteriosa* was Jean Marques-Rivière whose specialist topics were Tibetan Buddhism and Tantrism. Joscelyn Godwin[3] points out that Marques-Rivière in his Foreword to *Asia Mysteriosa* mentions that mystics Emmanuel Swedenborg and Anne Catherine Emmerich had both believed in a spiritual centre located in Tibet. Marques-Rivière wrote: "Now, the centre of trans-human power has a reflection on the earth; it is a constant tradition in Asia, and this Centre…is called in Central Asia *Agarttha.* It has many other missions, or rather as its reason for existence, the direction of the spiritual activities of the Earth." The importance of Tibetan Lamaism and ritual is central to a study of Otto Rahn's life and we will return to this theme.

Others who accepted the Oracle's provenance included alchemist Arturo Reghini. Reghini was responsible for introducing the mystic-fascist Baron Giulio (Julius) Evola to the works of René Guénon. Rahn sincerely admired the work of Evola (1898-1974), a

---

[1] Bhotiva 1929

[2] ibid

[3] Godwin, Joscelyn. *Arktos: the Polar Myth in Science, Symbolism and Nazi Survival.* Grand Rapids: Phanes Press, 1993

confidant of Mussolini, whose seminal work, *Rivolta contro il mondo moderno* (*Revolt against the Modern World*), was published in Germany in 1935. One can imagine Rahn, a voracious reader, boring into its pages in a single mammoth sitting, absorbing its startling premise that the cults of the Mother Goddess and of the Earth sprang from a splicing of the Atlantean civilisation with dark telluric elements of the yet more ancient Lemurian race. Evola's Nazi sympathies will be brought into sharp focus when we review the factors linking Otto Rahn's Nazi superiors to the founders of international fascism.

Evidently, Otto Rahn empathised with Evola's portrayal of prehistory's degeneration from a male dominated Golden Age to the Silver Age cycle of the Goddesses of Earth and Moon, the impure product of the marriage of the Sun-god warriors of the ancient North with the feminine cults of the South. Both Rahn and Evola believed, however, that one branch of the Arctic Hyperboreans did survive with its solar traditions largely intact. It was this race, unsullied by the inbreedings that befell its Aryan counterpart, which went on to populate Europe and India. Jean Mabire later observed the irony that Evola aroused too much emnity not to have been, like Rahn, a Luciferian: a "lightbringer." One wonders if Rahn and Evola corresponded. They may well have met on the occasion in 1938 when Evola was given a tour of the SS castles and praised the Order's "spiritual solidarity, which might become supra-national."[4]

Prominent Polaires member, writer and journalist Fernand Divoire (1883-1940), maintained a relationship with a group calling itself "la Société Initiatique Allemande Thulé," and he is believed to have helped Otto Rahn with his Grail research at Montségur. If Rahn did consort with Divoire, a man evidently known to associate with high level German esoteric society, one might ask if Rahn shared his helper's occult allegiances or whether their relationship was wholly a practical one to help expedite the Sabarthès explorations.

Interestingly, a considerably more famous associate of the Polaires was Sir Arthur Conan Doyle who, besides being world renowned for creating Sherlock Holmes, was a high profile Spiritualist. However, this connection with the Polaires began only *after* Conan Doyle's death on 7th July 1930. Following a series of psychic communications between England and France, Zam Bhotiva contacted London medium, Grace Cooke, in January 1931. Through her mediumship, Bhotiva heard Conan Doyle affirm that the Polaires were "destined to help in the molding of the future of the world...for the

---

[4] cited Parvelescu 1986

times are near." Mrs. Cooke's spirit guide, a Tibetan Sage named White Eagle, stated that Bhotiva had come on instructions from Tibet. The Chevalier Rose-Croix confirmed that Conan Doyle was to help the Brotherhood: "See the star rises in the East; it is the sign of the Polaires, the sign of the two interlaced triangles."

The *Bulletin des Polaires* of 9th June 1930 explained the seeming paradox between an Asian mystery centre and a Polar concept: "The Polaires take this name because from all time the Sacred Mountain, that is the symbolic location of the Initiatic Centres, has always been qualified by different traditions as 'polar.' And it may very well be that this Mountain was once really polar, in the geographical sense of the word, since it is stated everywhere that the Boreal Tradition (or the Primordial Tradition, source of all Traditions) originally had its seat in the Hyperborean regions."[5] Considering Otto Rahn's high regard for Montségur and its place in metaphysical European history, might we not assume that Rahn regarded its Pog as a Sacred Centre, an antenna of initiatory energy that transmitted its mystic rays to all those embarked upon a personal path of Quest adventure? There is abundant evidence in Rahn's writings that he regarded Montségur as an Apollonian Temple and in Chapter 26 we will look at this in more detail.

During 1929 and 1930 the Polaires made excavations in the Montségur area. According to a local newspaper, the Polaires had found traces of Christian Rosenkreutz's travels in the ruins of Lordat castle. This report corresponds with Zam Bhotiva's alleged discovery, via the Oracle, of the "Wand of Pico della Mirandola," which was said to shiver in the near presence of gold. With a lady companion, Bhotiva set off to find the lost treasure of Montségur (at one time in the early thirties there must have been a veritable queue of hopefuls scouring the grottoes), but having no success either there or in Spain (presumably around Montserrat) he quit the search and, thoroughly disgruntled, the Polaires.

By 1936 there were separate Polaires groups for men and women in capital cities in Europe and America, each dedicated to working for the good of mankind under Mario Fille's direction. Information on the Polaires is hard to come by. The Fraternity's papers were seized from the Paris headquarters of the Theosophical Society by German forces during the Occupation, an action which, according to Bernadac, was ordered by Alfred Rosenberg who sought the documents for his academy at Frankfurt, a cultural and learning centre established to provide a historical foundation for the justification of Nazism. One

---

[5] ibid

wonders why the son of an Estonian cobbler bothered because, as Godwin has astutely noted, Hitler did not for one moment regard Rosenberg's book *Der Mythus des 20. Jahrhunderts* (*The Myth of the Twentieth Century*, 1930) as representative of the truth regarding the revisionist Polar and Atlantean origins of Aryanism. Hitler had scant regard for the Thule Society or for any of its associated occult fraternities.

According to Joseph Mandement, the Polaires were looking for traces of Christian Rosenkreutz who, they believed, had passed through the area. Some recall Italian members of the group visiting Lordat as late as 1960.

An anonomous informant told Christian Bernadac that Otto Rahn, too, had shown a particular interest in Lordat *and had returned there several times after the war*. A Rosicrucian to the last, Rahn could evidently not resist, even in death, undertaking searches for the vault of the Rosicrucian founder, Father C.R.C., and the spiritual riches it is said to contain.

The commemorative stele erected at the foot of Montségur to honour the more than 200 Cathar faithful executed by the Roman Church in March 1244

Chapter FIVE

Germany 1933-1935
"...a precious treasure"

Early in 1933 Rahn was once more in Germany, taking up residence in Berlin-Charlottenberg. It is a period in which we see Rahn capitalising in his home country upon his activities in the Pyrenees. He became something of a media celebrity, which suggests that Rahn, either alone or with some PR support from others, succeeded in creating the image of an explorer who had made significant discoveries or had even brought home something of value to his native land. We will see that in this scenario Rahn at no time was recorded in his public statements as claiming to have made fabulous finds. Instead, we see Rahn describing (and embellishing) his adventures in the grottoes and offering these excursions as material deserving of high profile attention and, hence, a means to earn extra income for the impoverished writer.

In the first weeks of his arrival Rahn was concerned for his mother's health, informing Albert Rausch that she was very sick. Presumably, Frau Rahn made a quick recovery because a short time later Otto was telling Rausch excitedly about the marvellous prospects for his forthcoming book *Kreuzzug gegen den Gral*, leaving aside any mention of his mother's condition. Rahn's correspondence in this period focused predominantly on day-to-day, hand-to-mouth matters. Mention of his treasure hunting excursions in the Pyrenees and, more to the point, any successes he might have achieved continue to be conspicuous by their absence. We hear no more about his having made "one of the most important historical discoveries," an episode over which, if true, the Nazi leadership would have undoubtedly drawn a complete communications blackout.

Clearly, Rahn had his hands full in just keeping body and soul together. He complained to Gadal that he was going hungry, remarking that he had had to leave his watch at a bakery to buy bread; that his shoes were full of holes.[1] In his letters Rahn would always bemoan his financial plight and then, in contrite manner, try to put his poverty into

[1] cited Bernadac

context by emphasising the rich seams of European history that continued to guide and inspire his work. Rahn stressed that he did not want his material worries to pursue him to the special places of pilgrimage in and around Ussat-les-Bains. He evidently intended to return to the Sabarthès to resume his subterranean wanderings and, by implication, his search for riches (if he had not found them or identified their location already). But his life was taking a different course.

As knowledge grew of Otto Rahn's researches into the Grail histories, so did demand from German publications and radio stations for him to provide articles and broadcast material. He apologises to Gadal for rushing his letters and for his poor grammar, blaming it on his increasingly busy schedule. Rahn was excited that the *Berliner Tagesblatt* was about to print an introduction to his new book and to supply a table of contents. The *Frankfurter Zeitung* was going to run a feature article about him and he had also been interviewed in quick succession by both Radio Stuttgart and Radio Frankfurt. The radio stations commissioned him to compile two reports. The first would cover the battles at Vicdessos and La Gunarde, locations connected with the legends of the Grail Castle. The other would focus upon the plateau of Lombrives where "strange traces" had been found, the nature of which was not spelled out. Rahn told Gadal that having to concentrate on these two reports ensured he would not give up on their Sabarthès caves; that his caver's lamp was undimmed.

In the early autumn of 1933, following on from his library researches and his ground-breaking studies in the Pyrenees, Otto Rahn completed in Heidelberg *Kreuzzug gegen den Gral* two years after beginning the work. His publisher later recalled their first meeting in 1931. Rahn arrived at their office without a coat and wearing only a beret as protection against the bitter cold. His boundless enthusiasm for his project was infectious and the publishing house quickly completed a contract that spurred Rahn on to its completion. Otto Vogelsgang wrote to Albert Rausch in January 1934 remarking that Isabelle Sandy wanted to promote *Kreuzzug gegen den Gral* in the Parisian press. He was also pleased that Rausch was trying to organise an American edition.

Once published in Germany, *Kreuzzug gegen den Gral* was not a best seller, selling just two thousand copies and as many again in France. But it touched deeply those who came to it. Despite the initial sales figures, Rahn was buoyed by the overall positive critical response to the book and he told Gadal that, all things being equal, his future augured well.

At the same time Albert Rausch was writing in glowing terms to

Monsieur Delamain of the Paris publishing house *Delamain et Boutelleau* about the wonderful book that his friend, Otto Rahn, had written. Rausch paints a hugely complimentary picture of Rahn's oeuvre, which, he explains, is the result of two years research in the Pyrenean grottoes. In true spinmeister fashion, Rausch praises a masterwork which has already created a huge sensation in Germany and beyond because of its great breadth and scope of subject. Rausch invited Delamain to serve as Rahn's French publisher because, assuredly, the work would be a big success in France and, he emphasised, if Delamain was interested he had to act quickly (the obvious inference being that if his company did not pick it up then a competitor surely would). Rausch had obviously forwarded a copy to Delamain's wife because he mentions that she would also be briefing her husband after a day or two of reading.

Rahn writes from Frankfurt in late September thanking Rausch sincerely for his recommendations to Delamain. He is finalising radio scripts for Wolfgang Frommel of Southwest Radio, which are expected by the 22nd.

By October Rahn is writing once more to Rausch and musing on the ironies that had led to a young man from Hesse making historically important discoveries in the Languedoc. Rahn tells Albert that he believed it was his destiny to unearth the findings. Once more, having been presented with tantalising statements from Rahn about achieving important discoveries, we are left none the wiser as to their nature. Frommel and Rahn were friends but Joachim Kohlhaas confirmed in an interview with Hans-Jürgen Lange that Frommel often disputed Rahn's research findings.

Otto Rahn was in vogue and his correspondence with Antonin Gadal indicates that Rahn hoped that this positive exposure would reverse his fortunes and allow him to fund a return to his beloved Languedoc caverns. He makes it clear that the subject material of his writings remained loyal to the research matters that mentor and acolyte held most dear: the Pyrenean Mountains and their unique position in medieval metaphysical history.

Nevertheless, Rahn felt compelled a short time later to write once more to Gadal affirming afresh that he had not forgotten about him, the caves or his promises. To phrase things in this manner might suggest that a bout of amnesia had been exactly what had seized Rahn's mind within days of his heartfelt protestations. He pleads pressure of work and his customary cash difficulties, saying that he is making little bits of money, sufficient to help satisfy his creditors but leaving nothing for himself. He was pinning his hopes on income from the soon-to-be published French edition of his book, *Croisade contre le Graal*. He was also still in demand on the German media circuit with a forthcoming radio spot to talk about his *Story of the Thieves of Lombrives*, which had been commissioned by a "big German magazine." Presumably, radio producers hired Rahn's services on the cheap otherwise he would not have had so much opportunity to complain about his poverty.

This was also a period when Rahn was making new friends in the broadcasting world. These included Manfred Keyserling, son of philosopher Hermann Keyserling, with whom Rahn participated in a radio play, and Sven Schacht, son of Hjalmar Schacht who was one of Hitler's chief financiers from 1933 to 1939 in his capacity as President of the Reichsbank. (Schacht Sr.'s position did not prevent him from ending up in Dachau after he opposed the financing of Hitler's war plans.)

Another close friend of Rahn's was medical student (later Professor Doctor) Hans Grebe who, in the summer of 1933, provided Otto with accommodation and helped to prepare his radio scripts for Wolfgang Frommel. After this activity Rahn asked Hans if he would help with his planned book on Konrad of Marburg. He suggested that Hans accompany him on a driving trip to Wilnsdorf to research the area where in 1233 Konrad had destroyed a "heretical" school and put to death a number of unfortunates charged by the Church with apostasy. Otto and Hans managed the trip by car as far as Haiger and then they cycled the rest of the way looking for traces of Konrad's activities. In September 1933 Rahn gave his friend a signed copy of *Kreuzzug gegen den Gral*.

From this period also emerged a (homosexual) friendship with Dr. Dietmar Lauermann, a member of the Jugendbundes "gray corps" who wrote radio plays for the Jugendfunk.

Grebe later recounted a time when he came across Rahn wearing a black uniform and SS cap without insignia of rank. In answer to Grebe's enquiring remarks, Rahn said that he had been summoned by Rosenberg to discuss a collaborative project about religion in Germany.

In October Rahn wrote to Rausch remarking upon the irony that he should be the person to reawaken the Cathar-Grail legends: "Must a Hessian drive into the Pyrenees in order to determine that Montségur was Munsalvaesche, the grail-castle? Must a Hessian determine in South-France that Grail-Christians lived in Hesse? (The symbol of the German *amour courtois* was the rose-cross, incidentally, but that is only an aside.)[2] Is it not strange that I, the Hessian who, so often as a high school student, used to hike…where brothers of the Provencal Cathari were once burned, must write books like *Kreuzzug Gegen den Gral* and *Konrad of Marburg?*[3] The material lay before me. I was predestined for it, I believe."

Rahn's aside about the rose-cross is most revealing. It begins to open a line of study where we embark on a markedly different treasure hunt than that during which Otto Rahn sought to obtain King Solomon's fabled artefacts. His comment, offered casually to Rausch but which invites deeper reflection, leads us into the caverns of Rahn's philosophy and esoteric thought, a study of which may reveal treasures as equally alluring, if not more so, than ancient cups and shittim Arks. In Part 3 MEANING we will plunge along the metaphysical pathways of Otto Rahn's inner explorer and see what we may find.

Around this time, most likely in Heidelburg, Rahn wrote about himself: "Due to my book written while I was in France and dealing with clarifications on the relations between German and French Minnesingers, some of the very eager ones had already become suspicious and thought I was a Francophile. All of a sudden this suspicion was replaced by another suspicion called 'agreement with the enemy.' This French sympathiser has a friendship with a French female author who, an employee of Daladiers—dares to write—in the middle of Berlin—a book about the Third Reich! Attention, whispered some! This correspondence with a French publisher is too much to be harmless, whispered others. Why do French papers praise a near-unknown German author considering the still unsatisfactory French-German relations, they shouted? How is it possible that an author on fascistic Italy advertises this young German who has lived for years in France? There must be something wrong, clamoured some. After an article of mine was given to a formerly liberal paper after a press conference (to which I was recommended by a department of the Ministry of Propaganda, which still owes me my fee) and they printed it in one of their evening issues, my reputation was completely ruined. With a bitter aftertaste I left Berlin and tried to work from that point in Heidelberg, my hometown, peacefully. I thought that when somebody lives in Heidelberg and does not get in contact with famous Germans or even foreigners any more, people would see that this person is harmless. This optimistic line of thought was picked up by a radio channel; unfortunately just by the one, but my name was again part of

[2] Rahn's parenthesis

[3] This book was never published

the radio programmes, which was pleasant in a way since my eyes were looking forward to seeing the postman deliver money orders. I had been stony broke for some time, had lots of debts, did not get my royalties in and had wasted lots of time on work I had done for radio stations. And time, of course, means money. But people employed me again...! In Heidelberg I started to rework the French edition of *Kreuzzug gegen den Gral* (translated by a professor of the University of Bordeaux and subsequently published as *Croisade Contre le Gral*)."[4] The "author on fascistic Italy" is not named but can be none other than Julius Evola.

In late spring of 1934 Rahn wrote an article for the *Berliner Illustrirte Zeitung* titled "*Was ich in den Pyrenäenhöhlen erlebte,*" translating as "*What I experienced in a cave in the Pyrenees.*" There was also a radio broadcast of the same title for Rundfunksendung (South West German Broadcasting). I confess that when I first came across a mention of this interview my excitement levels rose by several notches guessing, incorrectly, that this might have been Rahn giving chapter and verse as to the nature of "the most important historical discovery" he had breathlessly proclaimed to Paul Ladame eighteen months previously. Nonetheless, the following extract does yield rich pickings:

Rahn: "My servant twice rescued me but I will speak of it afterward. I was climbing a precipitous slope leading to a cave in Fontanet. This cave is very long and was thought by locals to be such a very dangerous excursion that no one had previously entered it. I was looking for objects or inscriptions maybe. We had walked about two kilometres into the cave when it widened itself into a moderately high hall. Suddenly my companion pointed to a sculpted giant dog carved into the stone. The limestone carving was three metres high and nine metres long. Behind the sculpture the gallery came to a dead end and we could go no further."

Interviewer: "What meaning might this dog have?"

Rahn: "Ah, we asked ourselves that, also. We began looking, my servant searching around and under it; there were rocks everywhere. He managed to move one to reveal a new opening. Here must be found the puzzle's solution! We squeezed ourselves through the opening and crawled in on all fours, arriving shortly into another hall about ten metres high and thirty metres wide. Such galleries are commonplace thereabouts. However, this cavern had three peculiarities: its walls were blackened, a large mound occupied centre position and, lastly, it was dominated by a thunderous noise that we quickly discovered was the

---

[4] cited by Lange *Otto Rahn: Leben und Werk.*, p22-23

roar from a subterranean river that must be running under our feet through a ravine. The power of the water was such that it easily shook the walls of this cavern. We then scrutinised the blackened walls more closely, testing the nature of the rock with our fingertips and discovering that the walls were lined with soot! Mighty fires had burned here once! We turned our attention to the mound and set to it with hand-shovels, quickly unearthing a large number of objects."

Interviewer: "What were these objects?"

Rahn: "Vases, arms, jewelry and dogs! Mixed in with human skulls and bones of dogs!"

Interviewer: "Does the sculpted stone dog-figure you mentioned stand hereby in context?"

Rahn: "Indeed, see. That hall, whose discovery I have just portrayed to you, was two thousand years earlier a grave-chamber for the Celtic tribes then resident in that part of the Pyrenees. The Celts named the God of Death and the Underworld, Dispater. The ancient Greeks called him Pluto. And like the Greeks, the Celts also believed that the realm of the dead was guarded by a hell-dog. I don't know what the Celts named this dog but the Greeks called it Cerberos, as you know. Is it now not strange that a Mediterranean harbour, not that far from my caves, retains the modern day name of Cerbère but in antiquity, when Greek colonists excavated in the Pyrenees for gold, this harbour carried the name Kerberos?"

Interviewer: "How deep are your caves actually?"

Rahn: "The caves of Fontanet include one which has a length of seven kilometres. Another in Lombrives, and most beautiful, is twelve kilometres long and in parts eighty metres high, making it taller than most steeples. But that is far from being the full extent of it and both of those caves probably lead even more profoundly into the earth. In Lombrives I have hiked for more than two hours through a one hundred and fifty metre deep canyon but feared to go no further, and in Fontanet I tried to swim across a big subterranean lake but, again, my fears stopped me short. There have been times when I was surprised to get out of the caves alive. One incident was especially hairy. My servant and I crawled into an unknown part of the caves around Lombrives, a place in fact where we found some interesting inscriptions dating from the reign of the 16th Century French King Henri IV. Before his succession to the throne Henri was said to have been a leader of the French Huguenots, and hidden deep within the Lombrives caves lay the Huguenots' subterranean fortress.

"But I digress. My servant and I crawled in and came to a

cavern whose exit was a passageway a good two metres above floor level. I climbed onto my servant's shoulders to make my exit and then helped pull him up and in after me. We pressed on into the mountain but before long we heard the boom and thunder of rapidly running water and in moments we saw a channel of water approaching us, which quickly became a fast flowing stream. It was upon us!

"We rushed back to the small cavern but this, itself, was already half filled with water. There was nowhere to turn and the water was rapidly climbing. In seconds the level was up to my shoulders; I was sure I would have to swim for my life. But then my manservant came to my rescue. Habdu was his name: a strange name and an equally strange fellow. He was a tree-sized Negro from Senegal, almost two metres tall. Even though the water was up to his chin, Habdu lifted me onto his shoulders and waded through the waters guided by the lamp I had retrieved from my backpack. He carried me in this fashion and in such dreadful conditions for three hours, after which the waters began to recede. This item of good news was outweighed, however, by the fact that our carbide lamp burned out and we had no candles. All that remained to light our way were two boxes of matches! I'll never forget that awful journey, stumbling every step of the way, our bodies soaked, cold and shivering. As the last match burned down we finally reached the main cavern just one kilometre from the outside world. We walked this last stretch in near darkness."

Interviewer: "Where had this sudden tide come from?"

Rahn: "Oh, I have forgotten to tell. While we were crawling around in the cave there was a heavy downpour outside. The rains soaked sponge-like into the porous mountain limestone until it reached saturation point when it discharged its heavy volume into the interior caverns."

Rahn recorded his interview responses in manuscript form and what is revealing is the number of hand-written alterations he made suggesting that he was prone to exaggerate. For example, the sculpted dog is recorded in the first draft as having a modest dimension of just one by three metres but which was subsequently amended to read the three by nine metre measurement quoted in the interview. Evidently, Rahn had more than a little of the showman about him.

Central to this fascinating account is what Rahn regards as the strange transposition of the Mediterranean harbour name known in the ancient days as Kerberos with the modern day name of Cerbore. But what is so odd or noteworthy about it? The two place-name versions share an obvious etymological association. Perhaps by making an issue of it Rahn was actually wishing to draw attention to something else. This opportunity offers up a study that we will develop in detail in Chapter 20. In *Luzifers Hofgesind* Rahn mentions the tale of the Argonauts over and over again. For him it was clearly an extremely important piece of mythography. Like the timber spar from the sacred oak of Dodoni that Jason placed into the prow of the Argo to ensure the voices of the gods were heard, Rahn inserted it in his work to provide a key foundation (a *dietrich*) in support of his dreams and visions. It is on record that Rahn told Wolfgang Frommel he was searching for the Golden Fleece.

After the war Rudolf J. Mund, the last head of the Neu-Templerorden (O.N.T.) and author of *Der Rasputin Himmlers: Die Wiligut-Saga*, wrote to Rahn's first publisher Otto Vogelsang asking if there was any knowledge of Rahn having worked with a Negro shortly before his death. Lange has confirmed that at the time Mund wrote to Vogelsgang there were no references to Rahn's association with his Senegalese servant, Habdu, in any available sources of literature. Why Mund put this question and what prompted it is unclear.

In the same letter Mund also asked if Rahn had ever made any connection between the whereabouts of the Grail and Lake Chiemsee, situated between the towns of Rosenheim and Salzburg, and often referred to as the Bavarian Sea. Chiemsee is a popular resort area in the foothills of the Alps and is close to Berchesgarten. Apparently, the issue of a possible Grail connection with Chiemsee had arisen in the course of work carried out between Rahn and Weisthor. Mund might have been aware of this link.

For Rahn the pattern of daily living went on as before; much of it humdrum, hand-to-mouth activity, mostly underscored by hard luck, hard times and equally hard cheese. Rahn wrote to Gadal on 25th June 1934 from the Hotel Rothe in Heidelberg, telling his old friend that he had been in Paris over Whitsun. The French translation of *Kreuzzug gegen den Gral—Croisade contre le Graal*—had been completed, together with a new epilogue, but it would not be published before October (it would be published by Stock). The delay was a blow to Rahn who, as we have seen, had been counting on early income to reverse his impoverished status.

Rahn informed Gadal that urgent business in Germany had forced him to leave Paris before he could carry out his plan to make a return visit to the Midi. Rahn did not elaborate on the nature of the important business. However, Paul Ladame later recounted a story told to him, he said, by Rahn that while the latter was visiting Paris in 1934 he received a telegram from an anonymous sender, offering him one thousand marks a month to write a follow up to *Kreuzzeg gegen den Gral* and supplying an address in Berlin for a meeting. According to Rahn, the person who greeted him was none other than Heinrich Himmler. This story has never been corroborated by correspondence or by time witnesses. However, if there is any truth to it then by 1934 Rahn was at the call of the Reichsführer SS (and I have suggested that the relationship could have been initiated by the late 1920s), hence the necessity for a speedy visit to Germany.

From this time to his disappearance in 1939 there is no evidence that Rahn ever again returned to France but Jean Michel-Angebert states that he returned to the Ariège in 1937 and Colonel Howard Buechner repeats this claim, adding Rennes-le-Château to Rahn's itinerary. Records show that Rahn did later try to obtain entry visas through the French embassy in Milan but was turned down.

While in Paris, Rahn renewed contact with Antoinette Rives, the daughter of a wealthy Toulousian industrialist. He told Gadal that he was lucky in meeting her again as she was one of the few friends who had never lost faith in him, even when he was deeply in trouble over the Hôtel-Restaurant des Marronniers affair. In a conversation with Mme Rives Rahn told her that Napoleon had taken part in a mass for Jacques de Molay, Grand Master of the Knights Templar at the time of the Order's dissolution in 1307. Rahn remarked upon "the all powerful Templars of the Middle Ages...always present in their long night where we, the Germans, can see them, whereas the West does not want to know about them...Powerful yesterday and today like my country itself, they prepare the Future in silence." The latter part of Rahn's remarks clearly invoke the Arthurian theme of the Once and Future King resting in timeless sleep, awaiting the occasion when an imperilled world calls for his return as protector and saviour.

It was thanks to Antointette Rives that Rahn was introduced to Isabelle Sandy, writer and poet, who lived at Foix in the 1930s and who had published an article about him. Rahn quoted some of its text in a letter to Gadal:

"Germany has paid! Everybody should know that by now. A precious treasure was returned to us without fuss, without diplomats, and that is the cause of an incomparable success. However, Germany has paid and I for my part would like to show my appreciation to the young writer for his poetic jewels that he sent to us over the river Rhine. And the educated French won't stay ignorant towards the loyal gesture of the young German in making us aware of our Middle-Ages heritage, our own spiritual fortune. Not only in his books but also via the radio where he was particularly successful, he recreates the beauty of the romantic France, the beauty of the Ariège and Montségur, which are in his opinion the spiritual climaxes of Europe."[5]

Praise indeed. But what are meant by the enigmatic phrases: "a precious treasure returned," "poetic jewels," and the consequent "incomparable success" in restoring France's "spiritual fortune?" Was Sandy talking in purely allegorical terms or was there something more concrete that should command our attention. Sandy's are such adulatory statements that one might be forgiven for thinking that Rahn had discovered no less than the Grail, the Holy Lance, and the Philosopher's Stone all in one afternoon! That Sandy wrote in these terms indicates that Rahn's successes, however they might have been defined, were regarded in her circle as weighty achievements: the work of a visionary and at this early point in our review of Otto Rahn, a vote for the Grail Knight as opposed to the Nazi guru.

Sandy later wrote gushingly of Rahn: "Between the two wars, more closely the last, had appeared from the heavens a meteor over the valleys of the Ariège. He cut the Firmament like a diamond cuts glass and then disappeared forever. He carried a human name: Otto Rahn. Who was he? One knew not. Where did he come from? From Germany, his homeland, he was called a Tyrolean: pale with a golden breath, heavy hair, which pasted like wings on him, eyes from anthracite…He intruded a little childishly with his mystery, which accompanied him in death and into the beyond…"

Sandy said that the last words Rahn spoke to her were: "I cannot leave the German earth. It is pasted to my steps…the true home of a person is basically mankind, but first after that comes Geography."[6] It will serve us well to bear in mind these unequivocally patriotic and philanthropic sentiments of Rahn's when we review the reported circumstances of his death in March 1939.

We see that Rahn was warmly acquainted with a number of women influential in their fields. We might add to this list a friend named Bricon, an associate of Daladier who had come to Germany to learn all about National Socialism. Bricon's nom de plume for her writings for "*La Republique*" was Etienne. According to a letter Rahn wrote to Gadal, he saw in the 1933 New Year with her.

Rahn's correspondence with Antonin Gadal carried on unabated, mostly pining for the good old days with his friend in the

---

[5] Lange

[6] ibid

Sabarthès and how he wished he could return and do it all over again. However, this was impossible, he complained, due to his increasingly heavy workload that fully occupied his day and night-time hours. Quite what was filling his time to such a degree is not made clear. One assumes his writings but also quite possibly tasks entrusted to him by Karl Maria Weisthor on behalf of Himmler.

If it were possible to return to France, Rahn wrote: "important people will support us." In this context Rahn mentions Count Evola whom we have already seen was a major influence on Rahn's thinking. He described the philosopher to Gadal as the most influential Fascistic writer in Italy and one of Mussolini's closest advisors. He also told Gadal: that "we have influential friends in Germany, Switzerland, the Netherlands and France." We have no indications from Rahn as to the identity of these powerful allies, nor any feeling for their political and philosophical affiliations. Instead, we gain the impression that Otto Rahn, on the face of it, was very well connected in European learned and social circles, a fact we will do well to remember when examining the circumstances surrounding his destiny in 1939 and his AFTER LIFE (Part 2).

In his letters Rahn makes a meal out of various "what-if" scenarios, posing endless rhetorical questions to Gadal on where he should live in the Midi, whether he could bring his secretary (provided by Himmler, which confirms that in 1934 Himmler and Rahn were strongly linked), and how the locals might receive him in light of the "awful things they did to me…and I to them." Again, we have no explanation to which these matters refer; only Frau Winckler's forthcoming testament that Rahn was hated by the villagers around Montségur and by whose hands he had suffered physical attacks. Rahn complains to Gadal that: "these simple people can't understand that I advertised their country and that I will continue to do so. They judge me by what they have seen. I can understand them. But we are even now."

What inciteful things he did or said to provoke such hostilities and why he should say both sides were square have never been elaborated. Instead, we are left to surmise on whether Otto Rahn was a hapless victim of generic post-WW1 anti-German hatred or whether he was the butt of reprisals brought upon him by his actions or by personality flaws that inflamed violent responses. His writings reveal no such hard and fast character weaknesses. However contemporary descriptions of Rahn's behaviour in public attest to lapses of social protocol that provoked harsh words falling just short of coming to blows.

Correspondence is also characterised by an irritating penchant of Rahn's to harp on endlessly about his money troubles, explaining how he would write to A to pay off B so that he might achieve this and that objective. All his plans were based on the naïve assumption that the cost of living would remain low and that a buyer's market might prevail. "It is terrible," Rahn complained to Gadal, "how expensive my life is currently."

That the Comtesse Pujol-Murat still ranked highly in Rahn's thoughts is evident from his letters. He told Gadal that he had written to her, something he had not done for a long time. Rahn was making mention of her in the preface of his new book and he wanted her approval of the paragraph.

In mid-February 1934 Rahn was introduced to publisher Adolf Frisé (Adolf Altengartner) by Grete von Urbanibski, a Viennese journalist and a member of Otto Rahn's seemingly wide circle of gay acquaintances. (Rahn told Gabriele that Grete was a lesbian.) Frisé later published the works of Robert Musil, author of *A Man without Qualities* who later chose exile in Switzerland rather than remain in his home country of Austria after Hitler's Anschluss had merged it into the Nazi Reich. This would not be the only instance when Rahn would be observed associating with persons who held little or no sympathy for the Nazi regime. It is a matter of debate as to whether Rahn entered into these relationships naïvely or with eyes open; either way, it cannot have gone unnoticed.

Frisé's meeting with Rahn was in the Kaiserhof-Halle tearooms in the Grand Hotel on Wilhelmstrasse near the Reich Chancellery. The Grand was, in effect, Rahn's stage to the world of fame. He stayed there in a minimum price room under the roof but it was, after all, a prestigious address of a kind that status-conscious Rahn had been seeking.

A few months later Rahn's article *Heinrich Minneke* appeared in a Frankfurt newspaper. It alluded to the worship by the Cathars of Lucifer having falling from the heavens. The idea for this successful story was taken from Professor Dr. Henke's small book *Konrad von Marburg*. In this is a hint of the Lucifer theme where the fallen prince's diadem tumbles down onto the Cathar mountain. Adolf Frisé related in a radio broadcast how he read the article while in the Tyrolean Alps and, impressed by it, renewed his contact with Rahn because it was his custom to encourage young and talented writers.

Frisé was astonished to receive a response from Rahn not from Germany but by postcard from Geneva, and then another shortly after by telegram from Milan. Rahn was certainly getting himself about.

On making enquries, Frisé was led to believe that Rahn was on the run from the *Nacht der langen Messer* (Night of the Long Knives) cleansing operation following the Röhm putsch of 30th June 1934. In Volume III "*Les mirages de Munich ou l'Europe hypnotisée*" of his book *Un témoin du Xxe siècle*, Paul Ladame makes a number of unsubstantiated comments about Rahn, including the claim that, together with SS-Oberguppenführer Dr. Best, Rahn participated in the murder of Röhm at Munich-Stadelheim. The execution was carried out by SS-Brigadeführer and Konzentrationslager (KZ) Commander Theodor Eicke and SS-Haupsturmführer Michael Lippert, together with SS-Gruppenführer Schmauser, liaison to the Reichswehr. Ladame was of the opinion that Rahn was a protégé of Sepp Dietrich, leader of Leibstandarte "Adolf Hitler" and points to the appearance twenty times of the word "Dietrich" in *Luzifers Hofgesind* as proof of this suspect claim, adding that Rahn was later arrested at the Leibstandarte.

I find this supposition hard to believe. The truth of Rahn's hasty departure was far more likely to have been caused by his increasingly overt homosexual tendencies rather than his imputed membership of Leibstandarte SS Adolf Hitler. Moreover, Rahn's oft repeated reference to the *dietrich* in *Luzifers Hofgesind* is always in the context of re-affirming that to be personally equipped to appreciate the mystical-metaphysical qualities of life as extolled by the troubadours and demonstrated by the Cathars, each of us requires a *dietrich*, a "skeleton key" that can open the doorways to worlds of legend and enchantment. Personally, I believe that Ladame was missing Rahn's point in a big way, being so obviously far off the mark as to suggest that he might have had dark motives of his own to implicate Rahn so directly in one of the Nazis' most notorious murderous episodes.

Nevertheless, one man who played a key role in coordinating the Röhm episode, later claiming that he made seven thousand telephone calls to key figures in a seventy-two hour period (one every forty seconds!), was Karl Wolff, a pivotal link between Rahn, Himmler and Hitler. In the absence, therefore, of concrete proof one way or another, the question of involvement by Rahn in the Röhm case, however slight or tangential, remains open.

Rahn assured Frisé that politically he was "an unwritten page." At this time official intolerance towards homosexuality was one of the chief propaganda reasons for the liquidation of the SA leadership, a development that would have rattled the nervous and over-sensitive Rahn. This may be a contributory reason why in Rahn's estate there is no private correspondence on record except for a letter dated 16th September 1934 to an unknown woman thanking her for sending on mail to him at Alberto Alpino, Plancios, Bressanone (Brixen) in Italy. The embarrassing and shameful Rahn-Röhm execution rumours would also have discouraged Rahn's family from making correspondence freely available to outsiders.

While in Brixen Rahn wrote to Gadal to say that he had asked Monsieur Delamain to contact the historian for photos of the grottoes if more should be needed, albeit that Madame Sandy had already provided some very good photographic documents. Rahn expresses his optimism that one day not far off Gadal and he might collaborate on a book about the Sabarthès and the Tabor. However, the letter clearly highlights that their friendship had been thrown off balance by undeclared circumstances surrounding Joseph Widegger and Nat Wolff. Rahn adds that the Comtesse was no longer writing to him, supposing that this was because of Joseph. In face of these stresses Rahn confirms in his letter that he has decided to return to Germany as soon as possible where he will try again to raise the funds he would need to live abroad, either in Ussat-les-Bains or Bressanone, and press on with his novel *Laurin*, which is set in the forests of the Ariège. He would relieve the Comtesse of a lazybones by taking Joseph off her hands for a while. He concludes by telling Gadal that his address after the 20th of November will be care of his Aunt Nimis in Heidelberg. He encloses with the letter a little flower that he says he had picked at three thousand metres. What is its French name, he asks himself—an edelweiss? It is puzzling as to why Rahn should have bothered to do this. Might the despatch of the flower have been a coded exchange of some kind?

In November Joachim Kohlhaas, a young Tyrolean from the village of Czems born 9th July 1914, also received mail from Otto Rahn. Years before, Rahn had become acquainted with the winegrower's son from Erbach during a family party. In his letter Otto Rahn tells Joachim that he is in Brixen and wants to visit him in Meran where Kohlhaas was on a training trip. Kohlhaas assumed that Otto Rahn had obtained his address from Albert Rausch. Joachim went to the meeting place at the railway station and, despite the gathering dusk, he immediately recognised Rahn in the company of five other persons, including a German-speaking Italian officer, a man named Thomas Lambert, and two women. Together, Kohlhaas and Rahn’s group spent a convivial evening in the Batzenhäusel pub. Afterwards Joachim returned with the group to their pension near Meran.

Broke as usual, Rahn borrowed one hundred lira from Kohlhaas, not an insignificant sum in 1934 that amounted to roughly one hundred and seventy five Federal marks and equivalent to half a month's workman's wages. The men arranged to meet up again the next evening for another drinking session, after which Rahn and his company drove back to Brixen.

Kohlhaas never heard from Rahn again. Hans-Jürgen Lange asked Kohlhaas if he knew why Rahn had been in Brixen. Kohlhaas told the author that he wondered if Rahn had had suicide on his mind because of the latter's comment that he often climbed on the mountains while thinking to himself: "Lord, if I jump down there now…" Kohlhaas said something to Rahn in reply along the lines of: "Dismiss these thoughts, let God's will be done."

In these sombre conversations Rahn never mentioned anything to Kohlhaas about the Röhm-Putsch. One should not be quick to jump to conclusions that might on the surface seem obvious but, in reality, be far from the truth. Entertaining a lightning thought about the nature and consequences of a leap from a cliff or mountaintop is a far more common subject for reflection by those who find themselves in nature's high places than one might imagine. It is a fleeting, subconscious thought process and certainly does not mean that the world is full of latent suicides ready to do themselves in at the drop of a hat. In the case of Otto Rahn it does not, in my opinion, add any weight of evidence to support the view that Rahn was a willing suicide in March 1939. Nevertheless, Rahn's remarks also bring to mind the text and ulterior meaning of the article, *Jehan's Letzter Gang* (*Jehan's Last Steps*), which he wrote in 1934 for the *Berliner Illustrirte Zeitung* (reviewed in Chapter 25).

Curiously, Kohlhaas mentioned to Lange that Rahn's younger brother Karl (1906-1962) was some kind of high-ranking prosecuting attorney with strong Nazi sympathies; that Otto had once described his brother as an "old Nazi." Lange believes that Kohlhaas must be mistaken in these recollections because Rahn's younger brother Karl was, from the age of ten, a sickly person who suffered heart problems and rheumatism, and worked as a bookseller up to the end of the war. Why Kohlhaas should make such an obvious error in identification is a mystery. But this is not the only occasion when the identity of a Rahn has been confused or commingled together. In Chapter 12 we will examine the extremely curious claim made by Christian Bernadac that German WW2 ambassador Rudolf Rahn was, in fact, none other than

Otto Rahn. The conclusions are highly significant when assessing the wider picture of Otto Rahn's life and destiny.

Kohlhaas confirmed to Lange that Hans Grebe and Albert Rausch were linked to the Wandervogelbewegung movement (the Youth Wanderers) and were visitors to the home of "Uncle Willie" (Wilhelm Jansen, one of the movement's principle leaders prior to WW1) in Frankfurt am Main. This movement had strong homoerotic characteristics that were explored in Hans Bluher's 1912 book *Die deutsche Wandervogelbewegung als erotisches Phänomen.* Kohlhaas told Lange that Rahn, presumably through his friends' associations with the movement, found these overt erotic tendencies powerfully attractive.

In December Rahn wrote once more to Gadal from Brixen, still harping on about an imminent move back to France and settling down in Paris or Toulouse. However, he could not just pull up sticks and slip in; he had first to write to the French Embassy in Milan and hope it would be sympathetic to his travel plan. By now this nostalgic theme was wearing very thin. One cannot help wonder that if Rahn had truly wished to return to France to live and work then he would have done just that irrespective of any obstacles in his path.

He confides to Gadal that he is bothered by the increasingly repressive atmosphere building up in his native Germany. He had been in Munich for a fortnight, which was all he could stand, swiftly returning to his mountains. Rahn remarks in his letter: that "it is impossible for a tolerant and generous person to stay for long in this country, which used to be my wonderful homeland." He goes on to say that his father Karl, too, cannot get accustomed to the new German mentality and talks about his fond memories of France as a free country.

Rahn adds that his parents, living in Mainz since October, were fine but muddles this optimistic tone by adding that, once again, his mother's health is neither good nor bad, that she has a heart problem, she looks very old and that her lips are blue! Against that litany of problems Rahn comments that if his mother is allowed to take good care of herself she will live to a ripe old age provided that she heeds her doctor's advice not to become too agitated. His own health had improved over the last three months, he added, although it was still very unstable. The need to recuperate in solitude and sunshine had been a major factor in his decision to return to the country. He would finally forget the bloody observations he had made and the fact that he had almost been a victim in the way his friends had become victims. Rahn does not elaborate on these sombre and enigmatic statements.

However, the day after he had arrived in Munich all the bad memories flooded back; he could neither eat nor sleep. Rahn was of the opinion that he had had to endure the nightmare in order to feel better. Here we have fleeting but striking references to serious issues which, in microcosm, confronted Otto Rahn personally in 1934 but whose descriptions ("bloody observations," "enduring the nightmare,") conjure the nature of events befalling Germany at national level as a result of Hitler coming to power in 1933 and the consequent rapid rise of Nazism. The bloody events to which he refers could not have been observed by Rahn during his punishment period of guard duty in Dachau because that was still three years into the future. In which case, what were they? One might be tempted to return to the events surrounding the Röhm murder. Without firm evidence one can envisage a scenario in which Rahn was badly shaken at what had taken place during this notorious episode and felt little choice but to consider the ultimate escape route: suicide in the Tyrol. But that course of action neither took place in 1934 nor, I argue, in 1939.

Rahn told Gadal that he would return to France at the end of the month or by end of January 1935 at the latest. He would firstly travel to Toulouse and seek the Comtesse's permission to receive him and then move on to Gadal's as soon as possible because they surely had lots to tell each other. Unsurprisingly, the trip to France did not materialise.

Adolf Frisé bumped into Rahn again in mid-April 1935. By this time Rahn was completely broke and living in very poor circumstances in a Freiburg guesthouse. He was trading copies of his book for cigarettes. Frisé describes Rahn as a man who was trusting and generous to those who did not reject him and this trait made him very vulnerable. Rahn told Frisé that he had a vague hope of resuming his Pyrenean researches with the help of an unnamed Catalan aristocrat.

In the first days of May Adolf Frisé received a phone call from Rahn to say he was back in Berlin. Frisé wondered how Rahn had obtained his phone number. It must also have crossed his mind as to where Rahn had, in no time at all, found the means to upgrade his living conditions. Now, Rahn was living in Tiergarten Strasse. The houses along this street were very prestigious and even the cellar where Rahn had his apartment was paradise, a luxury den. When Frisé visited the apartment he saw Rahn was not alone but accompanied by an energetic young man seated at a table heaped with books. Rahn introduced him as his adjutant and secretary. Perhaps things were looking up

Later in May Rahn asked permission of his superior Colonel

Weisthor to travel to various places: Westerwald, Hessen and Bavaria. Documents prove that Rahn even at this early time had considerable operational freedom and was able to begin such projects without the need for special guidelines. Rahn wrote a letter to Dr. Alfred Schmid giving him the good news about the successful findings of his journey. Schmid was very curious about Rahn's "mental discoveries" during the Westerwald-Bavaria trip. Rahn, he reported, "saw things others couldn't, easy to people who are on good terms with imps and other cave-men."

Dr. Schmid moved from Basle to Berlin to market his inventions as a physio-chemist to two German consortia. A brilliant chemist, Schmid owned a large estate in Berlin-Dahlem. He was forced to leave Basle due to sex scandals. Schmid's Berlin apartment was filled with erotic male statues that led to a garish, pompous bedroom. The apartment also boasted a large bar painted with colourful fish illustrations, which Gabriele adored. She said that it was like being in an aquarium. Generously, Schmid offered to fund the artist's academic studies in exchange for his ostentatious painting of the bar.

Later Schmid became suspected of spying and was warned off secretly by Gabriele Winckler and Rahn. Winckler received a "friendly" warning from Major Karl Wolff just for sending Schmid a Christmas card.

Dr. Dietmar Lauermann, as previously noted a member of the "Grey Corps" associated with the Swiss and German Youth Movements, wrote of Schmid that the latter played a major part in the German Youth Movement and was also a founder of the "Ring" with seats in Basle and Berlin. The Grey Corps was prohibited by the National Socialist Government of 1934. Lauermann had already come to know Otto Rahn in 1933 in Frankfurt am Main at the university campus and at the local radio station for which he wrote radio plays for young listeners. He said that when Rahn visited Berlin he stayed with Schmid occasionally. Rahn also used to visit Lauermann's mother's house and on one of these occasions Rahn was accompanied by Raymond Perrier. Lauermann describes Rahn as intellectual, witty and garrulous but overall displaying an introverted personality, the latter trait being in surprising contrast to Lange's pen picture of Rahn as an outgoing, sociable individual.

Chapter SIX

Karl Maria Weisthor "Himmler's Rasputin"

Karl Maria Weisthor in 1936

We have mentioned in passing Frau Gabriele Winckler-Dechend, a close friend of Otto Rahn for two years from 1935 to 1937. Their warm but platonic relationship affords a rare glimpse into the milieu of Rahn's life in pre-war Berlin. It also offers further insights into Rahn's Grail-seeking endeavours. We will look at their relationship in depth in the next chapter.

At Himmler's request, Gabriele served as the "surrogate" daughter of one of Germany's most fascinating characters: Karl Maria Wiligut—he changed his name to Weisthor on joing the SS. It is the old Colonel under his pseudonym who now stands in our spotlight.

One of the oddest personalities of the Nazi era, Weisthor was born 10th December 1866 in Vienna. Weisthor claimed a royal lineage, issue of a long tradition of Germanic sages, the Uiligotis of the Asa-Uana-Sippe (clan), a link that would have conferred on him a most particular power: ancestral clairvoyant memory. Because of his history of mental illness Weisthor tried hard to disguise his past but could not help making brash claims. He asserted, for instance, that he had held a key position at the Austrian Kaiserhof, which had put him in a position of trust and influence with the archdukes. Weisthor claimed that his wife was the daughter of the last Doge of Venice. Gabriele believed this to be true. He boasted that before the 1st World War he had belonged to an esoteric circle around Baroness Maria Thaler, which included George Lanz-Liebenfels, Peryt Shou, Theodrich Czepl, Franz Spunda and even, allegedly, Adolf Hitler. Evidence has been subsequently found to show that Weisthor did have contact with Thaler and Shou.

With the help of the Salzburger police, Weisthor's family committed him to a sanatorium in 1924 because of his increasingly bizarre behaviour. His old friend Richard Anders, a member of the Order of the New Temple of Jörg von Liebenfels, had became an SS officer and introduced Weisthor to Himmler at a meeting of the Nordic Society in Detmold three years after his admission to the asylum. Details of Weisthor's mental health history were withheld from Himmler.

In September 1933, aged 67, Karl Maria Wiligut joined the ranks of the SS, adopting the name Weisthor, eventually rising to the rank of Brigadeführer.

At first Weisthor headed a Department for Pre- and Early History, which was created for him within the department of RuSHA (Rasse- und Siedlungshauptamt, principal race and population bureau of the SS). In October 1934 Weisthor became head of Section VIII, archives, of RuSHA. Weisthor moved to Berlin in early 1935 to serve on Himmler's personal staff. Very shortly afterwards Otto Rahn similarly transferred into Himmler's service. Some of the researchers grouped around Weisthor went on to form the backbone of the Ahnenerbe but, in common with many others close to him, Weisthor never joined the bureau whose members did not take him seriously.

Gabriele's mother had known the old colonel in Salzburg prior to 1933. She was interested in his family history and traditions. Her mother was also concerned that Weisthor had had to endure persecution in Austria, which had contributed to intolerable personal problems. She wanted to help the old man and invited him to the Dechend family house at Dingelsdorf, Lake Constance. A short time later Weisthor attended the conference at Detmold, which led to the introduction to Himmler. The Reichsführer SS was fascinated by Weisthor's family history and in the old man's occult theories. Weisthor agreed to come to

Munich and was provided with a small office and two colleagues: Suchsland and Feichtenbeiner, with a brief to work on a number of projects. Weisthor also had another helper, his ordnance officer Max Rieger. The pair soon paid Gabriele and her family a visit. They all hit it off at once and in a short space of time together made several excursions to ancient places.

Himmler wanted Weisthor to be adequately cared for and he asked Gabriele's elder sister, Lotte, to take him under her wing. Weisthor had suggested to Himmler that she might fill the role of his "vice-daughter," seeing that his own daughters, Lotte and Gertrud, were either married or engaged in important studies. Wisely, Lotte Dechend declined the offer, Gabriele volunteered and Himmler agreed to it. The prospect of being in the centre of all the action, seeing Berlin and mixing with SS officers, was a huge incentive for the young woman. Gabriele and Weisthor were introduced and straightaway she assumed the role of the old colonel's daughter.

At first it was uncontested that the colonel was a highly important personality. He was regarded as having an aptitude for matters of parapsychology and for being an authority on runes. Gabriele, herself, was proficient enough in translation and interpretation of runelore to write her own articles in magazines such as *Hagal* and *Nordin World.* An article on the subject of the Futhark rune, to which Gabriele contributed, was picked up by officials in Himmler's Ahnenerbe, the Ancestral Heritage section. On the strength of it she was offered a job, which she declined because she confirmed that her role had been as translator, the original information in the article having come from someone else. Gabriele expressed doubt that Weisthor had any clairvoyant powers of any kind and she never observed signs of such ability in the time she knew him.

Weisthor dabbled in other recondite areas of folklore. He was an advocate of Guido von List's philosophy of Wotanism introduced just after the turn of the century. This philosophy emphasised the initiation of man into natural mysteries based on the principles of the Edda and of the runes. Wotan was identified as a magician and necromancer who performed ritual acts of self-torture in order to win the magical gnosis of natural mysteries, thereby gaining shamanistic and psychic powers. In reconstructing this ancient gnosis, von List turned to theosophical thought but, more significantly in terms of the influence his teachings would exert upon the founder members of National Socialist Germany, he began writing thick volumes on the subject of sexology and eugenics, combining racial doctrines with occult notions derived from his increasingly bizarre interpretations of Teutonic mythology. Bizarrely, in subsequent interviews Frau Winckler has given about Weisthor she has mentioned that he was crucified on three separate occasions, apparently with the help of his sisters! One might say that enacting such practices was taking von List's Wotan masochistic rituals a shade too far.

The colonel also had a keen interest in the history of the gipsies and told Gabriele's family that he should have wished to have been their king like Hungarian magnates before him. During their excursions to ancient German sites Weisthor talked about the nine orders of the gipsies. One time on their travels they came across a collection of candlesticks featuring nine Roman numerals. Naturally, Weisthor the bombast claimed that these symbolised the gipsies and remarked that they were used for ceremonies such as weddings and baptisms.

Changes overcame Weisthor gradually. Gabriele maintains that her family was not aware of his previous mental health problems. He was later accused of charlatanism but well before then Gabriele became aware of his love affair with the bottle and of other distasteful habits (details of which Gabriele did not elaborate during our interview). Ultimately, Weisthor's behaviour deteriorated so badly that Himmler had no choice but to let Gabriele stand down from her position with the mentally degenerate colonel just prior to her wedding.

Gabriele's problems had also been compounded by intrigues that had built up around her by virtue of her special position with Weisthor and Himmler. Quite possibly these were created by those who would benefit by causing Himmler personal embarrassment. The Reichsführer SS took into account the debilitating effect of these trumped-up claims upon Gabriele's emotional state in making his decision to let her withdraw. Frau Winckler is very proud that Himmler was so fond of her family.

But before the pfennig dropped all was well in the Weisthor-Himmler-Gabriele relationship. When Gabriele described Rahn to her employer Weisthor wanted immediate contact with the Grail explorer and straightaway he briefed Himmler who gave Weisthor the order to get Rahn to Berlin. When Rahn first arrived at the villa at Grunewald Gabriele was delighted to have him to herself for several hours, She came away highly stimulated by Rahn's accounts of his researches. Rahn told Weisthor that he had been denied entry both to France and to Spain, dismissed by his publisher, and was on the skids. The older man laid on an apartment for Rahn and provided for all his basic comforts. Rahn made frequent visits from his home in Grunewald and got on very quickly with the much older man.

From May 1935 Rahn was commissioned by civil order to join Himmler's personal office to assist Weisthor. Rahn had entered the SS by the back door; formal admittance into the SS would take place in February the following year. His tasks and areas of responsibility in this department are not on record. However, available letters do indicate one area of research and study that is strongly indicative of sacred geometry.

It would appear that Rahn's involvement in the search for ancient treasures was far from over. More often than not artefacts of great value are associated with geographical areas characterised by significant earth energy grids and topologies. Rosslyn Chapel, south of Edinburgh, for example, is located at the heart of the so-called Reshel Grid energy matrix and has long been mooted as the hiding place for Solomon's treasures. It is believed that Rahn (and Rudolf Hess, significantly) held that the true location of the Grail Chalice was Rosslyn. The Sabarthès was perhaps always a blind. Similarly, the hilltop village of Rennes-le-Château in the eastern Pyrenees is regarded by innumerable enthusiasts today as occupying pole position in Europe for concealment of historical items of incalculable financial and philosophical value. The pioneering work of surveyor David Wood has established that Rennes-le-Château occupies a key and influential position in the area's remarkable pentagonal geoemetry.[1] In Chapter 21 we will review the likely associations between Otto Rahn, the Church and this tiny hamlet in the heart of the Corbières. Our conclusions will seek to reveal the true nature of Rahn's life of seeking.

In a letter to Weisthor dated 27th September 1935 Rahn stresses to his superior how hard he had been working in recent weeks on organising his acquired knowledge into a map library. Enigmatically, Rahn goes on to remind Weisthor of his earlier mention of the discovery of "big surprises." Rahn makes clear that because his work has been the fruit of many years of hard work he has not been talkative. He urges the Colonel to keep silent about his findings, with the exception of informing the Reichsführer SS, while his book *Montsalvat and Golgotha* was awaiting publication. However, this work was not published and the manuscript has never seen the light of day.

It is not clear from the letter whether Rahn intended to brief Himmler personally or if the task devolved upon Weisthor. Rahn asks Weisthor in his letter for official sanction to check some of the

---

[1] Wood, David. *Genisis: The First Book of Revelations*. Tunbridge Wells: Baton Press, 1985

locations and, in so doing, to travel for ten to fourteen days to the Odenwald, the Westerwald and the Sauerland. Ideally, Rahn adds, it would be preferable for the Colonel and Oberscharführer Folgmann to accompany him before the bad weather season sets in. Rahn then goes into more detail on his proposed itinerary.

Firstly, he would have a look at the Wildenberg ruin near Amorbach where archaeological work was currently in process. Rahn was in written contact with the responsible person on site. He would then move on to the Leichtweis cave near Wiesbaden from which it would be easy to get to the Sporkenburg, a ruin with a long history and, reputedly, where Emperor Nero was born.

From there the trip would continue to the Drutgerestein, the Steimel (a stone monument), the Hellenborn, the Widderstein, the great stone walls of the Dornburg (Thorburg), Rospe (assumed place of birth of the Heinrichs of Ofterdingen), Wilnsdorf (location of the German Kathars destroyed by Konrad von Marburg), Wambach and Asbach. (It was in Asbach in 1830 that a magnificent gold coin was found bearing the name Basileus Lysimachus, a general of Alexander the Great.)

More enigmatically, Rahn adds that from Asbach he would like to travel on to places about which he would only speak to the Reichsführer SS in person. Rahn says that he wants to leave after the wedding of Herr Lachner. He would conclude the trip with an extensive report which, duly written, was sent to Himmler on 19th October with a request that the Reichsführer SS contact him. On the 3rd of November Himmler's diary says about Rahn's trip: "Report returned and strictly confidential."

Where is this report today? And, far more to the point, what does it say?

Lange observes that almost all the locations in the letter derive from Karl Rehorn's book *Der Westerwald*, 1912, with three exceptions: Wildenberg, Widderstein and Wilnsdorf. Karl Rehorn believed that the Westerwald is the centre of an ancient cultural area and strove also to prove the presence of the Romans in the region. Lange suggests that the most secret locations—those whose identities Rahn would entrust only to Himmler—could have been in the area of Asbach where can be found the chapel of Uetgenbach, built on a German sacrificial area.

Lange points out that a careful study of Rahn's letter reveals that some key terms were not written properly. It says, for example, Kunis—for the German grail castle—whereas the correct title would be Wildenberg, the location of the grail castle in the Odenwald. Steimel does not derive from steinmal (stone monument). To put further emphasis on his discoveries, Rahn also uses unusual names for the places Rehorn had listed in his earlier writings: Hellenborn instead of Marienequelle, and Drutgerestein instead of "grossen Wolfenstein," both places near Bad Marienberg. These errors and misinterpretations would have been obvious to other scholars and archaelogists. One must ask why Rahn, an educated man, made them. Was it perhaps to draw attention to his activities away from those who might misuse or subvert the findings in some way? Or could it have been that Rahn was working at least in part to a different or private itinerary and just threw some other places into the list for effect? One thing he does not fudge is his emphasis on having worked so hard in recent weeks; here Rahn is evidently justifying himself to Himmler who probably had expected by that time to have seen better findings.

In February 1936 Rahn participated in an extraordinary report about the French mathematician and alchemist Gaston de Mengel who was visiting Berlin to present his research conclusions. His work was to be checked and translated by Weisthor's department with the assistance of mathematician SS-Sturmbannführer Schmid, author of esoteric books like *There Are No Stars*. The research of de Mengel was mainly about pre-Christian Indian, Persian and Chinese documents, focusing on various religious matters. The Frenchman also wrote for the Polaire Brotherhood's "Bulletin des Polaires," as well as for other esoteric reviews such as "Le Voile d'Isis." He was also known to have close ties with the (unknown) founder of an esoteric university in Nice.

Eighteen months after de Mengel's visit to Berlin, Weisthor reported under "strictly confidential" to Himmler the text of a very strange letter dated 23rd June 1937 from Helsinki in which de Mengel says something that will be of immediate interest to present day students of sacred geometry. He writes:

'The axis, which is northeast of Paris works very well. But the axis is neither near Berlin nor Helsinki. I was able to calculate the origin of the forces from the average of the axis. It is in Murm (Lapland) approx. 35 degrees eastern length and 68 degrees northern breadth in the vicinity of Lowosereo in Russia. I have also located the place of the big black centre. It is within the big triangle, which is formed by Kobdo, Urumtschi and Bakul, near Sin-kinag in western Mongolia.'

Weisthor tells Himmler that he is informing him of this letter because de Mengel was interested in the Colonel's opinions. It is information, Weisthor maintains, that should be appreciated. Then Weisthor makes the tantalising statement: "in my opinion the Russians, after agreement with France and Britain, set up air bases there. SD (Sicherheitsdienst) could try to find out if I am right."

The mysterious findings of Gaston de Mengel were forwarded to the Ahnenerbe. The correspondence between the bureau secretary Gertraut Schlarb and SS-Untersturmführer Kurt Ruppmann shows that they did not think much about them. There is no evidence that the SD acted on Weisthor's suggestion that it might look into the matter.

I have been unable to find further references to specific operational matters between Rahn and Weisthor but the de Mengel text indicates that sacred or grail geometry was a high research priority. It is my belief that Rahn's own travels in the Westerwald and associated regions were undertaken with similar objectives in mind. One may never learn of their exact nature but it suggests that Weisthor and Rahn sought to recreate a cult founded on the ancient Germanic traditions. In later chapters we will look closely at de Mengel's letter in the context of current science and opinion on earth energy grids and inter-dimensional realities. What we shall see makes for fascinating but uneasy reading.

On a social level the old Colonel introduced Rahn to new circles, for example at Schloss Malchow on Lake Malchow, which served as a place of relaxation for famous people from Berlin and for the flying squadron billeted nearby. Through these contacts Rahn made a great friend of the Russian immigrant Grigol Robakidse, a man described as having a "magical aura" and who came across as more shrewd and worldly than Rahn. Robakidse was obviously fond of Rahn and regarded each meal with the young German as a "cult" event. If he could not be in direct personal contact with Rahn he would spend all evening in silence, sulking, but on good occasions Gabriele and Rahn would be delighted to see an engaging Robakidse, eating excitedly and living up to his larger-than-life Georgian personality.

The relationship between Rahn and Weisthor was so close that in 1939 Weisthor received an invitation to Rahn's proposed wedding to Asta Baeschlin. Himmler was also invited. This mention of a forthcoming wedding was not what it seemed. In Chapter 10 we shall review Asta Baeschlin's own account of her relationship with Rahn.

In February 1939 Karl Wolff, chief of Himmler's office, announced to Weisthor that he should quit his duties. In the same month the Colonel retired from the SS on the grounds of age and ill-health. He was officially decommissioned of his responsibilities on 28th August 1939. Nothing in Weisthor's SS dossier indicates that he had failed in his duties. Weisthor's section was subsequently incorporated into the Ahnenerbe. On 13th November 1939 a dossier comprising Rahn's research file was sent from Himmler's office to the chief of SS personnel. The final sentence reads: "The decision concerning the former Brigadier General Weisthor is pending."

Weisthor was a man who had little difficulty in persuading authority figures to regard him as a rare remnant of an ancient clairvoyant German-Hungarian family line. He also had no problem in convincing Himmler that he needed young female company to compensate for the absence of his daughters. Apparently, Gabriele was only too keen to step in. I believe that the placement was neither purely altruistic nor its acceptance by Gabriele wholly naïve. Weisthor was a highly unstable man who needed close supervision. At the same time no one knew for sure if he really did have some kind of special link to the past. All the bases needed to be covered and Gabriele, an intelligent young woman with esoteric interests and skills of her own in runelore, was only too keen to fill the role.

Ultimately, Weisthor's behaviour became too much and Himmler had little option than to extricate Gabriele from the "vice-daughter" role (or else face the wrath, no doubt, from Gabriele's family who were old friends of Himmler and in a privileged position to press him to act if they believed that their younger daughter's life or wellbeing was endangered).

There is clear evidence that at least one important aspect of Section VIII's brief involved the investigation of earth energies and sacred geometry. We will shortly expand on this topic when we look at the relevance of the symbology of the Black Sun to esoteric Nazi ideology. For now we should be intrigued by Weisthor's enigmatic comment about the Russians entering into agreements with Britain and France and establishing airbases "there." Where is "there"—in the big black centre or in some other position within de Mengel's triangle of co-ordinates? Coincidentally, those co-ordinates tally very closely with one of the most favoured areas for the location of Shamballah.

Weisthor introduced Otto Rahn to social circles and through these new connections Rahn met Russian Grigol Robakidse. This relationship opens a doorway through which we will explore the ancient Order of the Black Swan, a group intrinsically linked with the desperate efforts of Dr. Karl Obermayer and his associates, if present day investigators are to be believed, to prevent Adolf Hitler from opening a timegate and creating an inter-dimensional incursion with horrifying consequences.

The old colonel was drummed out of his job in August 1939. There was no evidence that he had failed in his duties in any specific respect. However, Wolff brought to Himmler's attention in February 1939 the details of Weisthor's sanatorium confinement history. Rahn disappeared less than a month later—coincidence?

In November 1939 a dossier on Rahn's researches was sent by Himmler to the chief of SS personnel, stating that the Weisthor matter was still open. This raises more questions than can be answered. It is almost as if the author of the dossier is suggesting that, despite Otto Rahn having been officially reported dead eight months earlier, both the Rahn and the Weisthor matters were still live and pressing issues. Why might that have been the case?

Chapter SEVEN

Otto and Gabriele

Gabriele Winckler (born 1908) was a close friend of Otto Rahn in the mid 1930s. Unsurprisingly, considering Rahn's sexual orientation their friendship was platonic. Nevertheless, between 1935 and 1937 the two friends spent countless hours together engaged in conversation and light-hearted pastimes, more than enough time for Gabriele to explore the character and personality of Otto Rahn.

Gabriele Winckler-Dechend, Dingelsdorf, 1999

In 1989 Gabriele wrote to Dr. Wladimir Lindenberg following publication of his book *Rites and Grades of Initiation*, and told him that in 1935 she had read Otto Rahn's *Kreuzzug gegen den Gral*. She had been gripped by the book and passed her comments on to Weisthor to whom, as we have seen, she was an "adopted daughter" and employee. Gabriele's action in contacting Dr. Lindenberg brought her connection with Rahn and Himmler's circle into the public eye after a fifty-year period of relative anonymity.

In late 1998 London filmmaker Peter Boyce and I began making plans to interview contemporaries of Rahn who were still living and, crucially, who were willing to talk about their experiences. Fortunately, we were able to enlist the services of Stuart Russell, a British writer and historian resident in Germany, to act as our intermediary.

To our surprise and delight Stuart was quickly able to arrange for us to meet with Gabriele. Subsequently, Peter Boyce, Roy Dart (Peter's colleague) and I travelled to Lake Constance in March 1999. On a beautiful early spring morning we gathered in the Winckler-

Dechend's first floor apartment in the pretty lakeside village of Dingelsdorf and introductions were made.

Also present was Gabriele's husband, a frail but friendly fellow (now deceased) who was a favourite of Heinrich Himmler. Gabriele said that before her wedding (July 1937) she, along with her mother, had been working for Himmler. After she left his office in late 1936 Himmler paid her 100 Marks a month ("a lot of pocket money at that time") until the wedding so that she could have some degree of independence from her family.

Even up to the point that the pair became engaged, Gabriele was not aware that Himmler and her fiancé had been friends since they had been students together in Munich, writing leaflets and fliers together in the basement of the early NSDAP headquarters—the "Braunen Haus." The affection that Himmler held for Herr Winckler never diminished, and when Gabriele's husband injured his knee while fighting on the Russian front the Reichsführer SS sent him to Poland for treatment and provided the finance for the operation. Himmler then offered Herr Winckler the opportunity to recuperate at his official residence and afterwards sent his old pal to Kulmbach to work, in Gabriele's words, for Florian Geyer, a likely reference to the 8th SS Florian Geyer Cavalry Division, which had been actively involved in the invasion of Poland. During the invasion of Russia the Brigade was assigned to the Headquarters Staff Reichsfuhrer SS.

As the interview was getting underway Gabriele excitedly recalled the courier delivery made to her home of a large parcel shortly before the end of the war. In it was a valuable chandelier, a gift from Himmler. Gabriele had secretly longed for the item and had had no idea how Himmler had learned of her cherished desire. When it was fitted in place Gabriele said she had had the strange feeling that all the women with menfolk fighting at the front were seated together in front of the chandelier as if it brought them together in a wonderful way.

It is precisely this close familiarity permeating deeply through the Winckler-Himmler relationship that makes one question the true extent of the apparent disconnectedness of Gabriele from the heart of the Reich and its inner workings, especially in the context of the Otto Rahn story.

I confess to having been very nervous in the evening and early morning hours before the meeting. It struck me that I was about to come face to face for the first time in my long years of research on Otto Rahn with a living embodiment of WW2 history in the figure of an elderly lady who had both been Rahn's friend and confidante and a favourite through mutual family links of "Uncle" Heinrich Himmler. I had no idea what to expect. I was concerned that Gabriele might not be receptive to the interview and to the questions I planned to put to her. Frankly, I was also worried that Gabriele's advancing years and the physical and mental challenges that often confront the very elderly might make the session less productive. I should not have worried. Gabriele turned out to be more switched on mentally than many people I have met less than half her age. I have sought here to summarise the key elements of the interview and review how they help one arrive at a keener insight into the personality of Otto Rahn.

By 1934 Gabriele's mother had already known Weisthor for a long time. One day when Weisthor was with Himmler's attendant, Max, the old man came over to the family house and invited them to join him at the Buechener Tobel. Weisthor asked Lotte, Gabriele's elder sister, if she wanted to come to stay with him because his daughters were away from home and he did not care to live on his own. He said one daughter was married and the other one was still studying. But Lotte declined straightaway and Gabriele told her she was stupid, saying she personally would go immediately; she was really that interested. Weisthor was delighted, telling Gabriele that he would have never dared ask. The plan had first to be cleared with Himmler who said that Gabriele could come to Munich in August.

When the time came Gabriele received a telegram. Gabriele, accompanied by Weisthor's younger daughter Trude and her daughter, met up with Weisthor at Bogenhausen. A number of senior Nazis had their homes here, including Karl Wolff's seven-room family house. Straightaway, Gabriele and the others went off to attend an NSDAP meeting. She said that the occasion was a great thrill for each of them.

For the next eighteen months or so Gabriele kept the old man company as his "vice-daughter," and was required to call him Dad. He never went anywhere without her and Gabriele enjoyed this immensely because of all the people she met. In November they went to work in Berlin and it was in May 1935 when Otto Rahn came to join them.

In the three years or so that Rahn and Gabriele were friends they spent considerable time together. Gabriele worked in the office of the Director of RuSHA, Richard Walter Darré, who also held the offices of Reichsminister of Food and Agriculture and Reich Peasant Leader. (Darré was also Himmler's brother-in-law.) The office was next to Rahn's apartment and after knocking off she would often call on him. They would cook and talk together. Rahn would tell Gabriele about what he had written in previous evenings. His pad and pen were always beside his bed. Ideas seemed to come to Rahn most easily at nights and he would always discuss them with Gabriele. She found that process fascinating. At this time he was working and writing about Konrad von Marburg yet it is a fact that no work by Rahn focusing on this subject was published either in his lifetime or posthumously.

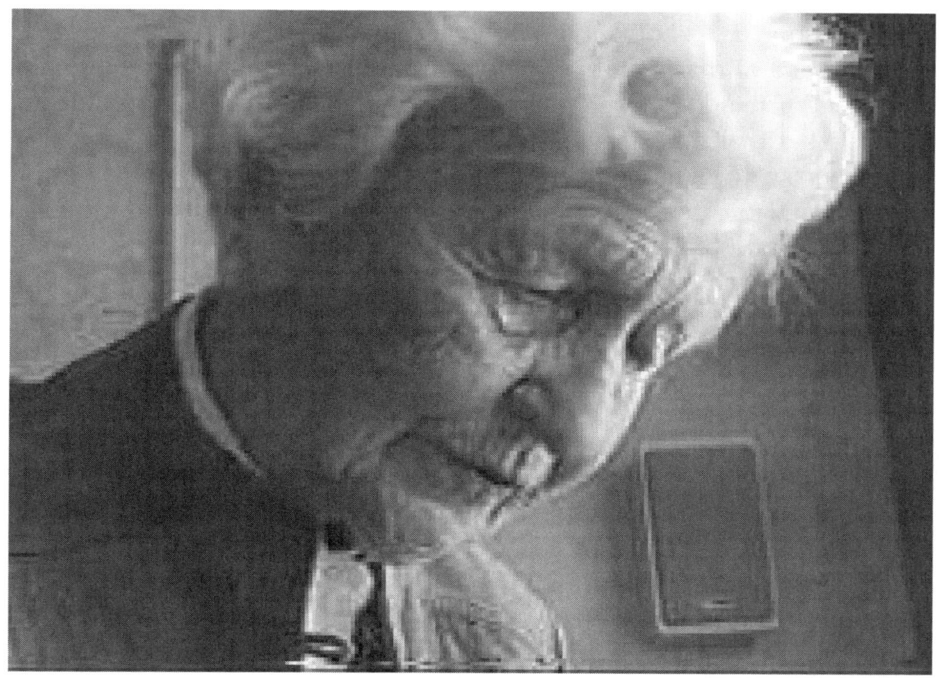

Now and again the pair would go off for weekend jaunts with Weisthor but Gabriele and Rahn enjoyed all manner of activities together. In her words they had become very good friends and being in each other's company was easy and fun. They seemed such a natural pair that one day Rahn told Gabriele that the Gestapo believed them to be engaged. That was a real source of amusement between them because had that been the case, Gabriele observed to Rahn, they would have quickly run out of tableware from the cupboard (with which to wipe their eyes) because both of them were such emotional characters. Because of the nights they spent together and Rahn not once making any kind of advances to her Gabriele, quite naturally, did wonder if her friend might be homosexual. But although she regarded Rahn's policy of keeping his distance from her as somewhat strange, on the whole she thought it was great because no complications were allowed to encroach upon the friendship. This allowed them to converse freely about literature and all manner of other topics.

Gabriele described how she had first become aware of Rahn's work. She had read *Kreuzzug gegen den Gral* and was fascinated by it, so much so that she passed it to Weisthor. He, too, became hooked and gave the book to Himmler who was similarly impressed. Himmler asked Gabriele to find out something about Rahn's circumstances: where he lived and so on. In her enquiries she learned that Rahn had been unwell. His book (*Kreuzzug gegen den Gral)* had attracted criticism and all the attention had got him down. Himmler did not like the sound of that and asked Gabriele to make arrangements to get Rahn to Berlin. At that time she was handling Weisthor's correspondence and so she wrote to Rahn via his publisher. He travelled to Berlin from Frieberg and on the day he arrived Gabriele was alone in the house, giving an opportunity for them to have a long and lively discussion about the book and all sorts of other topics.

One must question Frau Winckler-Dechend's recollection that it was in 1935 that she read Rahn's book and conveyed her enthusiastic impressions to Weisthor who, in turn, told Himmler. If 1935 was indeed the year she first read *Kreuzzeg gegen den Gral* then, as we have noted from Rahn's own remarks to Paul Ladame, Himmler had already been aware of Otto Rahn for twelve months or more (having set the ball rolling with his enigmatic telegram to Rahn in Paris in 1934) and therefore did not need to be re-appraised of the young writer's first book. Gabriele's stated timeline therefore begs the question as to the precise degree of her involvement in or influence upon the initial introductions between Rahn and Himmler.

What is clear, as we already noted and which Gabriele confirmed, is that from May 1935 Rahn joined Himmler's personal office. Gabriele said that Himmler brought this about so that Rahn could carry out tasks for him directly. It was only later that Rahn's time and expertise was also made available to Weisthor.

Rahn reported to Himmler directly but he made his own proposals on what he wanted to do. If Himmler agreed with his protégé's plans and went along with the travel arrangements then he would finance them. For all practical purposes Rahn was a free agent, a position of enviable power and opportunity. Although Rahn was always at Weisthor's apartment (where Gabriele lived in the capacity as the colonel's "surrogate" daughter and secretary) in the evenings, he did not work in their department. He had his own work and researches and he did not always take Weisthor and Gabriele into his confidence about what those duties entailed.

In 1936 Gabriele left Berlin. Rahn and she kept in touch for a while by letter but presently those communications dried up.

Gabriele remarked that although Rahn was a member of the SS he never wore any uniform and so she was surprised in later years with the public perception that he had been a willing servant of the SS. The only time when Gabriele saw Rahn in uniform was Christmas 1937 when he was on leave from his assignment to Dachau. Gabriele said that Rahn hated wearing the uniform but it was required of him. To Gabriele's astonishment, Rahn then remarked that all the things being told about Dachau were not true; that the prisoners were not all put together. The different kinds of prisoners—political, criminals, Jews—were distinguished by having their own colours and were kept in separate cells. Gabriele told us that she still remembers the remark vividly.

In April 1938 Gabriele's first son was born and she asked Rahn if he would be the boy's godfather. Rahn agreed but then he went off again, this time to Muggenbrunn where he holed up with his secretary Hans von Kalkstein, and set about writing a book. Gabriele presumed that the book was the one that Rahn had long been promising to write about Konrad, and so she was surprised when Rahn subsequently turned up at her parents' house later that year and gave them a gift of *Luzifers Hofgesind,* which had been published in April 1937.

This was the last occasion when Gabriele saw Otto Rahn, hearing no more about him until (Gabriele's words) "the strange death announcement appeared in the paper," strange because Rahn was actually popular. Gabriele could not make any sense of the story that Rahn had fallen off the Wilden Kaiser Mountain and had frozen in the snow and so she wrote to Weisthor's adjutant SS-Untersturmführer Hans von Lachner and asked him what he knew of it. Von Lachner was only able to say that Rahn had been caught with a homosexual friend *in flagrante* but had escaped with a caution from Himmler because the Reichsführer SS appreciated him a good deal. Rahn then got caught a second time and received another caution.

Let us remember that this was a time in Nazi Germany, and in the SS in particular, when being homosexual and getting caught was not funny at all and could lead to execution. It is worth noting that Rahn had no hesitation in introducing Raymond Perrier to Himmler and that the Reichsführer SS warmed to the Genevan. It seems inconceivable that Himmler would have had no inkling about the true nature of the Otto-Raymond relationship and, assuming that Himmler was not completely dense or blind to it, he seemed to have taken no action to bring it to an end or to persuade the pair to re-orient the nature of their friendship (Himmler believed that homosexuality could be "cured").

Nevertheless, von Lachner told Gabriele that Rahn was caught in the act a third time and on that occasion Rahn made the personal decision that he had sullied the good name of the SS once too often and that he should stand up for his actions and take the consequences. It was probably at that time, Gabriele suggested, that Rahn chose to take his own life and Himmler, recognising the inevitability of the situation, did nothing to deter his protégé from making the ultimate sacrifice.

This remark by Gabriele is important because it is the first and only occasion when anyone, especially one so close, has said that the decision to take his own life came about more from Rahn's own inner process of measured reflection than from the outcome of intolerable pressure brought to bear by Himmler or by those in the Reichsführer's circle. But how certain can Gabriele truly be about this?

Neverthless, Rahn's exit from life was three years away from the point we had reached in our interview and Gabriele had much more to say about their friendship, which was not all talk and earnest discussions about Germany's past but a time filled with outings and having fun. She described Rahn as always open and warm, good mannered and cheerful but when it came to his work he became serious, intensive and deeply involved.

Often, Rahn would join Gabriele, sometimes with Weisthor, at places like Schloss Molchow where German society figures congregated to let their hair down. Sometimes Gabriele and Otto would take over the bar and have fun making and serving cocktails. Rahn introduced Gabriele to friends of his from the Turkish Embassy. Gabriele mentioned that once they saw André François-Poncet at the Schloss. This was a passing remark during the interview but we will return to it because François-Poncet was not what he seemed and it provides us with an important avenue of investigation beyond Otto Rahn's "suicide" year.

Gradually, Weisthor became too difficult for Gabriele to handle and she determined to leave him. Her mother said he was becoming senile but his over-fondness for alcohol exacerbated the challenges brought about by advancing years. Gabriele asked permission of Himmler to be relieved of her surrogate daughter role but at first he begged to her to stay to help keep some degree of control over the colonel's drinking. Eventually, Himmler relented and Gabriele was released from her obligations to the increasingly unstable elderly colonel.

In discussing Rahn's 1935 travels in Westerwald, Hesse and

Bavaria, Gabriele provided an insight into the reasons for making the trip. She said that Rahn was on the trail of a French researcher who had been investigating the mysterious Kyot in Wolfram von Eschenbach's Parsifal. This researcher may have been Gaston de Mengel.

Rahn, too, wanted to get to the bottom of the Kyot character as did Himmler who, anxious to learn about Rahn's investigations into Eschenbach and the link with Kyot, gave permission for the trip. There is no record of Rahn having caught up with the Frenchman in question. However, we have already noted that in February 1936 Otto Rahn was participating in the SS review of Gaston de Mengel's religio-esoteric research work. One can therefore posit that a relationship between Rahn and de Mengel was forged some time before, and may have been consequent to the pair sharing an interest in von Eschenbach's story and its inner ciphers.

Gabriele told us also that Rahn believed that the Ark of the Covenant was included in the horde of ancient artefacts that the Cathars had cached during the Albigeois inquisition. This fact is critical to our post-1939 suppositions, which are explored in later chapters.

One of Gabriele and Otto's mutual friends was Alfred (Fred) Schmid, a chemistry professor from Basle whom we met earlier. On his return from Westerwald, Rahn wrote to Schmid giving him good news about the trip. Curiously, Schmid remarked that: "Rahn saw things people couldn't, easy for those on good terms with imps and other cave men." Gabriele believes that Schmid was talking symbolically because the chemist was a down to earth sort of person.

Schmid was in his early thirties and had moved to a Berlin-Grunewald villa because he romanticised about German soldiers and the army. Gabriele explained that because of his penchant for making useful (and money making) inventions Schmid had been given a job at Headquarters. He was homosexual and so it is not surprising that Rahn and he should have been friends. There came a time when Rahn had to warn his friend that there were those in the Gestapo who suspected him of being a spy. Those who had Schmid in their sights had weighed up what they knew: he was a multi-linguist, he worked in Headquarters for Himmler, and he came from Switzerland. Apparently that was sufficient to provoke suspicions and Gabriele and Otto went to his villa one night and urged their friend to make himself scarce. Schmid listened incredulously, thinking it laughable that anyone should suspect him of spying. A little before this Gabriele got into trouble just for sending Schmid a Christmas card. Somehow Karl Wolff saw the card and scolded Gabriele, reminding her that she knew very well that Schmid was *persona non grata* and she must not see him or make contact with him under any circumstance. If Wolff was involved in the Schmid blacklisting then whatever the Swiss was suspected of doing or being involved in must have been considered sufficiently serious to occupy the attention of those at the top around Himmler.

However, Gabriele told us that it was common practice for the Gestapo to spy upon SS activities and that she herself had been a target for suspicion. One day she had been at the opera with a cousin of her husband. Afterwards, the pair went for a drink in a café that the Gestapo had, for some reason, placed off limits to German citizens. The very next day, at work, both Gabriele and her friend got a note telling them they should have known that visiting the café was forbidden.

Another time Gabriele and some friends paid a visit to a store, going through the revolving door to see a sign saying "Jewish shop," and then straightaway turning on their heels and spinning right out again. Even so, Gestapo officials made a point of making it known that they had been seen entering Jewish premises.

One of the pals close to Rahn was Russian emigrant Grigol Robakidse, an eccentric fellow in every way. The Georgian was a published writer and both Rahn and Gabriele had read his books and been fascinated by them. Subsequently, they invited him to dinner one evening and a friendship began. Dinner with Robakidse was a bizarre affair. He did not allow any kind of conversation around the table, regarding the event as a kind of cult ceremony. If he wanted to chat then he would invite conversation afterwards. Robakidse was also a friend of Gabriele's mother who asked Grigol why he wore a wig (presumably a conspicuous one to provoke the question). He said that he was from a group called the "Schwanen" and that all the members wore them. This reference to the Order of the Swan is another clue to the deeper interpretation of Rahn's actions in the thirties and we will examine it in finer detail in Chapter 24.

Gabriele thought Robakidse was a great man and something of a white magician from the way he talked about his homeland. At the end of the war he fled from Berlin to an area occupied by the French. Gabriele later heard that two Russians in a jeep had picked him up and taken him to Russia. He obviously survived the encounter because from 1945 Robakidese lived in Geneva where he wrote philosophical essays. His earlier books include *The Snake-Shirt* (1928), *The Murdered Soul* (Jena 1933), *Demon and Myth* (1935), and *The Guardians of the Grail* (Jena 1937). He died in Geneva in November 1962.

Gabriele's husband was a friend of headmaster and politican

Heinz Pehmoller. On one occasion when Pehmoller and his family were visiting her parents in Konstanz he met Otto Rahn and they got into an intense discussion. His wife, the daughter of a landowner, took a dislike to Rahn but Gabriele said that she was a strange woman ("different to us"). Gabriele told of the time Pehmoller came home from the front and saw his five year old son standing in front of the workers in riding boots and commanding the group with a riding whip. Pehmoller was aghast but it was symptomatic of the way his wife wanted to raise their son in the manner of her own upbringing.

After the war Pehmoller travelled to the South of France in response to the claim made by a French youth group familiar with Rahn's books that the writer was still alive. They were aware of an old man living at Montségur who could be Rahn. This sounds unconvincing. In 1945 Rahn would have been just forty-one years old, not an age that the great majority of people reach such that they appear "old," even to youngsters. Even so, Gabriele obviously had lingering doubts about the official account of Rahn's demise because she told Pehmoller that one day she should accompany him to France so she could put questions to this "old man" that only Rahn could have answered. Unfortunately, that trip never took place.

Prior to Rahn's suicide he said he had been denounced. On asking Gabriele what Rahn might have meant by this, she said that in her opinion it was Wulf Sorensen who stabbed Rahn in the back. Sorensen accompanied Rahn on a research trip and later told Gabriele that she should take care of him (as if Rahn was under threat). Gabriele regarded that as a strange comment and could not work out why Sorenson might have said it. She told Hans-Jürgen Lange that during Rahn's latter months spies were assigned to him to test for evidence of his homosexuality. These spies, Gabriele believed, were not organised by Himmler and so one must consider the probability that Sorensen was one among the spy group working under the Gestapo's direction.

Research enquries on Wulf Sorenson bring up a reference to an identically named author of works of poetry, including *Freund Hein - Ein Buch des Lebens* (1940) and *Stimme der Ahnen* (1942), with the suggestion that Sorenson (or Soerenson) was a pseudonym under which Himmler wrote verse (Himmler is said to have written more than a thousand poems). During our interview Gabriele was clearly referring to a separate acquaintance of Rahn named Wulf Sorenson and not to the Reichsfüfrer SS. Remarkably, here we have yet another in a long list of "coincidences" in the Rahn story where identical surnames of persons have been conflated, thereby opening up other, unexpected lines of enquiry. In this case it is telling that one of the most notable examples of Sorenson's work is his story *Voice of our Ancestors*, a hermetic allegory in which he likens Snow White to the Goddess essence of the ancient Nordic people and the evil Queen to Christianity. This story contains many elements found in Rahn's masterly telling of the Legend of the Knight of Berne and the Roses of Bozen.

Frau Winckler has, of course, been interviewed by other researchers. In these we learn much that is of interest to students of hidden history, including the topic about the mystical Black Sun theme, which will be developed in Chapter 23. The context of Gabriele's remarks indicate her belief in an invisible or passive sun long since cooled existing at the centre of our solar system alongside the hot, active sun SOL. This description provides a fascinating and fresh insight into the Black Sun symbology and demonstrates that Gabriele herself was not a passive young woman on the sidelines of Nazi occult ideology but an intellectual player with contributions of her own, which were sought by others. Couple this knowledge with her evident expertise in the fields of runelore and one is encouraged to regard Gabriele and her part in the Rahn tableau in a different light.

In our interview we learned that the publication of *Luzifers Hofgesind* came as a complete surprise to Frau Winckler. In the two years or so that Rahn and she had been close friends, Gabriele observed that Rahn's priority project was a book on Konrad von Marburg: the work that he enthusiastically planned to publish as his preferred follow up to *Kreuzzug Gegen den Gral*. Instead, *Luzifers Hofgesind* was released, complete with ideological and racially insensitive insertions that differed radically from the writing and philosophical style associated with Rahn's earlier work.

Rahn was assigned a secretary named von Kalkstein. Gabriele said that Himmler picked von Kalkstein "off the streets" to work for the State and who, subsequently, he trusted to marry his sister-in-law. What possible cause might Himmler have had to do this or, more pertinently, what hold or influence might Kalkstein or others have had over the almighty Reichsführer SS? We will see in Chapter 16 the extent to which Admiral Canaris, for example, pulled Himmler's strings and we ask ourselves why there was never a satisfactory explanation as to why the head of the Abwehr (German Intelligence) held so much sway, not only over Himmler but over many other leading Nazis. In this scenario it is not impossible that von Kalkstein had two masters.

It would be surprising, even today, if Frau Winckler did not pause to measure deliberately the content and meaning of her words in addressing enquirers. There are still those alive today who might be compromised or offended should certain facts come to light. Nevertheless, it would be equally surprising if Gabriele did not, albeit at the unconscious level, offer a fact or comment here or there, which provided a clue to the enquirer. I did not appreciate until years later the value of the remark she made about the contacts at Molchow: "Rahn came with Weisthor and me to Schloss Molchow, I think, on weekends. We also met François-Poncet there once." A casual remark, perhaps, but its ramifications are far from immaterial in the debate on determining the nature of the political and ideological elements in Otto Rahn's life.

As Vice President, later President, of the Red Cross International Committee, André François-Poncet provided papers and passports to Nazis fleeing Allied justice along the Vatican's infamous 'Ratlines' escape channels." As early as 1936 U.S. intelligence in Austria knew that the International Red Cross was issuing temporary identity documents under assumed names…to persons operating under the protection of the Vatican, including war criminals."[1]

From 1931 to 1938 François-Poncet was French Ambassador to Germany and, in the latter year, Ambassador to Rome. François-Poncet's unprincipled nature was actually far uglier than that of a Mr Fixit for stolen identity papers. "France's highest ranking official in Germany had been an informant for Klaus Barbie and the Gestapo."[2] (Gabriele: "I don't know why everything that had to do with the SS was spied upon by the Gestapo. I can say that I experienced it myself.")

In 1943 François-Poncet was deported and interned by the Germans until 1945. During this time Klaus Barbie, the Butcher of Lyons, took an interest in François-Poncet and persuaded him to collaborate against the Resistance. By the late 1940's François-Poncet had become American intelligence operative Allen Dulles' channel for Red Cross identity papers so desperately sought by the Vatican's Nazi-smugglers. His services to Dulles were reluctantly approved by several sources in Western intelligence.[3] François-Poncet used to meet with Dr. Joseph Müller in a Munich safehouse but the Frenchman was unaware that he was actually meeting with the Black Orchestra's (Canaris') emissary to the Vatican.

Gabriele's comment that Rahn and she met François-Poncet one time does not, of course, preclude the possibility that either one of them

---

[1] *Ratlines*, p252

[2] IRS, HQ EUCOM 20th July 1949

[3] Confidential interviews undertaken by Aarons and Loftus in 1984-1985

met the French Ambassador on other occasions. Considering Rahn's role and responsibilities within Himmler's personal office and his proximity to Nazi dignitaries, it is more likely than not that there were further meetings, at least in a social context, but it would be unwise to discount operational motives. All things considered, it would have been in François-Poncet's interests to strike up a relationship with the young German. François-Poncet's homeland was the place where Otto Rahn had searched so avidly for the Treasures of the Temple of Solomon. Who would not have been curious as to the outcome of such efforts? Rahn's excavations were common knowledge. He had been the subject of newspaper reports over the Polaires links; he had been expelled from France for the Hôtel-Restaurant des Marronniers debts debacle; he had been shadowed by an odd group of hangers-on, one of whom, "Nat Wolff," had been exposed as travelling under false documents; the Montségur locals had attacked him with pitchforks and flails; and he had delivered radio broadcasts in Germany on the topic of "*What I Found in a Cave in the Pyrenees*."

If the French authorities became convinced that Rahn had dug fabulous treasures from French soil and transported them beyond their borders they might consider it a matter of urgent national importance to seek to retrieve them. Locally placed emissaries such as François-Poncet would have been invaluable in achieving that objective. Equally, the matter would have given Rahn a bargaining hand by which to secure a highly placed source (and who could have prayed for anything better than International Red Cross provenance?) for procuring false papers and a passport when the going got too hot. It is only speculation but the more one considers it the more one can see the logic and mutual benefits of François-Poncet—Rahn friendly relations.

Our interest in François-Poncet extends further still. U.S. Special Agent William Gowen discovered in 1946 the existence of a spy organisation called Intermarium, a group that had its origins in the early 1920s when "White" Russian emigrés fled to Paris in the wake of the Bolshevik putsch. By the mid-1930s the Paris group had grown into Intermarium "a secret organisation that desires as its members people whose homes are to be found in the 'Intermare,' that part of Europe between the Baltic, the Black Sea, the Aegean, the Ionian Sea and the Adriatic. Also included are the Caucasians".[4] "Intermarium proclaimed the necessity for a powerful anti-Communist, pan-Danubian Confederation. Before the war it had received strong support from both

[4] *Intermarium Bulletin*, number 5, January 1947

French and British intelligence for anti-Communist operations."[5]

Intermarium's goal was to create a *cordon sanitaire* against both Russia and Germany. In pursuit of Intermarium objectives Charles de Gaulle allowed François-Poncet to hold both the post of French High Commissioner for Germany (which controlled the issue of HICOG travel documents) and French representative to the International Red Cross. While Intermarium was being organised, Bishop Alois Hudal ran the first crude Vatican post-war escape network for fugitive Nazis. By his own admission Hudal's job was to protect as many Nazi Catholic soldiers and leaders as possible from "Allied vengeance." In 1948 Hudal obtained stolen identity papers from the Red Cross via François-Poncet. Monsignor Karl Bayer, Rome Director of the Catholic relief organisation, Caritas International, told writer Gitta Sereny (author of *Into the Darkness*, 1989, an account of interviews held with mass murderer Franz Stangl, head of Treblinka extermination camp) that money passed to Stangl by Hudal was authorised by Pius XII. Hudal said in 1933 at the time of von Papen's visit to Rome to negotiate the Concordat: "in this hour of destiny all German Catholics living abroad welcome this new German Reich, whose philosophies accord with Christian and National values."[6] Hudal was so openly pro-Nazi he held a Golden Nazi Party membership badge. He was delighted to meet even the very worst mass murderers. He was a friend of mass-exterminator Walter Rauff who oversaw the development of the mobile gas vans, the "Black Ravens," in which one hunded thousand people, mostly women and children, met a terrible death. In Chapter 12 we shall meet Hudal again in the context of his role in exchanges of correspondence between the Vatican (Pius XII) and Berlin on the subject of the deportations of Jews in Rome.

On reflection, I offer the possibility that Frau Winckler was more than a young innocent, pulled into the periphery of the Ahnenerbe's occult endeavours via Rahn and Weisthor, with little appreciation as to the scale and nature of its objectives. It is beyond question that Rahn and she were close friends. However, it canot be ruled out that Gabriele was tasked by Himmler with keeping a close-quarter watching eye upon both Rahn and Weisthor with a brief to keep him informed of any snippets of intelligence that might prove useful.

Coincidentally, while we were interviewing Gabriele at her Dingelsdorf home the telephone rang. Gabriele took the call and when

---

[5] Brown, Anthony C. *The Secret Servant,* London: Michael Joseph, 1988 pp. 143-4

[6] Hudal, Alois. *Die Grundlagen des Nationalsozialmus; eine ideengeschichtliche Untersuchung*. Leipzig: Johannes Gunther, 1937

she returned a few minutes later she said disarmingly that the caller had been Himmler's only child, Gudrun Burwitz. Himmler called his daughter "Puppi"—his little doll. Burwitz has never denied her involvement in helping to run Stille Hilfe (Silent Help) a charity organisation established in 1951, which was named by the Wiesenthal organisation as a 'ratlines' support centre for former Nazis. One of the most prominent Nazis helped by Stille Hilfe was Klaus Barbie, François-Poncet's one-time paymaster. In a rare interview Burwitz said: "It's true, I help where I can, but I refuse to discuss my work." It was plain during our meeting with Gabriele that Gudrun and she are friends.

There is absolutely no evidence or suggestion that Gabriele Winckler has ever been involved in helping Nazi war criminals escape justice. Notwithstanding, considering the tight-knit, clannish nature of such friendships born out of the Reich years one can only speculate upon what our conversation might have yielded if, having had foreknowledge of Burwitz's activities, we had travelled down those lines of enquiry.

After the 1999 interview Gabriele Winckler-Dechend proudly displays for the camera the personalised copy of *Luzifers Hofgesind*, which Otto Rahn gave to her family in 1938—the last occasion Gabriele saw Rahn in life.

Chapter EIGHT

Germany 1936-1937 serving the Reichsführer SS

On 29th February 1936, Karl Wolff, SS Divisional General, wrote to the SS recruitment office to convey Himmler's personal instruction that Rahn be admitted officially to the Order. He was accepted into the SS on 12th March 1936 and the following month, 20th April, he was promoted to SS-Unterscharführer, joining Himmler's staff.

Otto Rahn joined the Black Order, the Allgemeine-SS (as distinct from the Waffen-SS, the combattent branch), member 276 208. This was an ironic choice of SS branch membership for Rahn because the Allgemeine-SS was created around December 1935 consequent to Himmler's "house cleaning," which effectively ended the careers of sixty thousand SS members who were deemed to be opportunists, alcoholics, homosexuals or of uncertain racial status. Rahn scored at least twice on this list of unwanted traits, being homosexual while at the same time suspected in some quarters of having Jewish origins.

Three years prior to this, on 13th December 1933, Otto Rahn had complied with the law and joined the German Writers Association. In his SS dossier of candidature we read that Rahn affirmed himself to be "ready to defend without reservation German literature in conformity with the spirit of National Socialism."

Himmler regarded Rahn as a very important member of the team. Rahn seemed to incarnate the highest ideals of the SS, representing a savoir-faire founded in the most fundamental knowledge of the old traditions. Rahn's published works were required reading for all principal Nazi dignitaries, thereby attaining the status of Nazi gospel. It has been said that his writings contain the key to Hitlerian cosmogony.

Special Ordensburgen schools were instituted for candidates: leaders for all levels of the Nazi power structure to ensure absolute discipline and who were believed ready to be instructed in the new Gnosis. These schools or castles provided the metaphysical foundation for the creation of the Aryan super-race and for the establishment of orders destined to ensure the continuance of the party. There were never more than three in number and were located at Krossinsee in East Prussia, Vogelsgang in the Rhineland, and Sonthofen in Bavaria. Otto Rahn tutored at Vogelsgang (known as the Knight's monkscloth) where political and spiritual training was given. At these schools of instruction candidates were prepared to conduct and participate dispassionately in atrocities.[1]

Rahn's close position to the SS has always given reason for speculation about the man and his work. One example focuses around the establishment of Himmler's castle at Wewelsburg near Paderborn. It was at Wewelsburg that the ideological centre of the "thousand year empire" would have been established. This ambitious objective was proof of how seriously the men of action within the Nazi regime at this time perceived the project.

In 1935 Heinrich Himmler officially formed the Order of Blood and the Circle of Ritters SS. A few years later he reconstructed Wewelsburg Castle. In olden-days the site had been the home of a castle of the Teutonic Knights. It was at Wewelsburg that the circle of thirteen Knights of the Blood of the Schutzstaffel (SS) met regularly. Each of the elect donned the garb of the ancient Teutonic Knights, the symbolic red, white and black. In the main hall of the castle stood a great oak table carved with runic symbols. Draped across the table was a red velvet cover. On the frontpiece centre of the massive table was a great white square and in its centre two Runes side by side, symbolizing "Sig" and making the letters "SS."

Behind the table were thirteen massive oak chairs polished and finished to an impeccable degree of perfection, each upholstered in boarskin. Each Knight's name was etched into a silver plate affixed to the back of his chair. Knights progressively fulfilling the thirteen chairs had to travel to a remote part of Bavaria and fast for seven days and nights, taking no more sustenance than a little wine, bread and cheese on the morning of the following day. Their dress was the traditional red, white and black uniform of the Old Order of the Teutonic Knights.

In the initial designs the original triangular shaped form of the castle was intended to be the basis for a huge lance-shaped layout for the building. This suggests the creators behind the project intended to highlight the symbols used in the Grail, specifically a colossal grail lance from whose tip, as mentioned in the Grail legends, blood drips.

In the centre of the "spearhead" there is a dome-shaped crypt,

---

[1]Sklar, Dee. *The Nazis and the Occult*. New York: Dorset Press, 1977

built deeply into the rock, around whose unfinished centre are grouped twelve basalt pedestals. The architecture is minimalist but very well planned in every detail. The original purpose of this crypt is not known and so there is considerable room for speculation. Due to the absence of answers on these questions the complete complex at Wewelsburg is still referred to in literature as the "Order and Grail Castle" of the SS.

From time to time, Otto Rahn worked in this castle and it has been suggested that this work centred upon Rahn's search for the Grail on behalf of his Nazi masters.

Paul Ladame met up with Rahn during the Berlin Winter Olympics in February 1936. According to Ladame, Rahn elaborated on the circumstances in which he first met Himmler, referring to the telegram he received while in Paris in 1934. At that time Rahn was despondent about his difficulties in raising the finances for the French edition of *Kreuzzug Gegen den Gral*. The author of the telegram praised the newly published *Kreuzzug Gegen den Gral* and offered Rahn one thousand marks a month to write a second publication in the same vein. At the same time a sum was telegraphed to Rahn in Paris so he could settle his affairs and return to Berlin to an address supplied. When Rahn turned up at 7 Prinz Albrechtstrasse he was taken aback to discover that the secretive telegram sender was no less than Heinrich Himmler who welcomed him personally and organised an office and secretary for him. When Ladame quizzed his friend about his reaction to Himmler's invitation Rahn's response was: "What was I supposed to do, turn him down?"

Rahn's friends maintain, however, that his initial pleasure for his change in fortune soon gave way to worries as he realised the nature of the regime under which he had to work and the constant scrutiny under which he was observed. During his time with the SS Rahn believed that his telephone was tapped and that he was being spied upon. He was under orders to deliver a book to Himmler by 31st October 1937 and another by 1939.

In December 1936 Rahn's superior was arrested and Ladame (who had tried to intervene on behalf of the arrested man's wife) found he was under surveillance. It was, in fact, Rahn that was ordered to keep watch on him but he tipped off his old friend and Ladame left Berlin. Ladame said that this was was the last time he saw Rahn (but can we believe this?).

Opinions differ on the level of Rahn's commitment to the Nazi cause. René Nelli and Paul Ladame believe that his work was simply too useful as propaganda for the Nazis and that he was therefore co-opted into the SS, an offer that could not be refused.

Christian Bernadac, however, believes that *Luzifers Hofgesind*, published in 1937 and characterised by a distinct anti-semitic thread, was not written under orders as some claim but that it was based on personal and mystical exploration of the mythology of the Grail and, moreover, based on Rahn's journal kept before, during and after his time in France. Bernadac believes that, from their context, the anti-semitic passages were present in the original journal. Bernadac cites documents written by Rahn in his SS file. A note dated 23rd February 1936 is headed "My combat for the Third Reich before 1933" and states that "Before the taking of power (in 1933), I had written abroad...a book (*Kreuzzug gegen den Gral*) and articles that today represent an inheritance of the National Socialist thought..."

When Bernadac asked Fauré-Lacaussade whether Rahn was anti-semitic he replied that he did not recall Rahn ever talking specifically about the Jews but that he held racist attitudes towards Arabs and blacks. Nonetheless, we have heard evidence from Frau Winckler that *Luzifers Hofgesind* is a markedly different work than that which would have typified Otto Rahn's characteristic style of content, substance and delivery.

In April 1936 Himmler made private contact with Rahn about an earlier letter from his subordinate in which Rahn had said he might be able to help with investigations into Himmler's family links with the family Passaquei in Savoyen. Maria Magdalena Ottilie Passaquei, born 12th December 1775, was the wife of Himmler's great-grandfather. Her parents were Johann Michael Passaquei, born 1739 in Savoyen, died 18th September 1803 in Abensberg, and wife Maria Katharina Bartl from Greifenberg. At the same time a Sebastian Albert Passacuei, married to Maria Barabara de Michael a Francenoc is mentioned, whose daughter is Anna Katharina Maria Magdalena, born 17th January 1776 and died 3rd April 1861 in Abensberg.

Himmler was not sure if this second Passaquei was a relative of the first but was of the opinion that it seemed quite likely. Himmler makes a further point that on a graveyard in Chambery there is a headstone with the name Passaquei on it. He concludes by asking Rahn if he could try to find out some more about it and thanks him and his friends very much in advance. Himmler's obvious desire to seek confirmation of his ancestral line is from this point forward an important activity for Rahn.

In October Rahn writes to friends (indiscreetly as usual) about Himmler's ancestral link with the family Passaquay of Savoy, emphasising that he was keen to arrive at the desired conclusion. Rahn comments that he will probably continue the investigations in Switzerland seeing that Himmler had given him permission to take a rest there to recuperate from recurring illness.

From Switzerland Rahn planned to travel on to Turin and Annecy, again with Himmler's express permission. He advises Himmler that after several fruitless attempts to progress the genealogy enquiries he had invited his friend Raymond Perrier to join him between Christmas and January. Together they were discussing the known facts of the Passaquays, and Rahn had asked Raymond to add his own research efforts to the project. He would compensate Raymond for any out of pocket expenses he might incur. Their joint efforts had begun on a promising note, Rahn explains. The pair had received all the documents about the Passaquays and had had all of it translated, including the "useless bits." Rahn enclosed copies in his letter, retaining the originals, which he was taking to Switzerland for review. The researches had confirmed that Johann Michael Passaquay was, indeed, Himmler's great-great-grandfather who was, however, born in 1739 not 1736. Rahn marked certain sections in the copy documents with red pen to highlight facts concerning Himmler's family tree. Perrier, Rahn explained, was in Thorens doing his bit for the genealogy and Rahn told Himmler that he was curious about what his friend might unearth.

Rahn was granted permission to travel to Switzerland and given a monthly allowance of thirty marks against anticipated book income until April 1937. On completion of the enquiries Rahn's researches on Himmler were sent on to Wewelsburg Castle where Hitler's genealogy was also compiled.

Rahn was warned to produce his own family tree, the request being repeated in January 1937 when he promised to deliver it within eight weeks. Despite this omission he was promoted on 30th January to the rank of SS-Oberscharführer and further upgraded in rank on 20th April to SS-Untersturmführer. Evidently, the powers that be were more than pleased with Rahn's activities.

In July 1937 the commander of the Wewelsburg, SS-Sturmbannführer von Knobelsdorff, wrote to Himmler's Berlin secretariat and confirmed a very interesting genealogical fact. "There is indeed a mutual ancestral line with the plumber Wilhelm Himmler of Bergburgheim. The Reichsführer SS and the father of the plumber Wilhelm Himmler are cousins six times removed as it can be seen from the attached list. Vicar Kern/Bergburgheim also mentioned that there exists a mutual ancestral line of the Reichsführer SS with the family

Rahn Bergburgheim."[2]

The ancestral line of Otto Rahn does exist but unfortunately the mutual ancestors of the families Rahn and Himmler cannot be found on superficial investigation. However, the intriguing possibility of Himmler and Rahn being blood relations could help to explain the generous and tolerant behaviour the Reichsführer SS exhibited towards the young scholar.

More than once I have reflected upon the possibilities that Rahn and Himmler might have had closer links than might have been obvious to the casual observer. The student fraternity into which Himmler was initiated in 1919, for example, was named Apollo. We have seen also that Rahn enjoyed a keen interest in the German movie business and it is a fact that Himmler also had friends in the Munich film companies. The pair also shared a hatred of the Jesuits, Himmler regarding them along with Masons, Jews and Bolsheviks as the key protagonists in the conspiracy against the Aryan race. These mutual interests and antipathies might have been considerably strengthened if the two men were aware of a blood relationship, no matter how distant.

At the beginning of June 1936 Rahn journeyed to Iceland with twenty comrades on a study-commission for the SS-Führen. Very little is known about this expedition except that Rahn found the landscape boring and desolate. Frau Winckler confirms that Rahn derived little fulfillment or satisfaction from the trip. Rahn spent the summer solstice in Reykholt, the birthplace of Snorri Sturlusson, the Nordic Homer and author of the Edda. Rahn also visited Lake Laugarvatn where he celebrated the Summer Solstice. It is noteworthy that the ship sailed for Iceland flying a flag with a blue swastika on white background, in sharp contrast to the official standard of the Third Reich. It begs the question as for whom the explorers were actually making the trip.

En route to Iceland Rahn's ship docked at Leith, allowing enough time for Rahn to visit Arthur's Seat, the remains of an ancient volcano situated in Holyrood Park in the centre of Edinburgh. His description of this visit, warranting a brief chapter of its own in *Luzifers Hofgesind*, throws up many more questions than it answers. In Chapter 27 we shall explore Rahn's description of this visit for the light it shines on the author's mystical-metaphysical areas of interest.

Rahn wanted Gabriele to accompany the expedition and to serve as cook. She was keen to go but Himmler turned down the request as he did not think the trip was a place for women. Weisthor did not join them.

---

[2] Lange

The group did not have a firm brief; more likely they were supposed to be brought closer to the roots of the Germanic Edda-Saga by enjoying things together. Team members included the Iceland expert Paul Burkert (while in Iceland he ran up considerable debts at the Reich's expense) and Hans Peter des Coudres who befriended Rahn. Coudres worked as a scientist to set up the Wewelsburg library. He did mention to friends that Rahn at one point shouted out loud: "I want to see trees."[3]

According to Adolf Frisé, some other members of the team did not take Rahn seriously and behaved towards him in a dismissive manner. Rahn wrote in *Luzifers Hofgesind*: "I have no business being here."

The historian Armin Mohler (author of the encyclopaedia *The Conservative Revolution in Germany 1918-1932*) said that dreamers like Rahn were interested only in physical and comprehensible proof of their dreams. In Iceland, he said, Rahn saw very little other than monumental and threatening nature. In general, Rahn's ideas at this time were not generally appreciated or supported by other SS members. After Iceland Rahn's researches took him to the French part of Switzerland but details of these travels are not at hand.

During Rahn's absence in Iceland and Switzerland, SA-Sturmführer Herbert von Kalkstein answered Rahn's letters. As has been noted, von Kalkstein married in 1936 Berta Boden, the sister of Himmler's wife Marga. At the service he wore full SS uniform. In the questionnaire regarding the notice of intended marriage von Kalkstein wrote that he was employed as a secretary of Unterscharführer Otto Rahn between 1st February and 1st of July 1936. Some believe that Kalkstein was ordered to spy on Rahn.

At the 1936 Summer Olympic Games Rahn was seen wearing a uniform with a swastika armband and "Staff of Adolf Hitler" insignia. He wore boots and a dagger and carried a black cap with a shiny peak. His normal insignia should have been "Staff of RFSS." Ladame asked his friend: "my dear Otto, what are you doing in this uniform?" to which Rahn replied: "my dear Paul, one must eat," a comment mindful of the opinion trotted out by some Rahn theorists that the academic joined the SS to secure three meals a day and inexhaustible funds to support his research.

Rahn told Antoinette-Rives that he was a troubleshooter for the SS and that he was proud of his uniform and of his rank. Rahn's

---

[3] cited Lange *Otto Rahn: Leben & Werk.* p27

uniform and insignia on this occasion might lend weight to Ladame's charge that Rahn was a member of the Praetorian Guard established by Himmler in 1933 to protect Hitler from assassination: the Liebstandarte-SS Adolf Hitler, comprising one hundred and fifty select members under SS-Obergruppenführer Joseph "Sepp" Dietrich. The difficulty one has with this proposition is in trying to imagine Rahn with sufficient muscle and killer instinct to have been of any use whatsoever if push came to shove in the face of a determined and fanatical assassin. One struggles to picture it. No documents have come forward to prove any involvement. In my opinion, the balance of probability falls on the side of a non-aggressive history scholar as distinct from a cold-blooded thug prepared to kill for Hitler without hesitation.

In April 1937 *Luzifers Hofgesind—Eine Reise zu den guten Geistern Europas* was published by Schwarzhaupter Verlag in Leipzig. (Seventeen years would pass before the French publishing fraternity would regain sufficient confidence in Rahn as a writer of popular appeal to bring out a French language edition.) Rahn dedicates the book to his SS comrades. He had started the book in his home village of Ohm, Hamburg at the foot of Schlossberg, Haute-Hesse. Substantial progress was made in France and he completed the first draft in Iceland.

As we have seen, Frau Winckler has confirmed that Rahn always intended his second book to be about the despised archbishop Konrad of Marburg, the father confessor of the Landgräve Elisabeth, but what came out ultimately was *Luzifers Hofgesind*. If Rahn was so keen to produce his book on Konrad why would he go on to publish something completely different unless he was under pressure to change tack?

Karl Wolff had been responsible for much of the prior correspondence with the publishers. A hugely favourable review of the book appeared in the SS journal (SS-Leitheft) of 7th May 1937. Himmler ordered one hundred volumes of *Luzifers Hofgesind*, including ten bound in pigskin and another ten in luxury parchment. After Rahn's death, even with his hands full with the war and despite the paper shortages, Himmler had an additional one thousand copies printed. A copy of the parchment edition was sent by the Reichsführer to Hitler for his birthday. If at this time there had been the slightest hint that Rahn was homosexual then Himmler would never have made such a gift.

The *Volkische Beobachter* edition of 25th April 1937 writes that '*the book may be compared to a young brook which courses down the mountains, following by accident the slope in unpredictable jumps and zig-zag lines. Maybe it will not even rush to a stream because it will be a stream itself. Maybe a life's work prepares itself here. Many may be frightened by the title Luzifers Hofgesind because even the most beautiful and deepest meaning of a word, meaning Light-Bringer, can be turned into horror of hell by a thousand twists. But Otto Rahn is not worried to advance the true meaning of the word; the book is packed with lots of dark myths. But where is the root of the myth? Yearning and darkness! Night! Whoever has patience will see the lightbringer, the sun, arise from the night.*'

Arnaud d'Apremont wries in the preface to the French translation of *Luzifers Hofgesind—La Cour de Lucifer: Voyage au coeur de la plus haute spiritualité européenne*[4] that Rahn's second book is written in a more idealogical style, vaguely racist and anti-semitic, to all appearances national-socialist. We have seen that Christian Bernadac shared this viewpoint. However, other critics see Rahn in a quandary, having to toe the nationalist party line, sucking up to the censor and unable to write the fully objective and integrated text he would have liked, indicating the irony of his position in the book's title. The irony suggestion seems unlikely as Rahn did not see Lucifer as synonomous with Satan or the Devil; to Rahn, Lucifer was the Pyrenean Abellio, the Celtic Belenos, the Nordic Balder, the Greek Apollo, all luminous gods today asleep. The Cathars called this god Lucibel. These are the light bearers, an attribute that Rahn wished the world at large would accord to him personally.

Above all else, Rahn wished to reawaken the grand European dream. Paul Ladame said in the sixties that when he was asked by René Nelli to write the foreward of a new French language edition of *Luzifers Hofgesind* he was surprised to see a slightly changed manuscript to that which Rahn had permitted him to read thirty years before. The changes imbued the text with an anti-semitic emphasis that, Ladame stressed, was not present in the original. Ladame said: "Otto Rahn would never have written that."

The question therefore arises that if parts of the book were changed, as Frau Winckler also believes, who made the changes and why? It is known that Rahn did make changes to his manuscript prior to publication but it is not clear which version he worked on. Let us remember also that Ladame later published disinformation regarding Rahn. The jury is still out on the vexed issue of third party influence upon Otto Rahn's work.

---

[4] Paris: Pardès 1999

However, Rahn's publisher von Haller wrote: "The possibility of an influence by a political party towards the text of *Luzifers Hofgesind* is in my opinion non-existent. I followed the creation of the work from the beginning to the end. I don't know the French version. The question of style, however, is a different one. When Mohler (Dr. Armin Mohler) compared the text with extracts from former works of Rahn he stated: 'This is not Rahn.' That's why he approached me. Nevertheless, the book is completely written by Rahn, I was only the understanding publisher who developed more and more of the underlying parts, having gained some experience as a lecturer at the Deutsche Verlags-Anstalt. There were various versions in better stages of development, a complete confrontation of Christian fundamentalism and the freedom of the spirit—of course without being complete."

Hans-Jürgen Lange asked von Haller about this and he answered that nothing far-reaching was changed. He said that he would have known about any because he was involved with the book from its inception. Nevertheless, von Haller also told Lange that he had had a strong influence on the book and on its linguistic form. He said that the title had come from him and, crucially, that he had sat down with Rahn for two or three weeks in Hamburg and together they had reworked the text completely. This prolonged and substantial hands-on involvement clearly contradicts von Haller's past insistence that he only helped develop "underlying parts." It is clearly evident that the book is linguistically very different from *Kreuzzug gegen den Gral*.

That Himmler had some influence on the work before it was printed cannot be ruled out. This is proven by his letter dated 30th March 1938 to SS-Hauptsturmführer Professor Dr. Eckhardt: "Thanks for your note regarding Rahn's book *Luzifers Hofgesind*. I know the book very well since I had a chat with Rahn about it before it was even published. Heil Hitler, Yours Heinrich Himmler."

Hugh Thomas[5] reminds us that Himmler had a history of misrepresenting key documents to further his own ambitions. Shortly after he was made Reichsführer SS in February 1929, Himmler re-typed a brilliantly conceived report by Ludolf Haase, Nazi leader for Hannover South, which called for the establishment of a secret National Socialist order within the Party to keep the party in trim. Himmler presented this report to the Party chiefs as his own political thesis. This fraudulent action was the precursor to Himmler's establishment of his own Order of Teutonic Knights.

---

[5] Thomas, Hugh. *The Unlikely Death of Heinrich Himmler*. London: Fouth Estate, 2002

We have also seen from Frau Winckler's testimony that Rahn was not even especially motivated to write *Luzifers Hofgesind* until he had concluded a more cherished project on Konrad of Marburg.

Rahn's constant bragging about his researches and discoveries in the Ariège was exasperating a number of highly placed people, including Heinz Pehmoller who we met earlier in Chapter 7. Pehmoller, headteacher and Nazi politician with responsibilities to develop the direction of the Hitler-Jugend (Hitler Youth) movement, met Rahn in Konstanz at the Winckler family house in the summer of 1937 while on his honeymoon. Unfortunately, there was immediate tension between Rahn and Pehmoller's wife, which made conversation very difficult. During subsequent contacts, which remained very loose, Pehmoller and Rahn invariably discussed Rahn's field of research. Pehmoller was interested in Rahn's work although he did not like his research methods, especially what he regarded as Rahn's inconsistency. To him, Rahn's methods seemed to confuse hypothesis and proof. He was irritated by Rahn's principle tenet in his theory that the Cathars were central to the Grail legends while at the same time offering no evidence. There was even no proof, Pehmoller suggested, that the Cathars knew of the word "grail." He was also unimpressed with what he regarded as Rahn's illogical deductions that connected his theories with references in Wolfram von Eschenbach's *Parsifal*. Nevertheless, the headmaster thought highly enough of Rahn to travel to the Pyrenees after the war and make contact with the French youth group who did not accept Otto Rahn's 1939 suicide as fact.

Eight weeks later on 20th August 1937 Rahn was in Hamburg attending the wedding of Mrs Hartmann, née Gotz. Wearing an SS-uniform, Rahn tried to provoke an argument with Leutnant Horst Buchrucker during the reception. Rahn felt insulted and was unhappy with the fact that the Leutnant had placed him at the very end of the table among a number of youngsters. He sneered at the Wehrmacht and about the fact that Buchrucker was not a member of the party. This was sheer hypocrisy on Rahn's part as then and at no time later was Rahn a member of the NSDAP. On this occasion Rahn must have felt inferior because Buchrucker was in uniform, too. Both men had been drinking and Rahn felt he had to show off verbally in the face of the other man's physical superiority. In loud voice Rahn threatened to provoke action against Buchrucker by people of greater influence.

Buchrucker's impression of Rahn was that he was very devious. Moreover, he knew Rahn had connections but was not sure how far they extended. Rahn gave the impression at the reception that he badly wanted to get to the top. However, surviving acquaintances and friends of Rahn rarely made any critical remarks about him, mostly describing him as a pleasant fellow, albeit nervous and oversensitive.

After the wedding Rahn stayed on in Hamburg, the place where he had finished *Luzifers Hofgesind.* He was visited by Antoinette Rives who stayed with Rahn for more than a month. This gave rise to considerable speculation among Rahn's friends about the nature of their relationship.

1937 was also the year when Otto Rahn met Dr. Franz Riedweg, a young man who had become engaged to the daughter of Imperial War Minister Marshal Werner von Blomberg. The pair later married. Riedweg thought, correctly, that Otto's and Gabriele's chemist friend Dr. Schmid was homosexual. It is likely that by extension Riedweg must have harboured the same feelings about Rahn. Riedweg was invited by Himmler in 1938 to serve as troop doctor to the SS-Standarte Deutschland. This move was to cause Rahn significant difficulties a year later.

Later in the year Rahn was to be seen breaking bread at the Nobelrestaurant, Berlin, with top influential figures within or supportive of the Reich, among them the infamous Reinhard Heydrich. The other guests were Himmler, Dr. Best, Karl Wolff, Dr. Riedweg and Jean-Marie Musy, a Swiss politician who made the anti-communist film *Die Rote Pest* (The Red Plague) with Riedweg.

Rahn's presence at table begs the question as to whether this occasion was a one-off venture or if he was a habitué who craved high level Nazi social intercourse. Considering Rahn's role as Grailhunter, it is a safe bet that the top Nazi dignitaries knew of him and his activities. If Rahn was a willing party to these sort of rendezvous then we must ask ourselves if he embraced these opportunities as a loyal servant of the Nazi cause or if he deployed such occasions as a shroud to gather intelligence while concealing altogether different motives and allegiances.

Rahn continued to act rashly. Adolf Frisé describes how dangerous and unworldly Otto Rahn was at this time. He relates his account of the time Rahn saw a "big fish" one night in a restaurant bar. The man was drunk and accompanied by a “tarty” female companion. An inner voice told Rahn that he had to be the conscience of his Order and in the name of his boss, the protector, he had to puff himself up in front of the pair as a shining symbol and teach them a lesson. "They dirty our uniform," he said. "It makes us aware of our duty to act as an example." It was the case, he later boasted, that his appeal had led to decency, dignity and proper behaviour. On the other hand, and more frequently, Rahn's appeals and good intentions provoked laughter and he was unable to cope with this kind of reaction.

In August 1937 party court proceedings were instituted against Karl Mahler who was accused of defamatory behaviour (a euphemism for homosexual activity). In a letter dated 27th August written by senior party officials to the Gau Court in Berlin, one reads that Untersturmführer Otto Rahn, member of the personal group of Reichsführer SS in Berlin, was heavily incriminated because of behaviour contrary to the honour of the NSDAP.

In the preceding months Rahn had been living at Ohm, Hamburg and was working on *Luzifers Hofgesind*. He had relatives there and contemporaries have reported to Hans-Jürgen Lange that Rahn was having a sexual liaison with a young man at his workplace. Because of this denunciation Rahn was prosecuted and as a result he would have to undertake punitive service. In the records it says that alcohol also played a part, which was seen as a mitigating factor. Himmler was briefed on the matter but he was of the opinion that homosexuality was a disease and that, consequently, Rahn could be "cured" of his sexual orientation.

After the case against Mahler had been completed the Arolsen court files on the case and Rahn's involvement were sent to the Gau Court. In the meantime, action on Rahn's party membership application was suspended because any eventual refusal was to be based on collective evidence, including the outcomes of any legal proceedings such as those at Gau.

On 28th August, shortly after the Arolsen case, Rahn wrote in secret to Himmler. In his letter Rahn promises to abstain from alcohol for the next two years. He confirmed that in four days hence, 1st September, he would meet SS-Gruppenführer Eicke in the concentration camp Dachau to join the SS-Totenkopfverbände "Oberbayern" for at least four months active service. During this service, Rahn assured Himmler, he would remove his signets as an SS-Untersturmführer and wear those of a simple SS soldier. Rahn concludes by promising he would try very hard to compensate at least partly for his behaviour in Arolsen, so injurious to the SS and for which he was so very sorry, by doing his duties.

Dachau was the first camp run solely by the SS and over which Himmler had full operational and executive command. Until 1936 protective arrest was used to bring order to the domestic situation and later to isolate or destroy those outside mainstream society. The

"Reichskritallnacht" pogrom on 9th November 1938 vastly increased the number of inmates. During the re-organisation of the camp system by the Dachau commander Eicke the guards were brought out of conventional SS control, being subsumed into the newly created SS-Totenkopfverbände. After 1937 the three Totenkopfstandarten groups were formed: 'Oberbayern,' 'Brandenburg' and 'Thueringen.' The average age of the members of those groups decreased in 1936 to twenty-three years when more and more young men joined up. Ideology did not, however, play a significant role in the decision-making process for the younger joiners because Dachau was an important training centre for the SS and was a model copied by other camps.

The formal SS policy towards homosexuality was very strict; there were even claims that Himmler had had his own nephew shot.[6] In practice, Himmler's utterances about the issue were far stricter in public than the line he took in dealing privately with his own (favourite) subordinates.

On 27th April 1938 a letter from Dachau records that from 28th November until the 21st December 1937 Otto Rahn had been on a training course and had served at the front for one week from 1st September. He had shown some effort, being just able to cope with the physical demands of drill exercises (and this is the man alleged to have been a heavyweight praetorian troubleshooter for Hitler). However, Rahn always expressed eagerness and had been appointed as assistant trainer after fourteen days. Overall, though, his capabilities at the end of the training showed some deficiencies and, consequently, he could not be named as a fully competent group leader. Rahn's behaviour both on- and off-duty had been first rate and he had been an example to all his comrades.

After his punishment Rahn went skiing to Lake Schliersee in Bavaria with Raymond. Five months later Rahn wrote to Himmler: "By the way, I arranged for Mr Raymond Perrier to meet some leaders of the Totenkopfstandarten 'Oberbayern.' Although there were initially some language difficulties, in the end they got on with each other so well I really felt proud of these Dachau colleagues."

During this holiday the pair visited the Lauermann family in Neuhaus. Later Rahn rented a small farmer's cottage near Joseftal.

---

[6] Kersten F. *Totenkopf und Treue*. Hamburg: Robert Mölich Verlag, 1952

Chapter NINE

FRANCE 1937
Forbidden Merchandise

Colonel Howard Buechner asserts that in 1937 Rahn was sent back to the Languedoc for reasons never clarified, during which time he stayed briefly in Montségur and then left saying he would be back in 1939. Jean Michel Angebert also claims that Rahn returned to Montségur in 1937. There is no proof that Rahn made these visits.

It has been further speculated that during this year Otto Rahn visited the Corbières and made his way to Rennes-le-Château, the tiny hilltop village where in 1891 cleric Bérenger Saunière found undisclosed items in his church and thereafter attained fame and riches. Saunière died in 1917.

Rahn's purported trip to the Corbières is said to be connected with "forbidden merchandise." In this connection, rumours have been circulating for years that Rahn sought a meeting with Marie Dénarnaud, Saunière's housekeeper, the one person alive in 1937 said to have known the secret of Saunière's source of wealth. The story goes that Dénarnaud (known by villagers as the "priest's Madonna") entrusted to Rahn articles and/or documents concerning her deceased employer's fabled secret.

As we have noted, there is no proof of any kind that Rahn did visit the Corbières or Rennes-le-Château specifically. Evidently, however, there are many today who want to believe not only that Rahn's travels turned him in that direction but that he came away with riches or, at least, the information to find and retrieve them.

Before we look at the claim in detail it is worth reflecting on the singular and surprising omission that in neither of his published works nor, as far as one may ascertain, in any of his published articles and broadcasts did Rahn mention Rennes-le-Château by name. Saunière died only fourteen years before Rahn's commenced his explorations in the Languedoc and so the stories surrounding the priest's activities would have still been relatively fresh and in circulation, considering the intense interest they aroused among the highest quarters in Europe between 1891 and 1917. Otto Rahn, medieval historian and arch-student of Grail and Cathar legend, would have undoubtedly known of the affair and, it could be reasonably argued, would have been drawn to investigate matters on the ground. However, Rennes-le-Château in Rahn's writings is conspicuous by its absence. Why might this be?

The claim made is that villagers have confirmed that in the early nineteen thirties Otto Rahn was a welcome house-guest at the home of Marie Dénarnaud. Furthermore, it is claimed that during the visit (or visits) Rahn spent many hours in conversation with Marie and that she subsequently imparted to her visitor details of the local Grail secret. It is not possible to comb through Rahn's person correspondence for any relevant references to this episode because his mother burned the greater part of it after his death.

Hans-Jürgen Lange has strongly refuted these claims, basing his opinion on Rahn's own texts in which it is clear that he believed the Grail was cached in the caves of the Sabarthès after it was removed in 1244 from Montségur. Lange's view is that Rennes-le-Château and Montségur are two different stories, which have been artificially conjoined for journalistic purposes to deepen and prolong the mystery.

Lange also poses the obvious question as to why Dénarnaud would want to converse with a young German stranger with little or no obvious means, let alone proceed to entrust him with a tremendous secret. Besides, if Dénarnaud had been in connivance with Saunière (and villagers said that the pair were so close they basically lived as man and wife) and she was indeed privy to a big secret, then why was she was seemingly unable or unwilling to capitalise on it when compelled to burn her banknotes in response to de Gaulle's announcement to the citizens of France about withdrawing the old currency? Maybe the plain truth is that Marie knew nothing at all.

There is also the practical issue surrounding poor transportation links to the area. In the 1920s there was no handy bus service connecting the villages in and around Rennes-le-Château. Rahn would have had his work cut out to make visits to this geographically inhospitable location. Getting around the Montségur area was a little easier because Countess Pujol-Murat occasionally lent her car to Rahn. However, this facility was tied to Rahn conducting research into the Cathars to shed more light on the Countess' belief that she was the reincarnation of Esclarmonde de Foix.

Nevertheless, the belief continues to gain strength that Rahn went to the Corbières on the trail of something of great value and that the feverish search for "forbidden merchandise" was the brutal motive behind the subsequent massacre of the villagers of Oradour-sur-Glane by Otto Skorzeny's *Das Reich* in 1944. Skorzeny denied any participation in the matter.

Robin Mackness wrote a book called: *Oradour: Massacre and Aftermath,*[1] which described the affair in detail. Oradour-sur-Glane is a small village in the Limoges area that was visited by the III./SS-Pz.Gren.Rgt. "Der Führer." The declared purpose of their visit was to search for SS-Sturmbannführer Helmuth Kampfe who had been captured by the Resistance. The officer in charge of the unit was SS-Sturmbannführer Otto Diekmann. However, there are those who believe that there was a second, secret reason underlying the "Der Führer" visit, which was to search for "forbidden merchandise," said to be documents or archives of some description. Whether the SS found anything is not clear but they concluded their visit by exterminating the village residents.

Otto Skorzeny

Beginning at 2pm, it took just five hours for the SS troops to murder 642 civilian men and women on 10th June 1944. Among the killers were a handful of French countrymen, mostly young conscripts from Alsace, the eastern region of France that was annexed by Germany in 1940. Of the fourteen Alsatian men one was a volunteer; the others had been forcibly enrolled for the massacre assignment.

All the male villagers who had not fled or hidden were rounded up, machine-gunned, then burned. The 241 women and 209 children were herded into a church, which was ignited by exploding an ammunition box behind the altar. Before the Germans marched off they burnt 123 houses and more than 200 barns. Only about fifty villagers survived. After the war the obliterated village was preserved as a memorial.

In 1953 twenty-one of the one hundred and twenty strong SS contingent was put on trial in Bordeaux, including the twelve surviving Frenchmen. The French conscripts were sentenced to life imprisonment. The volunteer was condemned to death. This provoked

---

[1] London: Bloomsbury Books, 1988

outrage in Alsace where it was argued that most of these men had been forced into the SS. In the interests of "national reconciliation" the National Assembly swiftly voted an amnesty for the condemned Frenchman, provoking equal fury in Oradour-sur-Glane and the Limousin region. The village returned its Légion d'Honneur medal in protest.

It is said that after the massacre an SS team, allegedly led by Otto Skorzeny, went to the Corbières, the arid region around Rennes-le-Château and searched the mountains and caves. Rumour had it that Skorzeny's team found a cache of treasure containing artefacts as fabulous as the Ark of the Covenant and the Grail Cup. The story goes that the SS was so utterly focused upon its objective to find the hapless Sturmbannführer that its soldiers rapidly and clinically murdered 642 men, women and children. This was a grossly excessive act even by SS standards, out of all proportion to the professed nature of their rescue mission. It suggests that there were ulterior motives. A search for secret documents, especially those with a promise of great enrichment in some form or another, may well provoke extreme violence.

Otto Skorzeny and Adolf Hitler

Is there any evidence to support the secret document-archive theory behind Der Führer's actions? Yes, there is. The key documents in question are masonic-alchemical in nature which, some researchers argue, are the records sought so avidly in 1891 by Rennes-le-Château pastor Bérenger Saunière and his friend Abbé Boudet (and by Otto Rahn fifty years later?).

The development of mystical Christianity in the Languedoc was given substance by the gathering together of ancient texts and popular traditions. These documents included masonic-alchemical texts from the eighteenth century. In particular, the Primitive Rite of the Marquis de Chefdebien of Narbonne bears an especial importance if one considers the notion that the roots of the Rennes-le-Château affair trace back to that period.

According to a letter received from France by the UK Rennes group, whose members are verifying the provenance of the letter and its author, the "forbidden merchandise" concerns occult documents apparently stolen from Hector Dagobert in the Napoleonic era by the marquis Chefdebien of Narbonne. Hector is a candidate for the real identity of le Comte de Saint-Germain. Chefdebien was a member of the Philadelphus Society and it was he who introduced Bérenger Saunière's brother Alfred to aristocratic circles. The inference is that Dagobert's documents and the "forbidden merchandise" are one and the same.

In 1745 Luc Siméon Auguste Dagobert, Marquis de Fontenille and his two brothers established at the court of Versailles "The Lodge of the Three Brothers." Dagobert's Uncle Hector later initiated him into the Scottish Primitive Rite Branch. In 1771 the "Lodge of the Reunited Friends" was founded in Paris. Around this time Dagobert persuaded his Versailles lodge to establish a constitution called the "Commission of Grades and Archives" to investigate Masonic rites and rituals. In 1777 Dagobert was appointed Grand Secretary to the "Grand Orient," and at the same time he formed the "Régime des Philadelphes" lodge. Straightaway, Dagobert lost no time in raiding all other lodges in France for information, a foray in which he was apparently highly succesful.

In 1779 the Marquis de Chefdebien (son of the Vicomte), already a high profile mason, was initiated into the order with resultant access to the precious documentation Dagobert had seized over the preceding years.

Towards 1780, a little later after the foundation of the Grand Orient of France (1773), Narbonne was host to many masonic groups. The Philadelphus Lodge, claiming for itself the title of the first Primitive Rite in France, was established in 1779 by the family of Chefdebien d'Armissan and, at first, was allied with a board of Scottish directors. It recruited its members principally from the aristocracy. The seven founders of the society were the Vicomte de Chefdebien and his six sons. The Philadelphus Lodge enjoyed a strong association with the Lodge of Saint Germain. The masonic rite that the Marquis de Chefdebien created was particularly steeped in alchemical researches. This was not untypical for the area and a trip to Carcassonne library will unearth many documents concerning masonic-alchemical rituals of this period. Moreover, evidence suggests that Chefdebien's alchemical endeavours were intrinsically connected with the legend of the Golden Fleece.

Antoine Faivre, professor of esoteric philosophy at the

Sorbonne, reports in his *Alchemy and the Golden Fleece*[2] that in 1806 Jean Etienne-Juste d'Hermensen wrote to the Marquis de Chefdebien about the masonic grades he had reached, which were General of the Argonauts and Knight of the Argonauts. In Chapter 20 we will follow Jason's voyage as a powerful and illuminating allegory allowing us to examine the life Otto Rahn led between the lines of his public words and actions.

Alfred Saunière, Bérenger's brother and an individual in the Rennes affair who is little mentioned, was a private tutor in the Chefdebien family of Narbonne. However, it seems that in the accounting of Abbe Saunière much of the sums in his possession came, in fact, from his brother. Bearing in mind that Alfred has been accused of misappropriating items and belongings from the Chefdebien family, one might be forgiven for suggesting that the famous manuscripts of Bérenger Saunière also originated from this ancient family by an act of theft and not from the cellars of the church at Rennes-le-Château.

Certain essential elements in this scenario are worth reviewing. For example, in Bérenger's time there was an Occitan language revue published at Rennes-le-Château called "Montségur." The revue was overseen by the village primary school teacher who, apparently, had no association of any kind with the curé. Neither did the Abbé Boudet of Rennes-les-Bains contribute to the revue. This somewhat dampens the idea that there were links between neo-catharism and the abbé Saunière and his Church colleagues.

On the other hand, an alchemical thread appears more and more possible as deriving from the Chefdebien of Narbonne family, especially when we highlight the strong links between the Philadelphes and Dagobert de Fontenille, cousin by marriage of Jean-Pierre François Duhamel. Duhamel was commissioner of mines and forges for Louis XVI and publisher of a book entitled *Géométrie Souterraine* in 1787. This book speaks of mastery over metals and of the search for gold-bearing seams in the Razès, notably in the environs of Rennes-le-Château. On August 8th, 1780, Dagobert de Fontenille married the daughter of lord high justice Joseph-Gaspard Pailhoux de Cascastel. The wedding was witnessed by Duhamel.

In 1779 Pailhoux, Duhamel and a businessman called Peltier decided to reopen the mines in the Roussillon. Permission was given by the controlling owner, the Monastery at Lagrasse, for a thirty year operating period. By virtue of his relation with the Pailhoux family, Dagobert received a one-sixth share of the operation. Dagobert was

---

[2] State University of New York Press, 1993

later able to buy both Duhamel's and Peltier's shares, allowing him to gain complete control over the mines by 1782. Having made all this effort to secure overall control, it is a curious fact that there is no evidence to show that Dagobert had anything extracted. So what was Dagobert up to?

Dagobert was a direct descendent of King Dagobert. It is not beyond the bounds of possibility that he was combing the mines for physical evidence relating to his forebears' connections with Merovingian and Visigothic treasure.

Dagobert was arrested in the early days of the French Revolution. His Masonic friends argued for his release, claiming that Dagobert's incarceration was denying the French army the services of a loyal, highly trained officer. He was freed, promoted, and then joined his new commanding officer, Marquis de Chefdebien, the son of the grand master of the Philadelphes, in an army unit in the Pyrenees.

Concerned about how the approaching war might affect him personally, Dagobert left his archives: "Les Arcanes des Mines des Corbières" with the Grand Orient. Ironically, Dagobert died just a few days later, not in a theatre of war but in decidedly shady circumstances by food poisoning. Had Dagobert's cook not shown a clean pair of heels he might have been able to throw some light on his master's untimely end. If the chef was involved in the affair was he acting in the pay of the Chefdebien family? This powerful family did manage to obtain Dagobert's archives at a later date but no one knows what use they made of them.

Many believe that these records survived into the 20th century and that the Nazis, aware of their existence and of their significance, were determined to obtain them at any cost.

The history behind these matters (Alan Scott's well researched Rennes-Discovery website[3] is a principle and welcome source for the Dagobert-Chefdubien account) provides powerful evidence that there existed documents of such import that men would kill indiscriminately to obtain them. Their content is unknown but when we look in detail at the brilliant hermeneutics of the legend of the Golden Fleece and its associated philosophic outgrowths (in particular, Rosicrucianism) we will gain a much clearer understanding of what would have been at stake in securing ownership of these ancient esoteric texts.

---

[3] http://www.rennes-discovery.com/sauniere_and_martinism.htm

Chapter TEN

Germany 1938-1939 "Gral"

Rahn's writings, coupled with a high media profile earned by well-received radio spots and magazine articles, brought him recognition and esteem. His bright and ascending star quickly made him a hot property among the intelligentsia for lectures. We are fortunate to have details of one such presentation delivered in Dortmund to the Dietrich-Eckart Society during the second week of January 1938.

Kurt Eggers, the cultural director of the Society, gave an initial introduction in which he welcomed Rahn as a friend and briefly described the Lucifer issues with which Rahn was involved. In an enthusiastic delivery Rahn outlined the imagery in more detail, illustrating his talk with readings from *Luzifers Hofgesind*, which reported on his European journeys and researches in the South of France. In these places, on the trail of the Grail and the Albigensian people, Rahn drew a fertile picture of the Cathar faith crushed with such fervent hatred by the Roman Church. Witness reports of Rahn's presentation spoke of its sensitive treatment of a difficult matter that required of its audience great discipline and attention. It spoke volumes for both those present and the presenter that no word was lost and that the concept and image of Lucifer, celebrated by Rahn as the Lightbringer, came out very strongly.

There were clearly two parts of the evening that could be distinguished, namely Rahn’s succinct description of the Grail and Lucifer issues and, secondly, his use of concrete examples to draw conclusions from the presentation. By virtue of Rahn's skill in knitting together the various critical elements of his subject, his audience was treated to a persuasive reassessment of historical events, personalities and facts. With a sense of genuine dramatic tension Rahn led his audience back to the origins of a real longing for freedom and a return to nature, re-establishing shared and cherished opinions into the belief of an eternal kingdom to come and in the fear of hell. He declared himself for *Luzifers Hofgesind*, in whose name Kurt Eggers closed the evening by exclaiming “Lucifer, who was treated unfairly, we greet you!”

In Dr. Wolff Heinrichsdorf's review of the lecture we get a further perspective on the content:

"Otto Rahn, the young poet and researcher read and lectured Friday evening at the Dietrich Eckart Verein (club) in front of a rather large and highly captivated audience. Kurt Eggers, the person in charge of cultural events for the Dietrich Eckart Verein, made a few introductory remarks, greeting Rahn as a comrade and briefly outlining the "Lucifer-Problem" which Rahn would talk about. Rahn quickly sketched an image of Lucifer in such emphatic and compelling language that it could not be thought out in a more moving and explicit manner. The author read from his newest work Luzifers Hofgesind, which tells of his travels and findings in Southern France where he followed the traces of the Grail and the Albigenses (Cathars), the pure and true heretics. Developing this theme and highlighting new viewpoints, Rahn drew a prolific picture of this anti-Roman movement which had also spread throughout Germany at that time. The lecture covered difficult material and required a very high degree of discipline and alertness from the audience. It was a good sign for the symbioses of lecturer and audience that no word was lost, and that the image of Lucifer, which Rahn celebrated with the Albigenses as the Bringer of Light, was most effective.

Two parts of the evening can clearly be differentiated: the first, where Rahn reported on the research and current status of the Grail and Lucifer-Problem—here the most powerful words and the most exciting creative power came into play—and a second, which the lecturer based on concrete examples, drew conclusions from his new points of view and teachings, and arrived at not only an interesting but also a largely convincing re-evaluation of historical events, leading figures and facts. The hurdle of a rationalism of the old kind—a danger, which would without doubt exist for a less truthful and less strong acceptance of nature and re-evaluation—was avoided by Rahn very well. In true excitement, he again led back to the sources and origins of real desire for freedom and true closeness to nature.

The Albigenses have been exterminated. In Southern France, 205 leading followers of Lucifer were burnt on a giant stake (March 16th 1244) after a great crusade led by Dominican priests in the name of Christian mildness. The teachings of Lucifer, the Bringer of Light, and his followers were persecuted with fire and sword. The Albigenses are dead but their spirit is alive and takes effect, especially in these days, in a renewed and rejuvenated excitement and passion. Christ's representative could burn people but he was wrong when he thought he could burn with them their spirit, passion and desire. This spirit became alive again yesterday, took its effect and was visible in Otto Rahn—a descendent of the ancient Troubadours—in front of many people.

Rahn set a new limit to the spirit tied to the Romans, to the belief in a life after death, and the fear of hell; he negated Yahweh and the Jewish teachings, and professed the truth of Luzifers Hofgesind in whose name Kurt Eggers closed the evening with the following greeting: 'Lucifer, who has been done wrong to, greets you.'

Altogether the evening was a great success, which was a promising beginning for the future work of the Dietrich Eckart Verein. The Conservatory Quartet provided an excellent setting for the evening and furnished the artistic background for the multitude and richness of thoughts."[1]

Around the time of this talk, Rahn asked his superiors for leave to leave Munich and travel to Switzerland to recuperate. His health was worsening and permission was granted.

On 29th February 1938 Karl Wolff wrote an astonishing letter to the SS Office of Racial Questions, informing it that Rahn had been unable to produce a certificate of racial origin, a certificate, as this letter points out, that had been an absolute requirement for SS membership since 1st January 1935. Wolff's letter grants Rahn one more month to obey this rule. In mitigation for Rahn, Wolff explains in the letter that the delay had been caused chiefly by Rahn's training duty in Dachau (during the last quarter of 1937) and by his travel abroad on behalf of investigations for the Reichsführer SS. The letter adds a handwritten postscript that Rahn was in Switzerland to recover his health.

In April Rahn confided by letter to his friend Ullmann, SS-Obersturmbannführer and Stabführer of the Personnel Department RFSS, that he had interrupted his stay in Switzerland to resolve things in his absence that had gone wrong. Rahn did not elaborate on the details but said that he had been trying to avoid some unpleasant things, the nature of which he wished to pass on to Himmler and to Wolff. Rahn goes on to mention that he had been trying to take up an invitation to visit the home of the Swiss film-maker and former member of the Bundesrat, Jean-Marie Musy, but his health problems kept forcing him to postpone. He was, however, delighted that Musy and his wife had been able to enjoy the company of Mrs Dollfuss and children. Mrs Dolfuss' husband Engelbert, anti-NSDAP, was opposed to the attachment of Austria to Germany and was killed in the

---

[1] Berlin Document Centre/Bundesarchiv Potsdam: SS-Personalakten: Otto Wilhelm Rahn

Bundeskanzleramt in July 1934 during an attempted coup by eight Austrian Nazis, as a prelude to Anschluss.

Rahn mentions that he would be forwarding presently new documents regarding the Reichsführer SS family tree. He adds that his financial problems were solved and his health had improved but, strange to relate, his legs seemed not to work properly. Rahn's Swiss doctor had diagnosed general exhaustion that would take a long time to cure. Thankfully, his lungs were back to normal. He was planning to return to the Sonnmatt health clinic at Lucerne after sorting out his own incomplete ancestral line. Moreover, Rahn was keen to know as soon as possible if Himmler had other plans in the pipeline for him because sudden new trips and decisions were factors contributing to his physical problems. Rahn was certainly pushing his luck.

Despite all the delays, Rahn was finally able to provide a complete ancestral lineage back to 1750, the time period necessary for every SS leader. This ancestral proof is part of the legacy of the family Römer-Rahn. Suspicions were raised that Rahn dallied for a purpose, frightened by the thought that the surname of his mother "Hamburger" might indicate Jewish origins.

Even today there is still conjecture about Rahn's supposed Jewishness. The writer E. Mila, for example, claims that Rahn's Jewish status is irrefutable. Rahn's mother was Clara Margaret Hamburger and his grandfather was Simeon Hamburger, a name form frequently used by central European Jews. His maternal grandmother, Lea Cucer, was Jewish. Cucer comes from Cocer, a name of profession widely used by Jews of central Europe. However, Gabriele Winckler told us that based on her own knowledge Himmler would probably not have made too much of the issue had it been demonstrated that Rahn had Jewish antecedents. She quoted the example of Dr. Martini, a Nazi archaeologist who confided to Himmler that there was Jewish blood in his family. Himmler was personally uncritical but relocated Martini to Turkey to conduct archaeological work—out of sight, out of mind.

In April 1938 Rahn made an oral statement about the admission of Dr. Franz Riedweg, Jean-Marie Musy's former secretary, into the SS. Rahn clearly disagreed with the proposal. The intent for Riedweg to join the SS, together with adoption of German naturalisation, created bad press in Switzerland, Riedwig's native country. Rahn's sentiments mirrored this concern. He confided his feelings about Riedweg to Ullman who later recalled that Rahn thought little of the Swiss doctor because he was all image and no substance. Riedweg, Rahn claimed, thought little of his political life and looked only to opportunities for self-aggrandisement and that his desire for SS membership was no more than a calculated career move.

Musy, also, was not too happy about these efforts of Riedweg. In the film-maker's view the least courtesy Riedweg could have offered was to have advised him of his intentions. Unaware of Riedweg's ambitions, Musy continued with his latest film opposed to the Komintern. When the news broke about Riedweg and Swiss public opinion was unanimously hostile Musy was forced to change the ending of his film being made in Germany, which had already cost in excess of one hundred thousand francs. The film, Rahn remarked, now had to have a "democratic face" so that it could not be put about that Musy had financed the film with SS money.

Rahn's personal views about Riedweg's provocations were tempered to a degree because the physician was always perfectly affable and courteous when the two were in company together. Nevertheless, Rahn could not dismiss his feelings and his opinions weighed upon him heavily in deciding how far to stick his neck out in making his objections known to Himmler.

Two months later Rahn was asked to put his views about Riedweg into writing to Himmler who said he would advise on his response. Considering that the initiative to induct Riedweg into the SS as a medical officer was Himmler's own idea, Rahn chose to skate on very thin ice in criticising the Reichsführer's proposals. It was not the smartest of moves.

Around this time Ullman informed Rahn by letter that he had had an opportunity to meet briefly with Wolff about all the various issues. However, Wolff was busy preparing for a trip to Italy and would not be drawn into expressing opinions about the Riedweg matter and about other "things that had gone wrong" for Rahn. Consequently, Ullmann asked Rahn if he would write down all the bits they had discussed.

Ullmann's letter goes on to throw a little light on the "things that had gone wrong" when he asks Rahn to comment more fully on why he wished to publish in French and Swiss newspapers, giving the names of the various papers he had in mind. Additionally, Ullman advised, Rahn should give details on who had attacked him (not made clear if this was a reference to a physical, spoken or written attack) and how it had come about. Rahn was also invited to spell out what he wanted in terms of his holiday and salary arrangements, profits from his book, and to name an amount for any additional purchases he wanted to make. Ullman pressed Rahn to put down the details of "what we have discussed" and then the whole account could be handed to Wolff on his return from Italy for discussion with Himmler. Ullman went on to ask Rahn to write a separate letter about both Mrs Dolfuss and the visit of Musy to Berlin.

The SS-Obersturmbannführer added that he had also brought up the matter of Dr. Riedweg and professed to Rahn that he was not at all keen to get mixed up in the affair since the doctor had friends of some influence, somewhat of an understatement when we note Himmler's own degree of support. However, Ullman mentioned that Wolff considered Riedweg's recent support for Pan-Europe as a very important consideration among the various arguments and that it was Rahn's duty as SS-Untersturmführer to inform Himmler of all the facts. Wolff wanted Rahn to brief either the RFSS or himself on the content of the discussions between Rahn and Ullman on Riedweg.

Ullmann also asked Rahn to inform him of "those accusations you can prove yourself and those for whom you can name witnesses." The correspondence throws no further light on what circumstances were referred to in connection with these matters. Nor is there clear explanation on Ullmann's remark at the end of his letter that SS-Gruppenführer Wolff had no further information "regarding the matter in which you got involved with a commander of the airforce." Ulmann conveys the fact that Wolff was quite willing to forget about the whole thing, largely due to the dedicated service that Rahn had undertaken at Dachau for the SS-Totenkopfverbände but also because the officer in question was no longer with the airforce. The SS-Untersturmführer concluded the letter by stipulating that a detailed report on all these matters must be submitted soon and added rather limply that he hoped Rahn would soon feel better.

Later in June Rahn wrote confidentially to Himmler to convey both his opinions and those of his "Swiss mates" about Dr. Franz Riedweg. Straightaway, Rahn put his cards on the table by declaring himself biased against Riedweg, who had been introduced to him by mutual friend Professor Alfred Schmid. Rahn admitted, however, that there had always been courtesy and correctness between Riedweg and himself. Rahn explained to Himmler that his Swiss friends, some of whom he had met by introduction from Riedweg, believed that the doctor's entry into the SS was purely an opportunist move designed to hasten his diplomatic career and thereby make progress up the ladder, which he could not hope to equal or emulate in his home country. Rahn was extremely concerned that Riedweg, who had no previous soldiering experience, was manoeuvring to attain membership of one of the most powerful groups in a once more powerful Germany; all this via a senior position in the SS and a marriage of convenience to the Reichswehr. Rahn left it at that. He told Himmler that he would make no further comments nor speak more of the opinions of his Swiss friends, who were all members of the Swiss higher army corps and who played an important role in Swiss society. Each, also, had personally been attacked as Nazis by the Swiss press in the past. Rahn confessed that never had a report been so difficult to draw up for the Riechsführer-SS as the Riedweg matter.

After another bout of negative press in the Swiss newspapers, the head of SS Personnel, Schmidt, aware of Rahn's feelings, suggested that Riedweg should be released from the SS. Himmler wrote to Schmidt telling him in no uncertain terms that he was very upset by his suggestion, adding that good SS men came from places like Sweden and Flanders and that their countrymen naturally interpreted this as malicious, scandalous and treacherous and so what of it! He finished by emphasising that Dr. Riedweg would certainly remain in the SS.

Rahn's admonitions to Himmler had cut no ice at all. There was no going back and the gathering storm clouds offered no concealment for Rahn's growing problems. Hans-Jürgen Lange believes that Riedweg was aware of Rahn's very negative assessment of him. However, there may well have been another motive that drove Rahn to express such downright hostility to the Swiss.

In a recent book by Professor Hergemüller, *mann für mann,* (title is lower case in source) the author claims that Riedweg was also homosexual, similarly moving in the same circles as Rahn around Alfred Schmid. Lange believes that in this tightly enclosed environment, jealousies, wrangles and power and influence mixing powerfully below the surface were the order of the day. Moreover, Riedweg knew the right people, consequently having more leverage among higher circles than Rahn. The affair with Riedweg coincided with Rahn's star falling rapidly among Himmler's personal staff and these events taken in the round demonstrate a certain degree of inevitability with regard to Rahn's pathway that had little or no weaponry to fend off a one-way, ignominious ending just months later.

Riedweg became head of Germanic Volunteer Recruiting, a division of the Berlin Main SS-Office. He was also the inspirational figure behind the SS-Leitheft, often called the "SS-leadership magazine." It followed that Riedweg also became a combattant in the 'Germanischen Freiwillige' (Germanic Volunteers) in the Waffen-SS. He rose to the rank of SS-Obersturmbannführer and was awarded the Iron Cross. He was clearly a man who had the right stuff for Nazi business. In hindsight it is obvious that Rahn never had any real chance of swaying top level opinion about the appropriateness of the Swiss physician to undertake important work for the SS.

Meanwhile Rahn attempted to address the other issues for which Ullman had been pressing him for details. He told the SS-Obersturmbannführer that his health was vastly improved; he was working between eight to ten hours a day without getting too tired, devoting the mornings to writing and research and the evenings to his correspondence. He had allowed some letters to accumulate since his Dachau days. He lamented the poor sales of *Luzifers Hofgesind,* which most recently had trickled almost to a stop. His publisher, Schwarzhaepter Verlag, Leipzig, had told him that a new edition was simply not cost effective and therefore absolutely out of the question. Total sales over the past thirteen months were way below the two thousand copies that had been issued, a figure which included one hundred given to the author as free copies, a large number circulated to newspapers, magazines and radio, and a hefty batch gifted to Himmler. Rahn, incredulous, complained that his income was just 0.52 Reichsmark per copy, noting bitterly that sales of his first book *Kreuzzug gegen den Gral* had been much better.

Rahn also confirmed to Ullman that his ancestral line was almost complete.

At this time Rahn also enquired about an offer Ullman had previously made to him about a present to mark his thirty fourth birthday: a book of Rahn's choice inscribed with dedications from all his SS comrades. He would like, he said, the volume of the works of German lyric poet Friedrich Höderlin (1770-1843). He also wanted to take up an offer made by SS-Gruppenführer Wolff to cover his travel and clothing costs incurred during his convalescence trip. The sum amounted to RM-340 and he would advise later on the costs to be reimbursed for storage of his books, pictures and radio. He wanted his belongings delivered by the 1st of June to a quiet cottage in upper Muggenbrunn near Todtnau where the air was conducive to healing but where expenses could be kept to a minimum. He asked Ullman to leave it to Wolff to decide an appropriate sum for delivery but it would be no more than RM-50. In any case, he needed the cash as soon as possible.

In June Rahn wrote Himmler to update the Reichsführer SS on the status of his literary projects. In addition to the writing and "scientific" research for the sequel to *Luzifers Hofgesind,* whose working title translates in English as *The Will of Prometheus*: *a trip to hell and further beyond,* he was hard at work on a novel, *Sebastian.*

Rahn had high hopes for this latter work, which was substantially complete. He boasted to Himmler that it would be a work of art, his strongest and finest to date artistically, and one in which he would piece together the quintessence of his findings and their applications to present day life. Experts had reassured Rahn that this would be the case.

Then came the catch. Rahn explained that this work required more concentration than previous projects. This factor, combined with the high amount of work that remained to bring the novel to the printing presses, encouraged Rahn to seek the permission of Himmler to allow him to carry out these tasks in the peace of the Black Forest (Muggenbrunn). This period of creative retreat, Rahn suggested, would also provide an opportunity to heal the bronchial problems that continued to aggravate him (recall that this was very soon after Rahn had told Ullman how well he was feeling). Rahn added, somewhat lamely, that under these conditions he might also fulfil all of his neglected administrative duties. Wolff added a hand written note in the margin: "*yes*."

In this letter Rahn also tries to play a clever hand in emphasising the magnitude of his two thousand page opus, asking Himmler just how long one must write to arrive at such a magnificent number. If Rahn expected Himmler to go easy on him and give him all the time in the world in which to produce a work of high literary esteem he was sadly mistaken. In fact, Rahn's ploy created the opposite effect, encouraging Himmler to press for an early completion, thereby compounding Rahn's difficulties and escalating his overwhelming feelings of pressure and stress.

It was not long before Raymond had bedded in as a houseguest in the Muggenbrunn retreat and Rahn asked Brandt in Himmler's office to inform Himmler of it. His pal would stay until the end of August. Rahn recommended that Perrier be allowed to take a tour around Berlin and also to pay a visit to the “Leibstandarte Adolf Hitler” or to the SS-Totenkopfverbände Brandeburg. Raymond should also have the honour, Rahn suggested, of visiting Dachau (where he already counted friends among Rahn's former camp comrades) and observing the archaeological work carried out by the Schutzstaffel. These arrangements, Rahn suggested, would make Raymond very happy while at the same time, as a Swiss representative and nephew of the Genevan Chancellor, would make him an even bigger supporter of Hitler's Germany than he was already. Raymond sent the Reichsführer SS his respectful salutations. Evidently, Himmler approved Perrier's visit because in August Raymond wrote to him to convey his gratitude for his hospitality and trust.

And then Rahn did the oddest thing. He fell in love with a woman. Or did he? Writing to Himmler, Rahn exclaims: "Reichsführer! I found a female companion for life. I am glad to point out that even in my role as a member of the SS I can be proud of my choice. May I ask SS-Gruppenführer Wolff to give my bride and me some idea of the necessary formalities?"[2]

Otto's intended bride was a Swiss, Asta Baeschlin, née Holtz, aged twenty seven at the time she met Rahn. From a good family, Asta was married to a Swiss and the couple had a four-year old, blond haired son. Her divorce, brought about Rahn said by actions on the husband's side, was imminent. Rahn was aware that he could not announce their engagement until the divorce formalities were completed but they planned to wed by Christmas. Himmler was exceptionally pleased about this new development, writing privately to Rahn to express his happiness and to give his permission. He encouraged Rahn to go for an early date, giving an assurance that no obstacles would be allowed to hamper the formalities. This heaped further pressure on Rahn who had badly miscalculated if he thought that a radical announcement of this nature would get Himmler off his back. In 1994 Asta Baeschlin recounted the circumstances to Hans Jürgen-Lange:[3]

"I was never engaged to Rahn, he just wanted everybody to believe that; how I found out later. During my divorce in 1938 my son and I, together with a female servant, stayed during the summer in the Black Forest. By accident I met Rahn in a corner shop in the village. He told me about his books, and since I was quite interested in this matter he came to visit me a few times to tell me about this research. Not once did he touch me or attempt any overtures. On the contrary, he very much kept his distance, which suited me fine. Once he asked me if I intended to stay in Germany and if I would like to work on his research as well. I told him no, clearly. Rahn never once proposed to me. It seemed to me that he would have liked a fictitious marriage, since he was not at all interested in me as a woman. In my opinion his true interest was with men. My suspicion grew when his friend Raymond Perrier came to visit him for some time. Rahn introduced me briefly to Perrier and after that I saw neither of them any more until Perrier left. I happened to be in the village and witnessed the pair saying farewell. Rahn cried his eyes out and apologised to me later for that. I regarded this scene as additional proof of my assumption. Later I understood that

---

[2] Lange
[3] ibid

Rahn must have told his boss H.H. also of an engagement. An unpleasant thing to say; I assume he did it to camouflage his real tendency. I left at the end of August for Switzerland and sent Rahn a note that I wanted no further contact with him."

These comments are contrary to what Rahn told SS-Oberführer von Alvensleben in December 1938. Rahn regretted that a "flash" marriage to Asta (to meet Himmler's pre-Christmas deadline) was not possible due to pressures of work and his bride's residence in Switzerland where she was constrained by her job in a Zurich bookshop (Rahn and she had not met since September). Rahn also blamed Asta's parents for favouring a "rich lord" over him. As usual money came into the explanation. Asta had, Rahn said, agreed to support him and would come to Muggenbrunn at Christmas to talk things over. In the meantime, he proposed staying put in Muggenbrunn to concentrate on his new book, except to make a trip to Munich to see Professor Wüst and SS-Brigadeführer Johst, a meeting ordered by Himmler and overdue since the summer. Rahn's workload also included writing a contribution to Alfred Rosenberg's *Handbook about the Question of Rome*.

Wüst is a reference to Walther Wüst, former Dean of the University of Munich, who joined the Ahnenerbe in 1937 as curator-trustee, replacing Hermann Wirth as its intellectual leader. In this capacity Wüst worked to limit the influence of those he deemed "scholarly upstarts," which included excising communication links with the RuSHA office of Karl Maria Weisthor. Wüst's influential interventions in this latter regard may shed further light on the background circumstances under which Weisthor was relieved from his duties in 1939. In 1937 Gabriele's mother had moved on from Himmler's employ and was working for Wüst. Bearing in mind her daughter's increasingly rough time with her alcoholic "dad," Frau Dechend would have had ample grounds to side with Wüst in his efforts to sideline Weisthor. Equally, considering that Rahn was evidently in contact with Wüst and taking account of his longstanding friendship with Gabriele he, too, may have felt justified in adding his arm to the pincer movement to put the elderly and unstable Weisthor out to pasture.

The SS-Brigadeführer is writer Johannes Johst, a leading official and representative of loyal German literature during the time of the Reich. Until 1945 Johst was president of the Reich Chamber of Literature and of the German Academy of Poetry. It is not surprising that Rahn, a favourite of Himmler and a highly esteemed academic, mediaevalist and author who joined the German Writers Association in 1933, should have had high level relations with Johst.

Although it cannot be proven, it is quite likely there is a bit of truth in both Baeschlin's and Rahn's accounts of the "wedding" story, but probably more so on Asta's part. Baeschlin emphasised to Lange that she did not ever think of a relationship with Rahn: "For one, because I knew about his preferences—or at least assumed it—and on the other hand because my ex-husband, whom I had to leave because of debts, would have taken my son away from me if I had married an SS-member. How would Rahn have been able to feed a family? He lived even in Muggenbrunn very modestly. My parents were quite wealthy; maybe he thought I could finance all our needs. But this idea of a marriage was anyway very unreal."[4] Nevertheless, it can be imagined that there was disagreement at the last minute. The resulting trouble for Rahn can easily be pictured.

On 1st July 1938 the post-Romantic composer and conductor Hans Pfitzner wrote a short message to Otto Rahn, thanking him for "the sign of life" he had waited for so long (what this referred to is not explained). Gabriele Winckler remembers that Rahn mentioned his and Pfitzner's joint plans, which concerned the creation of an opera on the Cathars. She also remembers that Rahn was quite upset about the fact that Pfitzner was not invited to the official opening of the "Haus der deutschen Kunst" (House of German Art) in Munich. After Rahn intervened, the composer was mistakenly invited as "Rudolf" Pfitzner and, annoyed over this latest slight, Pfitzner decided not to go.

Hans Pfitzner

In the sixties eighty-year old Wilma Stoll, Pfitzner's wife's sister, told anthroposophist Karl Rittersbacher by telephone that: "Pfitzner liked Otto Rahn very much, he thought he was a pleasant young man but very self-opinionated. Rahn was a member of the guards in Dachau and told Pfitzner a good deal about it. Rahn was quite upset about what he had seen there. Hitler did not think much of Rahn for some time. Rahn intended to report better things about Pfitzner to Hitler and sent the Führer a book and wrote

[4] ibid

him a letter. Stoll then wrote to Rahn saying he should not tell Pfitzner too much. Rahn was once addressed by a Jesuit concerning *Kreuzzug gegen den Gral*. He also received threatening letters. Publications against the Society of Jesus and the Catholic Church like the 'Hoensbroech' one[5] would not stir up too much trouble but Rahn brought documents that would be unpleasant..."

This account is fascinating because it reveals for the first time that Hitler was personally aware of Rahn, and in this particular matter his interest would have been provoked by the composer's known opposition to the Nazi regime. Yet again Rahn was keeping dangerous company, bandying papers around that were of a sensitive or unpleasant nature. These matters were clearly being observed.

Some researchers have claimed in the past that Hitler and Rahn often had closed door meetings when the pair discussed the philologist's findings in his quest to find ancient and fabulous artefacts. It has also been suggested that Hitler personally made the Iceland travels the top priority in Ahnenerbe business. (After Rommel's assassination attempt against Hitler, Reinhard Heydrich assumed a far greater influence in top Nazi circles. Interestingly, it is known that Heydrich also placed great store in the Iceland-Hyperborean expeditions and supplied transportation and men for Rahn's travels.)

Nevertheless, Rahn and his Grailhunter talents were insufficient to insulate him against Hitler's swings of mood and something evidently happened to upset the Führer. But Wilma Stoll's account indicates that Rahn was only in Hitler's bad books for a period of time. Evidently, despite his occasional falls from grace Otto Rahn was a very important figure to the Nazis; far too important to have him suffer an early and untimely death?

We are also left wondering about the nature and identity of the documents that threatened the Jesuits. Rahn was scathing about the Jesuits because the Society and he differred so emphatically on scholarly opinion. He is on record as saying that in the Middle-Ages the Jesuits would have burned him. Did Rahn fear for his physical safety at the hands of Jesuit extremists? It is posible that in the course of his work for Himmler Rahn might have been associated with or even been instrumental in drawing up documents inimical to the Catholic Church. We know that Himmler and his confederates were not shy about about moving against the higher reaches of the Church when expediency

---

[5] possibly a reference to ex-Jesuit, Count Paul Von Hoensbroech, author of anti-Jesuit work *Fourteen Years a Jesuit*; London & New York: Cassel & Co. Ltd., 1911

demanded it.

On 11th September 1938 Rahn was awarded his final promotion, rising to the rank of SS-Obersturmführer. Within eight months the authorities would be reporting his death.

After Otto Rahn left Muggenbrunn, Afolf Frisé moved into the small house. In 1939 Frisé and Paul Ladame bumped into each other but according to Ladame, when interviewed by Hans-Jürgen Lange, they merely exchanged pleasantries and learned little about their old pal Rahn. Ladame said that Rahn had spent a few weeks at the house but insisted that he had had no concrete news about Rahn's movements or circumstances. They had last seen each other at the beginning of December 1936, more than two years before.

Ladame's account does not ring true. In the years following Rahn's death Ladame made a number of unsubstantiated comments, including the claim we examined earlier that Rahn participated in the murder of Röhm at Munich-Stadelheim. Ladame also said that Wulf Sorensen copied important documents. Again, Ladame offered no proof to back this up but we should recall Frau Winckler's description of Sorensen as a cowardly and duplicitous character and her belief that it was he who denounced Rahn.

In a face-to-face chat with Lange in 1994 Adolf Frisé said that everything he knew about Otto Rahn had been published in his book *Der Beginn der Vergangenheit* (*The Beginning of the Past*). In his photograph album there was a page with five or six photos said to be of Rahn taken in August 1938. In the photos both the interior and exterior of the Muggenbrunn house can be seen. Two of them show the balcony and in one of them Rahn can be seen with a younger man identified as Raymond Perrier. The second photograph is taken from a greater distance and shows again two men but the second figure is scratched out. One wonders who this other person might have been and why someone felt it necessary to delete their features.

In his book Adolf Frisé describes how Rahn confided in a Muggenbrunn shoemaker, Stubanus. Stubanus had described how Rahn had been in Muggenbrunn throughout July and August 1938, reading and writing extensively. Rahn returned in January 1939, staying until February and telling Stubanus that he could bring himself neither to read nor write. He could not say where he had been but he had seen things with which he could not come to terms. He said he had to see the boss, the boss did not know about it (whatever "it" was). He waited for the message that he could come (presumably for permission to visit Himmler).

Lange has confirmed that in 1938 a civil action was brought against Rahn. Based on his past record it is probable that Rahn's homosexuality would have been at the bottom of the affair and, possibly, it was connected with the time in the recent past when Rahn had become involved with a commander of the airforce.

As a likely consequence of these intemperate actions, on 1st October 1938 Rahn was called up for an SS autumn reserve duty training exercise by which his superiors hoped that Rahn would toughen up his image. A letter to the head of the concentration camps, Eicke, confirms that Rahn was serving in the camp of Buchenwald on 9th November, the day of the Reichskristallnacht. Prior to this time there were 2,912 inmates in Buchenwald. The arrests of 9th November throughout Germany increased this number sevenfold to 20,122. By all accounts, Rahn's initial experiences in Dachau had not had too much of an impact on his mental and emotional states of mind but it can be surmised that what he later experienced in Buchenwald inflated his growing personal difficulties dramatically.

In early December 1938, Ullman wrote to Eicke asking the SS-Gruppenführer to organise leave for Rahn so that he might work undisturbed on a new edition of *Luzifers Hofgesind.*

Ten weeks later Rahn despatched a report to Himmler about the cloister of Saint Odilien, a location that has long been favoured as a hiding place for Grail artefacts. This piece of work was in all likelihood the last research undertaking that Otto Rahn carried out for Himmler.

Trevor Ravenscroft has bequeathed a detailed account of the seventh century person of Saint Odilien and her family's key role in the subsequent establishment of dynastic Grail guardians in Europe.[6] Ravenscroft believed Walter Johannes Stein's theory that the Grail was hidden in the cloister. Evidently, there were those in the Nazi hierarchy who similarly leaned to that opinion.

Odille was the daughter of Eticho who inherited the dukedom of Alsace in A.D. 666. The girl was born blind and Eticho decided to murder her when he heard rumours in court that he was responsible for her infirmity. The mother gathered up the girl and fled to Regensberg where Erhard, the city's bishop, baptised the child whose sight was promptly restored. The bishop named her Odille, after *ool die*, sun of God, believing that the miracle was analogous with Christ's healing of the man born blind. Odille returned to her father's court where all went well for a while but in the best tradition of dark and dirty medieval tales her father erupted in anger when she refused to go along with an

---

[6] *The Cup of Destiny*. Maine: Samuel Weiser, Inc., 1982

arranged marriage. Odille went into hiding to the hermitage where Treverizent, Eschenbach's Grail hermit, later instructed Parzifal after his first unsuccessful sojourn into the Grail castle. Father and daughter were eventually reconciled.

Odille went on to found Christian cloisters in the Hochberg and in the nearby valley at Niedermunster. She meditated in the mountains and was entranced by visions inspired by the revelation of Saint John. Pilgrims flocked to the centres from all over Europe to be taught of the mysteries of the Grail and to undertake initiation in a new form of Christianity.

Chroniclers have placed great store on the bloodline of Eticho. Dionysos Albrecht wrote: "Just as Jacob's seed, according to the stars in their ordering, spread to all points of the compass, so also did the race of Odilla."

Eschenbach discovered the truth of the Grail race, stating: "...and in Anschau (Kyot) found the tale. There he read the true story of Mazadan (Eticho) and the exact record of all his family was written there..." Anschau was the term used by Eschenbach for a non-physical spiritual realm, which can only be accessed via higher states of (Grail) consciousness. This journey is achievable only by an initiate who has gained the requisite faculties (the *dietrich*) and, according to Eschenbach's stipulation in *Parzifal*, has learned "his ABCs without the art of black magic." The Odille Grail bloodline subsequently melded with nearly all the main dynasties of Europe, which henceforth believed they were the keepers and guardians of the Grail mysteries.

At the same time as Rahn submitted his Saint Odilien report, Himmler's diary records the receipt from Rahn of a copy of "Gral," copied also to Standartenführer Dr. Caesar, Head of SS Training Department. The entry contains no further information that might indicate the mysterious nature of this "Gral."

On the same date as Himmler's Gral note, 28th February, Rahn sent a handwritten note to SS-Gruppenführer Wolff saying: "Gruppenführer! Unfortunately I have to ask you to ask the Reichsführer SS for my immediate dismissal from the Schutzstaffel. The reasons for that are so deep and serious that I can explain them only orally. For that purpose I will come to Berlin in the next days and report to you. Heil Hitler, Otto Rahn."

Frau Winckler remarked during our discussion that she believed there is a link between Rahn's sudden resignation request and his announcement that Asta Baeschlin and he had become engaged. But even if this were true one struggles to see why it should have required

Rahn's immediate resignation from the SS.

Himmler scrawled a handwritten "*yes*" on the letter and made his signature.

On the 17th March Rahn was dismissed from the SS, retrospective from 22nd February and with immediate effect.

Chapter ELEVEN

Endura

A few days later Rahn visited Kurt Eggers' apartment in Dortmund in a state of extreme nervousness. Rahn's former liaison in Schwarzhaupter Publishing, Albert von Haller, told Hans-Jürgen Lange that he had never heard or realised anything about Rahn's homosexuality and therefore was surprised to hear about it during his last meeting with Rahn, which he believed took place in March 1939. This meeting was in Dortmund at the apartment of author SS-Sturmführer Kurt Eggers. (Von Haller was also the editor of Egger's book *The Birth of the Century* from which, Rahn records in *Luzifers Hofgesind*, Eggers recited extracts to him.)

Von Haller added that he did not have any written documents and so he could be mistaken with the dates but not with the facts. After a quarrel with Rahn in Berlin over publishing advances in the winter of 1937-38 von Haller did not expect to have any more contact with him since, in addition, he had switched publishers and was no longer Rahn's. Unexpectedly, Rahn turned up at Eggers' flat in a state of complete confusion. He said he would be fleeing towards suicide. The SS had asked him to choose an enforced death in a KZ or a "decent" self-directed death. It was a frightening, shocking scene.

In 1998 von Haller put further flesh on his earlier comments to Lange. He had been at Eggers' flat when Rahn arrived. Rahn was as thin as a rake and in a terrified condition, nervous to the point of complete breakdown. Rahn said: "I am pursued by the SS. I am accused of homosexuality." He pronounced that statement quite freely. "I have been given the choice: either I enter a KZ or I choose suicide in the mountains. No other choice is possible. I am at the end."

Von Haller took Eggers to one side and asked if one could just stand by and do nothing. He told Eggers that he had a passport with a departure-visa to France in his bag. How would it be if he gave the passport to Rahn, von Haller put it to Eggers? Why might von Haller have believed that the passport, presumably bearing his own details and photograph, would have passed muster in Otto Rahn's hands with police or immigration officials? Von Haller's remarks on this point lack credibility. In any case, von Haller told Lange, Eggers then turned on him, saying he was crazy. Understand, Eggers said, that the SS leaves a man no more than five minutes out of their sight. They are already standing outside of my home and are aware of something almost before it happens. If you do that then you are of no use to Rahn at all and you, too, will land yourself in the KZ. Our line is clear: Rahn has simply gone away. Eggers phoned for a taxi for Rahn who soon set off wanting, he said, to catch a train to Munich.

After Rahn's departure Eggers told von Haller that an arrested man (no name given) had admitted to having had sexual intercourse with Otto Rahn while he was in Hamburg doing labour service. Von Haller's view was that the whole thing had been blown up out of all proportion to the extent that it was evident it was not just Rahn's reputation at stake but something deeper and more sinister. The prize, von Haller suggests, was the highest positions of power among the Reichleitern, the in-crowd around Hitler. Bormann was ahead on points at this time and in the game of strategy being acted out he could block fellow players and increasingly isolate Hitler from other trusted sources of advice and counsel. Rahn, von Haller had been told, had gained a considerable position of trust with Himmler; he carried out for the Reichsführer SS secret and covert tasks. When the rumours about Rahn reached Bormann he was forced to act since he could not allow anything to happen behind his back. This was an opportunity to highlight a person in Himmler's trust who was homosexual and so weaken Himmler's own position with Hitler, the spirit of Röhm rearing its head afresh. In such a situation Himmler was surely prepared to sacrifice a less important person, even a man whom he held in such high esteem as Otto Rahn and who was even his own distant kin.

Looking back, Dietmar Lauermann felt sure that Rahn was no Nazi. His opinion was that Rahn was internally averse to the political system in the 1930s, even after Himmler decided to support him. Lauermann's view was that Himmler's offer of support forced Rahn into a state of inner contradiction that he simply could not resolve, a quandary which can only be truly understood by one who lived through those times.

According to Lauermann, Rahn's act in eventually quitting the SS was surprisingly brave. Of course, there was the issue of Rahn's homosexuality but, Lauermann observed, that was a red herring in that it is a way of life capable of only ever saying little because expressing such love can reflect as many colours as loving a girl or woman.

For her part, Gabriele Winckler is open-minded on the theory that Rahn quarrelled badly with Himmler after experiencing the inhuman conditions at Dachau and witnessing the cruel practices at one of the Lebensborn-Heim centres. Even if this were true it cannot be certain that such a quarrel would have necessarily invoked sufficient anger in Himmler to seal Rahn's fate. There are recorded instances of Himmler's closest officers standing up to the mighty Reichsführer SS in very dramatic circumstances without incurring drastic recriminations. In August 1943, for example, Karl Wolff had a furious row with Himmler, chasing him from behind his desk, intent on landing blows on his terrified superior.[1] Indications suggest that Wolff got away with it.

Von Haller must have stirred things up regarding Rahn's disappearance. Dr. Gerhard Klopfer, former secretary of state to Reichsleiter Bormann, soon accosted von Haller about the latter's opinions on the circumstances of Rahn's suicide. Klopfer told him that Rahn's failings were still a state secret and criticised von Haller for talking about it, telling him he was an anti-person. Prior to this their relationship had been much warmer and Klopfer had promised von Haller a copy of *Luzifers Hofgesind*. This abrupt negative reaction confirmed von Haller's suspicions that the Rahn affair was little about the writer but much about top level political intrigue. Von Haller also told Armin Mohler that Rahn was asked by his superior to commit suicide because of his homosexuality.

Rahn visited other friends while fleeing. On 8th March he was in Freiburg to meet his first publisher and friend Otto Vogelsgang in the Hotel Zahringer Hof. Paradoxically, Vogelsgang described Rahn's demeanour on that day in a letter in the sixties to Rudolf J. Mund as relaxed, positive and happy about the future. This description must be regarded as significant when making an overall assessment of Rahn's state of mind immediately prior to his reported death.

On the 12th March Rahn set off for Kufstein. During this trip Rahn visited the Lauermann family who owned a cottage in Schliersee. In 1994 Dietmar Lauermann wrote that Rahn went over to Neuhaus and Kufstein and then to Söll, most likely by the bus service that still runs between Germany and Austria. At Söll Rahn checked into a small hotel and the next day he travelled further into the mountains by bus, got off at a stop known as Der Steinerne Steg (Stony Path—reminiscent of the rock strewn trail leading from the outskirts of Montségur village to the Pog) and walked into the forest.

Neither family nor friends saw Rahn alive again. One wonders

---

[1] Jochen, von Lang. *Top Nazi SS General Karl Wolff*. New York: Enigma Books, 2005

how Lauermann came by the knowledge of the last leg of Rahn's trip unless the latter's movements were able to be identified by inspecting written records such as a hotel register and/or interviewing time-witnesses such as the bus driver, fellow passengers and/or hotel staff. Or did Rahn simply relate to Lauermann the details of his journey some time later? If that is the case then the reported circumstances of Rahn's death are obviously pure concoction.

On 17 July 1939 Rahn's father wrote to a writers' association to which Otto belonged, informing it that his son had died in a snowstorm at Ruffheim on 13th March 1939.

The *Die Welt* edition of 5th December 1979 reports that Rahn fell asleep in the snow and froze to death while climbing the Wilder Kaiser Mountain. This was in line with the SS position.

In the 25th May 1939 edition of the SS newspaper *Das Schwarzes Korps* appeared this notice: “During a blizzard in the mountains the SS-Obersturmführer Otto Rahn died tragically. We regret that, and lost with him a decent SS-member and the creator of marvellous historic and scientific works.” It was signed by the Head of Personnel, RFSS Wolff, SS-Gruppenführer. The protocol of death notices did generally begin with family but in the case of important individuals it was prestigious for the SS to acknowledge them with an "official" recognition. In the same issue of the newpaper there is a much larger death notice with Himmler's signature for another former SS soldier.

Bei einem Schneesturm in den Bergen kam im
März dieses Jahres der
SS-Obersturmführer
Otto Rahn
auf tragische Weise ums Leben.
Wir betrauern in diesem toten Kameraden einen
anständigen SS-Mann und den Schöpfer ausge-
zeichneter, geschichtlich-wissenschaftlicher Werke.
Der Chef des Pers.-Stabes RF SS
Wolff

Otto Rahn’s death notice in *Das Schwarzes Korps,* 25th May 1939

The SS regarded Otto Rahn's suicide as a declaration of faithfulness of the dead. Therefore, Rahn was immediately re-admitted into the SS and was put on the list of deceased SS leaders.

Additionally, Karl Wolff published an official obituary notice on May 18th 1939 in *Berliner Ausgabe*: "Due to a mountain snowstorm, last March, SS-Obersturmführer Otto Rahn tragically lost his life. We weep for our late comrade, an honest SS man and an excellent author of historical and scientific works."

Four years after Rahn's death, the Schwarzhaepter publisher enquired if a new edition of *Luzifers Hofgesind* could be printed. Himmler appreciated the enquiry and supported the allocation of the necessary paper. SS-Obersturmbannführer Brandt of the personnel department answered the publisher: "...find attached a copy of the proof-read material. There are some further corrections to be done. Please consider those before printing. Although there are quite some repetitions within the text, I fear that further changes would be rather difficult and endanger the original substance of the work." There are no indications as to the nature of the "further corrections" Himmler evidently wished to be made prior to the publishing of a new edition, or why he thought they were necessary.

The most powerful case for the March 1939 suicide account was made by Peter Maier in a written statement to Hans-Jürgen Lange in 1994. Maier was one of two children living at Rechenauer Hof, an outlying farmstead near Söll, in March 1939. The nearest neighbouring farm was half an hour away. In the chronicles of the gendarmerie post at Söll, Tyrol, an account of the find was recorded on 11th May 1939. The following day the body was identified as Otto Rahn from Berlin, missing since mid-March 1939, by Gustr. Lentsch. By what means did Lentsch identify the body? Did he know Rahn by sight? If so, how? Was Rahn carrying identity papers? Did someone in the vicinity happen to be carrying a handy photograph of Rahn? Were there others in the area at that precise time who could identify Rahn and who volunteered themselves to Lentsch for that purpose? The proximity of any such persons would have mocked coincidence, suggesting conspiracy and complicity.

The body was brought to Worgl Söll and buried there. The children of Josef Maier, a farmer of Eiberg, had found a body already badly decomposed.

Peter Maier told Lange that in mid-March 1939 his elder brother and he saw Rahn in the late afternoon; the snow was about one metre deep. The man was about thirty metres from the farmhouse. He stopped and checked his golden wristwatch. The two children were playing and the stranger spoke with them for a short time. Then he turned and went towards the valley down the winter path to the brook where the boys usually took the cows for drinking water. The children did not attach any further significance to this encounter but when it got dark they asked what had happened to the stranger who had walked further into the forest. The people there looked about but could not find him.

Lange regards this as "interesting" because the Maier family should have been able to see Rahn's tracks in the snow.

Of course, it is interesting. The fact that Rahn's body was nowhere to be seen just hours after he passed by the farm and walked deeper into the forest is a very significant vote in favour of acknowledging that something very odd was going on with regard to the reported manner and timing of Otto Rahn's death.

It is evident that at the time Rahn passed by the Maier's farm the weather was inclement, characterised by heavy snow and icy conditions. One wonders, therefore, why Paul Ladame later remarked that at that time of the year and at that altitude it would take up to two weeks for a person to die from the cold. Just what was it that Ladame, disinformation lecturer, was not saying by making these plainly incorrect remarks?

It was not until spring, two months or more after the thaw, that the boys found "Rahn's" body. It was 11th May. He was under a tree covered by a coat. The boys recognised him because of the coat. It was the man who had approached their house weeks earlier. He was wearing the same gold wristwatch. The Maier family concluded that Rahn must have backtracked to Kitzgraben brook, the small stream running by the farm, and had walked upstream to hide his tracks.

But how did the family know for certain that Rahn had walked in the stream? After all, a stream with running water usually cannot bear lasting witness to a person's footsteps.

Peter Maier told Lange that the deceased had lain down under a fir tree and ingested the partial contents of two phials of sleeping tablets. The two phials of tablets were found next to the corpse: one empty, the other still half full. Maier's opinion was that the deceased had not died from a drug overdose but had simply frozen in the snow. On what basis could Maier have made this conjecture? As a young boy he would have had no way of discerning if a deceased person had downed a handful of pills or had perished by freezing unless he had been told the precise cause of death; in which case Maier would not have had to venture an opinion but would have been in possession of the facts. Maier's opinion was proferred sixty years after the fact and little credence can be attached to it.

The address of the Rechau farm is Söll/Stockach, Eiberg no. 15. Nobody has lived there for ages. A similar statement concerning suicide with sleeping pills was made by Otto Rahn's mother to Karl Rittersbacher in the sixties.

Even after many decades Peter Maier was able to pinpoint the exact location of the suicide spot when he returned to the location in the autumn of 1995. The place is almost visible from the farm on the steep hill of the Kitzgraben brook. Behind the farm is a small memorial to the plague in 1630. In that year almost one third of Tyroleans died of the disease. Affixed to the farmhouse is a memorial plaque: "Plague grave of Rechau 1636." In the death register of the church of Söll it says in Latin: "The farmer Johann Zintinger buried next to his house his children who died of the pestilence on the 5th, 19th, 20th and 21st October. He and his cousin Anna Zintinger laid down in the grave which they had themselves excavated and died on the 22nd of October."

Along one of the mountaineering paths there is a signpost to the bus stop "Steinerne Steg" to Söll from where Rahn had travelled. According to Lange's researches there is a death certificate in the Söll registry, county Kufstein. It records the death of Otto Rahn, religious, resident of Berlin, who was found dead on the 11th May 1939, in the evening at Söll, Stockach no. 15. The deceased was born on 18th February 1904 in Michelstadt. Day and hour of death are not known, assumed to have been on the night of the 13th and 14th March 1939. The deceased was not married.

The details were registered from an oral statement of the gendarmerie post of Söll after submission of passport. The death certificate is dated 3rd June 1939, registrar Johann Ortner. Rahn had been reported as passing from this world almost to the day of the anniversary of the fall of Montségur.

In my considered view Maier's account does not offer the cast iron certainties that mainstream historians cherish. In this view I am not a lone sceptic and there are at least a dozen different accounts of the circumstances of Rahn's death. In the next chapter we will place these accounts in the beam of our caver's lamp and see what we might discern in the shadows.

Chapter TWELVE

Trompe l'Oeil

In the previous chapter we reviewed the commonly accepted account of Rahn's last days and the discovery of his body by the children of farmer Josef Maier. If only life were that clear and simple. Despite the firm convictions of writers such as Hans-Jürgen Lange, I remain totally unconvinced of the truth of those accounts. There are just far too many conflicting points between fact and opinion.

Compare the official account, for example, with the fruits of Christian Bernadac's findings. Bernadac found that no notice of death had been received by the town council of Michelstadt, Rahn's place of birth. The normal procedure was to send a notice within thirty days and this rule was strictly applied even for soldiers dying in combat. Rahn's father was a civil servant and would have known this rule.

Moreover, there is nothing on record concerning Rahn's inheritance, which would have included royalties from his books.

Bernadac and a fellow-researcher also went to Kufstein, the nearest town to the Wilder Kaiser. The mayor of the time remembered nothing of the discovery of the body and there is nothing in the town's archives concerning the event. They were unable to find any records in any of the relevant towns concerning the death, recovery of the body or of the inquest.

Bernadac compares Rahn's obituary to those of eleven other SS officers who died around the same period. In every other case the notice was signed by their family but in Rahn's case it is written and signed by Karl Wolff. In none of the other eleven examples is the press notice included in the officer's SS file but it is included in Rahn's.

In eight of the other cases the items included are the legal proceedings, inquest details and so on, but they are not found on Rahn's file.

And why was the letter from Rahn's father in the SS file? The letter ends "Heil Hitler," which was usually only used by Party members (Karl Rahn Sr. was not a Party supporter). The press obituary is dated two months (to the day) after Rahn's dismissal from the SS and sixty-six days after his death.

Let us also look at the additional comments Bernadac made for an eight-part television series *Le Passe-Montagne* in 1975. Bernadac believes that certificates attesting to the details of Rahn's death in 1939 are "bidon," phony. He says that he unearthed correspondence in the U.S. between Rahn and Himmler (but did not produce it for public examination). As evidence for Rahn's phony personality he says that half the cave drawings that Rahn reproduced in his books had been made up and drawn by Rahn himself.

Let us also compare various other accounts of Rahn's demise. Saint-Loup found information in Rosenberg's records after the war stating that Rahn killed himself with a dose of cyanide for politico-mystical reasons on top of Mount Kufstein in 1939. This was in line with other rumours that Rahn had committed suicide by swallowing a cyanide capsule while on the mountain.

Gerard de Séde wrote in *The Treasure of the Cathari* 1966 that Rahn was arrested and imprisoned in solitary confinement at Dachau and that he was beheaded in 1945 just before the compound was liberated by American forces.

An Austrian author named Kadmon relates that while walking towards the Totenkirchl, a promontory of the Wilderkaiser where, traditionally, war victims had come to commit suicide, he met an old man who told him that in 1939, while out climbing, he had come across Rahn's search party. The old man pointed to a small hill surrounded by saplings and told Kadmon that it was the place where the searchers had found the young man's body. There were no markings, nothing to indicate the scene. The man said that the group had searched for several days before finding in the falling snow a body. The back of the head and the shoulders were buried in the snow. He said there was something "sacred, the saintliness of a hermit, of a sage. The face displayed a great gentleness and softness; there was no sign of agony."[1]

If this account can be believed then it blows out of the water the claims made by the Maier brothers that the pair simply came across the body two months after they had seen Rahn walking past their farmhouse. In the old man's story he is clearly describing the activities of an organised search party, which had searched doggedly and determinedly for Rahn's body for many days before making their find. The Maiers never said that they had been part of or had observed an adult search group going about its business when they came upon the body. Moreover, if the old man's account is true then on what basis of intelligence or information was the party searching in that particular

---

[1] *Auf den Spuren von Otto Rahn*, in *Aorta 7*, c/o Petak, Postfach 778, A-1011, Vienna, 1991

area?

Otto Rahn's friend, Otto Vogelsang, described Rahn during their last meeting, days before the latter's disappearance, as relaxed and positive about his future. Vogelsgang believed Rahn to be buried at Mainz, giving the date of death as 10th May 1939 and interment on 20th May.

Heinz Pehmoller made several trips to the Pyrenees after the war to search for Rahn, a man with whom he had not really got on as a friend but who was prepared to give some credence to a French youth group's belief that Otto Rahn had survived an enforced suicide.

Gabriele Winckler told me in 1999 that she did not believe in the legend that Rahn lived on but in the same interview she threw considerable doubt on the certainty of that opinion: "*I still remember Pehmoller telling me that this group didn't believe that Rahn was dead. They were sure that he was still alive, that there was an old man living on the peak of that mountain (Montségur) who could be Rahn. I said to Pehmoller that they should take me with them one day. I could have asked the old man who was supposed to be Rahn some questions, which only he could have answered. Then we would have known if it was him or not.*"

Italian members of the Polaires were recalled visiting Lordat as late as 1960 and an anonomous informant with initials H.D. told Bernadac that Otto Rahn had returned there several times after the war.

Antonin Gadal believed that Rahn died in a motor vehicle accident in Iran in 1959.[2]

The *Die Welt* article of 13th May 1979 mentions that Rahn was said to have drunk a bottle of rum and expired in the mountain snows. Peter Maier's account makes no mention of the presence of an alcohol bottle on or near the body. The author of this article also throws further doubt on the official account when he says: "*writer Otto Rahn, born in 1904 in Michelstadt in Odenwald…died in mysterious circumstances in March 1939 in a snowstorm in the Kaiser-Wilden, supposedly suicide...the death of Otto Rahn is to this day unexplained.*"

Isabelle Sandy said that the last words Rahn spoke to her were: "I cannot leave the German earth. It is pasted to my steps…the true home of a person is basically mankind, but first after that comes Geography." The logical interpretation of this comment is that, by his own words, Rahn could not bear to leave this life prematurely and therefore had no intention of cutting it short by his own hand.

In October 1943 an intriguing letter was written to Brandt by

---

[2] cited Bernadac, p195

ministerial director for propaganda, Neumann. The letter confirms that paper, a very scarce and costly commodity during the war, had been made available for a print run of 10,000 copies of *Luzifers Hofgesind* to meet Himmler's request. The letter goes on to say: "*Otto Rahn tries to give in the form of a travel diary a description of those locations (in Europe) where rebels were chased by the Church, tortured and killed. Unfortunately, the author made a mistake and was searched because of paragraph 175, and killed in the mountains shortly before the beginning of the war.*"

I am indebted to Marcus Williamson for identifying the background to "Paragraph 175." Paragraph 175, also known as Section 175, was a provision of the German Criminal Code until 1994. It made homosexual acts between males a crime, committing thousands to concentration camps irrespective of guilt or innocence. The Nazis widened the law in 1935 and vastly increased prosecutions under the provision. Minister Neumann is telling Brandt, if he did not already know it, that Rahn had been found wanting under the provision. Critically, Neumann goes on to say that Rahn had been "killed in the mountains," not "died in the mountains," providing the definite impression that a third party had been at work in the affair. That is very different from saying that Rahn had killed himself and had been asked to make the ultimate sacrifice. Neumann could not have made it clearer that he was speaking about officially sanctioned murder.

Brandt replied to Neumann in early November. He mentioned that the Reichsführer SS was aware of the tragic (should that have read "homicidal?") circumstances of Rahn's death and that no more could have been done compared to Rahn's ultimate sacrifice in atonement for his mistakes in the SS. Brandt makes no mention of Neuman's seemingly unequivocal statement that Rahn had been "killed" in the mountains. Brandt went on to suggest to Neumann that they could have a chat at some time about the circumstances surrounding Rahn's death (as, obviously, all was not what it seemed and Neumann was breaking a silence he probably had no right to infringe). He also suggested that perhaps the Minister might see to it that people did not talk of Rahn's failures. In December the Schwarzhaupt publishing house was bombed and caught fire. Consequently the June 1944 print run was reduced to 5,000 copies.

On 23rd February 1944 someone repaid an outstanding loan made from Himmler's "black fund" to Otto Rahn in the sum of DM 5,471, about $6,000 in today's money. Who would think this necessary five years after Rahn's death?

In September 1949 Albert Rausch wrote to friend Werner Bock in Argentina. Hans-Jürgen Lange explains that Rausch is evidently writing indirectly about Rahn, saying that Rausch did not speak plainly because of the cover up over the scandal that had led to Rahn's suicide more than nine years earlier. However, Lange states that despite this indirect approach it is clear that Rausch is unambiguously referring to Otto Rahn in the letter because of his mention of an informant close to Himmler and of a person referred to as dying of the white starvation (Cathar Endura) in the high mountain region. In his letter to Bock Rausch reveals that he was always kept very well informed from a source within the inner circle around the "bloody Heinrich" because, he tells Bock: "One is only betrayed by one's own." Rausch writes this sentence in French: "*on n'est trahi que par les siens,*" another probable indication that he is referring to Otto Rahn, seeing that the latter made his name through his Grail explorations in France and was fluent both in French and in the Occitan tongue.

Rausch then makes mention of the "brilliant internal Secret Service" (the equivalent to MI5), implying that he received his secret intelligence on matters around Himmler directly from within the internal security services. He adds that he even knows a case that "nobody would believe." One of the "*siens*" (that is one of the betrayers close to Himmler) has helped fifteen younger Jews to flee before he, himself, departed full of shock and horror, dying in the mountains like a hunted down animal with the "white starvation."

The clear implication in Rausch's letter is that the person around Himmler who was working for German intelligence forces opposed to the Reichsführer and the person who helped the Jews escape is one and the same—Otto Rahn. One is steered towards this inevitable conclusion because of Rausch's description of the ceremonial manner of the person's death in the mountains.

This also adds weight to the opinion that there was a covert operational link between Canaris, head of the Abwehr and Rahn. When we review later in this chapter the strange case of the Rudolf Rahn-Otto Rahn interpolation we will see that Rahn was given a cover name and rank in Himmler's circle: *Oberst (Colonel) Wonnegut (retired).* Without knowing the content of Rausch's letter to Werner Bock one might simply be puzzled as to why Rahn should have been given such an identity but now, I suggest, it becomes clearer. It is likely that Himmler assigned Rahn an intelligence role but under that operational cover high ranking figures hostile to Himmler sought to capitalise on that situation to thwart high level policy, possibly even on behalf of the anti-Hitler peace initiatives that were underway from the earliest days of the war.

In this latter scenario one must also consider the possibility that Karl Wolff played a key role in the subterfuge. Jochen von Lang[3] describes Wolff as “a white knight within the Black Corps” because of the help that he gave to a number of Jews. Wolff gave this help voluntarily for no personal benefit and often in dangerous circumstances. Might Wolff and Rahn have been working in secret partnership, possibly with others who shared common cause?

Rausch’s letter goes on to describe how in autumn 1935 his book *Konstanze* appeared and was at once misunderstood and abused in a nationalistic way. It was quickly removed. Rausch informs Bock bitterly that "the megalomaniac Heinrich VI" delightedly saw in *Konstanze* material to provide the foes of the gipsy with even greater ammunition. Later the book underwent a revised interpretation and sold in the tens of thousands but Rausch had had his fill of Germany and was residing in Paris. Never again did he cross the border but, Rausch confides, he had very good protectors: "our foreign Secret Service (MI6 equivalent) worked more than well." This comment can only help to cement a deepening belief that Cecil Williamson, an MI6 operative (see Chapter 14), played a key role in facilitating the receipt of wartime intelligence from those around Himmler and, by extension, from confederates like Rahn in Himmler's immediate orbit.

Rausch tells Bock that: "in 1937 the second wave of hatred was launched against 'Galla Placidia’.” This is a curious comment. Galla Placidia (386-452 A.D.) was the daughter of Theodosius I and sister of Honorius, the Roman Emperor who moved the capital of the western empire from Milan to Ravenna. Captured by Alaric I in the course of his Italian campaign, she was held hostage by the Visigoths for a three-day period as they sacked Rome (during which they made off with the Treasures of the Temple of Solomon). Placidia later married Alaric’s successor Ataulf at Narbonne. After the murder of Ataulf she was at first ill-treated but was returned in 416 A.D. to her brother Honorius. It is stretching coincidence that Alaric and Ataulf are both integral to the fate and whereabouts of Solomon’s Treasures after the fall of Rome in 410 A.D. In light of Rahn’s commitment to the location and recovery of the Grail artefacts, might Rausch have been using Galla Placidia as a code name for Rahn? This may not be quite as farfetched as might appear considering Rahn and Rausch’s sexuality. Moreover, the decision by Himmler to punish Rahn in late 1937 by sending him to Dachau to undertake military duties can be described as an act of hatred

[3] ibid

against him.

Multiple accounts, multiple variations—suicide, ritual suicide, accident, act of God, execution, betrayal—take your pick. Did Rahn die in the Tyrol Mountains in March 1939 or did he not? Rahn's friend from the Iceland trip Peter de Coudres, for example, was very suspicious of the received wisdom that Rahn was more or less ordered to kill himself with a bottle of cognac in the ice.

We should pause to consider another very tantalising aspect of the Rahn mystery. This concerns an account of the activities of Swiss researcher, Karl Rinderknecht, who, prior to 1941, explored the mountains and caves around Montségur. The account appeared in a German periodical[4] and from the content and context it is evident that the unknown author is quoting Rinderknecht directly. It is probable that the author is, in fact, Rinderknecht. The article goes into the detail of Rinderknecht's activities, adding that he "later discovered notable evidence through his research and excavations." The passage states that "the Grail Castle is located on Montségur. Karl Rinderknecht had to master many difficulties during his search (*the article does not say when the searches were made*) for secret hiding places and catacombs. Old grail symbols were found in the underground corridors of the holy mountain. One fresco depicted a red disk, a lance and a cross, all of which were emblems of the Holy Grail." Each aspect and component of the article is matched in corresponding detail to the discoveries Rahn had made ten years earlier. Seven photographs were included with the article, all very similar to those attributed to or associated with Otto Rahn during his Sabarthès explorations.

It is of especial significance that nowhere in the article is Otto Rahn's name mentioned, an astonishing omission considering that barely ten years previously Rahn had made his Pyrenean travels and that news of those activities had been made public by newspapers, periodicals, radio programmes and, most relevantly, by Rahn's own writings on the subject. I can find no trace of any photograph of Rinderknecht or any biographical information about him. One of the most obvious inferences one could draw is that Rahn and Rinderknecht were one and the same person. Considering the number of times Rahn is supposed to have been observed by various parties in the Pyrenees after the war it is a possibility that must be very seriously considered.

As a diverting aside, the name "Rinderknecht" can be deconstructed phonetically to read Rin der Knecht, which translates as Rin the Servant, even Rahn the Servant. This word play is not as whimsical

---

[4] *In Quest of the Grail*, Koralle Magazine, #42, 19th October 1941

as it might first appear. In the next few pages we shall see that *Die Welt* described Rahn in 1979 as *"a founder of a sort of secret movement."* That is a remarkable statement to make and one can only speculate as to why the journalist of the piece chose to do so; there is no evidence that Otto Rahn instigated any such order. However, the word servant comes from the Latin *familia*, meaning household of servants. In the Latin context *familia* does not refer to nuclear or blood family specifically but more usually to a small group dedicated to upholding a high ideal or principle. Looking at the phrase "Rin der Knecht," albeit lightheartedly, revisits the premise that within the Nazi cabal there existed a small group of men and women united in their opposition to its ultra-negative regime and that Otto Rahn was a member of that brethren.

The overwhelming opinion says that Otto Rahn committed suicide but why would he have taken this course? He was working on a number of projects: a book on Konrad of Marbourg (as stated in *Kreuzzug gegen den Gral*), *The Will of Prometheus: A Journey to Hell and Beyond* (sequel to *Luzifers Hofgesind*), *According to God and to Right* (a book for the French, according to Rahn's SS dossier), *Laurin* (a novel as per Rahn's letter to Gadal of 14th July 1934—Rahn's niece Ingeborgh Römer-Rahn has the manuscript in her possession, according to an inventory list she gave to Hans-Jürgen Lange), and *Montsalvat and Golgotha* (per letter to Weisthor 27th September 1935). In addition he was preparing a grand novel *Sebastian*, a 2,000 page manuscript that he had been working on for several years and which he described in a letter to Himmler as his "masterpiece…the quintessence of my perception, realization and thesis, with exclusive references and practical applications in connection with life as it is viewed today. This will be my strongest artistic and intellectual achievement. Experts have assured me of this."[5] Himmler had granted Rahn a one-year leave of absence from his SS duties with complete freedom to devote himself to writing and research.

The mountain on which Rahn died, the Kaiser-Wilden, is comparatively low and it is rare to find life-threatening conditions there. (However, it is just forty kilometres from Hitler's 'eagle's nest' at Berchtesgaden and was in the defensive zone surrounding it.)

On 13th November 1939 a confidential note containing appendices on Otto Rahn was sent to SS-Gruppenführer Schmidt at the office of the Chief of Staff SS.

APPENDIX 1 said that Rahn had been receiving a Captain's pay ever since he had been a Leutnant. APPENDIX 4 said that Rahn had

[5] Otto Rahn's letter to Himmler 9th June 1938

been "decorated" with the "Julleuchter," the Candlestick of the Winter Solstice, which certified the spirit of the SS and its Nordic renewal. This was an exceptional measure for Rahn as the Julleuchter was exclusively reserved for couples and families. APPENDIX 5 said that Rahn had stayed in one of the fourteen houses of the Lebensborn Association dedicated to racial purity.

Himmler dreamed up the idea of Lebensborn, a chain of maternity homes that looked after unwed mothers and provided foster homes for illegitimate babies. He believed the organisation would result in several thousand more choice births annually. Every SS officer had to join and support it with his dues: 5% to 8% of his salary.[6] This was a commitment to prove that one had handed over one's life to Himmler as a "Man of the SS" (Himmler's Order). We have already noted Gabriele Winckler's remarks about the possibility of a falling out between Rahn and Himmler caused, at least in part, by events Rahn may have witnessed in a Lebensborn home. Might Rahn's Lebensborn connection, seen in conjunction with his Julleuchter award, even suggest that Rahn fathered children for the good of the Fatherland? If so, what happened to his offspring? Might they still be alive? Might fatherhood not have further strengthened Rahn's desire to hang on to life (and by the same token have discouraged Himmler from exerting pressure on Rahn to kill himself)?

Bernadac believes that in his last year Rahn held a directorial post in an American society in Düsseldorf. At this time, Bernadac suggests, Rahn was employed both by Himmler and by Heydrich. Heydrich had made hundreds of people "disappear" and then given them a false identity to use them in his secret service. Bernadac is persuaded that Rahn fell into this situation, was posted to Paris, then to Italy and to Lebanon.

Bernadac is also on record as saying that Rahn established mysterious orders in Holland, France and Switzerland, and as leader of this movement was irreplaceable to Germany. If we are prepared to lend even an ounce of credibility to a survival theory then it is not beyond reason to suggest that one or more of these mysterious orders would have been instrumental in providing a haven and, more importantly, a sense of personal and professional direction for Otto Rahn beyond March 1939.

The unanimous opinion is that Rahn killed himself. Very few researchers consider the possibility that he was murdered. Personally, I do not believe either theory. Consider for a moment the statement Rahn

---

[6] Sklar ibid

made at Kurt Egger's apartment: he had been given a choice—enter a KZ or choose suicide "in the mountains." By that remark is one to conclude that someone in power, maybe Himmler, had voiced those precise choices? But think on it—death in the mountains? That sounds stagey, contrived; almost as if Rahn manufactured the remark to provide a plausible story. Why might he have done that except perhaps to shroud a planned disappearance? Might they have been the words of a man in control of his next step, a man with life on his mind, survival?

Before we move on let us to consider one other extremely important factor in the Rahn survival scenario: the alleged links between Otto Rahn and Rudolf Rahn, German ambassador to Italy in WW2, let us pause briefly to reflect upon Kurt Eggers, the friend to whom Rahn turned in extreme agitation en route to the Tyrol.

In March 1933 Eric Jan van Hanussen (real name Harshel Stein Schneider, a Czech Jew born in 1889 and better known as the "mage of Hitler"), disappeared and his bullet-riddled corpse was found in a forest near Berlin on 7th April that year. He had acquired a certain reputation in astrological circles and had been allied with Karl Ernst, Röhm's debauched adjutant, and with Count von Helldorf, Prefect of Police in Berlin, later hanged by the SS in July 1944 after plotting against Hitler. Obviously, someone in power decided that Hanussen had outstayed his welcome in the world of the living. His two assassins were Kurt Egger and Rudolf Steinle, both members of the NSDAP and both controlled by Himmler. Kurt Eggers: Otto Rahn's friend and provider of fleeting sanctuary while Rahn was en route for suicide, and Kurt Egger: SS assassin—are they really two unconnected people? If they are one and the same or linked in some way, perhaps through family, did Rahn know this? Are Rahn's disappearance and Egger's assassin role linked in some way?

Let us also pause to reflect on one single but supremely important fact in considering the suicide question. With all his heart and passion Rahn empathised with the Cathar ideal. Living those ideals requires the faithful to practise the rules of the order, without exception. Rahn wrote in *Kreuzzug gegen den Gral*: "Their (Cathar) doctrine allowed suicide but demanded that one did not put an end to his life because of disgust, fear or pain but in a perfect dissolution from matter. This kind of Endura was allowed when it took place in a moment of mystical insight of divine beauty and kindness...It is only one step from fasting to suicide. To fast, requires courage but the final act of definitive ascetism requires heroism. The consequence is not as cruel as it may look."

According to Rahn, when the Cathars elected to die according to the rite of Endura, a ceremony in which members wittingly chose to cross the threshold, unafraid, and filled with the light and power of God, it was always carried out in pairs. Rahn wrote in *Kreuzzeg gegen den Gral*: "This brother with whom the Cathar had shared the most perfect friendship and years of striving together mightily for ideal spiritual life looked forward to sharing with him the life to come, the true life, the beauty already glimpsed of the Hereafter and the knowledge of of the divine laws which move worlds."

Moreover, Rahn added, it was necessary, according to Cathar dogma, that after death a passing soul should suffer no sadness in the life to come. This sentiment extended to caring for the feelings of one's close brother in life, whom they loved as they loved themselves. One did not have the right to inflict on one's brother the pain of separation otherwise the act had to be paid for in the Hereafter, on the Mountain of Purification, degree by degree, as told by Dante.

For these compelling reasons the pair had to travel to the next life together.

If Otto Rahn did take his own life the question therefore remains. Who was Otto Rahn's "Cathar" brother with whom he would have been obliged to share the act of self-immolation?

More to the point, if it was the case that the pair had determined to end their lives together in ritual Cathar fashion where was the second body?

It is purely academic, seeing that each of the various accounts speak of finding one dead person, not two, but who might this second person have been? It can be argued that Rahn's closest companion in life was Raymond Perrier but he lived on for another fifty-nine years.

No, the closer one looks at the Rahn suicide scenario, the less it supports even the most cursory scrutiny.

Christian Bernadac advances the startling theory that Otto Rahn and Rudolf Rahn, Germany's ambassador to Italy in WW2, were one and the same person, which was the subject of a carefully conceived cover-up within the higher echelons of the Nazi regime.

In April 1941 a German diplomat was sent to Beirut with a pro-German Frenchman named Guérard to handle the delivery of arms to rebels in Iraq. The diplomat, chosen because of his excellent command of French and knowledge of the country, was Rudolf Rahn. He was the advisor to Otto Abetz, the German ambassador to France, and subsequently became Nazi Germany's last ambassador to Rome. However, in both the memoirs of Jeanne de Schoutheete (the wife of the Belgian diplomat in the Lebanon) and Henri Seyrig (director of the Institut Français in Beirut) he appears under the name Otto Rahn. There are some correspondences in respect of this theory that must be examined.

Otto Rahn and Rudolf Rahn employed the same secretary, the former in 1932 calling her Tita, the latter in 1943 in Rome. Otto Rahn at one time wrote to Gadal saying that his secretary was "indispensable." It was Paul Ladame who wrote to Bernadac confirming this curious fact of coincidence. Rudolf Rahn said he was often called Otto, even preferring it, in memory of his brother who died in infancy in 1904 aged three. Rudolf was born 16th March 1900 at Ulm. During his mission in the Midle East Rudolf also went under the name of Robert Renouard. He explained to Mme Schoutheete that he had chosen the name Raynouard (his initial choice, he told her, was Renoir) after a 19th-century Provençal writer but that his superior officer had mistakenly spelt this as 'Renouard' on his papers. Otto Rahn was in a rush to leave the Hôtel-Restaurant des Marronniers at Ussat-les-Bains and in his hurry he left behind in his bedside cabinet a book of Occitan poems translated by Raynouard.

In his memoirs Rudolf Rahn writes of the mystical "jeu d'images" phenomenon he experienced as a young child. He had the "gift," as it were. He said it was always at his shoulder, impossible to escape from. He could foretell coming events. His phantoms often took the form of numbers. He could visualise numbers and geometric lines to form pathways to locate missing objects, the numbers being footprints and the lines the direction to take to find the missing item. These memoirs have several identical elements to Otto Rahn's own writings. For example, Otto Rahn in *Luzifers Hofgesind* writes: "Soon, my little alarm clock will ring seven times. In two hours it will be night..." Rudolf Rahn writes: "The clock rings two chimes first, seven after...."

In Rudolf Rahn's *Une Vie sans Repos* we read that after attending University (Berlin and Heidelberg, the latter also attended by Otto Rahn) Rudolf, like Otto, lived in Geneva where he worked as a teacher and translator. Here he met an elderly spinster who took him to Provence. He does not name this benefactor who Bernadac thinks is strongly mindful of the Comtesse Pujol-Murat. Rudolf Rahn was Germany's ambassador to Italy in the final days of the war. Karl Wolff at this time was head of the German military in Italy. Bernadac showed photos of Rudolf Rahn to Paul Ladame and photos of Otto Rahn to Jeanne de Schoutheete. Both said there were resemblances.

In 1979 *Die Welt* reviewed Bernadac's theory and attacked it with clinical precision. It is worth reporting in full because its neat dissection opens up a number of other critical strands of enquiry into the Otto Rahn story.[7] This is the article in full:

"Two photos accompany this text. One (left) was taken in 1933. The other, which shows a man with a medal around his neck, originated from 1944. The writer of a sensational book shortly to appear in France claims that both photos show the same person. It is physiognomically improbable since the younger man has a hooked nose, which is apparently curved eleven years later and which could only be done by an operation...today's plastic surgery is not that advanced and was even less so in the 1930s.

However, we do not wish to limit ourselves to physiognomy; we know who both are. The young man, of slight build, is the writer Otto Rahn, born in 1904 in Michelstadt in Odenwald, who died in mysterious circumstances in March 1939 in a snowstorm in the Kaiser-Wilden, supposedly suicide. The other is the diplomat Rudolf Rahn, who was born in 1900 in Ulm and who died in 1975, and who is remembered as a powerful, almost colossal man. Both are persons of their time.

The diplomat became well known due to his involvement in dramatic situations—firstly in 1941 in a German attempt to trek through Iraq, then at the end of the war as the German representative to Mussolini. He published well-written memoirs in 1949 (Life without Rest).

The writer enjoyed a more esoteric reputation. With his books 'Kreuzzug gegen den Gral' (1933, 1934 in French) and 'Luzifers Hofgesind. Eine Reise zu den guten Geistern Europas' (1937, 1954 in French), he has brought to the notice of people from many countries the pilgrimage he described through the French Pyrenees, and in particular to the Burgberg (castle hill) of Montségur in Ariège, which he described as the Grail-Castle of Wolfram von Eschenbach. He has popularised the history of the Cathars who were destroyed in the 13th century in a bloody Crusade led by the Pope and the King of France, and he

Rudolf Rahn

[7] *Die Welt* article of 12 May 1979: *Der doppelte Rahn und sein heiliger Gral. Wie ein toter deutscher Schriftsteller als Botschafter weiterlebte* (The Double Rahn and the Holy Grail. How a dead German writer lived on as a diplomat).

became known to many French people as a reluctant/unlikely father of the Occitan resistance.

Therefore we have two basically different people—one a founder of a sort of secret movement and possessed by his own visions, the other a wandering diplomat renowned for his tendency for chic. However, the author of this book is set on the idea that they are one and the same person.

The author is bothered a bit that as Otto Rahn was documented as being established in his Pyrenean nest in 1931/32, Rudolf Rahn was in another part of the world starting his diplomatic career. Fortunately for the author, the death of Otto Rahn is to this day unexplained. He was taken into the SS in 1936, within Himmler's close group, and appointed a secret alias as Oberst (Colonel) Wonnegut (retired), where other interesting people such as the astrologer Krafft from Basel and the clairvoyant Hanussen came under his wing.

At the end of 1939 Otto Rahn enquired with SS Group Captain Karl Wolff about leaving the SS on grounds of 'difficulties.' In the 'Volkischer Beobachter' (newspaper) of 18 May 1939 a notice signed by Wolff appears—'SS Obersturmführer Otto Rahn dies tragically in a snowstorm in the mountains in March this year. We mourn our dead comrade, a decent SS man and creator of outstanding academic work.' What occurred with this SS-Leutnant who was for a long time a favourite of Himmler? Comrades gave information after the war that because of 'personal tendencies' which Himmler detested, Rahn was pushed into suicide (he is supposed to have emptied a bottle of rum and passed away in the snow). However, our French author knows nothing about this. He believes instead that due to the discovery of his half-Jewish ancestry (for which no evidence is presented and which is denied within SS circles) Rahn was pushed into a corner. The suicide was faked in order to allow Otto Rahn, who was irreplaceable for Germany, to reappear in the person of Rudolf Rahn, the diplomat.

This nonsense is long-winded and the details are not convincingly explained by Christian Bernadac—who up to now has published 13 books of mostly contemporary historical content about Hitler's doctors, the women's Konzentrationslager (KZ) and similar. The title of this book reads 'The Mystery of Otto Rahn—The Grail and Montségur—From Catharism to Nazism.'

As a publisher, France-Empire does not have a clear political identity, but has a clear tendency for contemporary history thrillers.

Bernadac's argument is astonishingly disjointed and without thought. His main argument is that long after Otto Rahn's death, a guilt attaching to his name was removed with no ascertainable reason. What we have, however, does not concur.

Then a great fuss is made that a witness mixed up the first names of the Rahns. Above all, Bernadac wants to forcibly inform us that the autobiographical works of the Rahns deal with the same life, only with changed names and places. In this respect, Bernadac finds it very meaningful that both Rahns felt a pull towards France, and the midi, south of the Loire, was particularly attractive to them.

Bernadac the historian, who has written a lot about Germany, appears not to know that this area is a traditional destination for German intellectuals since Seiburg and Ernst Robert Curtins (and to a lesser extent is still so today).

In addition, Bernadac's translation from German is not too exact, sometimes due to a lack of knowledge. One cannot believe it when comparing his translation of Rudolf Rahn's memoirs with the original German text. It is significantly amended/simplified in order that Rudolf's text becomes more similar to that of Otto's. In this respect, non-French names are often spelt incorrectly so that one can only guess at the correct spelling. If the name is spelt correctly apart from one letter, as in the case of Wilhelm von Schwamm, then this gives greater credibility to the emigrants of 1933, although Schramm thought of things other than emigration at that time.

It is no wonder, if historical revelations are presented in this way, that Himmler and Abetz would have sent Otto Rahn as a spy to the Pyrenees in 1931. At that time Abetz was still miles away from the NSDAP and Himmler was busying himself with his party's seizure of power—not with factories in a Pyrenean valley.

It is a shame about this book as it is a good source of material still not generally available about new Catharism and the Occitan revival, although it is laid out in a scattered and arbitrary way. Whoever is interested in the secret 'history of ideas' of our time should, in spite of Bernadac's crude intentions, turn to this book."

It is noteworthy that *Die Welt* should refer to Rahn's "supposed" suicide. Clearly, the newspaper's editorial staff had doubts that Rahn took his own life in 1939. Personally, I was not persuaded of a link between Otto Rahn and Rudolf Rahn until I read John Cornwell's excellent book *Hitler's Pope: the Secret History of Pope Pius XII*[8] because *Die Welt's* brusque riposte to Bernadac's assertions introduces

us to Otto Abetz, Rudolf Rahn's superior in France the early thirties, an individual who played more than a bit part in the evolution of the post-

[8] Viking, 1999

war fascist international movement. It is my belief that, equally, Abetz does not play an insignificant part in the development of a survival theory for Otto Rahn. All things considered, it is likely that while in France Rahn was under the heel of Abetz, a German Embassy official in Paris and a spy for Ribbentrop from 1933 until he was found out and expelled from France.

Otto Abetz and Rudolf Rahn were both involved in the Neumann Kreis (Circle). Rahn was the last German ambassador to Italy. He had previously served under Abetz in the Paris embassy's Culture and Propaganda section where he helped organise anti-Masonic and anti-Jewish exhibits.[9]

John Cornwell reveals that Rudolf Rahn was directly involved in the passage of secret communications between Hitler and Pope Pius XII (Eugene Pacelli).[10] In October 1943 the SS, led by SS-Hauptsturmführer Theodor Dannecker, began the round up of Jews in Rome. Characteristically, Pacelli said nothing personally but gave Father Pankratius Pfeiffer permission to speak in his name. However, Pfeiffer was deemed to be of too low a rank and Bishop Alois Hudal, rector of the German Catholic Church in Rome, was called upon to serve as the pontiff's mouthpiece. A letter was drafted to the German ambassador at the time, Weizsacker, and to General Rainer Stahel, senior German miltitary authority in Rome. The letter of protest, phrased so that it appeared as if Pius was speaking directly, was telegraphed to the recipients on 16th October by Rahn's office. This letter and the fact that it was despatched by (Rudolf) Rahn was referred to in a follow-up letter from Weizsacker to Berlin confirming that Hudal's letter represented the Vatican's official reaction to the deportation of the Jews of Rome. The deportations took place two days later and by the 23rd the 1,060 deportees had been gassed.

Considering the arguments Bernadac has advanced on the Rudolf Rahn—Otto Rahn interpolation, the severe unease Otto Rahn felt about the Catholic Church (especially the Jesuits' opinions about his writings and activities), the known links between Rudolf Rahn, Otto Abetz and Karl Wolff on the one hand and between Otto Rahn and Wolff on the other, and the curious remarks from Joachim Kohlhaas about Otto Rahn's "bookseller" brother Karl having strong Nazi sympathies, we must seriously consider the strong probability that there is much more to all these links, conflations and coincidences than meet the eye. Abetz and his French born wife died an "accidental" violent

---

9 Tauber, *Beyond Eagle and Swastika*, Vol.1 p 295

10 Cornwell ibid

death when their car exploded in May 1958 near Düsseldorf.

There are far too many ifs, buts and maybes casting a pall of uncertainty over the true circumstances of Rahn's death. Obviously, Rahn did meet his Maker. I waste no energy in promoting absurd notions of immortality even if the Tibetans and their spooky conjuring tricks are rumoured to have featured in Rahn's post-1939 survival plans.

I have no argument with Hans-Jürgen Lange's findings that there is a death certificate in the Söll registry, county Kufstein, a document recording the death of Otto Rahn, religious, resident of Berlin. I understand that Ingeborgh Römer-Rahn can show enquirers a grave where she says her uncle is laid to rest. Again, I do not doubt it for one moment. The critical question for me and other doubters is not if Otto Rahn died but *when* he died. When exactly was Rahn interred in that grave? I have huge problems accepting a March 1939 time of death but, frankly, there is just too much fog swirling around the headstone.

Too many post-mortem activities have been ascribed to Otto Rahn to dismiss them wanly as stuff and nonsense. No, my instincts tell me that Rahn left this life many years later than the official line would have us believe.

Here we might leave the vexed issue of mixed identity were it not for the curious circumstance of a document, reproduced for the sake of interest and completion by Hans-Jürgen Lange in *Otto Rahn: Leben und Werk*, purporting to be the NSDAP identity card of one Otto Rahn. Lange speculates that the document derives from Christian Bernadac's sources:

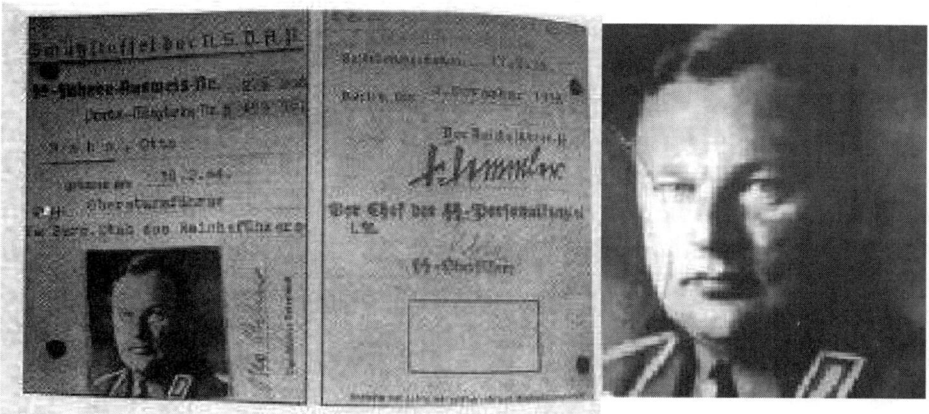

Lange states that the document is a pure forgery and, clearly, it is not a photograph of the person of Otto Rahn who would be most familiar to family, friends and colleagues. Moreover, Rahn was never a member of the NSDAP. However, Lange remarks that, except for the date of birth, all other details on the card are wrong. That observation may well be substantially correct but it is unarguable fact that Otto Rahn's final rank *was* indeed SS-Obersturmführer and that he was promoted to this rank on 11th September 1938. It is clear, at least, that that description of rank and particular date do appear on the card.

Undoubtedly the card and its make up do provide cause for concern in terms of its legitimacy, provenance and purpose. The photograph is only roughly stuck on and the stamp on the picture does not continue onto the paper of the card. The key question that springs to mind is why someone thought it necessary to create such a clumsy forgery in the first place. For whom was it intended? It was obviously not made to fool anyone who knew Otto Rahn in any degree of familiarity.

It could have had no useful purpose as an identity document. For example in connection with the curious alias *Oberst (Colonel) Wonnegut (retired)* that *Die Welt* claims was allocated to Otto Rahn on his induction into the SS in 1936. Moreover, if the passport comes from Bernadac, as Hans-Jürgen Lange suggests, then from where did he obtain it?

Could Rahn himself have made it or had it made for his own purposes? If he was behind it, then what were his motives and rationale? If he was not the originator then did whoever forge it or cause it to be forged ever tell Rahn that the card had been made and, if so, did they give him instructions as to the circumstances in which it was to be used?

We will probably never know the answer to these and a whole host of other questions about this matter but it is yet another ill-tasting ingredient in the Otto Rahn casserole of dissemblance and uncertainty. Doubtless, there are many more such ingredients to bubble up out of the pot of history before we may lay claim to anything approaching a more complete and accurate understanding of Rahn, his life and his work.

Chapter THIRTEEN

Troj de Reses

Here we must leave Otto on the Rose trail, at rest in the snow, the curriculum of the physical endured, eternity before him. In Part 1 LIFE, we have filled our canvas with all the paintstrokes and shades that reflect light upon Otto Rahn's activities in the external world between 1904 and 1939. I have drawn from all available texts in presenting a comprehensive picture and enhanced it with primary source material in the form of Gabriele Winckler's recollections of her friendship with Rahn. I trust that his life's account presented in the preceding pages is faithful to the facts and is comprehensively informative for the diverse audience of readers who might be drawn to this work. Further original material arising from interviews with key personalities of the day will help us to see beneath the canvas in Part 2 AFTER LIFE.

By all accounts Rahn's sexual peccadilloes had led him to an impasse. He was offered the choice: jump or be pushed. But who can say that the crack would have widened to a fissure, even allowing for Rahn's brittle temperament? Mood swings can get us into all kinds of difficulty but bad grace and poor manners rarely bring an offender to death's door. That route requires contempt for the rules of society way above the threshold of commonly acceptable behaviour. It is evident that Rahn could easily get himself worked up, most often when he perceived his work undermined by those who ought to know talent when they saw it and, moreover, should reward it in due proportion. Rahn wore his chip with bitter pride, thereby providing kindle and match to those who would fan his misfortune and enjoy a healthy slice of *Schadenfreude*. But to advance from being our own worst enemy to being so out of emotional kilter as to turn friends into homicidal foes is a giant step.

I am not at all sure we have seen sufficient evidence that Rahn created the conditions that made an unnatural death inevitable. Certainly, he had an enduring knack for exciting those around him into sharp provocation. We have Bernadac's account of Rahn's beating at the hands of Joseph Mandement for reportedly faking cave drawings. Frau

Winckler tells of the violence of the Montségur farmers. Rahn's travel companions will not give him the time of day in Iceland and give him the brush off. The wife of influential Nazi politician Heinz Pehmoller could not stand his company. Leutnant Horst Buchrucker displayed remarkable restraint at Mrs Hartmann's wedding party. Rahn shouts his mouth off in a restaurant in the name of the Nazi order and provokes hoots of laughter for his absurd and highflown sentiments. People skills were not always high in the armoury of Otto Rahn's talents but, frankly, academics are often neither noted for their sparkling bonhomie nor for their tact. However, such lacunae in the socially inept are rarely the cause of murder or enforced suicide.

On the other hand, Rahn was at least on the periphery, if not within the inner ring, of an extremely vicious circle of key players in the Nazi hierarchy. It is more than possible that he could have got on the wrong side of a bigshot and paid the price. We have read Hans-Jürgen Lange's description of the occasion in 1937 when Rahn sat in the Nobelrestaurant with Heinrich Himmler, Reinhard Heydrich, General Karl Wolff and Dr. Franz Riedweg. Rahn hated Riedweg but failed completely in his efforts to overturn Himmler's respect for the Swiss. It is entirely possible that the loathsome Heydrich may also have supported Riedweg and that he quietly determined to put Rahn in his place, perhaps permanently.

But as always with men at or near the top their own survival is a delicate act of balance. All too often they are open and vulnerable to those with the real influence who work beneath the shrouds of power. With this in mind it is legitimate to posit that, consciously or not, Otto Rahn might somehow have played a part in determining the longer-term fortunes of certain well positioned Nazi powerbrokers.

Rahn can be forgiven if his biographical legacy appears short on remarkable achievements or heroic discoveries. We note that he darted about here and there, his footsteps covering large swathes of mythical and inquisitional Europe. Nonetheless, I do believe that the details of Rahn's life are of vital historical significance. But the substance is not so much to be found on the surface but deep within the fabric woven around him. Whether he spun this himself or it was knitted by others is another matter.

Evidence of Rahn's footsteps are scarce enough; he wrote very little about his personal day to day life, and enlightenment from friends and family scarcely adds much to the overall picture. If Rahn's surviving family members possess documented material that could expand upon his interests, hopes, dreams and wishes then let us hope that one day it might be brought into the public domain. For now we must make use of what we have. But if we stand back and review the material perhaps we come to realise that, in point of fact, we have more than sufficient to develop our canvas into an Impressionist work, worthy of a Renoir or a Degas, wherein all is revealed to the keen observer.

Otto Rahn identified with the Knight of Berne and his Quest to find the magical Elfin Kingdom of Laurin. We shall look at this beautiful tale in Chapter 21. Let us recognise that when a man or woman undertakes a sacred quest, a task or goal against whose conclusion nothing is allowed to stand in opposition, their pathway is private, personal and special. We are not meant to be able to follow in their tracks because every person's journey is unique. However, the nature and quality of personal quest conforms to ancient archetypes of universal law, which can be interpreted by the patient observer. Otto Rahn did not leave us with an Ordnance Survey map. He did not need to. He willed to us his writings and broadcasts, and it is within these media that we will find and explore the mountain pathways by which he travelled in private search for truth and meaning.

In the third part of this book, MEANING, we shall follow the scent. One cannot say if Rahn came off best in his battle with the windmills or if he found and won to his heart his own Dulcinea. It is my reading of Rahn, however, that he *was* a man of honour and integrity, qualities that stood him apart from those around him and which placed him in very great danger. We shall look beyond his footprint and focus on the impression it made in the inner worlds of quest, enchantment and ancient truths. Rahn did have a personal quest. He sought his Grail; he thirsted for the (Philosopher's) stone; he tugged at Caliburn buried hilt deep in ancient rock. And like all mystics who similarly went before him in preceding millennia Rahn knew better than to speak of his journey. Himmler and his circle were the last people to whom such knowledge could be safely entrusted. Their journey was one of murder and madness. Otto Rahn's, on the other hand, was in the grand tradition of the man of La Mancha who sought the impossible dream and succeeded in fastening a pendant of stars around the neck of the Goddess, his beloved Dulcinea.

But right now let us look in PART 2 AFTER LIFE at the principle figures in and around Otto Rahn’s life up to March 1939 and how their lives and destinies might have impacted upon or intertwined with a post-mortem survival scenario. We will begin by recounting the story of Cecil H. Williamson, WW2 MI6 agent and a pioneer member of the Service's fledgling occult section. His actions, statements, opinions, philosophy and, not least, his circles make a direct pathway to all of the major personalities around Rahn, in life and in "death," laying the groundwork for a close review in ensuing chapters of those figures and the synergies that bound them together.

Otto Rahn in the Odenwald, circa 1937

Heinrich Luitpold Himmler
Reichsführer-SS

Cecil H. Williamson, WW2 MI6 Occult Bureau operative and founder of the British Witchcraft Research Centre. Photograph taken by the author in 1998.

PART TWO

AFTER LIFE

Chapter FOURTEEN

MI6

Several years ago, Gary, an American friend of mine researching Otto Rahn's life, received a letter from an ex-WW2 MI6 agent named Cecil H. Williamson. Williamson's brief note explained that a present day member of MI6 had passed Gary's address to him and suggested he get in touch.

Straightaway, this manner of approach arouses suspicion. Why would a serving MI6 officer be so open and upfront about his status, even with a long since retired member of the security services? It is equally possible that Williamson concocted the story for reasons he kept to himself. In either case, the circumstances surrounding the introduction smack of dissemblance, a clumsy attempt to divert a person from their present line of research perhaps because they are getting too close to the truth for comfort. But a diligent researcher looks for opportunities in whatever may come his or her way, knowing that a red herring when viewed from the correct perspective can sometimes point the way to better and bigger catches.

With these thoughts in mind Gary reflected upon Williamson's approach. He concluded that it must have been made in connection with his research enquiries about Rahn and, in particular, the skein of thought he was then attempting to unravel, namely that Rahn had belonged to a small esoteric group, which had worked in great secrecy within the heart of the Nazi regime to oppose Hitlerism.

Coinciding with the receipt of Williamson's letter was Gary's relocation from the U.S. to Australia and so, nothing ventured, nothing gained, he asked if I would make contact. In 1997 I interviewed Williamson by phone and a year later in person at his home at Witheridge near Taunton in Somerset.

When I met Williamson he was eighty-nine years old and as sharp as a razor; indeed it was hard to get a word in edgeways. Certainly there was no hint in his physical or mental demeanour of the stroke that was to cut him down so swiftly a year later, and which led to his passing in December 1999. Williamson remembered much from his early life but maintained that he could not recall the name Rahn. However, he did say he remembered a man named Han or Hahn from the Berlin film studios in the mid-thirties (recall that Otto Rahn was a movie enthusiast who wrote screenplays and acted in bit parts).

But firstly, prior to receiving Williamson's letter Gary had corresponded with Reverend Lionel Fanthorpe, a Cardiff based cleric who is well known for his work and writings on the Rennes-le-Château mystery and for hosting television programmes on Fortean phenomena. Gary's objective in writing to Fanthorpe was to try to obtain information or a lead on the suggestion that Otto Rahn travelled to the Corbières in the 1930's and visited Marie Dénarnaud, Abbé Saunière's housekeeper, in Rennes-le-Château. We looked at this claim in Chapter 9 and concluded that there is no evidence to support it.

Subsequently some brief exchanges followed which did not produce any new earth shattering facts about Rahn's life or his alleged connections with Rennes-le-Château. However, Williamson's letter arrived shortly after the American's exchanges with Fanthorpe. It was Gary's intuitive opinion that these earlier enquiries might also have had a bearing on the decision by someone in "British Intelligence" to encourage Williamson to write to him, thereby making a direct link between Otto Rahn's life, Williamson's unique activities as a member of MI6's "occult" bureau founded in 1938, and the secrets of Rennes-le-Château. These alleged links between Rahn and MI6 had not previously been made by any researcher on Otto Rahn.

I wrote to Lionel Fanthorpe in September 2000 to see if he recalled these earlier exchanges and if they might be fleshed out further. Fanthorpe soon replied, saying: "*Delighted to hear from you, especially on the subject of the Rennes mystery, in which we've been keenly interested for many years. Unfortunately, I don't currently have any copies of the correspondence with your friend, and I never actually met Hahn (alias Rahn, perhaps). There are various intriguing leads in the Rennes puzzle suggesting that Marie Dénarnaud possibly had a number of contacts with characters who were involved with curious religio-political organisations and/or espionage. Hitler's interest in the paranormal might have led some of his minions to investigate whatever he thought might have been hidden at Rennes but it's all highly speculative.*"

There are elements of this letter that are noteworthy. Firstly, Fanthorpe does not address the main MI6 issue but in not doing so he succeeds in emphasising it by omission. Secondly, Fanthorpe provides a strange syntax in the piece in his letter about Hahn: "…I never actually met Hahn..." Expressing the phrase in that manner is like saying such a person did exist but I never got around to making an acquaintance. It is as if Fanthorpe wanted to affirm something concrete about a Hahn-Rahn interpolation without actually coming right out and saying so.

I was struck also by Fanthorpe's reference to "*curious religio-political organisations and/or espionage.*" We have mentioned already a number of candidates that warrant the "curious" tag such as the Polaires and the hotch potch of Nazi occult groups. We know that Rahn was linked to the first and that he was undoubtedly knowledgeable about the Thule and allied groups in light of Rahn's telling of the legend of the Knight of Berne, a tale which corresponds closely with a Thule initiation ritual.

Moreover, Rahn can be objectively described as having been one of "Hitler's minions," seeing that his boss was Himmler, the Ignatius to the Black Pope of the Third Reich. We know also from Wilma Stoll's testimony that Hitler was personally aware of Rahn and his activities. Again, I get the feeling that Fanthorpe was laying a chalk trail that leads back to Otto Rahn and his covert activities.

Williamson's appearance in the increasingly complex topology of Rahn's life provides the connection linking the German with a number of critical strands of enquiry which, ultimately, will shine a light upon Rahn's true fate and, dare we say, survival post-March 1939. These elements involve Tibet, the occult and metaphysical underground in Germany in the 1920's and 1930's, Rudolf Hess' still unexplained flight to Scotland in 1941, (which links, as we shall see, with strange bedfellow relationships between the Nazi hierarchy and British establishment figures) and, possibly and intriguingly, mysterious U-Boat activity in British waters.

The emergence of Cecil Williamson and his ensuing testimony convinces me that there is a good deal more to be learned about the life and destiny of Otto Rahn than has been hinted at since 1939. Williamson's remarks, his nuances, the gaps between words spoken and things left unsaid created a strong impression that the former MI6 agent not only knew Otto Rahn beyond the periphery of a clapper boy's brief encounter but, crucially, knew of Rahn in an operational context, the precise details of which have yet to come forth. A deeper evaluation of Williamson's biography helps us to stand back and see a bigger picture of Otto Rahn in the context of the hidden strata of European affairs in the first decades of the twentieth century.

Knowledge of Cecil Williamson did not land in our lap by accident. Via events still unexplained, Williamson's appearance on the scene, coupled with his secret service pedigree, brought forward the scenario that Otto Rahn and British Intelligence circles were known to each other.

Williamson was born into a well-to-do family on the 18th September 1909 in Paignton, Devon. His father had a long and distinguished career in the Fleet Air Arm of the Royal Navy. The family later moved to Carrington House, Curzon Street, Mayfair. Previous occupiers of the house included Nell Gwynne and Lord Nelson. The house boasted a sad female ghost and a hyperactive poltergeist!

Williamson told me that in his early teens he confided in an elderly woman that he was being bullied at school. She showed him how to cast a spell against the bully. The spell took the form of sitting on a garden swing and swinging over a lighted and smoky bonfire. A short while later, Williamson claimed, the bully had a skiing accident, leaving him crippled and unable to return to school. Williamson was delighted. As far as he had been concerned the spell had worked a treat. This had a dramatic effect on him, sewing the seeds for a lifelong quest for knowledge and research into witchcraft and occultism.

He was educated at Malvern College in Worcester and spent the summer holidays in Dinard, France, visiting with his grandmother and her friend, medium Mona Mackenzie. The latter pair shared a house in Thurlo Square. Mona was an astrologer and it was from her that Williamson learned abour clairvoyance. Mona's great frend was Madame de la Hey, a palmist, Tarot reader and necromancer (caller up of spirits).

After coming down from Malvern College, Williamson was sent at the request of his father to what was then Southern Rhodesia to learn about tobacco cultivation. His "house boy" was a seventy-year old native named Zandonda who taught the young man the principles of healing and shamanism and how to step into the secret world of the "never-never land."

Having been initiated into this nature-based form of tribal sorcery at an early age, Williamson told me that he did not want anything to do with today's witchcraft scene, which is removed from the pure and positive nature-healing-feminine orientation of the past. Interestingly, in *Double Standards: the Rudolf Hess Cover-up*[1] by Lynn Picknett, Clive Prince and Stephen Prior we learn that it is likely that the young Hess had a similar learning experience when he was growing up in Alexandria, Egypt.

In 1930 Williamson experienced a seemingly magical train of

[1] Picknett, Lynn; Prince, Clive; Prior, Stephen. *Double Standards: the Rudolf Hess Cover-up*. England: Time Warner Paperbacks, 2002

events that pitched him into the Motion Picture Film world, working first for Sir Oswald Stoll at the Stoll Studios in Cricklewood, North London. Three years later he married Gwen Wilcox, niece of film producer Herbert Wilcox. Gwen was working as a makeup artist for Max Factor of Hollywood.

Williamson then worked for a number of film employers, among them Wilcox, Paramount, Sound City, Ealing Studios and British International. In 1935, around the time that Rahn was struggling to make ends meet in Berlin and, among other things, working as a film extra and screenwriter, Williamson, aged eighteen, travelled to Cologne and Berlin with British filmmakers to meet German exponents of the avant-garde film movement. As the junior member of the team he served as focus puller and clapper boy. The British crew wanted to see and learn about German avant-garde cinema techniques, including the art of filming in close-up. (For readers who are interested in the occult aspects and techniques of early film-making I strongly encourage a reading of Theodore Roszak's excellent novel *Flicker*, which contains a number of extremely interesting correspondences—the Cathar and Templar references being of special note.)

The German director/producer who hosted the British visitors was named Han and he became interested in Williamson because of his interest in witchcraft. In light of Rahn's own involvement in the German film business (as extra and budding writer) it is not at all unlikely that during Williamson's visit, Rahn (Han, Hahn…) and he would have met.

Williamson nurtured his occult contacts, meeting Aleister Crowley at the Folklore Society. He joined the Golden Dawn, which he described to me as all sets and theatre: calling up spirits, charging them to do this and that, and then banishing them. He said that Crowley's ritual magic was "codswallop" although Crowley, he maintained, was brilliant and a great writer.

In January 1938 a family friend of Williamson's father, a Colonel Maltby of the Foreign Office Section MI6, met with the nineteen year old. He asked if Williamson would be interested in helping the Section on occult matters in Britain and Europe from time to time because war with Germany was inevitable. Williamson explained to me that the German middle and upper classes at that time were being swept up in a wave of interest in all occult subjects: astrology, horoscopes, graphology and prediction among them, together with an extraordinary interest in the works of Nostradamus. Part of the reason for these obsessions, Williamson suggested, were the shockingly hard terms of the Versailles Treaty. The Foreign Office felt it would be useful to have someone with contacts in these areas to keep an eye on the phenomenon and see how it might be exploited to Britain's benefit. They wanted an early indication of which Nazis, especially in the upper echelons, might be addicted to and influenced by this kind of "nonsense." Williamson readily agreed to help.

As a direct result of this initiative, Williamson formed the Witchcraft Research Centre. When war started Williamson was promptly summoned by Colonel Maltby and then reported for duty to Brigadier Gambier-Parry at Whaddon Hall, the requisitioned home of the Selby-Lowndes family adjacent to Bletchley. Later the unit also sequestered Wavendon Towers, another large house close to Bletchley, which Williamson and his team converted into sound recording studios and related facilities.

Williamson was involved in a number of missions, which he briefly described. One involved Rudolf Hess' defection. Williamson desribed to me how his witchcraft group re-wrote a page from Nostradamus and had it inserted into the prophecies in a masterly way helped by the Bodleian Museum, forgers and paper-makers. This fake copy was 'discovered,' according to plan, in France by occupying Germans and fed to Hess and others by Williamson's group's connections with Nazi astrologers, especially the Japanese astrologer close to Hitler. This man was bribed with gold. Hess' wife was also worked on by German astrologers in the pay of the allies. The Hitler circle was then 'tipped' off about the discovery and Hess' defection followed, the clear implication being that the Deputy Führer's flight was a direct consequence of the deception. Williamson says it was a tragedy that the Hess mission went the way it did because he was a very brave man who deserved better than he got. Another of Hitler's astrologers, Louis de Wohl, was lured to New York by MI6 in 1941. He also told of his role in MI6's Nostradamus-Hess ruse.

Another of Williamson's operations involved broadcasting radio messages to U-Boat crews to demotivate the Kriegsmarine sailors, especially younger members, in order to make them feel homesick.

Williamson also described to me his involvement in the famous "Witches Ritual," a magical ceremony undertaken during WW2 against the Nazi high command to prevent the invasion of England. The whole thing was no more than an elaborate hoax to fool Hitler, an ardent believer in occultism. The ritual took place in Ashdown Forest in Crowborough, Sussex, and employed the services of Aleister Crowley and his son Amado. The service was said to have involved forty

Canadian airmen draped in blankets embroidered with symbols from the Key of Solomon. British wizard Gerald Gardner claimed that he and his coven were involved and that the ritual actually took place in the New Forest in Hampshire. Five members of the coven died shortly afterwards, their deaths blamed on the power drained from them during the ritual.

A number of new covens were created in the New Forest in 1939. Principal among them was the Rosicrucian Order Crotona Fellowship, an occult group of Co-Masons located in Christchurch and established by Mrs Besant Scott, daughter of the Theosophist Annie Besant. This group claimed to have established the first Rosicrucian Theatre in England, which presented plays with occult themes. Gerald Gardner was a keen participant in this Order and in 1947 Crowley gave Gardner a charter to revive the Ordo Templis Orientis (O.T.O.) in Britain. In the summer of that year Gardner sailed for America to meet the American O.T.O heads, which included the enigmatic rocket propulsion researcher and occultist, Jack Parsons, one of Crowley's most loyal supporters.

After formally joining the O.T.O in 1941 Parsons, together with L. Ron Hubbard (founder of Scientology) and Parson's second wife Marjorie Cameron, participated in what is probably the most famous and certainly one of the most bizarre magical rituals of the twentieth century, the Babalon Working. This extraordinary ritual, commenced in 1946, was designed to fashion a Moonchild, a construct of etheric energies created by powerful thought-forms conjured by sex magick, as a means to raise the Antichrist. Parsons believed that by succeeding in this ritual the patriarchal power structure of the Piscean era would be supplanted by a resurgence of the Goddess energies, which had characterised and guided humankind in previous millennia. The Babalon Working was an exhausting ritual designed to open an interdimensional doorway for the goddess Babalon, the Mother of the Universe. It has since been widely rumoured that Parsons and his co-sorcerers succeeded in creating a rift in space-time, a doorway to the "other side." The culmination of these experiments is said by those who buy into these extraordinary accounts to have coincided with mass UFO sightings and the infamous Roswell incident, the latter occurring just prior to Crowley's death.

In 1952 Parsons was mortally wounded in his home in an explosion of fulminate of mercury, dying hours later. The incident was treated as accidental although considering Parson’s scientific expertise the affair is regarded as highly suspicious. (Werner von Braun remarked that Parsons, and not he, should be regarded as the father of the American space programme.)

Many believe that Parsons and his cohorts' misguided occult efforts opened a gateway to unimaginably terrible forces, much as Hitler was feared to have done years earlier in Europe. Cecil Williamson operated at least on the fringes of these activities through his association with Crowley and Gardner but my observations of him encourage me to consider that his involvement was substantially deeper.

In our discussions Williamson talked at length about occultism, witchcraft and Tibetan shamanism. He talked a lot about our 'familiar spirit,' that we all have a shadow: the equivalent, he said, of the Christian Holy Spirit. He said that one has to lead a perfect life to be a powerful and positive witch. He said that we have to clean ourselves inside to be fit for spirit growth, spiritual advancement and the attainment and development of healing powers.

These pronouncements on the right attitudes for personal spiritual enhancement were in sharp contrast to the extreme tenor of Williamson's comments on other issues such as the Jewish race. He told me that he had little time for the Jews whereas he had a great deal of respect for Hitler. It is clear from what Williamson said that he was an ardent supporter of the Nazis. Disarmingly, he emphasised that this view was commonly shared by the British upper classes and had been prevalent in the wartime security services. He said Himmler was a decent chap and that an awful lot of bad press had unfairly been thrown at Hitler. Author Kevin Coogan[2] states that many conservative Britons believed that Hitler threatened Russia not England. Equally, Williamson sympathised with the Vatican in face of the criticism towards it for providing Nazi escape routes.

Our first telephone conversation took a turn that astonished me. After I had broached the subject of the deceased Tibetans found by the Russians when Berlin fell, he said that at his home he had an authentic Tibetan temple. Williamson's story was that when the Chinese communists overran Tibet in the 1940's a group of five Tibetan exiles settled in Cricklewood, North London, and established a temple inside their temporary English home. Not long after their arrival the Dalai Lama ordered the priests to return immediately to Lhasa. The monks had no money for their airfare and obviously knew Williamson well enough to ask him for assistance. He advanced the cash and in return

---

[2] Coogan, Kevin. *Dreamer of the Day: Francis Parker Yockey and the Postwar Fascist International.* New York: Autonomedia, 1999

the monks donated to him their entire temple accoutrements. The items include headdresses, costumes, signed mementos and a host of other paraphanalia. I saw a number of these items when I visited Williamson's house in 1998 and toured its outbuildings, which were crammed with occult bric-à-brac. He stressed that the important thing to note was that the priests of the Bönpo cult worked with the "evil" side of occultism, involving daemonology. He said that the monks received numerous visitors. It would appear, therefore, that the London based monks were involved in less than pure and positive practices. One wonders what kind of persons might have been drawn to visit this unique Bön cell in North West London.

In 1999 when Peter Boyce and I visited Taunton Hospital where Williamson was incapacitated after suffering a stroke the ninety-year old made no response to any of the items of conversation we put to him until we mentioned Tibet. Straightaway, Williamson opened his eyes, alert, attentive. Sadly, moments later his eyes went blank and he retreated into his former state of all round unawareness.

In early 2005 I made efforts to get in touch with any other persons in British intelligence (present or former), who might have known Williamson, his colleagues or those to whom he reported. Subsequently, I made contact with Tony Sale, a member of MI5 between 1956 and 1963. He did not know Williamson but had met Colonel Maltby. Sale's boss had been Peter Wright (of "Spycatcher" fame). Wright was in tune with Maltby's old line of work and asked Sale to try some experiments on "action at a distance" by the influence of mental pressure or focus on a random number generator. The experiments produced no tangible results. Sale, however, was interested to inform me of these activities because their nature chimed closely with the work undertaken by Williamson for Maltby and Gambier-Parry twenty years before. The only significant difference, Sale pointed out, was that whereas Williamson's occult work was directed against the Germans his own ESP experiments were undertaken in the Cold War era to gain an intelligence advantage over the Russians. The fascinating element of Sale's account is that the psychic work Wright asked him to undertake closely mirrored the telepathy experiments Otto Rahn and Gabriele Dechend carried out in the streets of Berlin in the 1930s. Not only do Rahn's association both with Ernst Schafer and Tibet and Williamson's with the London based Bönpo priests link with Sale's story, but his account also strengthens the case for a likely operational connection between Rahn and British Intelligence, especially in the esoteric research fields of remote viewing, ESP and other like phenomena.

Williamson's abiding passion was witchcraft, practised in an atmosphere of far-right conservatism bordering upon anti-semitic, fascist philosophy. His views were not restricted to himself. By his account, many fellow British Intelligence officers shared similar extreme sentiments. Himmler admired the English upper classes and promoted Anglo-German friendship. He contacted pro-German elements in England and liked to discuss their problems with them. Himmler had begun cultivating English connections earlier through the Christian evangelical movement, the Oxford Group, founded in the late 1920s by American Frank Buchman and which morphed into Moral Rearmament in 1938. It is little wonder Himmler held Buchman in high regard, seeing that the fawning American made public statements of support for Nazism such as in the 1936 interview when he said: "I thank heaven for a man like Adolf Hitler, who built a front line of defense against the anti-Christ of Communism..," a remark Buchman quickly came to regret. Rudolf Hess was also a member of Buchman's group.

Williamson expressed strong support for eugenics. In his own words, he supported the cleansing of "riff-raff," which, he said, were the dullards of society and even more of a problem for developed countries. Shockingly, he referred to them in our discussion as semen.

Jim Keith, editor of a collection of articles under the title *Secret and Suppressed,*[3] published an account by an anonymous Vatican priest which highlights the key role alleged to have been played in European history by an ancient Semite order of sorcerers which, according to the article, has worked in alliance with Teutonic cults of similar occult persuasion since around A.D. 900 and which derives its power from human sacrifice.

The priest's account claims that the alliance has been the secret power cartel behind major affairs in the western world for two thousand years. This group has marked correspondences with the Semitic sorcerer elite opposed to Landig's Thuleans in *Götzen gegen Thule*.[4] Throughout its history, the priest states, the clique has been composed geographically of northern and southern European factions whose respective policies and aims have often been in conflict. The unifying force between them, said the priest, has been their practice of mass eugenics achieved through human sacrific and cannibalism (an example, he claims, being the systematic introduction of bubonic plague into Southern Europe in 1348), from which abominations the

---

[3] Feral House, 1993

[4] Hanover: Volkstum-Verlag, 1971

clique derives its occult power. The Jesuits, representing Rome and the southern faction, are said to have been instrumental in furthering the order's objectives since the time of Martin Luther's Reformation activities and the subsequent nuisances caused in the south by northern infiltrators.

The priest goes on to say that in 1897 the Teutonic-Semite alliance convened a conference in Basle to plan the blueprint for the elimination of European Jewry. To achieve the clique's aim of mass sacrifice required a world totalitarian government. To this end, so the account continues, the First World War was instigated but their plans were thwarted by the activities of the British Fascist movement, the Bolshevik uprising in Russia, and by the intervention of the United States sub-clique in which the Theosophical and Golden Dawn Societies were principle protagonists. The priest's account concludes by claiming that after this period of internecine disorder within the clique all the various sub-factions became united in their determination to enact the Final Solution and to indulge in mass slaughter of "useless" races to appease their satanic deities. By 1933 regular ritual sacrifice of Jews had been commenced in the Nazi camps, which proliferated in number and in prisoner stock as the thirties progressed.

If any of this remarkable, grisly and frankly astonishing account is true did Otto Rahn become aware of the terrible truth during his brief spells of duty at Dachau and Buchenwald? Could knowledge as mind wrenching as this have been the final straw that drove him to breakdown and flight? Jean-Michel Angebert state in their Introduction to *The Occult and the Third Reich*: "Those who induced Germany to embrace the swastika are not dead. They are still among us, just as they have been in every era, and doubtless will continue to be until the Apocalypse…what they are now trying to do is to revive the myth by other means." Whatever the truth of the priest's claim, it offers considerable food for thought in providing a hideous occult and historical perspective to the emergence of legalised euthenasia practice in Europe.

If we have been pushed headlong into all the nightmare aspects of the eugenics issue by the cold reminiscences of a WW2 MI6 agent who is likely to have known Otto Rahn, then this can only provoke many more questions. Recall that Rahn in the latter months of his life was desperate to "see the boss." He had "seen things." His mind was tipping over in the sight of unnamed horrors. We can only shudder to visualise the nature of the abominations witnessed by the young explorer. Williamson's sudden appearance in 1995 and his ensuing testimony raises the obvious but inevitable debate about the extent to which Otto Rahn's life was influenced by or, more relevantly, was itself an influencing force upon other figures who made a contribution to the political foundations of post-WW2 Europe, especially in the rapid development of the international fascist movement and the forces opposed to it. In the next chapter we will examine this theme in detail.

Chapter FIFTEEN

"We slew the wrong pig"

A figure, probably Otto Rahn's research companion, Edmond Abatut, looking at a pentagram in the caves of Ornolac (Archives Stock)

Such is the remark attributed to Winston Churchill after the Second World War. Whether the words are apocryphal or not they illustrate the Allies' profound fear about the threat posed by communism. What is of especial interest to our Rahn study is the extent to which this sentiment brought together in common purpose during and after the war men who, on the surface, were implacable enemies but who, in truth, were united in a pathological hatred of Russia and its ambitions. Many of them knew Rahn, indeed ordered and directed his day-to-day actions throughout the thirties and possibly earlier. Their actions, therefore, inform and influence Rahn's directly and significantly.

What is all the more extraordinary about these unlikely alliances is the extent to which Churchill was regarded by many in Britain, America and Germany as an enemy of peace: "The British Foreign Minister in 1939, Lord Halifax, reluctantly became the focus for peace overtures for those who were disenchanted with Churchill, who was seen by powerful financier and industrialist factions as an impediment to peace."[1]

Two of the names from within the ranks of the upper echelons of the Nazi regime that come up again and again in this context of strange bedfellows are Heinrich Himmler and his close subordinate Karl Wolff, both men exerting a very close control over Otto Rahn's actions up to spring 1939 (and even beyond).

Before we look at these two men and their secret agendas in detail we shall profit by reviewing briefly the early years of Nazism and the invaluable support given it by the Russian aristocracy and others who would form the backbone of the twentieth century rise of international fascism. Equally profitably, we shall look at those who worked behind the scenes to oppose Hitler.

In the mêlée of these depictions we will encounter personalities who, by virtue of their associations with characters whom we have linked already to Otto Rahn, will provide us with more choices in building a clearer picture of a post-suicide survival scenario. I am indebted to Jonothon Boulter for his work in gathering a substantial part of these facts.

In response to the growth of Communism in Germany (the Spartakus League), the authorities established unofficial groups of ex-servicemen called Freikorps and in March 1920 the volunteer troops of the Freikorps Erhardt Brigade marched into Berlin and installed an east-Prussian leader, Wolfgang Kapp.

The Freikorps included Ignatz Timotheus Trebitsch-Lincoln, a Jewish Hungarian adventurer who allied himself with the Munich members of the burgeoning Thule group. Gabriele Kruger (*The Ehrhardt Brigade*, Hamburg 1971) wrote that Trebitsch-Lincoln's role within Thule circles was to make the acquaintances necessary to succeed in procuring weapons for the ill-fated Hitler putsch. Author Hennecke Kardel offers the claim that Trebitsch-Lincoln purchased the *Volkischer Beobachters* newspaper in 1920 as a means of providing a powerful channel of support for Hitler's campaign for power.

After the putsch Trebitsch-Lincoln fled to China where he studied Buddhism and became adviser to the Chinese branch of a

[1] Thomas ibid

Tibetan secret society in contact with the mysterious Order of the Green Dragon. In 1929 Trebitsch-Lincoln moved back to Europe and in 1932, calling himself Djordi Djen, established a monastery in Berlin. He is reputed to have subsequently introduced Hitler to the Tibetan members of the Society of Green Men and their leader, the Man with the Green Gloves. This is the person said to have had the Keys to Agartha. The intermediaries for these introductions to Hitler were the Russian émigré circles of early Nazism, which had included members of the Green Dragon Society in Moscow. Author E.R Carmin[2] goes so far as to claim that Trebitsch-Lincoln *was* the Man with the Green Gloves.

The Ehrhardt Brigade wore the swastika on their helmets and on their vehicles as they marched and sang their way to Berlin. Although the Thule Society used the swastika as a form of rune in their symbology it was the Ehrhardt form, combined with the black, red and white of the Prussian flag, that became the synthesis organised into a new form by the early Nazis using the black swastika in a white circle on a red background. This was a distinctly Prussian design and derivation (Bavaria had its own flag and Germany as a whole did not have a national flag of its own). After the Kapp putsch top right wing Russian émigrés took refuge in Bavaria.

The Russians gave the Protocols of Zion to the Nazis and identified Bolshevism with Jews. In July 1920 a Warsaw newspaper accused the French occultist Papus of fabricating the Protocols with the aim of discrediting Martinist Master Phillipe. Martinism was a major force in the European occult underground from 1890 to the 1920s. Baron Ungem von Sternberg wrote a declaration of war to the West called No 13, which included a quote from Book of Daniel about the coming of Mekal the great Prince.[3] The Russian Court, including Nilus, saw Martinism as part of a Jewish plot. As we have seen earlier, Papus was the most successful populariser of occultism in Paris. His friends in Paris, Joséphin Péladan among them, thought that Papus' Martinist activities were a deliberate meddling in European politics. According to Victor-Émile Michelet most Balkan princes were Martinists.

At the time of forging the Protocols in 1896 Papus enjoyed cordial relations with notorious anti-Semite Gaston Méry. The Société

---

[2] *"Guru Hitler", Die Geburt des Nationalsozialismus aus dem Geiste von Mystik und Magie*, Zurich 1985

[3] Glinka, Yuliana. *Secrets of the Jews* (according to James Webb, author of *The Occult Underground*, Glinka, daughter of a Russian diplomat and a devotee of Madame Blavatsky, founder of the Theosophical Society, was probably the first person to introuduce the Protocols of Zion forgeries into Russia).

des Sciences Psychiques had appointed a committee to investigate Méry's protégée, the seeress Henriette Couedon, whose prophecies included the claim that someone was trying to poison the Tsaravich and that the Jews were to make a move for power. Papus spoke for Couedon at the hearing.

A collaborator with Papus was Jean Correre who began his political life as an anarchist Bohemian associated with the Symbolists. A note discovered among Papus' papers apportioned responsibility to Papus for the Protocol materials and to Correre for drafting them. Correre's wife sold the articles to the *Echo de Paris*.

The Russians donated major funds to the early Nazi party and built up the Nazi newspaper *Volkischer Beobachter*, using it as a mouthpiece for White Russian propaganda. The Ehrhardt Brigade members who had had to flee to Berlin became members of the early Nazi party. The Russian émigrés linked to the Brigade and who organised the Kapp Putsch brought the Protocols into the Nazi orbit, which included Alfred Rosenberg, a Baltic German who had lived in Russia. Rosenberg understood Bolshevism and was regarded by the Nazi leadership as a link between the White Russian émigrés and the Nazis. The anti-Bolshevik ideas instilled into Rosenberg were inherited from the Black Hundreds (an anti-Semite, anti-Bolshevik monarchist group) who had lost Russia in both the revolutions of 1905 and 1917.

Otto Rahn and his mother in the garden of Hôtel-Restaurant des Marronniers

Of all the claimants to the Romanov throne, Grand Duke Kirill, first cousin to Nicholas I, maintained the closest links with the Nazi Party and was one of its biggest sources of funds. Kirill declared himself Czar in August 1922.

A White Russian source claimed that Hitler hid in the Munich house of Kirill's aide-de-camp General Vasily Biskupsky, a friend of General Ludendorff who led the most anti-Semitic wing of the exiled White Russians. In 1939 Biskupsky told a Nazi official that Kirill had given Ludendorff half a million gold marks between 1922 and 1933 for

German-Russian national matters.

Eventually the Russian influence in pre-WW2 Germany faded due to the efforts of Rosenberg to foster anti-Russian attitudes. Some Russians who were part-German were absorbed into the Nazi party but pure Russians could not stomach the anti-slav ideas and some went over to the Soviet ideal, seeing it as a preserver of Russian tradition rather than as a destroyer and as a way to advance their Eurasian empire ambitions.

Others became National Bolsheviks and with other circles worked against Hitler in the Resistance. Key members of this group included Ernst Niekish, Ernst Jünger and Friedrich Hielscher, the latter leading a resistance cell within the Ahnenerbe. The early Ahnenerbe group believed in a wide embracing concept of Aryanism and was pro-Russian and pro-Islamic.

The principle groups within the German Resistance to Hitler were former National Socialists. They became National Bolsheviks and also called themselves National Revolutionaries. These resistance cells worked also with Van Stauffenberg in the Kreisau Circle and with Van Moltke who looked to the model of the pan-European, pro-Islamic Hohenstauffen Dynasty whose courtiers had included members of the Van Stauffenberg dynasty. The Kreisau Circle had previously existed in small groups made up of Prussian officers including members of the SS and the Ahnenerbe. These groups included the Circle Hielscher organised by Friedrich Hielscher, a name that crops up again and again in efforts to identify who really steered the reins of occult power in the Third Reich.

Friedrich Hielscher, a member of the "left of the right" wing of the Conservative Revolution, was an expert in many occult and historical fields and always worked behind the scenes. A friend of philosopher Martin Buber, Hielscher never joined the Nazi party and was always talked about in hushed tones. Heinrich Himmler and Wolfram Sievers held him in awe. After Hielscher was jailed by the Gestapo in September 1944 he later said he was only saved from a most unpleasant fate by Sievers' intervention.

Hielscher appeared in court to offer testimony on behalf of Sievers at Nuremburg, explaining that the accused was really a member of Gruppe Hielscher, the anti-Hitler resistance network, and that Sievers had entered the Ahnenerbe in that capacity. When Sievers was found guilty Hielscher conducted a rite for the condemned man called the L'Air Épais (Ceremony of the Stifling Air). Sievers then went to the gallows. Considering the weight of accumulated evidence that Otto

Rahn was allied against the Hitler factions, it is not beyond the limits of credibility that he was associated with Gruppe Hielscher.

Nigel Pennick[4] said that Hielscher had major connections with German occultism through his association with Swedish explorer and Tibet expert Sven Hedin who was also a friend of Karl Haushofer. Hedin brought a good deal of Tibetan occultism into the Nazi sphere, having lived in Tibet for many years. Rudolf Hess is supposed to have been carrying a phial given to him by Sven Hedin on his flight to Scotland.

In connection with our Rahn review, Hielscher was associated with Harro Schulze-Boysen, top Red Orchestra conspirator executed by the Gestapo in December 1942. Both men advocated close ties between Germany and Soviet Union. Schulze-Boysen ("Schu-Boy" to his friends), regarded as a "drawing room Communist" by many of his co-conspirators, provides another possible link with Otto Rahn and the Berlin film industry. Harro and his socialite wife used to mix regularly with the German movie cognoscenti in and around Grunewald, a focal point for the film business and, coincidentally, where Rahn and his superior Weisthor used to meet at the old colonel's home to discuss Rahn's work and findings for the SS.

Hielscher's decentralist return to regionalism attracted support from the elements of the "New Right." One of the movement's key supporters was Otto Abetz, whom we have already met in passing in looking at Christian Bernadac's Otto Rahn-Rudolf Rahn theory.

Abetz did not become a Party member until 1937. His most interesting French connection was an organisation called Ordre Nouveau (ON). In August 1931 ON helped sponsor a youth meeting in the Ardennes and Abetz, co-organiser, joined with future Hitler Youth leader Baldur von Schivach to create Reichsbanner, a group that sought to find a third way between Communism and Nazism. Abetz played a key role in developing links between Germany and France as the French expert for Joachim von Ribbentrop's private intelligence service inside the German Foreign Ministry. Ribbentrop also subscribed to ON's journal. He attended the February 1932 Franco-German Youth Congress at Frankfurt am Main with none other than Harro Schulze-Boysen.

Abetz employed Gerhard Heller on his propaganda staff. Heller's mentor was Jean Paulhan, a Resistance member and lover of Dominique Aury (pen-name Pauline Reage), author of the famous sadomasochistic work *The Story of O,* which started out as a sixty-page

---

[4] Pennick, Nigel. *Hitler's Secret Sciences.* Suffolk: Neville Spearman, 1981

love letter from Aury to Paulhan. Paulhan had a longstanding fascination with secret societies and in the 1930s became involved with the College of Sociology organised by French theorist of eroticism Georges Bataille. The College was fascinated with groups like the Assassins, Templars, Jesuits and Freemasonry. The College and Bataille's "Acéphale" group became enamoured by human sacrifices and Bataille even began planning his own religion based upon human sacrifice to create a neo-pagan society organised around sacrificial death rituals. According to James Miller in his book *The Passion of Michel Foucault*, Bataille's group even targeted a specific individual but never carried it out. We know that Rahn was terrified of something. It is not beyond the pale of possibility that he blundered into these very worst kinds of occult circles.

In the alternate version of *The Story of O*, O asks permission to kill herself as an act of ultimate offering.

Dusty Sklar said in *Nazis and the Occult*[5] that Scott Littleton, professor of anthropology at Occidental College, California, told her of original Nazi depositions taken at Nuremberg of the periodic sacrifice of a fine Aryan specimen of an SS man, whose severed head was used as an oracular medium for communication with Secret Masters in the Caucasus. These Masters were believed to be not earthly and were looked to for guidance.

In 1943 Julius Evola, whom we recall was greatly admired by Otto Rahn, undertook a project in Vienna, scouring arcane and occult texts and rare book collections. The SD bureau that provided him with these documents was Amt VII, an obscure branch that served as a Reichssicherheitshauptamt (Reich Security Main Office—RSHA) research library. With this material Evola translated certain esoteric texts for a book called *Historie Secrète des Sociétés Secrètes*, a work that never appeared because Evola claimed that all of his manuscripts were seized by the Russians. In a 1938 SS report it was stated that Evola was at work on "efforts to establish a secret international order."

Is it beyond the bounds of consideration to put Julius and Otto together on the same workbench, between them building the structure of a new mystical edifice, a collaboration which would go some way towards vindicating Christian Bernadac, who has been severely criticised for suggesting that Rahn was immersed in just such covert but grandiose activities after 1939?

According to Kevin Coogan,[6] Evola's work in Vienna was in all

[5]Sklar ibid
[6] Coogan ibid

certainty involved with this task to create a new kind of Knights Templar to function beneath the surface of mainstream European political and social levels. Additionally, while in Vienna Evola performed vital liaison services for the SS as Nazi Germany sought to recruit a European army for the defence of the Continent against the Soviet Union and the United States.

Well before the end of WW2 the financial and intelligence networks of the Third Reich were hard at work preparing underground networks to survive the coming defeat and Allied occupation. Evola had been fascinated by knightly orders as expressions of the Kshatriya caste of Hindu warrior aristocrats. Evola saw in the formal structure of the SS the precursor to a new Ordenstaat, a State ruled by an Order, an Invisible College. This would be a vessel for those "Hermetic" elements of the Conservative Revolution, the old ruling class, and the new Nazi elite not entirely beholden to the political, cultural and religious "Guelf" wing of the European aristocracy, which remained loyal to the ruling Christian status quo. Evola's task was to help create the inner organisational and ritual structure for the Grand Masters of a secret Shamballah whose financial nerve centre was carefully hidden away in Swiss bank accounts.

Many of the principle actors who strode the Nazi stage, both for and against Hitler, were directly associated with the life and work of Otto Rahn. We have established that these personalities wrought influence and power whose consequences reached way beyond their immediate office or community of interest. Men of cruelty vied with men of compassion to shape a new Europe and, ultimately, a new world order in the image of their respective beliefs.

From a study of his writings, supplemented by a reflection upon the memories and opinions of his friend Gabriele Winckler, I believe that Rahn was a man of compassion. In ways we cannot yet fully appreciate Rahn contributed to the efforts of a brave minority to throw open the lid of the Ark to unleash the Holy Fire upon Hitler and the invisible men of power who backed him.

Chapter SIXTEEN

Himmler, Wolff and Canaris

It does not require a "Eureka" moment of illumination to review the available facts and to observe that the men who most clearly defined and directed Otto Rahn's working life throughout the latter years of his life: Reichsführer SS Heinrich Himmler and General Karl Wolff, also played key roles in the clandestine intitiatives to secure (self-serving) post-WW2 accommodations with the allies. A third personality, Admiral Wilhelm Canaris, stands stage left in this scenario but merits inclusion because of the emergence of his name in the less obvious membership of the Nazi cadre that is believed to have played a pivotal role in determining Rahn's destiny in a post-suicide survival scenario.

In Himmler's case we are indebted to Hugh Thomas[1] for unearthing many new facts about Himmler's strenuous behind-the-scenes efforts to secure from the earliest days of the war a peace deal and a First Minister status in a post-war Germany.

As we have noted, Himmler admired the English upper classes and his love affair with things British did not dissolve once he had risen to Reichsführer status. His empathy with England no doubt encouraged the peace overtures he orchestrated *sub rosa* from 1939 onwards. Himmler never communicated directly with the allies in handling these initiatives but sought intermediaries. Among the go-betweens willing to serve as key active agents were a number of well-connected bankers, including Swede Baron Knut Bonde. Himmler had considerable financial interests in Sweden, including strong links to the Bofors armaments family. As we shall see, Bofors were implicated in shadowy post-war share activities concerning the giant German company, Bosch. Among Himmler's principle stockholdings Bosch shares featured prominently.

John Foster Dulles, U.S. Secretary of State, urged Roosevelt to take German peace proposals seriously precisely because they originated from Himmler and certain Wehrmacht generals, and not from German resistance groups. Quite by coincidence Dulles served as

[1] Thomas ibid

attorney to the holding company that owned American Bosch. As Hugh Thomas has pointed out, this is just one example of the shady alliances of self-interest that existed throughout the war and which allowed Nazi leaders to influence Allied policy at the highest levels.

Negotiations were channelled through Special Operations Executive (SOE) agent Peter Tennant who met with Dr. Walter Jacobson, a friend of Leipzig Mayor Carol Gordeler, who represented Himmler's financial interests in Sweden. Lord Vansittart, chief diplomatic adviser to the British Government, gave hesitant approval to the Tennant/Jacobson negotiations. Subsequently, Michael Balfour of the Ministry of Information made preparations to see Helmut von Moltke, leader of the Kreisau Circle resistance group. Churchill heard about this in advance and acted swiftly, but with great difficulty, to put a stop to the meeting. The British understood from Swedish intelligence sources that the Moltke-Gordeler group was backed by Himmler.

It is interesting to note in relation to our study of Scotland's probable place in a post-1939 context for Otto Rahn (Chapter 27 onwards) that one member of the British peace faction was Baron Knut Bonde, a Swede who married a Scotswoman and who had a home and business in Scotland. Knut Bonde represented Göring. His grandson, Baron St. Clair Bonde, has stated that his grandfather was instrumental in making the arrangements for Hess's flight.

Cecil Williamson told me that he remembered a man named Han or Hahn in the context of our discussion on his visit to the Berlin film studios in 1935. He may also have been thinking of Dr. Kurt Hahn (1886-1974), a German Jew, educationalist and founder of Gordonstoun, a school in Scotland favoured by the Royal Family and attended by Karl Haushofer's grandson. Hahn was co-author with the Duke of Hamilton of a letter written to The Times in October 1939 about the escalating conflict with Germany. The letter sends a signal to Germany that it is looking forward to making peace with "honourable men." Hahn also wrote a report for Churchill about Hess' arrival and a copy of the report was given to the King by Hamilton.

Sir Charles Hambro, a peace faction member, was also connected with both Allen and John Foster Dulles through the international banking house of Schroder. On 27th November 1940 a highly secret meeting was held in San Francisco. Present were William Wiseman, representing the American Kuhn Loeb Bank, Captain Fritz Wiedemann representing I.G. Farben, and Princess Stefanie von Hohenlohe-Waldenburg, a very close friend of Himmler and a regular covert visitor to Sir Alexander Cadogan, Foreign Office adviser to

Churchill. The trio agreed that Himmler, a "monarchist," was the practical choice to succeed Hitler. Wiedemann also met with other peace supporters in the U.S. such as Herr Volkers who had previously worked for Canaris and subsequently married into the Bofors family. The Bofors were later heavily involved in the post-war cloaking of Bosch shares.

Von Hohenlohe, born plain Stephanie Richter in Vienna in 1891, acquired her title by marriage to a member of the Austrian nobility. In 1933 she met Hitler who referred to her thereafter as "my dear Princess" and who allowed her to stroke his hair. To the FBI she was a deadly spy and "worse than 10,000 men," described in their files as "extremely intelligent, dangerous and cunning" and capable of resorting to any means to get her way. Having inveigled herself into the "Cliveden set," the group centred round Nancy Astor and the future King Edward VIII, von Hohenlohe was able to keep the Nazis informed of what was happening in the political landscape of Britain. Hitler used her to plant stories favourable to the Third Reich in the Daily Mail, including passing off Nazi atrocities as isolated acts of vengeance, via Viscount Rothermere who became a lover of the Princess in 1925. Subsequently, Rothermere and Hitler met in Berlin in December 1934. Hitler rewarded von Hohenlohe with a golden swastika and a castle in Austria, overlooking the fact that she was half-Jewish. Considering her strong attachment to Hitler and his circle, the years in which she forged these alliances in Berlin, and her support for Himmler as successor to the Führer, it is entirely feasible that von Hohenlohe came into contact with Otto Rahn.

Bank of England Governor Montague Norman and his Deputy Cyril Tiarks made an alliance with Lord Halifax in which their chief objective was to achieve the removal of both Churchill and Hitler, both regarded as obstacles to peace and, jointly, as a threat to the financial stability of rich and powerful European dynasties.

In March 1941 General Aranda of Spain told British Military Attaché Colonel Torr that Himmler wanted Hitler assassinated followed by a speedy settlement to finish the war. Pearl Harbour and America's entry into the war helped Churchill to divert allied attention away from what he believed were ill-considered peace moves but negotiations continued. These culminated in July 1943 when Allen Dulles, U.S. Special Representative for Berne (his Office of Strategic Services cover) met with Himmler's agent Count Max von Hohenlohe-Langenburg and a Nazi Sicherheitsdienst officer named Bauer. Dulles' OSS assistant, Gero Schulz von Gavernitz, was a supporter of the

Kreisau Circle.

Dulles' messages to England in 1943 reported that the German resistance still placed a good deal of emphasis on Germany having a free hand to expand towards the East to quash all vestiges of Bolshevism, noting paradoxically that in this regard the objectives of the SS and of the resistance were effectively the same.

The pressure from the Americans to strike a settlement as a means to dealing Bolshevism a deathblow was enormous. Churchill reacted by proposing stringent conditions: Hitler to be put under house arrest at Berchtesgaden, and a temporary government to be put in place comprising a Council of Twelve in Germany established under Himmler. Only then, Churchill insisted, could negotiations commence. Nothing came of these intitiatives.

Alarmed by Soviet military successes in 1944, the Americans hatched a plan to kidnap Hitler (alive to expose the man and not the myth). A consortium of secret services led by the Vatican planned the abduction in intricate detail. A special SS unit would carry out the kidnap and whisk Hitler off to the Mediterranean coast near Valencia from whence U.S. military would take him to America. Plans were dropped when mission-planning papers were sold to the British Secret Service.

At a meeting of top industrialists and military leaders at the Hotel Maison Rouge, Strasbourg, 10th August 1944, the delegates confirmed that Himmler was vigorously seeking to control one hundred percent of Germany's finances post-war via a process of transferring all the funds outside Germany to fund the economic basis for a Fourth Reich. So horrified was the British Government to learn of the vast extent of Himmler's plans that he was the only Nazi leader subjected to the Special Operations Executive (SOE) German Directorate's "analysis"; that is, picked out for assassination.

In December 1944 the British Secret Intelligence Service (SIS) reported their view that Himmler was "a thousand times worse than Ivan the Terrible—the most frightful monster that ever lived on earth." After all, this was said about the man who, before an audience of the top echelon of the Nazi leadership at Posen in October 1943, said of the extermination of the Jews that the SS had: "persevered, when 500 here or 1,000 there…this is a glorious chapter in our history that was never written and never will be written." Karl Wolff said under questioning at Nuremberg that Himmler decided "to relieve the burdens…from the shoulders of the new messiah Adolf Hitler. The Fuhrer was to remain free from sin." Incredulously, Wolff appeared to be saying that the

Holocaust was a misunderstanding between Himmler and Hitler.

Himmler amassed a great deal of personal wealth. One contributor, a member of the "Circle of Friends of Himmler," was Kurt Schroder of the Schroder Finance House. He set up a special account in the Stern Bank and was rewarded for his generosity with promotion to SS-Brigadeführer. Schroder was part of an unholy alliance with Allen Dulles who sat on Schroder's board. Between them the pair created an impenetrable web of companies to siphon off illicit SS assets. Dulles was generally regarded by the allies as an insurmountable obstacle to any effective challenge to Himmler and his plans.

Adolf Eichmann, subsequent to his abduction by Israeli intelligence, gave his testimony in 1961 about Nazis who had escaped justice. Included in the entry on page 4 of 4 of the list under the heading Anomolous is the comment: "*Reichsführer Heinrich Himmler, alive Germany? c, Lorenz.*" The "Lorenz" could have either been Obergruppenführer Werner Lorenz, the man in charge of resettlement of German forces in the Baltic Sea, a very useful man for someone looking for a hiding place, or Himmler's secretary Erika Lorenz. Even in 1942 when Himmler's appointments diary was stuffed full of key meetings he used to spend at least two hours with Erika in their "private chat" meetings. It could also have been a reference to the company AG Lorenz, the most important German subsidiary abroad.

SS-Obergruppenführer Otto Ohlendorf said while in custody in May 1945 that Himmler had gone to Arolsen in North Germany to seek refuge with Prince Waldeck. There are synchronicitous elements in this account that are allegorical both with an extreme low point in Rahn's life, the drunken Arolsen episode, and with the highlight, his Pyrenean searches symbolised by the stone bench at Waldeck fashioned from Montségur stone. This is a stretch of coincidence, which invites the consideration that if Otto Rahn's superior might have been resourceful enough to have survived the hangman then why might Rahn have not been as equally enterprising in organising his own escape?

Frau Winckler told me that after Rahn's 1939 suicide Himmler once told a visitor to his office that Rahn had "cleaned his plate." What might Himmler have meant by that curious remark? It does not need a flying leap of tortuous logic to interpret it in the context that Rahn had owed a debt or favour and had repaid it. It certainly does not automatically smack of a confirmation that Rahn had killed himself.

We saw in Chapter 3 that during his Pyrenean explorations Otto Rahn was accompanied by a gang of minders, chief among whom was

Nat Wolff, also known as Karl. Taking all the facts together, we concluded that Christian Bernadac may be right; that it is plausible that this person was none other than Karl Wolff, the most senior officer between Rahn and Himmler. Wolff was far from being a subordinate soldier on the sidelines of Nazi intrigue and he played a key liaison role in conducting high-level secret wartime machinations between Germany and the allies.

For example, we have the affidavit testimony of Wolff in which he told Father Paul Molinari about Hitler's 1943 plot to kidnap Pius XII. In September of that year Hitler discussed with Wolff his plan to occupy the Vatican and to move Pacelli to Liechtenstein. The Führer told Wolff never to disclose these plans to anyone, except to Himmler who "was aware of everything." Hitler pressed Wolff to come up with a plan to occupy the Vatican, seize its treasures and archives, and spirit them all away by December 1943. The plan called for soldiers of the SS Florian Geyer Cavalry, disguised in Italian uniforms, to invade the Vatican shielded by night, kill all members of the curia, and take the pope prisoner. Then troops of the Hermann Goering Panzer Division would pour into the Vatican to "rescue" the pontiff and kill the disguised SS men as if they were Italian assassins rather than SS compatriots, thereby leaving no witnesses. Wolff convinced Hitler not to proceed because of the likely ferocity of the backlash from the German Catholic population. Ironically, had the mission gone ahead Gabriele Winckler's husband, according to his wife a soldier in the Florian Geyer division, would in all likelihood have taken part in it. The papers regarding Wolff's testimony are held in the archives in the keeping of the Jesuits responsible for the case of the beatification of Eugenio Pacelli.[2]

There is more to this story. In July 1991 Roman Catholic monthly magazine, *30 Giorni*, dug into its archives and reported the account of Hitler's plan to take over the Vatican and to seize Pope Pius XII and his cardinals. In the same month Italian newspaper *Il Tempo* quoted from minutes of a meeting of the Nazi high command in which Hitler supposedly talked about wanting to enter the Vatican "packing up that whole whoring rabble." The *30 Giorni* article based its conclusions in large part on statements made by Rudolf Rahn in a letter he wrote in the 1970s to Reverend Robert Graham, an American Jesuit scholar researching the kidnap plot. Rahn's letter described the plot and attempts by him and other senior officials to head it off. Rahn told Graham: "We agreed that carrying out such a plan would have had

---

[2] ibid

tremendous consequences and that it had to be blocked at all costs." Rahn went on to say that he and others had finally succeeded in persuading the Nazi leader that storming the Vatican would be a mistake. As a result, the article reported, Rahn was instructed to draft a note stating that it was Hitler's wish that "nothing whatever be undertaken against the person of the Pope, the integrity of his entourage and the inviolability of Vatican institutions." It is an increasingly fascinating exercise to discover just how many times Rudolf Rahn plays more than a walk-on part in the circumstances surrounding high-level Nazi intrigue orchestrated by senior figures close to Otto Rahn.

Julis Evola once wrote a poem about "black monks who will burn the city" and who "when the time is full...will guide the forces of the resurrection." In Vienna Evola helped to conjure a new Order of black monks. At the same time the black monks of the SS were desperately attempting to reach an accommodation with future CIA head Alan Dulles to agree the foundations for a new Order of Knights Templar, a caste of warrior aristocrats that would flourish long after the Führerbunker went up in flames. However, with the war coming to a rapid end the Order lacked the time to implement its plans. With support from the top RSHA leadership a deception game was initiated with both American intelligence and with the Vatican. Himmler's top men, principally SS General Karl Wolff, became converts to a "kinder, gentler" SS eager to establish friendly relations with the Americans and with the Holy See.

In September 1943 Wolff was appointed German military governor of northern Italy and plenipotentiary to Mussolini, outranked only by Himmler in this role. With Hitler's knowledge and support[3] Wolff began negotiations with Alan Dulles about ending the war in talks codenamed Operation Sunrise by the OSS. One of Wolff's top men in the talks was SS Colonel Eugen Dollman, the SS agent who was Evola's friend inside the German embassy in Rome. Wolff and Dulles knew that the American government was locked into a policy of unconditional surrender; what was really at stake was the future of Europe from the day after surrender. Wolff used Operation Sunrise to hammer out a private understanding with elements of the American elite represented by Dulles.

Pius XII received Karl Wolff in private audience in May 1944, the first and last occasion when the Pope met with a leading SS officer. Wolff wrote in his journal that during the meeting the Pope told him:

[3] Von Lang, Jochen. *Top Nazi SS General Karl Wolff—The Man Between Hitler and Himmler*. New York: Enigma Books, 2005

"How much misfortune could have been avoided had God led you to me earlier." At the end of the meeting Pius was heard to say cryptically: "You are doing something difficult, General Wolff!"[4] One may only speculate on what prompted the Pontiff to make these surprising and candid remarks—Wolff was evidently playing a risky game.

In this regard Jochen Von Lang records that while in Italy Wolff took a huge personal risk in smuggling a young Czech radio operator, Hradecky, into his HQ at the palace of the Counts of Pistoia in Bozen so that he could keep in secret contact with the allies through neutral Switzerland.

In 1945 Wolff and his Germany army forces surrendered to the Allies in Italy six days before the agreed general ceasefire. Wolff's actions effectively shortened the war, saving the lives of those who would have been killed in action had it gone on for those extra six days.

Wolff was never tried by the Americans at Nuremberg. In 1948 he was handed over to the British who treated him very severely. When brought before the British court he was sentenced to four years imprisonment but released because he had already served equivalent time in incarceration since the end of the war.

In September 1964 Wolff was sentenced by a court in Munich to fifteen years imprisonment for arranging railway cars to transport 300,000 Jews from Warsaw to the gas chambers at Treblinka. Five and a half years later he was released on grounds of ill-health. Wolff died in 1984.

Some years ago I received a report from a confidential source that Otto Rahn was linked with Admiral Wilhelm Canaris, the head of the German secret service: the Abwehr. I would have thought no more about the suggestion but Albert Rausch's letter to Werner Bock, in which he writes that there were those among Himmler's innermost cadre who were not what they seemed and who were, in reality, working for both the internal and external Nazi intelligence services, brought fresh and urgent focus to the consideration. Rausch's letter indicated that one of the informants was a person who, before dying like a hunted animal of the "white starvation" in the mountains (an unmistakeable reference to Rahn and his Cathar affiliations as Hans-Jürgen Lange has stated) saved the lives of fifteen young Jews. This clear reference to Rahn as a member of a group of anti-Nazi informers within and around Himmler's office not only goes some way to substantiating an alleged Rahn-Canaris association, but also contributes

[4] ibid

to the belief in some research quarters that within the heart of the Nazi regime there indeed existed a coterie of brave individuals who were truly not what they seemed.

Ian Colvin's 1951 book *Chief of Intelligence* named Canaris as a British Agent. In his introduction to André Brissaud's 1972 book *Canaris*, Colvin adds that in 1942 Major-General Sir Stuart Menzies, wartime Head of MI6, offered him the opportunity to meet Canaris after Colvin had explained his theory that the Abwehr Chief was working against Hitler to shorten the war. Menzies confided that he knew "what was going on his (Canaris') mind," thus demonstrating the powerful entente between Canaris and Britain. Roosevelt's Casablanca declaration in January 1943 about unconditional surrender ensured the meeting could not go ahead.

Canaris despised Himmler (as he did all of Hitlerism) and exerted a hold over the Reichsführer SS such that Himmler refrained from alerting Hitler even when Schellenberg handed him a fat file on Canaris' treasonable activities. When Arthur Nebe, Chief of Police, asked Canaris why Himmler was so afraid of him Canaris just smiled. No one knew until recently what information Canaris had that could seriously have compromised Himmler. Hugh Thomas has now provided a probable explanation.

As we have seen, Thomas' painstaking research, conducted over a twenty-five year period, indicates that between 1939 and 1945 Himmler attempted to secure peace with the allies and to put himself at the head of a post-war government supported by a powerful alliance of financiers and industrialists. Himmler never entered into direct negotiations personally but was represented by bankers and lawyers. The Reichsführer SS also exploited the activities of other, less effective, resistance groups as and when it suited him.

Many senior British figures, including the Royal Family, were open to these overtures because of the overriding need to protect the capitalist system by keeping Stalin at bay and, in parallel, to see an early end to war to avoid the terrifying prospect of having to borrow huge sums of U.S. money to fund a long fight. Churchill held different views, however, and was seen by many in British and American circles as being a barrier to peace. The subject of German peace overtures is far too wide to cover in any detail. However, the fact that Thomas has now disclosed that Himmler, Otto Rahn's boss, was at the forefront of clandestine peace efforts and, moreover, that the man believed to be Himmler arrested by the British in 1945 may actually have been Heinrich Hitzinger, a rural policeman and Himmler's double, conjures some far-reaching questions.

Email postings in January and March 1997 from a correspondent named "Siriuss" claimed that the Reich sent many valuable artefacts out of Europe to U.S. sympathisers. These postings serve as a reminder of a rumour that an unusual item was removed from Germany and taken to the U.S. before the outbreak of the war. The emails claim that an item with what is now termed superconductive capabilities came to Los Angeles about 1938. Observers have often wondered how German scientists came close to discovering nuclear power. It is speculated that they had something which defied Einstein's theories. In 1921 Tesla and Einstein worked together on problems of superconductivity. Around this time a young graduate student named Linus Pauling began working on covalent bonds of copper and iron and finally created a coil in 1938 for a U.S. project using Tesla designs. Einstein's laboratory assistant, Dr. Herbert Fleischmann, made documents referring to these experiments but the German scientists to whom the details were passed were unable to fully develop the algorithms that would allow modelling for nuclear production.

In the summer of 1939 Canaris was briefed by Baron Ernst von Weizsacker, Principal Secretary in the German Ministry of Foreign Affairs, on studies by German scientists into nuclear fission and the question of chain reactions. When Canaris understood the terrible consequences of a chain reaction he was appalled and determined that Hitler must never be given such weapons of mass destruction. Immediately, Canaris extended protection to the scientists of the Kaiser Wilhelm Institute against SD and Gestapo investigations. The Vatican priest who confided information to Jim Keith for *Secret and Suppressed* also claimed that Rudolf Hess travelled to Scotland to deliver to the British authorities Germany's atomic research secrets.

Canaris and his close colleagues in the Abwehr also considered what steps might be taken to bring about a compromise peace with the British. Subsequently, talks conducted by Dr. Josef Muller opened in Rome. Muller sought an assurance from the British that might encourage the generals to turn their weapons against Hitler. Canaris supported these developments but moved with extreme caution, exercising a natural sense of self-preservation if, even in these early stages of the war, he was actively working with the British as a double agent. Vatican staff members close to Pius XII sounded out Sir Francis D'Arcy, British Minister to the Vatican, about his views and were encouraged to understand that there was still a chance for peace if Hitler could be removed from power. It was also confirmed that Lord

Halifax, the reluctant channel for peace overtures behind Churchill's back, accepted the broad lines of the German argument. Canaris was at the heart of these covert German initiatives to secure peace but, crucially, it is important to recognise that he was never a part of the Himmler-Wolff faction that sought to make accommodations with the allies for post-war personal self-aggrandisement and high political advantage.

Many of the Abwehr papers ended up in the hands of the British Secret Service, which, in itself, is an absorbing fact. Canaris took four suitcases to Spain in 1943 containing private papers and his diaries and did not return with them. Canaris buried canisters of microfilm in his son-in-law's garden containing evidence against Himmler concerning appalling concentration camp atrocities.

Canaris also had proof of Heydrich's Jewish parentage. Heydrich told Schellenberg at one time: "it was complete madness to have taken up the Jewish question," a quote distinctly at odds with the manner and cold efficiency with which Heydrich chaired the infamous 1942 Wannsee Conference convened to secure the commitment from top Nazi figures for deployment of the Final Solution. But even within the four walls of that ultra-secret conclave Heydrich was not safe from fingerpointing. Behind cupped hands the generals present rumoured among themselves that Heydrich's father was a Jew. Of course, none present dared pose the question to the man who months later would die an agonising slow death at the hands of Czech resistance fighters acting under the direction of the British secret service.

Canaris was a sensitive and cultured man and was devastated when the Scholl siblings, Sophia Magdalen and Hans, were beheaded in March 1943 for their leadership role in the White Rose passive resistance group. On the day of execution Canaris reluctantly met with the detestable Ernst Kaltenbrunner who had just been appointed Heydrich's successor as Chief of the Reich Central Security Office. The admiral was stunned by Kaltenbrunner's description of the young couple as vermin only fit to be exterminated along with all of their kind.

Rahn was not isolated from the Nazi hierarchy. Hans-Jürgen Lange mentions the occasion in 1937 when Rahn attended the dinner at the Nobelrestaurant where Himmler, Heydrich and Wolff were among those present. Karl Heinz Abshagen believed that Heydrich, Himmler and Schellenberg were prepared to see the plots against Hitler explode so that the SS could intervene and take over power while restoring the Government's authority.

The British and U.S. Secret Services were deeply implicated in the plot to kill Hitler carried out on 20th July 1944. Colonel Claude Arnoud, Chief of British Intelligence in France, confirmed that prior to the assassination attempt his agent Keun visited Canaris twice. Former agent Peter Tennant has admitted that the British provided direct assistance. SIS officer David McEwan gave Himmler intermediary Adam von Trott British fuses for the bomb (some of which malfunctioned) and the SIS supplied Abwehr officer Freytag-Loringhoven with the explosives. Cyrus Sulzberger, U.S. diplomat, confirmed that U.S. Intelligence had advance knowledge of the bomb.

Himmler's role was probably more direct than appreciated. It was Himmler, not General Fromm, who authorised the recommendation that Stauffenberg be promoted to a key position on Fromm's staff to give him access to Hitler's HQ. Himmler signed the recommendation, having met Stauffenberg only two weeks earlier. Himmler had no formal right to interfere with such promotions. When Canaris was arrested for his part in the plot he asked Schellenberg to plead for an interview with Himmler because "all the others are filthy butchers." [5]

When the Gestapo searched the office of Hans Dohnany (a senior Abwehr officer) in April 1943 they found papers relating to Abwehr contact with Pius XII, via a Jesuit intermediary, about Vatican peace overtures. We have seen evidence of Rudolf Rahn's centre stage liaison involvement with the Vatican regarding the Church's policy position vis à vis the despatch of the Jews in Rome, and we should concider this in light of the arguments voiced by Bernadac that there are marked similarities in the facts distinguishing the lives of Otto and Rudolf Rahn. It is evident where Canaris' allegiances lay.

In passing, being an admiral as well as a spy-chief, Canaris would have had authority and influence in deployment of a U-Boat should he have so wished and to have orchestrated the disembarkation of "special" passengers. This is worth remembering when we read the short story finale in Part 4.

Himmler and Canaris—polar opposites. The former was Rahn's superior and the model of German clinical efficiency in discharging his role as expeditor of the Final Solution. According to Albert Rausch, Himmler was surrounded by "*les siens,*" inner circle confidants and subordinates who betrayed him to others secretly working against Nazism. Rausch's letter clearly indicates that Otto Rahn was among those around the Reichsführer SS who risked terrible personal danger to subvert the Nazi course. We have also seen that Canaris was one of the

---

[5] Manvell, Roger; Fraenkel, Heinrich. *The Canaris Conspiracy*. New York: David McKay, 1969

most likely senior ranking recipients of this intelligence and that he would have passed it on to the British. Perhaps we are beginning to see far more clearly what specific nature of role Cecil Williamson might actually have undertaken as a case officer for a young, courageous German intellectual who risked his life daily for the love and liberation of his country.

Gabriele called Himmler "uncle." The SIS described him as being “a thousand times worse than Ivan the Terrible—the most frightful monster that ever lived on earth.” Admiral Canaris was the intelligence grandee who worried about nothing because he had files on everyone. Ultimately, this did not save him from death by hanging on Hitler's orders in the latter stages of the war. Both Himmler and Canaris enjoyed covert connections with Britain. Himmler wooed the Peace Party members opposed to Churchill, seeking from 1939 onwards an end to hostilities so that he could take the helm in a Fourth Reich administration. Canaris on the other hand, if we believe Ian Colvin, was a British agent. It would be ironical if both men had, unwittingly, treated with the same British security and political personnel, each believing that their contact in MI6 shared their respective personal principles. In Canaris’ case these principles had convinced him to betray his country for the promise of a world free from evil while in Himmler’s they had persuaded him that far too few millions were dying for his liking.

Did Otto Rahn have the savvy and courage to walk a different path and make a break from the madmen who were dragging his beloved Germany and as many others they could seize into the pit? Remember Lebesgue's statement: "*There was behind Hitler an order of chivalry, a secret order…the esoteric expression of Nazism…we neither know its name, its nature nor its rules.*" I believe that Otto Rahn was an active and inspirational member of that small but enlightened kernel of hope and enterprise working against terrible odds deep inside the Nazi machine.

There were numerous resistance and opposition groups working to thwart Nazism including the Kreisau Circle, the Edelweißpiraten and, later, the White Rose. It is more than possible that Otto Rahn was working in and around the activities of these groups with Admiral Canaris filling a Merlinesque role in orchestrating between them a combined force of opposition to Hitler’s ambitions. But my belief is that if there was a single group to which Rahn dedicated his allegiance it was to the “order of chivalry” in the heart of the viper’s nest described by Lebesgue. The main objective of this group, it is claimed, was to counter the greatest threat of all: the opening of dimensional thresholds and doorways by unnatural means.

The notion of other universes existing alongside ours is no longer fanciful. In fact, quantum physicists now routinely talk about the topic in terms of certainty rather than conjecture. However, even though we humans do not have the physical sensory mechanisms to enable us to perceive other dimensions, there is nevertheless much to suggest that the veil separating our world from other planes of existence is a flimsy caul. And if, as many posit, UFO and Fortean types of phenomena originate not among the planets and stars of this universe but from dimensions outside it (and some even believe from *within* it) then it is evident that those realms are home to life forms whose form, substance and intelligence are beyond our experiential competence to know and to understand.

Making a tear in the veil offers an invitation to energy forms to make passage and instances of it are common. One only has to look at the countless appearances of UFOs and the host of weird and wonderful animal-like agencies (goatsuckers, yetis and bigfoots among them) to evidence this phenomenon. But some energy forms may be more inimical to this plane than others and their entry on a mass scale would cause incalculable imbalance.

Such an eventuality had to be prevented at all costs. Rahn had seen things. He had to see the boss. Had he witnessed at first hand the early results of a concerted effort by Hitler and his disciples to fling open a door that should never be opened?

PART THREE

MEANING

Chapter SEVENTEEN

Over the hills and faraway

We have climbed to the peaks of the visible slopes that determine the topography of Otto Rahn's life and times. From our vantage point we have enjoyed a three hundred and sixty degree lighthouse view that has shone a beam into the smallest fissures. Our horizon encompasses an ever-widening circle of exploration, taking in the power centres of Europe and stretching beyond the continental shore northwards to ancient Iceland.

Otto Rahn with Asta Baeschlin and her son

From the lower slopes we trained our binoculars upon Rahn's childhood and his teenage years. The field of vision has been scant but a picture has emerged of a quiet upbringing surrounded by the timeless features of the Odenvald that instilled in Otto a love for nature that never deserted him. He grew up in the company of ancient trees and even older gods. In these early years we do not have a superabundance of facts by which the historian might adduce the direction that Otto Rahn's life would take in later years. Nevertheless, his mother, a strong influence in the boy's early years, was assiduous in instilling into her impressionable son knowledge and appreciation of mystical Christian and gnostic episodes in past times. She did not hide her loyalties and was clearly on the side of those who were vilified and murdered by the Roman Church.

Rahn's parents were Protestant but the depth of feeling imparted by Frau Rahn to her elder son suggests that her Protestantism was infused with a deep appreciation of early gnostic Christian sentiments by which the Roman Church felt extremely threatened. The mother's words would have been as pen on blank paper and Otto assimilated her opinions until his mental processes had developed to a point of maturity when he could make up his own mind on difficult historic and philosophical issues. Ultimately, there is no doubt where Rahn sided. He grew up listening to harrowing accounts of sustained, official murder on an unimaginable scale told from the perspective of those tied to the stake. He listened avidly and when he was old enough to form his own opinions he did not discard his mother's sentiment but filled his every pore and nerve with it. Every climb has its tumbles and in his early years Otto's ascent into adolescence was marked by the onset of the Great War and its attendant chaos.

Ostensibly, Otto Rahn was a member of the mainstream Christian faith but his recorded thoughts, words and actions indicate the workings of an innate mysticism founded upon the highest ideals of western European esoteric tradition. As we move beyond the tree line of Otto Rahn's personal Mount Meru towards the rising snow slopes, we can imagine the landscape that we might find from the telltale features of the lower pathways. We are following a man whose kindred spirit was steeped in every bloodied footstep leading to the stake and scaffold of Inquisitional Europe. True to form, when we clamber up the mountain's mid-slopes and observe Rahn's activities in and beyond his university years we see him empathising with and focusing upon the victims of mainstream religious intolerance. Rahn's university thesis was based upon "*the Research of Master Kyot of Wolfram von Eschenbach,*" a subject centred upon Parsifal's search for the Grail. To cement his allegiances Rahn dedicated his thesis to the troubadours, a body of poets and storytellers who provided a voice for the mystical Christian groups that abounded in the Middle-Ages and which, ever active, had had to remain in hiding since the Christian schisms of the early 4th century. Members of these gnostic groups adhered to a Grail philosophy, which taught that God resides within the spirit-soul of human beings, and that the pathway to discovering this eternal treasure and oneness with God does not need the intercession of priests who are prepared to murder on a genocidal scale both to rule the hearts and souls of men and women and to protect their authority.

A few years passed and Rahn published his seminal work—*Kreuzzug gegen den Gral*. The title did not beat around the bush in declaring the writer's personal philosophy in the battle between Catholic patriarchy and the pre-Christian era in which the ruling Goddess represented the magical essence of woman as symbolizing the true Church. In gathering the material for this first writing venture, Rahn embarked upon his travels and in the early chapters we charted his treasure hunting expeditions in the caverns of Ornolac and Sabarthès.

The highest and most physically challenging slopes of Rahn's life-mountain correspond with the last six years of his public life. In this time Rahn was pressed into the Nazi party and inducted into the inner sanctum of Himmler's SS. By all accounts Rahn was tested to extremes and, unsurprisingly, he did not make the last step to the summit to plant the swastika pennant into the red earth of new Thule. But this is to assume that the goals and objectives that drive a person's life should be in plain sight for all to see.

One has only to examine the bibliography of *Kreuzug gegen den Gral* to appreciate that Otto Rahn was an extremely well read fellow. He lists in the index nearly two hundred works sub-divided into categories ranging from general interest to the birth of Roman culture, druids and manicheism, the poetry of the troubadours, the Albigenses, the Merovingian Crusade, and the Pyrenean caves. Rahn's French publisher, Stock, also make the point that the original German edition cites many more works and references. Rahn was no intellectual lightweight. Study on this scale requires determination, patience, passion and a brilliant mind. Rahn had read all these works and arrived at his startling conclusions by the time he was twenty-six years of age. Notably, a number of the authors Rahn cites were associated with the nineteenth century European occult and Rosicrucian revival: Edward Maitland, Jules Michelet and Joséphin Péladan among them. This fact is important to note when we come to examine Rahn's empathy with the Rosicrucian ideal in Chapter 19.

Our brief re-examination of Otto Rahn's outer ascent of his climb through life has served to refresh our memories of his public profile. If we thought that the scree would be scattered with emeralds or the slopes paved with gold then our hopes are dashed. Let us retain the thought that at no point along our mountainside reconnaissance trail can we see the tiniest glimmer of gold, fabulous jewels or other precious booty. Nothing was reported found.

However, legends do not grow out of the dust (or snow) of empty lives. In the matter of the Grail let us pause for a moment's reflection. According to present day mythology Rahn *did* find the legendary Grail Treasure of Eschenbach's *Parsifal*, in which pages he believed he had discovered the cypher identifying the seat of the Grail: Montségur. Angebert claimed in *Hitler et le Tradition Cathar*[1] that Rahn did succeed in locating the Grail Cup, which was subsequently taken from its Sabarthès place of concealment by an Ahnenerbe archaeological team and displayed in the Realm of the Dead under the great hall in Wewelsberg. There is no evidence to support this claim.

Nevertheless, what things said, suggested or inferred support the theory that Rahn achieved the task that had eluded so many before him? We should be reminded of these salient points:

Colonel Howard Buechner says it was Rahn's task to steal the Treasure of Solomon for Germany and other fabulous artefacts including the Tablets of Moses, Ark of the Covenant, the Sword and Harp of David, the Sacred Candelabra and the Golden Urn of Manna.

In 410 A.D. Alaric sacked Rome and seized the Grail, taking it to Carcassonne and concealing it in a Sabarthès grotto. When the Grail had been safely removed from Montségur by the four companions a beacon was lit on the neighbouring mountain of Biaorta. The evidence suggests that Rahn did find something of fabulous historical provenance but left it behind in its place of concealment.

Ladame learned about Rahn's aims—to discover the secret of the Grail that he believed would unify Europe.

Rahn was convinced that he had made one of the most important historical discoveries, which would bring him worldwide fame and riches.

Rahn said that Arnaud, the Polaires engineer and Theosophist, would never find the treasure, which was hidden in the forest of Thabor guarded by vipers, the entrance blocked by an enormous stone. In *Luzifers Hofgesind* we read that Rahn finds an article among a trawl of his papers entitled *Has the Grail been Found?* The account relates that in the Oronte Valley between Antioch and Hamath in Syria an English archaeological expedition found in a grotto close to one of the first Christian churches a chalice, which was allegedly the one used by Jesus at the Last Supper. The cup had been sent back to England to be meticulously examined by scientists. Rahn never heard any more about this object or the story *nor, he wrote, did he ever expect to*. Why was this unless Rahn was convinced that he knew where the Holy Cup was

---

1 Paris, Laffont, 1971

to be found, that where it was cached was beyond reach, or that he knew it was already in private hands? I find the correspondences between this account and Spielberg's storyline for *Indiana Jones and the Last Crusade* startling and far too close for coincidence.

Rahn is said to have visited the Corbières near Rennes-le-Château, an expedition connected with "forbidden merchandise."

Enigmatically, Rahn reminded Weisthor of his earlier mention of the discovery of "big surprises." Rahn wrote to Weisthor in September 1935 telling him excitedly of a place he was visiting in his search for the Grail, and asking for complete secrecy.

Rahn despatched a report to Himmler about the cloister of Saint Odilien, a location that has long been favoured as a hiding place for Grail artefacts. Himmler's diary (February 1939) records the receipt from Rahn of a copy of "Gral."

"*I have reason to believe that many artefacts, including some found by Otto Rahn, were shipped to the U.S. in 1938.*"

Rahn's friend Joachim Kohlhaas told Hans-Jürgen Lange of Wolfgang Frommel's comment in 1937 that Rahn had been searching for the Golden Fleece of the Argonauts.

Gaston de Mengel's letter to Rahn 1937 said: "*...I have also located the place of the big black centre. It is within the big triangle that is formed by Kobdo, Urumtschi and Bakul, near Sin-kinag in western Mongolia.*"

These indicators are no more than chalk marks on the ground and in no way are they conclusive evidence that Rahn struck lucky. Nevertheless, taken together they offer a seam of possibility from which one might reasonably infer a hint of successful industry in the Grail-seeking business.

Equally important is the suggestion imparted by statements that the Grail expedition is also associated with a search for other worlds or dimensions, a theme to which we will return in later chapters where we will read:

There are so many allusions in stories, myths and legends to doorways, gateways and labyrinths that it is hard not to believe that there may well be a key to the portals of the Gods.

The Bönpo monks brought to Germany were said to have the ability to open dimensional doors by means of the Chod discipline. It is believed that this was what interested a certain group of Nazis because they knew the war was lost.

The whole Shambala theory was prevalent around the turn of the century, and one imagines that this was worked on by Otto Rahn. It may be that Rahn physically worked out these ritual practices and actually disappeared.

The Phisummum project and the purpose of the secret order behind it, the Order of the Black Sun, was time travel. Elizabeth van Buren has called WWII a War of Time.

These are more foods for thought and maybe a vote that the substance of the Rahn legend is not just quixotic vapour rising from a warming glass of *Fée Verte*, casually sipped while retouching Sabarthès cave drawings.

All of these references allude to a search in an external physical realm whose location and characteristics one cannot divine.

However, there is a third trail to the Grail Castle that Rahn vaunted at every opportunity in his writings. Like all mystics before and since, Rahn makes the case that fabulous treasures are to be found in a country we should know so well but acknowledge the least. The inner spirit worlds provide unlimited adventure to a brave traveller. Again and again, Otto Rahn pointed a finger to the Worlds Within—*I have the dietrich*, he oftened intoned.

Personally, I have never believed that Rahn's ultimate objectives were solely related to a search for fabulous artefacts, no matter how legendary their provenance. There *is* a treasure to be found in tracking Rahn's footsteps but one may not stoop down to retrieve it nor break sweat with pick and shovel to excavate it. To begin to understand the disciplines and challenges confronting one that seeks to turn the *dietrich* and fling open the doorway to the inner worlds, we must look beyond the obvious. The reward is to be found in disaggregating Rahn's words and actions and a dissection of his philosophy provides the tools we will need.

First and foremost, Otto Rahn was a modern day alchemist and we will thoroughly pursue this line of thinking. To do this, we need to stand on the slopes of Rahn's mountain and not peer outwards but look instead for the caves and hidey-holes with which it is ribboned.

Rahn took his tumbles but observers should not be quick to judge. Ancient Wisdoms teach that the seeker's path becomes increasingly narrow until eventually it disappears altogether. At that point the true seeker is in the position of Indiana Jones faced with crossing the bottomless chasm to reach the cave of the Grail Knight. It is then that pure unadulterated belief supports the hero's first step across the bottomless divide, thereby revealing the stone bridge leading across to the Grail cavern. I believe that Rahn attained this state of grace, albeit briefly, but enough to make the stepping stones take shape when the only options seemed to be a blind canyon or a deep Tyrolean crevice.

The power of belief also endows the seeker with the wisdom not to put faith in cups and baubles; he understands that the true treasure is within. Indiana Jones knew well enough to leave the Grail goblet behind and, instead, to accept the wisdom that his father had spent a lifetime pursuing—Illumination!

An excavation of Otto Rahn's writings quickly unearths substantial references and allusions to the Emerald Tablet/Rosicrucian/Alchemic thread of Western Hermetic metaphysics. I have endeavoured to highlight these links and to bring a sense of order to a complex area of study. The archetypal themes that are revealed—the concepts of timelessness, eternal life, transmutation to higher states, and the joys of the journey, are absolutely fundamental to all Ancient Wisdoms. Their representatives do not teach directly. They impart a sense of quest and positive restlessness by means of tales of power and allegory that signpost the seeker to one's innermost pathways of discovery. I have presented evidence to indicate that, in all probability, Rahn adhered to this noble tradition and sought to convey unequivocal mystical truths under an academic and literary shroud.

The Hermetic fabric (the Fleece) that Rahn stretched across his philosophic loom served as the cloth into which various patterns of specific esoterica might be knitted. The striking placements of these mystery elements, among them: Tibetan occultism, the legend of Shamballah and other inner earth traditions and earth energy sciences tend to divert the eye from the pure foundation. In turn, this preserves its strength. Nevertheless, the dabs of colour provided by some of the more sensational and often controversial esoteric episodes are vital to the whole. Light with shade. In the next few chapters we will look at each of these episodes and adduce further the connections to the thread of order attesting to Otto Rahn's mystical allegiances.

Chapter EIGHTEEN

Philosophy

What did Otto Rahn believe in? What were the principle philosophic and metaphysical drivers that underpinned his intimate thought, word and action processes? What are the components of Rahn's life that indicate possibilities of specific pathways of discovery?

To offer an intelligent answer one can excavate Rahn's writings and back "engineer" to a discrete point of philosophical origin; this we will do. Additionally, one can employ the tools of the metaphysician and search for the gouache, half tones and daubs of synchronicity that can guide the experienced observer toward illumination. An excavation of this kind reveals many clues as to the nature of the philosophical imperatives that gave Rahn keener sight to see better the sacred oak and the Golden Fleece draped over its boughs.

Clearly, also, Rahn was immersed in the tale of Don Quixote and never lost an opportunity to convey in his own writings what Cervantes wanted his intelligent and searching readers to discover: the true meaning of Quest (Quixote=Quixt=Quest). We will explore this theme.

We must also bring our caver's lamp over to the world globe and hold it fast over the tabletop country of Tibet, which merits a chapter of its own. It is there, I suggest, that we find one of the hidden keys, a *dietrich*, to help identify the circumstances surrounding Rahn's destiny. The study of Tibet is laden with symbolism and, among other motifs, returns us to the Black Sun theme, a study of which brings us to the work of Wilhelm Landig and his 1971 book *Kampf gegen Thule*—Battle against Thule, (later republished as *Götzen gegen Thule*—Godlets against Thule). This fascinating work is rich with clues and mentions Rahn. Tibet also steers us towards other inter-related topics, specifically the ancient Order of the Black Swan and the time-technology work of Dr. Karl Obermayer, Nikola Tesla and Rudolf Steiner on behalf of the Prometheus Foundation, carried out allegedly to thwart the worst excesses of Hitler's true agenda.

We should recall Rahn's question: "Must a Hessian drive into the Pyrenees in order to determine that Montségur was Munsalvaesche, the grail-castle? Must a Hessian determine in the South-France that Grail-Christians lived in Hesse? (The symbol of the German *amour courtois* was the rose-cross, incidentally, but that is only an aside…The material lay before me. I was predestined for it, I believe.") These strongly held sentiments of Rahn's lead one to explore powerful correspondences between his beliefs and Rosicrucianism, a hugely influential philosophy that emerged in the early seventeeth century when Shakespeare was still alive and Queen Elizabeth's magus Dr. John Dee was still a vibrant memory. In *Indiana Jones and the Last Crusade*, the indomitable Brothers of the Cruciform Sword, Grail guardians, are a thinly veiled representation of the Brothers of the Rosy Cross.

Moreover, in Chapter 5 we read Rahn's account of his subterranean adventures with his servant Habdu and their discovery of the sculpture of Cerberus. In this account Rahn makes a play on what he calls a strange transposition of the Mediterranean harbour name known in the ancient days as Kerberos with the modern day name of Cerbère. It appears that Rahn was wishing to draw attention to something else. In looking at the possibilities, it is worth examining the various myths relating to Cerberus and associated figures of Greek myth.

The Rosicrucian interpretations adduced from the canon of Rahn's writings receive nourishment from two other critical strands of metaphysical significance: the legend of the Argonauts' search for the Golden Fleece and the inner content and, briefly, the meaning of Shakespeare's plays.

While journeying to Iceland with his companions, Rahn disembarks for a few hours upon Scottish soil and his experience encourages him in *Luzifers Hofgesind* to wax lyrical on the plight of English heretics, in particular John Oldcastle, the principal figure among the 12th century Lollard sect of anti-Papist Christians. In narrating the history of this heretical figure, Rahn delves into Shakespeare, explicitly Henry IV and Henry V, and we shall seek to understand why.

Chapter NINETEEN

The Rosy Cross

"...the tongues of Flame are in-folded
Into the crowned knot of Fire,
And the Fire and the Rose are One!"
T .S. Eliot

Rahn's digression about the rose-cross was clearly intended to draw attention to its time-honoured symbology. Why? He went on to state, matter of factly, that "the material lay before me." I have established that Otto Rahn made a practice of presenting important information obliquely, between the lines. He laid the material before his readers. He indicated that its inspirational source is the immortal beauty of *amour courtois* illuminated by the ageless and incorruptible rosy-cross. What is it about this timeless symbol that evoked so much passion and high learning among the mystics and philosophers of the 16th Century? What thread of order might link the genesis and unfoldment of Rosicrucianism with esoteric teachings gone before, and of which Catharism was such a distinct and powerful forerunner?

The word Rosicrucian derives from Christian Rosencreutz or Rose Cross (or possibly from Ros and Crux—an alchemical meaning connected with dew as a solvent of gold and crux as the equivalent of Light). The term Rosicrucian is also said to derive from the Latin ‘rosa’ (rose) and ‘crux’ (cross). These two symbols of the Order, however, are not to be confused with similar Christian symbols and meanings. At least in some cases the swastika, not the cross, has been linked to the rose. In the monastery of Loudum, founded in 1334, several Carmelite brothers left their names engraved in a staircase, which has for this reason been named the staircase of the graffiti. Among the names of these brethren is that of a Brother Guyot, who added to his signature a rose overlaid by a sinistroverse swastika.[1]

The correspondences between the name of Brother Guyot and Eschenbach's Kyot, the Provencal master sage who was mentor to

---

[1] Charbonnay-Lassay, Louis. *L'Esoterisme de quelques symboles geometriques*. Paris: Editions Traditionelles, 1960

Parsifal, are startling. Curiously, Professor Karl Haushofer's infamous geopolitical *lebensraum* illustration of the swastika radiating out into a map of the extended Nazi ruled globe bears striking similarities to Brother Guyot's design:

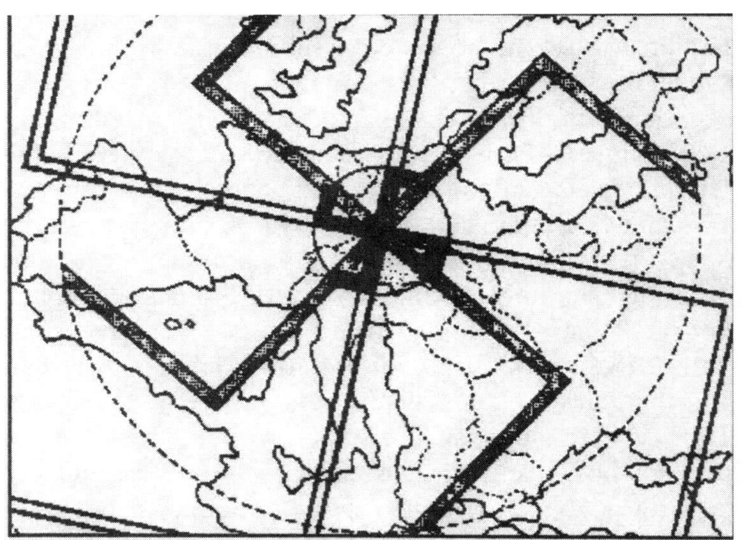

Haushofer advised Hitler to enlarge the living space of the Third Reich by moving out from a powerful territorial hub and by accomplishing this conquest progressively, step by step, following the accelerating movement of a growing spiraling sinistroverse swastika.

The Rosicrucian manifestos are two short pamphlets first published in 1614 and 1615, abbreviated as the *Fama* and the *Confessio*. Frances Yeats regards the manifestos as combining Magic, Cabala and Alchemy.[2] The hero of the manifestos is Father C.R.C. or Christian Rosenkreutz who is said to have been the founder of an Order or Fraternity and which the manifestos now invite others to join. The

[2] Yeats, Frances. *The Rosicrucian Enlightenment*. London and Boston: Routledge & Kegan Paul, 1972

preface to the Fama suggests that the Rosicrucian manifesto was setting forth an alternative to the Jesuit Order. This alternative constituted a brotherhood more closely associated with the true life and teachings of Jesus. To the Rosicrucian, the Jesuit-Hapsberg alliance (not a relationship approved by all Roman Catholic authorities of the day) was simply Antichrist. Yet it is ironical that of all the shoots of the Roman Catholic Church the Jesuits were the most like the Rosicrucians. The Order made great use of the Hermetic tradition in appealing to Protestants and to other creeds it encountered in its missionary work. Its pseudo-esoteric approach was given a great boost by the efforts of Athanasius Kircher who constantly cited the works of Hermes Trismegistus and, to a lesser extent, of Dr. John Dee. The Rosicrucian-Jesuit relationship was of a love-hate nature, which, nevertheless, was characterised by a number of similarities.

In observing the similarities between the establishment of Rosicrucianism and the Society of Jesus, we arrive at a point of particular irony. We have seen that Rahn hated the Catholic Church, the Jesuits in particular. It is likely that Rahn would have been aware of the similarities between the nature and establishment of both orders and took an opportunity in his writings to illustrate what he regarded as the beauty of one (Rosicrucianism) compared with what he perceived as the stultifying and conspiratorial nature of the other.

In *Confessio Fraternitatis* Chapter VIII says that God had sent a sign that the Great Council of the Elect was to be convened to usher in the Reformation. In this the Fraternity was to play a leading role by creating new stars in *Serpentarius* and *Cygnus*: snake and swan. This proved that God reveals in visible nature signs and symbols of all events that are coming to pass for those who have the sight and vision to discern them. Rahn made reference to both of these symbols in his work. Swan symbology is especially important in mapping the exegeses of Rosicrucianism with Otto Rahn's philosophy. We will look at these correspondences in later chapters.

In his *Secret Teachings of All Ages* (1928) Manly P. Hall describes four distinct theories regarding the Rosicrucian enigma.

The first proposes that the Order existed historically in accordance with the description of its foundation and subsequent activities published in its manifesto, the *Fama Fraternitatis*. To assist in bringing about the reformation to counter past egotism and greed, a poor person called "The Highly Illuminated Father C.R.C.," a German noble by birth, instituted the Secret Society of the Rosy Cross. At the age of five, C.R.C. was placed in a cloister, much later associating himself with a brother of Holy Orders who died while they were travelling in Cyprus. After studying in Damascus, Damcar (a place that has never been identified) and in Fez, C.R.C. journeyed to Spain where he was ridiculed by the intelligentsia. Not discouraged, C.R.C. returned to Germany for five years of contemplative study before renewing his struggle for a reformation in the arts and sciences of his day. He went to the cloister where his early training had been received and called to him three brethren whom he bound by an inviolable oath to preserve the secrets he would impart. Consider here the associations between the cloister of C.R.C. with that of Saint Odile, the legendary home of the Grail and the place to where Himmler despatched Rahn to locate and retrieve the Chalice. In around 1400 the four brothers founded the Fraternity of the Rose Cross. The number in the fraternity was soon increased to eight (coincidentally, the same number that comprised the founding members of Inigo Loyola's Society of Jesus).

Others, Hall pointed out, believe that the Fraternity originated in medieval Europe as an outgrowth of alchemical philosophy. This theory proposes that Johann Valentin Andreae was the true founder, reforming and amplifying a society that had been previously founded by Sir Henry Cornelius Agrippa. Some believed that Rosicrucianism represented the first invasion into Europe of Buddhist and Brahmic culture. Still others held that the society was founded in Egypt and that it also perpetuated the mysteries of ancient Chaldea and Persia. Whatever its origins the Order, incredibly, was able to retain absolute secrecy for many centuries. A number of very great scholars such as Francis Bacon and Goethe are said to have been affiliated with the Order.

Dr. Franz Hartmann, in his *Secret Symbols of the Rosicrucians*, believed that the brethren were able to command the elemental spirits and nature folk (a dominant theme in Rahn's wonderful recounting of the legend of the Roses of Bozen) and knew the secret of the Philosopher's Stone, a knowledge which rendered its possessor immortal and all-wise. Many suspected the Rosicrucian rose to be symbolic of the Hindu lotus blossom. In *Luzifers Hofgesind* Rahn draws his readers' attention to the theory held in the Middle-Ages that the Golden Fleece and the Philosophers Stone were one and the same.

The word Rosicrucian is said by many (Godfrey Higgins was the first) to derive from Ros=dew. A. E. Waite agrees with Higgins and says that the process of forming the Philosophers Stone with the aid of dew is the secret concealed within the name Rosicrucian. Alchemists took a great interest in what might be described as the Source: the energy of inner nature or the nucleus of the personality as neutral observer, which does not participate in the conflict of the opposites. That solid nucleus was called the Philosophers Stone, which had the capacity of penetrating every object. Alchemists believed that all material phenomena went back to one basic material—the Prima Materia, chief among whose symbolisms is the Divine or Bitter Water, the result of the Coniunctio: the bringing together of the Opposites. Water in general carries the projection of Knowledge. It is a very great paradox that liquid and stone are, according to the alchemist, one and the same thing. They refer to the two aspects of the Realisation of the Self. Something firm is born while at the same time something very much alive is brought forth, which takes part in the ebb and flow of life without the restrictions of consciousness. The alchemists believed that after the Philosophers Stone had been produced it began to circulate, to pass through winter, spring, summer and autumn: the essence of the individuation process and the accumulation of Wisdom-Sapientia.

The cross is symbolic of the human body and the two symbols together—the rose and the cross—signify that the soul of man is crucified upon the body and held by three nails. Speculators have stated that modern Freemasonry has completely absorbed Rosicrucianism, while others declare that the Rosicrucian Brotherhood still exists, preserving its individuality as the result of having withdrawn from the Masonic Order. Mystics explain that the symbolic cross seen by the "inner" eye is created by the diameter of a horizontal and a vertical wheel. The only place where the two make a link is the "hole" at the point of nothingness (the Hebrew Shamir) and the Abyss (Prometheus), sometimes called the Window to Eternity. Before Rahn disappeared he had completed the greater part of a manuscript entitled *The Will of Prometheus: A Trip to Hell and Beyond*. This work has not since seen the light of day and more is the pity. It is likely that its contents and sub-texts would be an illuminating experience for the modern day mystic.

The third theory, Hall submitted, denies that there ever was such a Rosicrucian Order, which was no more than a satire to ridicule the gullibility of Europe's intelligentsia. Nevertheless, the mystery has resulted in endless controversies and has occupied some of the finest minds in the history of Europe mysticism: scholars such as Michael Maier, Eugenius Philalethes (Thomas Vaughan) and Robert Fludd among them.

The final proposal, Hall explains, has a transcendental premise, asserting that the Rosicrucians actually did possess all the supernatural powers with which they were credited; that they were literally citizens of two worlds being able to function fully consciously in both a physical and an etheric body, the latter not subject to the laws of time and space. These adepts were conversant with the very highest mysteries that concerned the quest to regenerate, through a process of transmutation, the "base elements" of man's lower nature into the "gold" of intellectual and spiritual realisation. Under this alchemical process Rosicrucian adepts were believed to be able to teach men how to function away from their physical body at will by assisting them to remove the "rose from the cross." Rahn never forsook an opportunity to stress that he had the *dietrich*—a skeleton key whose function in an alchemic context may be construed as providing the means to open the doors to the invisible, allowing one to function away from the physical body and travel freely in the inner worlds.

Rosicrucian initiates taught that spiritual nature was attached to the physical form at certain points, symbolised by the three nails of the crucifixion. By three alchemical processes they were able to draw these nails and permit the divine nature of Man to come down from its cross. They concealed the processes by which this was accomplished under three alchemical metaphorical expressions: "The Casting of the Molten Sea," "The Making of the Rose Diamond," and "The Achieving of the Philosopher's Stone." The mystic believes that the true Brethren of the Rosy Cross exist in the inner planes of Nature; that they can only be reached by those who can transcend the limitations of the material world. To substantiate this view the mystic quotes the *Confessio Fraternitatis*: "*...wherefore now no longer are we beheld by human eyes, unless they have received strength borrowed from the eagle.*"

In mysticism the eagle is a symbol of initiation (the spinal Spirit Fire), and by this is explained the inability of the unregenerated world to understand the Secret Order of the Rosy Cross. In this theory of the Fraternity's beginnings the Comte de Saint-Germain. was its highest adept and is believed to be the same person as Christian Rosencreutz.

Max Heindel, Christian mystic, described the Rosicrucian temple as an etheric structure located in and around the home of a European country gentleman that was later moved to the American continent *("I have reason to believe that many artefacts, including some found by Otto Rahn, were shipped to the U.S. in 1938...I think the Grail you may be looking for is a superconducting stone that Hitler shipped to the L.A. area.*").

Rahn closes *Luzifers Hofgesind* with the words: "*I am going to follow the ancient path of the thief, my eyes constantly fixed on the Great Bear: Arktos, Artur, Arthur, Thor. Thor, the Grand-Father, loved honey. A little bee flies towards the table where I write, and disappears into the evening. Perhaps it will spend the night inside a wild rose. And tomorrow is a new day.*" To enter the wild rose is to cross the threshold into Nature's secret worlds of enchantment. According to Ancient Wisdoms, the bee is the symbol of the doorway or threshold to the soul. Hermes was a friend to thieves. In bringing forward mention here of Rosicrucianism, albeit tangentially, was Otto Rahn indicating to his more discerning readers that not only was that branch of philosophy alive and well but that he was one of its dedicated adherants?

Hargrave Jennings describes in *The Rosicrucians, Their Rites and Mysteries*, 1887, an elaborate genealogy of the arms of France in which the bee motif is all-important. It is symbolised by the Fleurs de Lis (Lucifers, Lisses, Luces, Lucies, Bees, Scarabs, or Imperial Bees of Charlemagne, of the Merovingian line of Kings, and of Napoleon the First and Napoleon the Third). The bees of Charlemagne are scarabs or figures of the same affinity as the Bourbon lilies. Via a complex examination of heraldric devices Hargraves associates these bee-insect motifs with the Lady-Bird which, in the ancient nursery rhyme, is representative of the Virgin Mary (Mary=Mare=the blue and salty bitterness of the sea) and Mother Nature-Isis. In the armorial bearings of the Frankish kings, the Lilies are represented as insects, seeded or spotted upon a blue field. These *scarabaei* were dignified by the Egyptians as the emblems of the "Enlightened." The *scarabaeus* or crab plays a large part in the grand rite of the Mithraic Sacrifice of the Bull. The motto placed under the lilies of the arms of France is "Lilia non laborant, neque nent." (The lily neither toils nor spins.) One recalls the parallel words of Jesus: "Consider the lilies of the field, how they grow; they toil not (like bees), neither do they spin (like spiders)."

Jesus said that the end would come like a thief in the night. At the close of *Luzifers Hofgesind* Rahn looks out at a moonlit sky and muses on following the path of the thief. Perhaps with shocking and clear sentience he knew what was to come; he had an insight into the unbridled cruelty and chaos that would follow. He was looking down the pathway of time with apocalyptic vision; he wanted us to share in these insights.

German peasants believed that bees were the survivors of the Golden Age. Above all other trees, bees love the ash: Yggdrasil, the Tree and the World of Life. The Cathars of Provence were known as *Tisserands*—weavers. The Tisserands is a constant theme in Rahn's writings. The three Norns wove the threads of Destiny and it was The Norns who sat under one of the three roots of Yggdrasil. The Norns make the laws, weaving and fixing the lives of the sons of men and the destiny of mortals. The three heads of Cerberus and the ancient practice of invocation of Hecate where three roads meet are illustrative of the image of the English broad arrow, representing the Three Nails of the Cross, the Fleur-de-Lis and the Crux Ansata of the Egyptians. The arrow symbolises the sudden directedness of the Living Force within. It has to do with projected energy and creative focus, the coming together towards a single goal or purpose of all disassociated forces of thought and of soul.

The legend of the Knight of Berne and his quest to find the doorway to the kingdom of Laurin offers striking correspondences. In Chapter 21 we will read Rahn's account of the dwarf who was tossed in the water because he had toiled insufficiently for the greedy mouths of men, this action causing the mill wheel to stop and to overgrow with roses. Later in the tale we read of the Knight's discovery of the mill cellar from which runs a deep passage leading to the garden paradise of King Laurin. It is guarded by the web of woven silk covering its entrance, spun by powers beyond mortal comprehension.

Since ancient times the bee has been regarded as the keeper of the keys to the inner-self. It is a mediator, a bridge or channel through which consciousness flows, like a flower's influence, from one kind of life to another. Each natural element interlocks with all others like a honeycomb arrangement. In contemplating these metaphorical allusions, we begin to better appreciate Otto Rahn’s mystical insight, which he offered in his writings to those with the sight to follow the flight of the bee to reveal the fabled entrance to worlds of enchantment.

"Lis/luces" is also related to lech or leche. Lich-gates were a sort of triumphal arch called *propylaea* placed in front of a church. *Propylaea* was also the name of Hecate, Cerberus' mistress. The link with Hecate suggests passage to the underworld or a perilous pathway to initiation when the heirophant undergoes death during a three-day period before being reborn anew into the Light. Rahn's account of his explorations in the grottoes, aided by his Senegalese servant Habdu, and his essay on the origins of Port Vendres in the south of France are filled with allusions to Hades and Cerberus, its ferocious protector, a beast finally vanquished by Hercules, the Hellenist Perceval who found the Grail after undergoing many labours.

John Heydon, prominent Rosicrucian thinker, wrote in *The Rosie Cross Uncovered* that the mysterious brethren possessed polymorphous powers, appearing in any desired form at will and had the gift of appearing in more than one place at the same time. Thomas

Vaughan corroborated Heydon's claims of the brethren's powers of invisibility, saying that they "*can move in this white mist. Whosoever would communicate with us must be able to see in this light...*" Brethren were buried in a womb, a glass casket, sometimes called the Philosophical Egg, out of which from time to time they would emerge to function before returning to their shell of glass. *Glas* in German means amber. In his writings Rahn explains that amber is a stone of a very particular kind. These descriptions are mindful of the Arthurian legend in which the Once and Future King is residing in a crystal cave on Avalon, the Island of Apples. We look at Rahn's meditations on Arthur in a Shakespearian context in the coming pages.

The Rosicrucians carried the great secret of Lucifer—Apollo, the Lightbringer by which epithet Otto Rahn proferred his mystical credentials to like-minded twentieth century alchemists.

The overall theme of the *Fama* is the discovery or, rather, the re-discovery of an ancient philosophy, primarily alchemical and related to the healing arts, but also concerned with number and geometry, all ingredients underlining the importance of the document as a pathway to illumination of a religious and spiritual nature. The story emphasises the importance of the miraculous discovery in 1604 of the vault housing the body of Brother Rosenkreutz who died in 1484. The allegory of the vault and its everlasting light is a central feature of the Roscicrucian legend. The sun never shines in the vault, which is eternally lit by an inner sun. Geometrical figures adorn the walls. Treasures lie all around, including the works of Paracelsus, magical bells, lamps and "artificial songs." In this imagery we are reminded once more of Rahn and Habdu tracing Hercules' steps in their search for the Solomon's treasures in the Pyrenean labyrinths. Interestingly, Falstaff, whom Rahn likens to the English lollard and Son of Apollo Sir John Oldcastle, makes this telling remark to Bardolph: "...thou art the Knight of the Burning Lamp," and we will return to Shakespeare's Henry IV works to examine further allegorical links with Rahn's secret agenda. The exemplar Rosicrucian is epitomised by Shakespeare as the Knight of the Burning Lamp.

Rahn wrote endearingly of the Knight of Berne embarking upon a quest to find eternity, eventually finding the key, the *dietrich*, in Nature, peeling aside the spider's web and penetrating into the fulgurant Middle Earth Kingdom of Laurin, becoming in the process an Immortal. Rahn wrote the story so powerfully that it is evident that he identified in every respect with the brave and fearless Knight. In his sojourns into the Pyrenean grottoes Rahn re-lived the Knight's archetypal journey, a caver's lamp before him lighting the dark, a brother of the Rosy Cross in quest and in belief. Was Rahn alone in his time in walking this philosophical pathway? The evidence suggests otherwise.

The many tributaries of Rosicrucian philosophy along which one is encouraged to explore from a careful reading of Rahn's writings are seemingly endless. Another rewarding line of investigation surrounds the Bacon-Rosicrucian-Shakespeare enigma, which Otto Rahn begins to explore in *Luzifers Hofgesind*. Chapter XII of the Rosicrucian *Confessio Fraternititas* says that one of the philosophers who make light of the Holy Trinity was "a stage player, a man with sufficient ingenuity for imposition." In *Luzifers Hofgesind* Otto Rahn quotes from Henry IV Part 2. Manly P. Hall strongly believed that Andreas' "stage player" was Francis Bacon (Lord Verulam). The *Anatomy of Melancholy*, 1621, by Democritus Junior, pseudonym for Robert Burton, an intimate of Bacon, contains a short but significant footnote: "Joh. Valent. Andreas, Lord Verulam" indicating Burton's belief that Andreas and Bacon were one and the same person. Abundant evidence exists to convince many, Manley P. Hall among them, that Bacon wrote the works of Shakespeare. Hall states that no one but a Platonist, Qabbalist or Pythagorean could have written *The Tempest, Macbeth, Hamlet* or the *Tragedy of Cymbeline*.

In 1604 a very curious work dedicated to the Duke of Wurttemberg was published in Stuttgart. It was a book of huge length entitled *Naometria* by Simon Studion and its theme focussed upon apocalyptic prophecy. It involved a system of numerology based on Biblical descriptions of the Temple of Solomon, leading to prophecies about future events. We see here close correspondences with the *Oracle of Astral Force* of the Polaires.

Apart from the Andreae-Bacon synthesis, two writers are acknowledged as the chief protagonists of Rosicrucian philosophy: Robert Fludd in England and Michael Maier in Germany. Maier gave expression to the theme of spiritual alchemy while Fludd gave more focus to the philosophy of macrocosm and microcosm. In his second work, *Viatorum hoc est de Montibus Planetarunt Septem,* Maier sets out his alchemical foundation of beliefs. The theme of the book is the search for the *materia philosophica,* the truth hidden in the arcana of nature, by holding fast, like Theseus, to Ariadne's thread, which will lead one through the labyrinth (and, equally, through Pyrenean grottoes to the place of concealment of the Treasures of the Temple of Solomon). In his 1652 work *Themis Aurea* Maier make a description of the R.C Fraternity as both an Order of Chivalry and as an Order of the

Golden Fleece.

In general terms Rosicrucianism stood for the individual's quest to undertake private and personal religious experiences by which his total being—body, mind and spirit—was refined and strengthened. As Dee and Fludd conceived it, the movement was to be inclusive of all religious attitudes. However, especially in Germany, it rapidly encouraged anti-Catholic sentiments as it evolved into a broad evangelical system of belief attractive to all denominations of Protestants. Anti-Catholic Rahn would have experienced little or no internal opposition to embracing these beliefs and expounding Rosicrucian principles *sub-rosa* within his own writings.

Chapter TWENTY

The Argonauts

Having sketched the history and import of Rosicrucianism in the sub-context of Rahn's philosophy, let us follow the wake of the Argo and its principal passengers. In *Luzifers Hofgesind* Rahn mentions the tale of the Argonauts over and over again. He remarks that Wolfram von Eschenbach celebrated Hercules as the prophet of the Grail (the grotto at Lombrives said by locals to be the tomb of Hercules). The oak has always been sacred. The troubadours (*sauveurs*) found in its branches the laws of Love and Courtly Poetry (*amour courtois*). Rahn said that in the Middle-Ages there were those who believed that the Golden Fleece was the Philosophers Stone. He sided with this belief, adding that the Philosophers Stone-Golden Fleece was the Great Work. Moreover, Rahn believed, like Eschenbach, that Hercules was a Hellenic Perceval who found the Grail. "I think it so," Rahn says in *Luzifers Hofgesind.*

In *Kreuzzug gegen den Gral* Rahn compares the legend of the sacred forest where hangs the Golden Fleece with the tales of the enchanted forest of Oberon, which surrounds the magical Castle of Monmur, protecting it from the rest of the world. Rahn built on this imagery by referring to the legend of the Argonauts in Nannos where the navigators see a cup floating on the 'Mountain of the World with the tree of lights.' In Rahn's synthesis Monmur (the seat of Oberon's enchanted castle), the Mountain of the World and Montségur are one and the same. They meld together to emphasise the symbolic significance of the ancient stories that link the voyage of the Argonauts, both with the Pyrenees and with the legend of Yggdrasil, the Tree of Life. Interestingly, in terms of Grail mythology the Argonaut's Nannos episode resonates closely with the Welsh account of the Nanteos Cup, a sacred life-giving cauldron with reputed healing powers, which was found near Aberystwyth in West Wales. The Nanteos Cup is thought to have been the basis for many of the later Grail stories.

Rennes-le-Château was the site of the grove of Oak trees sacred to the Francs Saliens, descendants of the Merovingiens and of the Celts. In later pages we will examine more closely the many layers of philosophic and metaphysical meaning linking Otto Rahn with Rennes-le-Château.

The interpolation of the Argonauts' adventures with the historical growth and evolution of alchemy (the Royal Art or Great Work) has been a cherished tenet among philosophers, mystics and seers for centuries. In our time one of the most powerful champions of the link between them is Professor Antoine Faivre, Directeur d'Études à l'École Pratique des Hautes Études (Section des Sciences Réligieuse) of the Sorbonne. In *The Golden Fleece and Alchemy*, Faivre examines the euhemeristic[1] and esoteric backgrounds to the myths and adventures of Phrixos and of the Argonauts. Faivre remarks that they gravitate towards two powerful archetypes: the journey towards the East and the "Holy Spirit Fire." His astute observations provide a powerful argument to encourage a belief that Otto Rahn's secret philosophic agenda was rooted in timeless hermetic-alchemic truths, protected from the profane by brave men and women over the centuries.

The ceremonial collar worn by members of the Order of the Golden Fleece consists of eight golden links joined by flintstones in which the spark of fire lies latent. We see here close correspondences with the three nails said by Rosicrucian adepts to affix the spirit to the cross of the physical body. The stones also contain steel components called "acies" (German Staale). Suspended from the collar is a pendant clothed with the golden wool of the fleece. In ancient times sheep's wool was used in panning to attract gold in aurific streams. The sacrifice of the lamb conjures a wealth of mythical imagery.

In the criobolium ceremony of antiquity the initiate was literally bathed in blood, whereas Christians are only figuratively washed in the blood of the lamb. The ram's skin has often been represented as a parchment with an alchemical text upon it. Henry Corbin, Faivre's predecessor, associated the Golden Fleece with the aureum vellus (the oriflamme), and in turn drew comparisons with the Avestian concept of the Mazdaznan *xvarnah* or light of glory. In the Iranian epics the light of glory of the Knights represents a link between the image of the ram and chivalry and was established long before Philip the Good brought them together in his founding of the Order of the Golden Fleece. Corbin said that this Zoroastrian notion refers to "victorial fire," characterised in the Christian tradition as the nimbus or halo of the Saints. He believed that the *xvarnah* and the Holy Grail were one and the same.

The Greek agnus was the name of the stone or stones that the

[1] Interpretation of myth derived from analysis of actual historical events or evidence, as distinct from reaching conclusions based upon esoteric or metaphysical insight.

weavers hung from their canvas in order to weave them. Many times in his writings Rahn refers to the oft-quoted description of the Cathar faithful as *tisserands*—weavers, which is how many of them made their living. The stone hanging from the weaver's canvas and the ram hanging from the stone of the fire-giving flintstone collar come together in the image of the lamb. Ancient Greek chronicler, Dionysius Scytobrachion, suggested that the Golden Fleece was really the skin of young Mr Ram, Phrixus' page. Recall the error made by *La Dépêche* in naming Rahn as Mr Rams at the time of the Polaires affair in 1932.

Raoul Lefèvre wrote his *Histoire de Jason* in 1456 in which the remarkable feature is the inclusion of both the Golden Fleece and the parchment of the Emerald Tablet of Hermes Trismegistus. A king called Apollo received a parchment from the god Mars containing "all the mysteries that should be discovered and preserved to achieve such a lofty thing." The lofty thing is the Fleece. Apollo, the discoverer of harmonic chords, played an instrument strung from the nerve sinews of a ram.

Authors writing on the theme of the Fleece have referred to it as a chrysographic medium, a method by which one can write a parchment in gold letters. Moreover, Chrysopoeia is also another term for alchemy and, therefore, the Golden Fleece is also a book of alchemy, written on skin and expounding a way to produce gold chemically. In the Renaissance we see an increasing number of allegories and publications depicting the Golden Fleece as an alchemical medium. Pico della Mirandola and Gregorio Giraldi also tried to draw the secrets of the alchemical art from both the myth of Hercules and the Golden Apples and the myth of Jason.

Splendor Solis, a German alchemical treatise, was translated into French in 1598. Its dedication says that the Odyssean voyage "gathers from the flowers of the best Philosophers a hive of sweet honey." We have already seen the high importance of the bee motif to the Rosicrucians and, later, to Otto Rahn, but the remark in *Splendor*

Solis established a link between the Golden Fleece and the esoteric role of the bee as the guardian of the threshold to the inner self.

In 1715 Ehrd of Naxagoras' treatise *Auruem Vellus* was published in Gießen. The 1733 re-print describes how Phrixus took the treasure of his father Athamos and set off in a ship (Schiff) called "sheep" (Schaaf). In the eighteenth century there was still a type of ship called a schaaf. The treatise also examines the verb "vello, vellere" (to pull out). Before scissors were invented sheep's hairs were pulled out by hand. From vello we derive wolle (wool) and so Vellus Aureum is the golden wool taken from the Ram "in whom the Philosopher's Sun is exalted." Naxagoras said that the Ram's skin is "none other than Hermes' Emerald Tablet." All things considered, the interpolation of Rahn and Ram in the Polaires business can be construed as a symbolic indication of Otto Rahn's attachment to the ancient Hermetic arts.

During the Renaissance period we also see decorative motifs made for the homes of the wealthy in which the Golden Fleece is guarded by dragons. The famed Hotel Lallement was one such residence. The villa of the Marquis Maximilian Palombara had inscriptions on a marble door that read: "the dragon of the Hesperides watches over the magic gardens and, but for Hercules, Jason would not have tasted the delights of Colchis." In this description we glimpse the elements of the story of the Knight of Berne and his quest to enter the Kingdom of Laurin and attain immortality, a magical tale that Rahn expounds so poetically in *Luzifers Hofgesind.*

The Argonauts set off from the Port of Venus. Rahn muses on the placename's transliteration with Port Vendre (where, legend tells, the Argo moored) and nearby Cap Cerbère, evoking the guardian of Hades whom Hercules vanquished and chained because he had no fear of death. Hercules knew he was immortal. Apollonius of Rhodes, 3rd century BC, said that the Argonauts returned along the Eridanos, the Nordic river of amber. The Argonauts placed a beam pruned from the sacred oak at Dodoni in the prow of the Argo so that they would not be deprived of the prophetic voice of their god.

Orpheus, son of Thracian King Oeagrus and the Muse Calliope, was the most famous poet and musician that ever lived. Apollo presented him with a lyre. After his journey to Egypt, Orpheus joined the Argonauts in their quest to find the Golden Fleece. Orpheus later married Eurydice. Eurydice was accosted by Aristaeus who tried to rape her. She trod on a serpent (as Rahn informs his readers he did while in the Pyrenees, a mountain range that is intrinsically bound up with the legend of the Hercules and, by extension, with his participation in the voyage to search for the Fleece). Eurydice died of the serpent's bite but Orpheus descended into Tartarus to try to get her back. Otto Rahn trod on a snake and then descended into the grottoes of the Sabarthés to find and restore his true love—the Holy Grail of the Cathars and of the Templars.

Aristaeus visited Arcadia and then went on to Tempe where all the bees died. (By now the bees have become a veritable swarm in our review of Rahn's cosmology.) Aristaeus was advised by Cyrene to bind her cousin Proteus to find out from him why the bees had sickened. Cyrene advised Aristaeus to raise four altars to the Dryads. He also had to bring poppies of forgetfulness to propitiate the ghost of Orpheus who had joined Eurydice below. Nine days later a swarm of bees rose from the rotting carcasses of the cattle and settled on a tree. The Arcadians now honour him as Zeus for having taught this method of raising new swarms of bees.

In the Austrian Tyrol men are not admitted to the flax harvest. The ruling spirit is the *Harpatsch*, a terrifying hag whose hands and face are rubbed with soot. Any man who meets her accidentally is embraced, forced to dance, sexually assaulted and smeared with soot. In *Luzifers Hofgesind* Rahn remarked upon an "abominable woman" from his village who in the Middle-Ages sold out her husband's parents to the Inquisitor Konrad of Marburg who promptly sent them to be burned.

The search for the Golden Fleece is one of the most powerful and enduring legends in mythological history. Today, our twenty-first century familiarity with the story is largely shaped by Hollywood's interpretations, rather than by the classical texts. I happily confess that even today one of my all time favourite movies is *Jason and the Argonauts* with Ray Harryhausen's fantastic and ingenious effects. Rather than feel despondent that such treatments cheapen the myth, let us be thankful that they keep it alive and available for successive generations to appreciate and, should Zeus be willing, to understand it in some small way.

The sacred oak of Dodoni is symbolic of the human body. Draped around it is the immortal *xvarnah*, held in place by twig and branch, the three nails of the Rosicrucians. Written upon the Fleece in words of fire is ultimate wisdom—Dr. Henry Jones' cherished pearl of Illumination.

Rahn confided in Wolfgang Frommel that he sought the Fleece. Maybe someone who could not see the Fleece for the trees took him at his word and tracked his every movement in the hope of stealing Rahn's secrets and a fast route to enlightenment.

But a true Argonaut is not washed overboard as easily as all that. Maybe Otto Rahn had the presence of mind to grab that bit of the prow brought from Dodoni—the mouthpiece of the gods and a guide to a safe harbour.

Chapter TWENTY ONE

The Church

"She has seen a door stealthily opening and she vanishes through it."
Sancho: "where may this Eden be?" Don Quichotte: "I alone know the way."
"He has the key to riches and happiness, he has the key."
"An azure wave laps its shores, 'tis beautiful and pleasing, it is the Island of Dreams."
"The jewel, in itself, is nothing, but the cause is sacred."
Excerpts from Henri Cain's libretto for Jules Massenet's *Don Quichotte*

Aerial view of Rennes-le-Château

In Chapter 9 we looked at the claim by Colonel Howard Beuchner that Otto Rahn visited the Corbières in 1937. This visit is not substantiated. However, there is little doubt in my mind that there is a strong connection between Rahn and Rennes-le-Château. I find these connecting links, which, in the following pages, will be explored in the context of the Rennes-le-Château story:

- Rahn's link to the Cathars whom he loved with great passion;
- The war waged against the Cathars by the Church and the French King, a war of such ferocity that it brings into question the true

nature of the secrets for ownership of which the crusade against Albigensian and Cathar was really launched;
- Rennes-le-Château seated in the Cathar heartland; Saunière discovering something linked to the "real" story of Catholic geopolitical involvement in the West over the centuries;
- The Vatican not speaking out against the Nazis until close to the end of WW2. What was the Church afraid of?
- Jules Massenet and his librettist Henri Cain for the opera: *Don Quichotte* and the metaphysical concepts of the necklace image and of the Island of Dreams;
- The various legends of the seven sleepers—Mary Magdalene and the Sleepers of Ephesus, Otto Rahn's account of the Roses of Bozen, even the story of *Snow White*;
- Nacht und Nebel/Société Angelique (Le Brouillard).

And finally a long shot:
- Feodor Chaliapin, the renowned Russian baritone, and his links with Pius X and with Bérenger Saunière.

How do we link Rahn and his brief life to Rennes-le-Château? We must remember first and foremost that Saunière was a Catholic priest. What was it that Rahn loved with all his heart but that the Church hated with such vitriol? The Cathars. The Cathar movement was crushed by the Catholic Church and the King of France with extreme brutality.

One hundred and fifty years after these Crusades came the witchhunts during when an estimated six to nine million people, eighty five percent of them women, were executed. The only crime of the Cathars was to believe in another way. At the heart of all major religions there is a pearl of great beauty. Its light cannot take sides. By definition, those from within the Church who allow these acts are at the same time outside the true church. Aggression on such a scale has to have another motive. And was this motive what Rahn was seeking?

What prevented the Church deploring the Nazis atrocities when they became evident early on in the war rather than waiting until the very end to speak up, and then only halfheartedly? Some say it was the secret Kirchensteur funds Hitler paid the Church during that time, but was it just that (as a lifelong Catholic Hitler personally continued to pay his taxes to the Church until his death)? What could the Nazis hold over the Church to keep it quiet so all those Catholic soldiers did as they were told? Otto Rahn was privy to the inner secrets of the Nazi elite. It is a safe bet he would have known something of the pressures the Nazis exerted over Pius XII to deter him from voicing public criticism of

Hitler's policies and actions.[1]

The Catholic Centre Party emerged from the Great War as a major force in Germany after forty years of suppression instigated by Bismarck. Its renewal allowed the Party to gain rapidly in influence and it succeeded in forcing a repeal of the anti-Jesuit laws passed in 1872. From that time the Society of Jesus was free to to enter Germany and to found colleges, schools and communities. It engaged in these activities with great vigour. It is perhaps of little wonder that Otto Rahn, therefore, was deeply distrustful of the Jesuits in Germany (and they of him) considering the subject, tone and passion of his pro-Cathar/anti-(Catholic) Church writings.

In 1933 Fritz Gerlich, outspoken editor of the Catholic publication *Der Gerade Weg* (the Straight Path), was almost beaten to death in his office and then thrown into a KZ. A year later he was murdered in the Night of the Long Knives. Considering the mud that has been thrown at Rahn by commentators and historians seeking to implicate him in the associated event of the Röhm putsch, it is possible that the Catholic Church regarded Rahn as not merely an impassive foe of Catholicism but one prepared to wield knife and gun in physical acts of terror.

The Reich Concordat, signed on 20th July 1933, legally (but certainly not spiritually or ethically) bound the Catholic Church in Germany to silence on outrages against the Jews because by that time the persecution and elimination of Jews in Germany was stated policy. Also in place by the 20th was the adoption of the Law for Prevention of Genetically Diseased Offspring, which called for sterilisation of all those suffering from hereditary mental or cognitive diseases, including blindness and deafness. Consequent to the passing of this law, nearly three hundred and fifty thousand people would ultimately be sterilised in the Third Reich, most without family permission.

In strict legal terms the Concordat bound the Church's hands from speaking out against such atrocities, or at least it was a major excuse trotted out to try to appease those who railed against the Church's pusillanimity. The guiding hand behind the drafting of the Concordat and the lengthy process of agreeing it with Hitler was Eugenio Pacelli who in 1933 was Vatican Secretary of State and who assumed the pontificate a short time later.

Through time everyone keeps looking for a treasure and ignores the Church but I am convinced that it is within the Church that we will

---

[1] Monsignor Mayol de Lupe, Chaplain of the French S.S. Brigade Charlemagne, was a personal friend of Pius

(eventually) find the key to the Rennes-le-Château mystery, which leads us to the influence of the Hapsburgs in the inner sanctums of the Church. The Hapsburgs still controlled who would become the Pope through the Curia. Franz Joseph exercised his veto as head of the Austrian-Hungary Empire against Leo XIII's candidate for the papacy, Cardinal Rampolla.

Nazism was a religion with Adolf Hitler as its object of veneration. Many of its principles were Catholic, including Hitler and Himmler. Practically every right-wing dictator in the 1930's and 1940's was brought up as a Catholic: Hitler, Franco, Petain, Mussolini, Tiso and Pavelic (whose lust for sadistic and bloody mass murder in Croatia was arguably even more rabid than that of Hitler).

Hitler saw himself as the Anti-Pope, referring to Himmler as "my Ignatius." In boyhood, Hitler attended the school at Lambach where he sang in the choir. There the young Adolf became acquainted with the symbol of the swastika because it was the heraldic design of Father Hagen, the abbey's administrator.

Himmler's castle at Wewelsburg represented a mystical warrior-monastery. The Reichsführer SS consciously modelled the SS after the Society of Jesus. He was greatly impressed by the Jesuits' order, discipline, authority and their sense of collective intellectual endeavour. Himmler sought to recreate this by pumping billions of dollars (at today's prices) in constructing the Ahnenerbe and executing its worldwide network of research programmes and initiatives.

Like many members of the Nordic Revival Himmler particularly hated the Catholic Church. After Ahnenerbe genealogical research showed that Himmler was related to women killed in the great Middle-Ages witchhunts, he held the Church responsible for genocide. In 1935 Himmler even set up a special Ahnenerbe unit called Sonderkommando H (H standing for Hexen—witches) to study the question. This unit included Himmler's cousin Wilhelm Patin, a Catholic priest before joining the SS.

There is more than a hint of irony in Himmler's resolute position on the Church, considering the entry he made in his diary as a nineteen year old: "…I shall always love God and pray to him, and shall remain faithful to the Catholic Church and defend it, even if I am expelled from it."

Further evidence of Jesuitical influence at the highest levels between the Church and the Nazi high command has been related by Edmond Paris in his book *Secret History of the Jesuits*. Paris' claims are summarised as follows:

Hitler's "Mittel-Europa" plan was very similar to the objectives of Halke von Ledochowski, Jesuit General, which was the creation of a Federation of Catholic nations in central and Eastern Europe: Austria, Slovakia, Bohemia, Poland, Hungary, Croatia and Bavaria. Hitler's plan, in effect, was Ledochowski's adapted to the needs of the time.

Eugenio Pacelli, Papal Nuncio in Munich and the future Pope Pius XII, shared this dream and aided Hitler in bringing the plan together. Franz von Papen, the Pope's secret chamberlain, also was instrumental in giving support for the plan.

By 1933 there were forty-five concentration camps in Germany holding more than 40,000 prisoners. Von Papen said: "Nazism is the Christian reaction against the spirit of 1789." He also said: "The Third Reich is the first world power which not only acknowledges but also puts into practice the high principles of the papacy."

Jesuit Cardinal-Archbishop of Milan Alfredo Ildefonso Schuster, head of the sinister-sounding "École de Mystique Faciste," called Mussolini's activities a "Catholic Crusade."

In 1936 primate of Poland, Cardinal Hland, said: "There will be the Jewish problem as long as the Jews remain."

In 1937 Abbe Jean Vienjeau wrote: "to accept the principle of the Inquisition one only needs a Christian mentality and this is what many Christians lack...the (Catholic) Church has no such timidity."

The Vatican issued a bulletin to the Spanish *Reforme* on 3rd May 1945, the date of Hitler's death, saying: "Adolf Hitler, son of the Catholic Church, died while defending Christianity...with the palm of the Martyr, God gives Hitler the laurels of victory."

Goebbels was brought up in a Jesuit college and was a seminarist before devoting himself to literature and to politics.

Heinrich Himmler's father was a director of a Catholic school in Munich. His brother was a Benedictine monk and his uncle, a Jesuit, held the key and influential position of Canon at the Court of Bavaria. According to author Walter Stagen, Ledochowski was ready to offer some collaboration between the Gestapo and the Society of Jesus as a weapon against Communism. Subsequently, an appropriate organisation was created inside the SS and Jesuit Father Himmler assumed the responsibilities as one of its superior officers. It is clear that Halke von Ledochowski and Father Himmler played a much more important role behind the scenes in influencing the Nazi heirarchy than previously acknowledged.

As we have seen Rahn hated the Jesuits and in all probability their action against him amounted to considerably more than outspoken criticism of his heretical writings and sending him threatening letters. I believe it likely that the denouncement which Rahn mentioned to his friends prior to his disappearance involved Father Himmler's SS office.

For a brief period Otto Rahn was an inside member of this "Nazi" church, which further enhances the perception of history that major first-level actions (wars, crusades, pogroms) are, more often than not, shrouds that conceal deeper levels of action on behalf of dark and unidentifiable secret interest groups, invariably male dominated, and equally invariably, at the expense of the personal freedoms of commonfolk. In the early summer of 1914, it was evident to observers that events in Europe were building to a catastrophic conclusion. What follows is an unsubstantiated account:

A young priest, gifted in languages, was despatched by the Vatican to Vienna in July 1914 to meet with Emperor Franz Joseph. The papal emissary's mission was to beg Franz Joseph to use his enormous influence to avert conflict. The priest was ushered into the presence of the living legend, the Hapsburg monarch who had been the crowned head of Europe for over forty years. The Emperor humbly welcomed the priest and then sank to his knees in tears, distraught that he had not been able to use his power and influence to save the lives of his family who had met with recent violent death. Franz Joseph asked the priest if he would hear his confession. The young man fell into the old devil's trap. During the confession the Emperor revealed that in the coming days he would declare war on Serbia, an act he knew would gather apace and ignite the Great War. Franz Joseph finished his confession, rose, and laughed at the priest, saying: "priest, you have heard my confession and, therefore, you have assumed my guilt. I shall put the world to the sword free from sin..."

Perhaps in this account we have a reason why the Nazis had a stick with which to beat the Vatican during WW2. Merry del Val was soon pressing Prince Schonberg, the Austrian ambassador to the Holy See, to encourage Austria to react vigorously to the events in Serbia. Del Val signed the concordat a few days before the assassination that started the war.

So what is the prize that the Church and the Anti-Church (are they interchangeable?) were prepared to kill for in such huge numbers? What were the real objectives of Himmler's worldwide Ahnenerbe initiatives? I believe we have to focus on the concept of the Grail. If the quest was for something tangible then the thing would have been found long before 1945, considering all the massive resources, manpower and money that have been thrown at it over the centuries. The heat would have dissipated. But if the pearl was less material and more Taoistic in nature (that which is, isn't), then slaughtering in ever vaster numbers only makes sense if these actions were mounted to conceal the nature of the real conflict—the eternal battle for the souls of humankind.

The Court of Lucifer is an expedition through the "garden of roses," Rahn's affectionate term for the Middle Earth Kingdom of the Asgardian Elfin, Lorin, and a realm closed to non-believers or the uninitiated. Rahn dreams of a return to Thule, the primordial centre of the European Hyperboreans. He pines for a return to the Golden Age. Here is Rahn's account of the Elfin legend:

"*One day, a Knight of the lineage of Dietrich de Berne was out riding in the Tyrol along the ancient Troj de Reses, the pathway of roses. He was trying vainly to find an access to the Kingdom of Laurin. Each time he believed he had attained this goal insurmountable walls would rise up in the mountains around him. He then came upon a gorge and he passed through.*

Close by a stream he heard the marvellous singing of a multitude of birds. He stopped to listen. Then the Knight saw a shepherdess in a sunny meadow. He asked her if the birds always sang so. She replied that she had not heard them sing for a very long time, but that now that they were it was possible, she thought, to rediscover the windmill and again put it to work for the good of men. What sort of windmill is it, asked the Knight? It is an enchanted windmill, the shepherdess replied. In the past, she said, it was dwarfs who worked it on behalf of Laurin who owned it and who milled flour for the poor.

But there were those who had become greedy and one day one of the dwarfs had been tossed in the water because he had not given enough flour. Since then the mill wheel had stopped and no one knew where it was.

It would be thus until the birds sang again. The windmill will be found at the bottom of a gorge. It is well concealed and even its wheel turns no longer. People call it the windmill of roses because it is covered in wild roses.

The Knight finds it. The mill is covered in moss, its wooden sides are blackened with age and its wheel is stuck. The roses form a thicket around it such that a passer-by would not see the mill. The Knight tries to open the door but it will not budge. In the wall he sees a tiny window. The Knight climbs on his horse's back and peers through. Inside are seven dwarfs stretched out, sleeping. The Knight calls and taps on the window but there is no response.

Defeated, the Knight returns to the meadow and sleeps for the night.

The following day he climbs on a high point overlooking the gorge. Three rose bushes are in bloom before him. The Knight picks a rose from the first bush.

An elf cries out from the foliage: "bring me a rose from the good old days!"

"Willingly" replies the Knight, "but how will I find it?"

The elf disappears in lament.

The Knight approaches the second bush and picks a flower. Again, an elf appears, asks the same question, getting the same answer, and withdraws lamenting. The Knight then picks a bloom from the third bush and another elf asks: "why do you knock at our door?"

"I wish to enter the garden of roses of King Laurin, for I seek the fiancé of the Month of May!"

"Only the child and the poet may enter the garden of roses. If you can sing a beautiful ballad then the way will be open to you."

"I can do it."

"Then come with me" said the elf who picks some wild roses and descends into the gorge followed by the Knight. They reach the windmill. Its door opens. The dwarfs sleep still. The elf brushes them with the roses, crying:

"Awaken, sleepers, the young roses are in flower!"

The dwarfs wake up, open their eyes and commence to mill.

The elf shows the mill cellar to the Knight. From there runs a gallery deep into the mountain and finishes in a dazzling light. This is the garden paradise of King Laurin, with its multi-coloured flowerbeds, exquisite groves and resplendant roses. The Knight sees also the web of woven silk covering its entrance.

"Now, begin your song" asks the elf.

The Knight then sings the song of Love and of the Month of May. And the paradise of roses opens before him.

The Knight penetrates into Eternity."

This tale is filled with powerful themes and images that might provide a clue to the real mystery, among them: Knight of the lineage of Dietrich, Troj de Reses, shepherdess, enchanted windmill, seven dwarfs, fiancé of the Month of May, web of woven silk. Taking them in turn:

Knight of the lineage of Dietrich—a Knight of the line of the Key (*dietrich* means skeleton key). This is a classic image of initiation of someone pursuing a Quest, a thread of order, under the protection of ancient guardians wherein over time they must develop a clue-key to their Higher Self, unlock the door and enter the worlds within. In Cervantes we read of Don Quixote's sojourn in the Caves of Montesinos. The old Knight, protected by his revered and battered Mambrino's helmet, pushes through the "membrane" separating the World Without from the World Within and enters the realms of initiation before returning to Sancho fully armed to complete his life's Quest. Sancho, whom Quixote calls *hombre de bien* (the *bonhomme* epithet beloved by the Cathars—too obvious to be a coincidence on Cervantes' part), asks his cousin while en route to the grotto of Montesinos who was the first *saltimbanque* (travelling performer or jongleur) of the world. His cousin cannot answer so Sancho answers his own question. It was Lucifer, he said, when he was tossed from heaven into the abyss. Amazed by his squire's knowledge, Quixote tells Sancho that he must have got both question and answer from the lips of another. Sancho retorts that when he starts the Question and Answer game he does not finish until the following morning, meaning he has wisdom a-plenty. Quixote tells Sancho that he could not have spoken better. Quixote had been struck by Apollo! Similarly, Rahn was struck by Don Quixote. It is evident that Apollo's reach to Quest adventurers recognises neither limit of time nor distance.

Troj de Reses is the Rose Trail, again the suggestion of an unbroken metaphysical link with the timeless power of Nature. The Knight picks a rose and is asked why he knocks at the elf's door. But picking and knocking are quite dissimilar. Once more, we get the impression of gaining access into hidden realms simply by being at one with Nature's rhythms at the right place and at the right time.

Shepherdess conjures images of Poussin, of Arcadian and Eleusinian initiations, of the feminine aspect of Jesus the Shepherd, which in the context of Western mysticism equates with Mary Magdalene, Jesus' wife and mother of their son who ensured the continuance of the mystical bloodline.

Enchanted windmill returns us to Cervantes and the messages that he tried to convey "between the lines" to those of his readers with the ears to hear and the sight to see. It is no coincidence that Jules Massenet and Henri Cain created similar themes in their opera Don Quichotte and that Massenet continued them in the titles of other works such as *Bérengère and Anatole* and *La Coupe du Roi de Thulé*.

Think of seven dwarfs and we think of Snow White (the Goddess) and her guardianship of Middle Earth. It was Snow White's purity and innocence that protected her and the dwarfs against the over-negative aspects of feminine power, the hag who can weave a shroud around the beauty in our lives.

Consider the Month of May, the fifth month and the number of the female pentacle. The double M is mindful of Mary Magdalene, High Priestess of the Temple of Ishtar. During his travels Don Quixote meets two prostitutes at an inn. He names them Tolosa and Molinara—Toulouse and Moliniers. The Cathars called the Vaudois: *Moliniers=meuniers=millers*. It was by virtue of seeking the millers that the Knight of Berne found their cave in the paradise Garden of Roses and from there walked the pathway to eternity.

Web of woven silk alludes to the timeless thread of order that is ever-present in the midst of chaos. It is the Guide between this world and the Otherworld, personified in mythology by Ariadne, Circe, Ceridwen and Hecate.

The Cathars and the Templars were reputed to be the guardians of the Grail and Rahn wrote (quoted from *Croissade contre le Graal)*: "*quand tombe la nuit meridionale, des étoiles d'une invraisemblable grandeur scintellent et rayonnent, si proches qu'on imagine presque pouvoir les atteindre de la main.*" As we have seen, to touch the stars is to fasten the necklace upon the Goddess.

The story of the Goddess is very powerful. She reined supreme long before Christianity, and the West welcomed her with enthusiasm. Lyons was already the city of Cybele by the third century. In Paris, Isis reigned until Saint Genevieve took over as patroness of the city. As late as the fourth century it seemed probable to an observer that if the Roman Empire survived, a religious consensus would prevail based on the worship of the universal Great Mother. But the Christian Church that Constantine established became strongly patriarchal with the growing emphasis on the martyr qualities of defiant steadfastness and simple faith of Christian soldiers rather than more subtle or gentler qualities. The feminine principle, so predominant throughout both East and West in centuries past, was rapidly transplanted by a patriarchal order that would know no limits in its efforts to bury any re-emergence of the mysticism and magic of the Goddess and her priestess representative, the Sacred Prostitute. The Temple of Isis at Soissons was re-dedicated to the Virgin Mary in the fifth century. The transition was almost complete. In the twelfth century the Church carried out its most brutal stage of its feminine-principle extermination programme with the advent of the Albigensian Crusade. The courts of the Inquisition replaced the courts of the Minne—courtly love—with mass torture.

The Quest for the Grail is a quest to find the Goddess within because it is she who stands at the threshold to all other worlds of mystery and enchantment. Artists and key historical figures have long sought to illustrate the timeless and poetic nature of this most personal and special of adventures, and it is they that provide us with some of the less obvious links.

As we have seen, Cervantes brought us to Don Quixote. Centuries before, the troubadours related the legend of the Kingdom of Laurin, the world of the nature folk, and resurrected by Rahn so richly in *Luzifers Hofgesind*. This magical realm is only accessible by a child, a poet, or a Knight with a song in his heart: "The Month of May." (Bolzano, the site of the legend, has a small mountaintop church dedicated to Mary Magdalene. Interestingly, a friend of Bormann's wife reported seeing Hitler's henchman, alive, in Bolzano in September 1945.) Poussin painted a tomb; Lewis Carroll wrote of a child and a white rabbit; Tolkein of Middle Earth; C.S. Lewis of Narnia. These authors believed in their creations. More than that, I am convinced that they believed them to be every bit as real as the world outside their window. Their belief system was such that these major figures banded together in secret groupings to ensure the continuance of universal truths through their writings and their art. Sir Walter Raleigh was a member of the esoteric School of Night (reminiscent of Shakespeare's mysterious line from The Tempest: "*what seest thou else in the dark and backward abysm of time?*"). Cervantes, Hugo and Verne were among the members of the Société Angélique (Le Brouillard). Tolkein and C. S. Lewis were members of the Inklings group. However, the Société Angélique became politicised in the late 1800's, interfering in the business of French succession and other affairs of state and Jules Verne bade them farewell. A short time later he died. Le Brouillard invited something bad into the fog. Thirty years later the Nazis created their own unholy fog: the Nacht und Nebel.

The Catholic Church is the hub for the spokes of the Otto Rahn—Rennes-le-Château connections. Who were the personalities on the field of play? The Pope in office at the time Saunière made his discoveries was Leo XIII who was succeeded in 1903 by Pius X. Pius was an admirer of Feodor Chaliapin, the larger-than-life Russian baritone who is said to have sung privately for Pius at Castel Gandalfo in the months before the outbreak of WW1. In his biography Chaliapin makes a cryptic comment in the opening pages, referring to "*that Bérenger volume, that precious Trio I had composed.*" The words are too direct to be coincidental but what are we intended to infer from them? Jules Massenet composed *Don Quichotte* specifically for

Chaliapin. Henri Cain's libretto for the opera is full of striking allusions to "keys (*dietrichs*), vanishing doorways, Islands of Dreams, jewels and sacred causes." These men were trying to tell us something.

After Pius' death a movement arose calling itself the Society of Saint Pius X, an extreme traditionalist group. It claimed to have a great secret, linked to the 3rd Fatima Prophecy, which is said to be connected to Rennes-le-Château. This secret, they claimed, would bring down the papacy.

Pius X struggled to staunch the Modernist tide. He excommunicated the key protagonists, among them the Jesuit scholar and author George Tyrell and his friend Abbé Loisy. Abbé Bieil of St Sulpice, the seminary where Saunière was said to have taken the parchments he discovered during his refurbishment work at Rennes-le-Château, had a nephew, Emile Hoffet, who launched the Modernist rebellion.

The Vatican in Pius' day was even said to have nuns serving the pontiff who were linked to an ultra-secret Parisian guild of Sacred Prostitutes located in the Rue d'Amboise, priestesses who provided an unbroken link to the original Temple of Ishtar and its feminine-based rites and initiations. Saunière went to great lengths to emphasize the Magdalene, both in the church at Rennes-le-Château and in his Villa Bethany.

Otto Rahn wrote: "to open the Kingdom of Lucifer you must equip yourself with a Dietrich, I carry with me the key." Let us indulge in a little wordplay: Dietrich...Marlene...Mary Magdalene. One of the many legends surrounding Mary Magdalene has her buried at Ephesus near the grotto of the seven sleepers residing in enchanted slumber. Compare the seven sleepers imagery with the dwarf elements of the legend of the Roses of Bosen and with the story of Snow White.

Maybe the Marlene Dietrich wordplay is not so fanciful. Hans-Jürgen Lange writes that Marlene Dietrich and Josephine Baker were said to have figured among Otto Rahn's guests at the Hôtel-Restaurant des Marronniers in Ussat-les-Bains. The legendary wartime actress and singer was born Maria Magdalene Dietrich and combined her first two names in this way at the age of twelve. She was brought up by a French nanny, always professed a great love for France and became anti-Nazi for that reason. At one time she travelled on a boat called the "Berengaria," a name that has a curious synergy with Bérenger (Saunière).

Dietrich was a close friend of Jean Cocteau, Grand Master of the Priory of Sion. Similarly, she was also a friend of André Malraux, a top member of the Priory[2] and a close friend of Pierre Plantard. Malraux was a key Free French resistance officer in the war and a member of de Gaulle's cabinet after it. Malraux's name features strongly in Baigent, Leigh and Lincoln's *Messianic Legacy*, their follow up to *Holy Blood and the Holy Grail*.

A principle contributor to the Prioré de Sion hoax, Philippe de Chérisey, claimed that Paul Éluard's poem—*La terre est bleue comme une orange*—was a veiled reference to the mysterious "blue apples" component in the Saunière parchments. Chérisey expanded on his theory, saying that Éluard's conflation of bleu, ange, l'or (phonetically Blue Angel) finds expression both in the 1930s Marlene Dietrich film Blue Angel (which alludes to a discovery that refers to Mary Magdalene—Madeleine the Sinner) and in the window of the Chapel of the Angels in Saint Sulpice (purportedly linked to a map of the Rennes-les-Bains area). It also alludes to the mystery of the raising of Lazarus (recorded as having taken place on 17th January). Many believe that the Biblical Lazarus episode is an allusion to the practice among Ancient Wisdoms of an initiation ceremony in which the neophyte enters a deep near-death trance state for three days while their spirit-soul travels in the inner worlds to receive teachings from sages and masters. Rahn's depiction of the adventures of the sleeping millers and the Knight of Berne's search for the fabled Kingdom of Laurin is a close parallel.

Josephine Baker also sailed on the Berengaria when she emigrated from the U.S. to France. Baker visited Berlin in 1928 and Munich in 1930. Intriguingly, Baker also had a song written for her called the *Black Sun in the City of Light*. Josephine later became a Lieutenant in the Free French Air Force (smuggling messages, chiefly to North Africa, in her sheet music), and was the eponymous inspiration behind the *Josephe B* mission undertaken by the French Paras of the Free French Forces in May 1941. This force was established by General de Gaulle on 29th September 1940 under the command of Captain Georges Bergé (father of the French S.A.S).

Marie Dénarnaud

[2] Baigent, Lincoln and Leigh ibid

Both Dietrich and Baker received the Légion d'Honneur. The French equivalent of dietrich (skeleton key) is passe-partout (known as a Peterken, little stone, in Lower Saxony). Passe-Partout "happens" to be the name of Phileas Fogg's companion *in Around the World in Eighty Days,* which gives us a link with the ubiquitous Jules Verne and the allusions in his work to the Rennes area (Bugarach, for example). Perhaps it is of note that Himmler was an avid reader of Verne's novels. His reading list also included Herman Hesse (Himmler was particularly impressed with Siddartha, which tied in with his personal belief in reincarnation and the laws of Karma), Zola, Dostoevsky, Homer and Oscar Wilde's *The Priest and the Acolyte.*

The Passe-Partout connection is further strengthened if we consider that Philibert de Brouillard (the latter word meaning fog) was the bishop in office at the time of the La Salette affair of 1846 when the shepherdess Melanie Calvet saw there an apparition of the Virgin Mary. Grail writer Jean Markale believed that Melanie was a cousin of the famous opera singer Emma Calvé who was linked with the Rennes mystery. The La Salette business attracted all sorts of characters. One of these was the infamous Abbé Boullan who, when asked by the Church Fathers to care for Sister Adèle Chevalier drawn to La Salette, she said, on heavenly instructions, had a child by Chevalier and then murdered it by ritual sacrifice in 1860. The pair founded the Oeuvre de la Réparation des Âmes, a front for diabolical practices. Boullan was investigated by Rome between 1864 and 1869, imprisoned by the Holy See for twelve months then exonerated, but was later defrocked in 1875. He died in 1893, rumoured to be the victim of the black magic of Marquis Stanislas de Guiata.

De Guiata was a close associate of Joséphin Péladan in the development of the Occult Undergound in late nineteenth century France. Otto Rahn greatly admired Péladan's work. Paris in the 1880s and 1890s was a hotbed of occult intrigue and Péladan was in the thick of the action. Although it had started earlier, the occult revival in Paris really began to take off in 1884 with the publication of two novels: one by J. K. Huysman called *À Rebours* (the inspiration for Oscar Wilde's *The Picture of Dorien Gray*) and, more pertinently, one by Péladan titled *Le Vice Supreme*, which ran for twenty editions. The latter was the first of a series of novels that the author called *La Décadence Latine*. De Guaita was so impressed with the work that he entered into relations with Péladan that endured for many years.

Péladan freely positioned himself on the extreme of Catholic sentiment, an attitude he maintained throughout his occult enterprises.

Péladan was an impassioned art critic, prolific essayist and novelist. He campaigned tirelessly for the revival of Italianate art with strong Catholic overtones. De Guaita and Péladan took it upon themselves to revive the Rosicrucian Brotherhood. In September 1885 Péladan declared himself Grand-Master of the Rose-Croix on the death of his brother, Adrien (whom Joséphin suspected had been murdered by a Protestant chemist).

In 1888 Péladan and de Guiata co-founded the Cabalistic Order of the Rose-Croix, joining forces with Jules Bois, Count Leonce de Larmandie, K. Huysmans and the painter Count Antoine de la Rochefoucauld, in reviving the movement that can be traced back to Charles Edouard de Lapasse (1792-1867) of Toulouse. Dr. Gérard Encausse (the famous "Papus") was affiliated with the Order. Papus was a friend of Jules Doinel, Carcassonne librarian and founder of the neo-Cathar Church where Papus and he served as co-bishops.

In 1890-1891 Péladan, concerned that the Cabalistic Order had become anti-Catholic, split the group he had established with de Guaita and founded the Order of the Rose-Croix of the Temple of the Grail in order to reveal the mysteries and prepare for the coming Kingdom of God. De Guiata divorced himself completely from Péladan, calling his former friend a schismatic and an apostate.

Tellingly, Péladan claimed his new Order had links with the power players in German occult circles, principally the Holy Vehm and the Illuminatus of Bavaria. Papus claimed that his friend was also under the influence of the Counts of Chambord who were the pretenders to the throne of France and promoters of the myth that Loius XVII had escaped from his pre-execution imprisonment from the Paris Temple.

During the course of his Grail researches Rahn happened upon a document of Péladan's in the Bibliothèque Nationale entitled *De Parsifal à Don Quichotte (le Secret des Troubadours)*. In the document Péladan hypothesised upon the close correspondences between Montsalvage and Montségur, anticipating Rahn's own research findings by thirty years.

Péladan died of seafood poisoning in 1918. At the time of his death Péladan's secretary was George Monti who affected the name Count Israel Monti and who inducted composer Eric Satie into Péladan's order.

Monti was born in Toulouse in 1880. He was Jesuit educated and at twenty-two he became a high level Scottish Rite Mason. In 1909 he was living in Munich. After the Great War Monti travelled frequently between Berlin and Rome and earned a living in films, a professional circumstance in which Monti may well have met Otto Rahn. Monti's life was a mass of conflicts, always appearing to be on the periphery of events but desperately seeking to play a major occult role. He spent time between the wars in Germany and was reputed to have been Aleister Crowley's representative in France in the early twenties.

Any possible relationship between Rahn and Monti may have remained a peripheral affair had it not emerged that Gaston de Mengel, the Frenchman who would contact Rahn and Weisthor about the curious geographical co-ordinates and the *"place of the big black centre,"* joined Monti in 1924 in founding *Groupe Occidental d'Études Ésotériques*, a small elitist order dedicated to bringing about a lasting world peace and reconciling all esoteric orders with the Church of Rome.

De Mengel's involvement increases the likelihood that Rahn consolidated his access to the European occult underground by virtue of his relationship with the French earth energy enthusiast, alchemist and mathematician. In fact, *Groupe Occidental d'Études Ésotériques* was a far right cadre whose members believed they wielded vast influence over the political leadership of the day. Robert Richardson has presented a compelling argument[3] that the Priory of Sion is an outgrowth of Monti's group, which itself was a poor successor to Joséphin Péladan's Rose-Croix cabalistic order.

In 1936 Monti was denounced by the Grand Lodge of France as a Jesuit informer trafficking in secret information and making a fraudulent claim to nobility. He died mysteriously by a form of poisoning that covered his body in black spots. This was the supposed murder method of the Holy Vehm. According to occultist Anne Osmant, Monti had a plan to "destroy all that is dear and precious, to build an illusory society."

Rahn was anti-Catholic and especially anti-Jesuit. Monti, a disciple of Péladan, shared his former master's extreme pro-Church sentiments. On the face of it, Rahn and Monti would have been polar opposites. However, Rahn was an admirer of Péladan's work and the inclusion of Gaston de Mengel, evidently a person of learning with insights into the exotic field of earth energies, in the circle of relationships may well have brought the men's interests together into a shared and valued experience. It is not at all clear as to why Rahn should have named one of the characters in his Jehan short story (Chapter 25) as "lively" Gaston. Seeing that Rahn named Jehan's elder

---

[3] Rennes-le-Château Observer No 21, December 1998

son as Antonin (after his number one pal, Antonin Gadal) and his younger as Gaston, it might indicate that Rahn regarded the two men in real life as equally valued friends. It certainly begs the question as to whether the relationship between Rahn and the energetic de Mengel was far more significant than may be initially evident.

Otto Rahn's love for the Cathars, his involvement with the inner Church of Nazism which, in turn, had a stranglehold on the papacy, his narration of key fables and legends suggestive of worlds of enchantment attainable by those with a key, (which they all carry with or within them), and his alleged connection with Dagobert's "forbidden merchandise" episode of 1945, all link him to Rennes-le-Château and its environs.

Before we accompany Otto Rahn out of the environs of Rennes-le-Château we should make brief mention of a purported yet tantalising link between Rahn and the Nazis' search for the Arma Christi, the Instruments of the Passion used during the Crucifixion (crown of thorns, nails, scourge, spear et al). In 2006 Dutch author Karl Hammer-Kaatee published his novel *Satans Lied: De Jacht van de CIA op Jezus. Waargebeurd verhaal*—"Satan's Song: the CIA Hunt For Jesus. A true story." The book, not yet available in an English language edition, relates the testimony of countryman "Tom R.," who worked in Munich for the Art Looting Investigation Unit (ALIU), the U.S. secret service body investigating German art thefts during WW2. During this work Tom R. learned about the theft of two panels of Jan van Eyck's 'Adoration of the Mystic Lamb'. One of the panels, the Just Judges, was said to contain the key to the geographical location of the Arma Christi. It had been missing since April 1934, six months after Otto Rahn had allegedly undertaken on Himmler's behalf a mission in Ghent to make preparations for its theft. It would appear that when the panel was stolen the following spring a different party of thieves was involved because it later became the subject of a three-year search by the Nazis with Rennes-le-Château featuring significantly in the search led, once again it seems, by Rahn. The story goes that Tom R, having been ordered by the CIA to find the holy instruments, got very close to actual discovery and went into hiding. In his book Hammer-Kaatee states that at one time the Arma Christi, guarded by a Franciscan network calling itself the Ebionites, were transported twenty kilometres south from their hiding place at Notre Dame de Marceille at Limoux to Rennes-le-Château, only to be taken back to Limoux when Rahn got too close for comfort. The Arma Christi story is fascinating but there is no proof of any involvement by Otto Rahn. At the same time there is no way at present one can prove or disprove that Rahn might have taken time away from promoting *Kreuzzeg gegen den Gral* to travel to Ghent in the autumn of 1933.

The Franciscan element within the Arma Christi story introduces us to another fascinating piece of Indiana Jones mythography. Film cognoscenti claim that at one time Spielberg and Lucas wanted to make 'Indiana Jones and the Vatican' but were prevented from doing it. One can only speculate upon the circumstances but if there is any truth to the claim it would be fascinating to unearth the details of the story and to understand why the pair were deterred from turning it into the episode of their choice.

In the Rennes group's *Rennes Observer 1.1* we read that just prior to June 1993 a team from the Vatican were allowed to scan places at Rennes-le-Château, an activity forbidden to others over the years. They went away "mouths shut."

Chapter TWENTY TWO

Tibet and Thule

Members of the SS Tibet team pose at Berlin airport 1939

In May 1999 I addressed an audience at Gullane, a coastal town near Edinburgh, on the life of Otto Rahn. I talked about his passions as revealed in his work, in his correspondence with friends and mentors, and in reminiscences with time-witnesses, in particular Gabriele Winckler-Dechend who has provided a wealth of information about Rahn in the mid-1930s. I concluded by suggesting that Otto Rahn had a rare quality, an indefinable element that set him aside from his contemporaries and, indeed, from most adventurers that followed. His love for the Cathars was evident throughout his life but that, in itself, does not explain the remarkable attraction Rahn exerts on those who seek to peer into their inner world, into the secret rose gardens of Laurin where, by his own admission, Rahn kept the *dietrich*, the Key.

It was in 1995 when I first heard the radical and intriguing opinion that within the Nazis there had been a small but special group which, within a very brief period of time, pulled together information, understanding, insight and balance, even with such negativity surrounding them. The important thing, so the story goes, about some of these individuals who were said to be involved within the occult agency of the Nazis is that they became a self-contained group within themselves, with abilities to move in and out of places and zones because of a kernel of inner wisdom in face of the appalling degredation of human morals and decency. They were very "metaphysical" in their own right. In this scenario Otto Rahn is a key to something that has been lying dormant, and which may have been uncovered by members of this secret cadre who, though apparently committed to the goals of the NSDAP, were truly not what they seemed.

It was in consideration of this far-reaching and, admittedly, highly controversial opinion and my desire to know more, that I embarked on my study of Rahn. I was engrossed in developing my research plan for examining these fascinating elements of hidden history when, a year later in Paris, a trusted but confidential source put it to me that Otto Rahn did not die in March 1939 and that, furthermore, he was helped in his survival by the Tibetans in Germany. Although stated unequivocally, those remarks could not be corroborated. But because they were put to me at the same time as my own intuition was telling me that Rahn escaped his inquisitors I noted and appreciated the evident synchronicities. Rahn had told us: "within me I have the key, the *dietrich,*" a declaration of faith and power that echoed the profound teachings conveyed by Pythagoras to his students at his school in Crotona. I was convinced that the true story of Otto Rahn's life and work was to be read between the lines of what was obvious. I remain so convinced today.

I determined to understand more about Rahn and his activities, especially to explore the Tibetan connections. Frau Winckler had confirmed that Rahn was acquainted with Dr. Ernest Schafer and was knowledgeable about the latter's Ahnenerbe-financed expeditions to Tibet. I was certain then and now that there is a wealth of information to be unearthed about the Nazis' relationship with Tibet and its occult traditions and Rahn's own agenda, but today the empirical proofs continue to elude the researcher. I do not think we have to go too far to understand why this should be so. I believe that Rahn's deepest actions were designed to create a controlling balance upon a systematic policy of unsurpassed negativity, and that the agencies responsible for promulgating that policy are at least as busy today as they were in the Nazi era.

There is no hard and fast evidence to link Rahn with the Tibetan colonies in Germany. However, Rahn's fascination for grottoes and subterranean caverns, magical doorways to middle earth kingdoms (Laurin), and other allusions mesh very closely with the legends of Agarthi and Shamballah, mythical realms said to be accessible to Tibetan priests and mystics. Interestingly, while in Lavalanet, Rahn was told by an old man of a book he had found in the castle at Montségur written in script like Chinese or Arabic. But it could equally have been Tibetan; how might an old shepherd know otherwise?

It was Pauwels and Bergier who, in their 1960 book *Le Matin des Magiciens*, first mentioned the Tibetans brought to Berlin in the late 1920s. Maurice Bessy also mentioned it. Pauwels and Bergier described the Russians entering the ravaged city in May 1945 and finding a large number of Tibetan corpses in the eastern sector dressed in German army uniforms bereft of any insignia of rank. The authors put the number at a thousand but this is certainly a gross exaggeration. The number would have been limited to ensure that the lamas' presence was not over-conspicuous. Moreover, one can guarantee that the Nazis' mania for tidy records would have documented every dot and comma of the Tibetans arrival and purpose. Those documents have not surfaced.

In the cellar of one building the Russians found six Tibetans lying in a ritual circle. In its centre was a monk wearing green gloves. (In *Luzifers Hofgesind* Rahn tells of the discovery of a dozen skeletons found lying in a wheel formation in an Albigensian tomb, a practice related to solar worship.)

According to Pauwels and Bergier, a small trans-Himalayan colony was established in Berlin and Munich in 1926. One of its members was a Tibetan monk known both as the 'man with the green gloves,' and as the 'Guardian of the Keys' since he was said to have the keys to Agartha. Note the key symbolism once more. This monk took a keen interest in the growing Nazi movement and gained notoriety by accurately predicting how many party members would win seats in the Reichstag. Hitler consulted with him regularly.

Alongside the state religion of Lamaism was Tibet's aboriginal religion of Bön. Its priests had a reputation among the common people as magicians and dark occultists. The religion of Tibet is Buddhism but like the Zen of Japan, it is a brand of Buddhism far divorced from the Indian original. Many scholars prefer the term "Lamaism" to distinguish between Tibetan Buddhism and its parent root. The religious life of the country is concentrated in a multitude of monasteries, many of them built in nigh inaccessible mountain regions.

The Bönpo follow a primitive, animistic creed, full of dark rituals and spells. Its poetry and writings are full of references to ritual killings describing extreme acts of torture such as pulling a victim's entrails through his mouth so as to leave the corpse unscarred. If the holy Lamas of the Buddhist sects were looked on as personifications of spiritual wisdom, the priests of Bön had a potent reputation with the common people as cruel and all-powerful magicians not to be crossed under any circumstance.

The Tibetans believed in an esoteric history of mankind and it was in the archives of Tibetan monasteries that this history was preserved in its purest form. Already, in the latter half of the previous century, tantalising hints about Tibetan secret teachings had been carried to the West by Helena Blavatsky who claimed initiation at the hands of the Holy Lamas. Blavatsky taught that her "Hidden Masters" and "Secret Chiefs" had their earthly residence in the Himalayan region.

As soon as the Nazi movement had sufficient funds, it began to organize a number of expeditions to Tibet and these succeeded one another, practically without interruption, until 1943. One of the most tangible expressions of Nazi interest in Tibet was the party's adoption of its deepest and most mystical of symbols: the swastika.

The swastika is one of mankind's oldest symbols and apart from the cross and the circle it is probably the most widely distributed. It is shown on pottery fragments from Greece dating back to the eighth century BC. It was used in ancient Egypt, India and China. The Navaho Indians of North America have a traditional swastika pattern. Arab-Islamic sorcerers used it. In more recent times, it was incorporated in the flags of certain Baltic States.

Before Hitler perverted its meaning the swastika had been used for thousands of years to symbolise the positive solar aspects of creation. It is a representation of the seven-starred celestial pole, Arktos. Nearby there is another set of seven stars of very similar shape but reversed, the Little Bear. Between the two Bears lies Draco, the dragon that guards the Apples of the Hesperides. The twin counter-clockwise motions that man has observed for aeons are the reflections of the earth's daily rotation and its annual revolution about the sun. A record of the nightly and yearly cycles of the Great and Little Bear constellations reveals them in four positions that are strongly suggestive of the swastika, hence their use as a Polar symbol and the motion that takes place around it. The "left-hand" clockwise swastika traditionally depicts polar revolution and the "right-hand" swastika (counter-clockwise) the course of the sun.

The idea for the use of the swastika by the Nazis came from a dentist named Dr. Friedrich Krohn who was a member of the secret Germanenorden group. Krohn produced the design for the actual form in which the Nazis came to use the symbol; that is reversed, spinning in an anti-clockwise direction. As a solar symbol, the swastika is properly thought of as spinning and the Buddhists have always believed that the symbol attracted luck. The Sanskrit word "swastika" means good fortune and wellbeing. According to Cabbalistic lore and occult theory, chaotic force can be evoked by reversing the symbol. Accordingly, the symbol appeared as the flag of Nazi Germany and the insignia of the Nazi party, an indication for those who had eyes to see of the inherent occult nature of the Third Reich.

Bön was introduced to Tibet by immigrants from north-east Persia. The Bönpo lamas are, without doubt, one of the oldest and most continual unreformed religions in existence and in studying them it is not difficult to see where shamanism may have its roots. These Aryan settlers brought with them the Aramaic alphabet, named after Aramaiti, the Iranian Earth Goddess. The actual founder of Bön is known as Shenabe but was said to have originated in Elam where he was known as Mithra. Shenabe taught a doctrine known as Kalachakra. Specifically, Kala refers to vaginal emanations in Hindu tantra or sex magick. The Goddess was symbolised by the Black Sun, representing the void of creation from which all life emanates.

The Bönpo lamas were tolerated by the Buddhists but not welcomed at great ceremonies, although one connection with the old religion was the Oracle of Tibet who predicted the oncoming year at the New Year celebrations. Dr. Hugh E. Richardson, the British representative in Lhasa from 1936 to 1950, explained to Scottish filmmaker and historian John Ritchie how the ceremony worked. Ritchie describes Richardson, a personal friend of the Dalai Lama, as a remarkable man who translated the historical pillars in the main Potala temple in Lhasa and wrote five books on Tibet. He spoke to Ritchie at length about the Swastika Mountain and its reference to Bönpo. Richardson described the Oracle of Tibet as a very tall man for a Tibetan. His ceremony was preceded by the dance of death. He then danced himself into a trance and a very heavy ancient hat was placed on his head weighing about fifty-six pounds (mostly ancient gold items of great antiquity) to stop his soul from flying away. After dancing himself into frenzy he collapsed, then rose to make the predictions for the coming year.

Tibetan legends recount that the first kings of Tibet came to Earth along a celestial axis or Sky-cord. A traditional poem explains:

“From the mid-sky seven-stage, Heavenly sphere, azure blue, Came our king, lord of men, Son divine, to Tibet land so high, made so pure, without equal, without peer, Land indeed! Best of all! Religion, too, surpassing all!” This illustrates the founding of the Yarlung Dynasty and almost resembles Christ coming to earth.

“Mid-sky” reminds one of Laurin, the middle or inner earth Kingdom of the Elfin race that Rahn so lovingly described in his account of the Knight of Berne and the Roses of Bozen. “Seven-stage high” recalls the Temple mysteries of Ishtar and her Priestesses’ sacred labyrinthine dance of the seven veils, which opens the gateways to the threshold of the Mother Goddess. “Azure blue” conjures up the words in Henri Cain’s libretto for Jules Massenet’s *Don Quichotte* where we hear sung: "...an azure wave laps its shores, ‘tis beautiful and pleasing, it is the Island of Dreams. He has the key to riches and happiness, he has the key"—the *dietrich*, always the *dietrich*.

The Thule group believed in an esoteric history of mankind and that knowledge of it was preserved in Tibetan monastary archives. The three godfathers of the Thule Society were Guido von List, Jorg Lanz von Liebenfels and Rudolf von Sebottendorff. The monastery libraries were said to hold extremely important scrolls for the history of mankind, hidden in grottoes. (The secret manuscript relating to the history of Atlantis is said to reside in the Vatican library with a copy placed in a Tibetan monastery.) One theory is that Tibet was the refuge of the survivors of Hyperborea. Nietzsche wrote in *Antichrist*:

"*Neither on earth or the waters shall you find*
The way leading to the Hyperboreans."

Believers in this new "volkisch" thinking formed the Germanenorden in 1912. Handicapped and "unpleasant looking" persons were forbidden to join. At Pentecost in 1914 the Germanenorden hosted a conference at Thale in the Harz Mountains to unite with various disparate volkisch and anti-semitic groups, the common bond being a shared belief in the Northern (Hyperborean) heritage and the legends of Thule.

Edmund Fuerhoelzer, in *Arro! Arro! So Sah ich Tibet*, 1942, wrote that while in Tibet he met with the Pantschen Lama and commented to him upon the great German interest in Tibet and its culture. The Pantschen immediately expounded upon the virtues of the German leader, Adolf Hitler, observing that the Führer's Tibetan appellation was Hsi Tale, where Tale meant "all comprehensive," much in the same way as the Dalai Lama is regarded by his countrymen. This unique appellation corresponds very closely with the extraordinary esteem in which the German dictator was held by such enrapt supporters as Savitri Devi, "Hitler's Priestess," who "elaborated an extraordinary synthesis of Hindu religion and Nordic racial ideology involving the polar origin of the Aryans, the cycle of the ages, and the incarnation of the last avatar of Vishnu in Adolf Hitler." [1]

In 1919 René Schwaller organized his Paris based Theosophical companions into a group called L'Affranchis. This group renamed itself in July of that year as an anti-Judean group, styling itself Les Veilleurs (The Vigilants). Pierre Mariel (alias Werner Gerson) said that the young Rudolf Hess was a member. Its members wore riding breeches and dark shirts and called its leaders Chef, all very similar to Hess' style. In Schwaller's 1916 book *Les Nombres* he describes the swastika alongside the book's numeric and geometrical figures as a representation of the archetypal movement of any body around its axis. This is reminiscent of Rudolf Rahn, the German ambassador believed by Christian Bernadac to be Otto Rahn's post-1939 identity, experiencing mental phantoms in the form of numbers, a trait that helped him visualise numbers and geometric lines to form pathways to locate missing objects. The Affranchis-Veilleurs eventually split themselves into two groups: the *Centre Apostolique* and the *Mystic Group Tala,* tala translated as the `link.'

Thule—Thale—Tale—Tala, near identical expressions, which denote the same meaning: the all-knowing, all-comprehending unbroken thread connecting with the secrets and traditions of the antediluvian Golden Age of Hyperborea.

The Thale conference gave birth to a Geheimbund (a secret band) whose objective was to breathe fresh vigour into the true and lasting Nordic traditions. An advertisement was placed in 1916 to attract suitable members and Rudolf von Sebottendorff answered the call, going on to establish the group's ultimate imperative: the creation of a spiritual community named the Halgadom, the Nordic equivalent of the context of the Ark of the Covenant and the Israelites. The Halgadom was to be the spiritual focus of all Germans but also for all other Europeans who remained faithful to the ideals of their Hyperborean beginnings—Scandinavia, Netherlands, Britain, France, Italy, Spain and Russia.

In 1918 Sebottendorff's colleague, Walter Nahaus, proposed re-christening the Germanenorden the Thule Gesellschaft. Its symbol, predictably, was the swastika. The Thule group's initial members

---

[1] Goodricke-Clarke, Nicholas. *Hitler's Priestess: Savitri Devi, the Hindu-Aryan Myth and Neo-Nazism.* New York University Press, 1998

included seven with Jewish origins or relations. Paradoxically, its members, including the Jewish element, promised to combat the "world conspiracy of Freemasons and international Jewry." Writer Wulf Schwartzwaller[2] described the Thule group as a "secret organisation of conspiring right wing radicals with rigorous anti-Marxist, anti-democratic and anti-Semitic opinions."

Writer Elizabeth van Buren regards WW2 as a colossal attempt by the darkside of humanity to harness the secrets of Time. Similarly, Maurice Magré believed that the swastika symbolised the power of Time. Thor's hammer, Mjolnir, is associated with the alchemical characteristics of the swastika, symbolising the transmutation and origins of matter.

The Bavarian branch of the Thule was to assume precedence above all other lodges in shaping the profile of history. Its membership roll mostly comprised aristocrats and professionals. Himmler's father, Gebhard, was a regular visitor to its Munich meetings held in the Hotel Vierjahreszeiten but was regarded by the regulars as somewhat of a nuisance. It was this group that propelled Anton Drexler, the radical intellectual who was to play a key role in thrusting Adolf Hitler into the role of demagogue.[3]

As a vehicle that might appeal more to the working classes a sub-group, the NSP of Anton Drexler, branched out of the Thule, becoming the German Workers Party (DAP) in January 1919 and, in the following February, the NSDAP. Sebottendorff stated: "Thule people are the ones to whom Hitler first came." He also created the exhortation of "Sieg Heil" (Glory Hail) to be used as a rallying cry for the group's members. Intererestingly, Herman Pohl's Bavarian bank took the cover name of Thule. Also curious is the fact that the journey undertaken by the Knight of Berne and described so passionately by Otto Rahn is, almost word for word, an account of a Thule Society initiation ceremony in which the Knight is named Herman.

The Thule group practised a form of divination using a special Tibetan "Tarot" pack, used also to keep contact with the secret master, the King of Fear. H. Brennan suggests that this "King" was Gurdjieff. Both Gurdjieff and Aleister Crowley are believed to have sought contact with Hitler.

Adolf Josef Lanz (better known as Jörg Lanz von Liebenfels), one of the founders of the Thule Society, created the O.N.T. in 1907 and it subsequently became the prototype of the SS (Schutzstaffel).

---

[2] Schwartzwaller, Wulf. *The Unknown Hitler*. U.S.A.: Berkeley Books, 1990

[3] Thomas ibid

Lanz said that non-Aryans were the result of bestiality by the ancient Aryans after their departure from the Northern Garden of Eden. He theorised that the original homeland of the Aryans was Arktogaa (Green Northern Earth). Lanz was a renegade Cistercian monk, having been expelled for dubious practices in 1899 from his monastery. Like Rahn he was fiercely anti-Jesuit. Lanz maintained that he had initiated Hitler, "tapping" him as a young man in accordance with the practice of Tibetan dalai-lamas. Hitler called into the Vienna offices of Lanz's Ostara publication in 1909. Lanz also claimed to have similarly influenced Dietrich Eckart who was later imprisoned, like Hess, with Hitler in Landsberg Fortress and who edited Mein Kampf (written in Landsberg).

We have seen that Rahn adds a curious reference in a letter to Antonin Gadal about the *edelweiss*, the white flower, as if he is trying to draw attention to a greater theme. Compare this with the story in Chapter 23 of the Master (King of the World) who erased the flower after fleeing the Occident, leaving the swastika as the sole symbol of his authority. Marcus Williamson has provided me with a number of names by which the Edelweiss (*Leontopodium alpinum*) is known in France. These include *Immortelle des neiges* (immortal of the snows), which has a distinctly ironic and prescient ring considering the emerging belief that Otto Rahn did not die in the snow on the Wilder-Kaiser Mountain in March 1939 but instead lived on. Does Rahn's choice to mention this flower to his friend and mentor indicate, perhaps subconsciously, a clairsentient personal foresight into what would unfold?

The leader of the Tibetan Berlin colony, the Man with the Green Gloves, was affiliated with the Verdant Society. Joscelyn Godwin suggests that the Thule Society is linked with the work of Dr. John Dee, Queen Elizabeth I's astrologer and magician. In accounts of Dee's work we learn of a conjuration of a spirit named "Madimi." She said she saw "the coming of the end of the three year cycle and…the Nine Guardians of the Vert act(ing) against fire by…the Scorpion and watch(ing) for the chimney of smoke." The reference to a three-year cycle suggests an allusion to the concept of the Third Reich; while "fire," "creatures of the Scorpion," and "chimney of smoke" conjure striking images of the stench-filled concentration camp ovens and of the inhumanity of the planners and personnel who made a practice of mass murder on an unimaginable scale.

Between 1582 and 1589 Dee is said to have conducted a series of ritual communications with discarnate entities known as the

Enochian angels. At the core of these rituals was an objective to plant among mankind the ritual working that would initiate the period of violent transformation between the present aeon and the next, commonly known as the Apocalypse. The angels' formula was designed to open the locked gates of the four great watchtowers that stand guard against the extremities of our physical universe. Dee was not given permission in his lifetime to enact the ritual and, so the story goes, the baton passed instead to Aleister Crowley. Crowley believed he had successfully invoked some of the forty-nine Keys that would open the Watchtowers but that the task of ushering in the Apocalypse must fall to another who would come after him: Adolf Hitler, born exactly three hundred years after Dee completed his Enochian rituals.

In Chapter 24 we review a claim that Aleister Crowley participated in a bizarre, but apparently deadly serious, magical experiment undertaken in Germany in 1923 involving time and inter-dimensional travel. In this respect, we shall look at the work of the mysterious Order of the Black Swan. We will need little encouragement to consider a close link between the objectives of Dee's magic, its reprise in the early twentieth century by Crowley, and a claim by U.S. sources that Hitler and his Bönpo confederates strove to open a doorway between this world and the "fallen" universe with terrible consequences.

The Vril Society or Luminous Lodge of Light was at the heart and soul of Nazi occult doctrine. The first news of this society leaked out to the western world through Willi Ley, the rocket scientist who fled Germany in 1933. According to Ley, the disciples of Haushofer believed that they were unveiling a secret knowledge with which they would be able to create a mutation in the Aryan Race: the Superman. Vril derives from Baron Edward Bulmer-Lytton's *The Coming Race*, a nineteenth century book that describes a subterranean race, which has developed a unique and all-powerful energy—Vril. Bulmer-Lytton is said to have been initiated into a German occult lodge, the Rising Dawn (or simply the Jewish Lodge).

The Luminous Lodge was formed by Berlin Rosicrucians after attending a lecture by anti-Christian Louis Jacolliot. Jacolliot was inspired by several sources, chiefly Emmanuel Swedenborg, Jacob Boehme (celebrated 16th century alchemist and one of the founders of Rosicrucianism), and Louis Claude St Martin, the pontiff of French Illuminism in the 19th century. The first members of the Lodge called themselves Wahrheitsgesellschaft, "Society for Truth," and later the Luminous Lodge or Vril Society. The society had close links with various theosophical centres at home and abroad, among them the British Golden Dawn Society, founded by J. S. L. Mathers and briefly headed by Crowley.

It is a striking fact that the physical character of Dr. Henry Jones in the Indiana Jones films bears a very close resemblance to Welsh author, Arthur Machen. Machen was a member of the Golden Dawn. In his 1915 book *The Great Return* Machen delved into the Grail myths and associated esoteric topics. Machen was also the first writer to introduce into his work the notion of the Grail surviving into modern times, precisely the running theme in the Indiana Jones films, which Machen developed most pointedly in his novel *The Secret Glory*.

Golden Dawn members engaged in "spiritual" exercises in an attempt to harness and acquire the mysterious Vril force that was regarded as a tremendous reserve of energy of which man uses but a fraction in his earthly life. They endeavoured to make contact with supernatural beings in the centre of the world with whom they would make alliances to rule the surface and all its inhabitants.

Karl Haushofer, a professor of Geopolitics at the University of Munich, and Rudolf Hess' mentor, was a principle contributor to the establishment of the German-Japanese plan for world domination (having visited the Far East and possibly Tibet). He was known as the “wizard of Germany.” Haushofer was a member of the Yellow Hats, known as Dughpas in Tibet. Haushofer's connection with the Bönpo led to the formation of Tibetan and Hindu colonies in Berlin and Munich in 1926. In these endeavours he was helped by Hungarian mystic, Ignatz Trebitsch-Lincoln. Haushofer also played a key role in the establishment of both the Thule Society and the Luminous Lodge. From 1907 to 1910 Haushofer lived mostly in Japan where he was initiated into the Green Dragon Buddhist society. It is possible that Rasputin was also a member of this society for its Lodges fringed Russia. Rasputin gave a gift to the Tsarina of a pair of small emerald green dragons, the Order's insignia, which were discovered in 1918 sewn into her dress.

Alexandra, the last Tsarina, inscribed the left-hand swastika with the date 1918 on the wall of her prison quarters at Ekaterinburg where she and her family were subsequently murdered. Her doctor, Badmaiell, was a practitioner of Tibetan medicine. The Tsarina also used the swastika as a secret sign of recognition in her correspondence. The swastika was also used by Russian monarchists who, after defeat of Germany in WW1, allied with General Ludendorff's entourage as protector to Hitler.

Rudolf Hess was carying the visiting cards of both Haushofer and the professor's son Albrecht when he flew to Scotland (Albrecht, a white magician and a plotter against Hitler, was beheaded by the Gestapo). Karl Haushofer was said to have committed hari-kiri on 14th March 1946 but records from his interrogator, Father Edmund Walsh, show that he died by arsenic on 10th March that year.

Rahn lived and worked in Berlin for the greater part of the 1930s. His work for Weisthor's department and the host of tasks demanded of him by Himmler personally would inevitably have brought him into frequent contact with every conceivable esoteric group in Nazi Germany, including the Tibetan Bönpo contingent whose locus of activity was centred round occultism and associated beliefs. Rahn's erudition and language skills would have made him an ideal intermediary between the Tibetans and Himmler's offices. Gabriele Winckler and Rahn were on friendly terms with Ernest Schafer, the leader of the Ahnenerbe's Tibetan expeditions, from whom they learned about phenomena like telepathy, which they practised enthusistiacally in busy Berlin streets.

Rahn's tale of Jehan and his death at the hands of the Huguenots is a thinly veiled treatise on the Tibetan traditions of the dead, particularly the Ceremony of Chod by which the deceased spirit's passage through the Sea of Souls proceeds unhindered and all past attachments to the earth plane and its memories are severed.

Paradoxically, it is known that during the time of the Reich Tibet and its traditions had a significant British context. As we have seen, the man whom some regard as the leading contender for the true identity of the head lama of the Berlin Bönpo, the Man with the Green Gloves, is Ignatz Trebitsch-Lincoln. Trebitsch-Lincoln entered British politics in 1910 as Member of Parliament for Darlington. He is believed to have been an agent for the Abwehr from 1912. This latter role would have brought Trebitsch-Lincoln into Wilhelm Canaris' direct sphere of influence during WW2. We have already reviewed the significant indications that the covert activities of Canaris and Rahn were not entirely unrelated.

Moreover, wartime MI6 occult operative Cecil Williamson was a frequent visitor to the Cricklewood enclave of exiled Bönpo lamas in North London. In fact, Williamson gave them the airfare to allow them to return to Tibet in exchange for receiving the Bönpo temple and ritual paraphernalia they had brought with them to London.

Many members of the Thule group, disenchanted with Hitler's policies from 1934 onwards, came to England and settled in London and Oxford. Howard Buechner says that there is fragmentary evidence that Rahn's explorations in France were financed by the Thule. Examining these alliances alongside the wider links that Himmler and other top Nazis orchestrated with members of the British Peace Party to find an early to the war, we see that Britain in the 1930s and 1940s was a cauldron of occult intrigue. Moreover, the pot was seasoned with a wide array of mystical condiments in which Tibetan Bönpo demonism was a significant element.

In *Luzifers Hofgesind* Rahn writes about being in Arthur's bosom by virtue of having made a brief disembarkation on Scottish soil to visit Arthur's Seat while en route to Iceland. Is that truly how he felt about being in Britain, that for a few brief hours he felt safe and, paradoxically, at home, a Knight errant receiving the hospitality at the mystical court of Camelot? All indications point to Rahn enjoying precisely these sentiments. It is therefore of little surprise that Arthur's Seat is an integral part of the sacred geometry generated by nearby Rosslyn Chapel, a "Christian" edifice called the Grail in Stone, and named by Tibetan Tantric buddhists today as a centre for world peace.

Chapter TWENTY THREE

The Black Sun

The Bönpo recognised the land of Shambhala, a Sanskrit word meaning "source of happiness," as Olmolungring, reduced to Og or Oz as in Frank Baum's famous children's tale. The great mountain in its centre is Mount Meru. A good reference work on Bönpo is Andrea David Neal's book *With Mystics and Magicians in Tibet.* Written in 1898 about Neal's travels and searches for unusual Lamas, it gives a good account of her extraordinary meetings with Bönpo faithful and their religion.

One of the extraordinary Bönpo rituals is the Chod or Starwrighting ceremony where the Lama sits up through the night with the body of the departed and releases the soul, guiding it through the Sea of Souls. By this ceremony the deceased is encouraged to recognise its own soul so it can travel on to the next world. The lama, after releasing the soul and making sure it is well on its way, cuts up the body and distributes it to be eaten by the birds of the air and the beasts of the field before the dawn. The body must not be buried to ensure that the departed soul has no earthly point of reference that might serve to draw it back to a lightless, etheric existence.

The Bönpo monks brought to Germany in the 1920s were said to have had the ability to open dimensional doors by means of the Chod discipline. Although not present in anything like the large numbers that Pauwels and Bergier reported, the ancient structure and hierarchies of the lamas would have enabled them to achieve "impossible" possibilities, even a mass Chod. This ability later excited many Nazis because they knew the war was lost and they were going to have to make an immediate getaway at some point. The Nazis would also have picked up on the necessary research and traditions through its extensive resources and, in particular, through the work of Himmler's Ahnenerbe section. It would have been aware of Gurdjieff, Blavatsky, Neal and many others who had spoken and written about the Bönpo. The suggestion has been made that Otto Rahn, associated on a day-to-day basis with the Tibetan monks by virtue of his role and responsibilities in the SS and having mastered the necessary Bönpo techniques, may have made his escape in March 1939 in such manner. Rahn was the SS officer to whom occultists and psychics such as Eric Hannussen, the Jewish seer, reported. In this role it is logical to assume that he was also a key liaison figure between the SS and the Tibetans.

The whole Shambala theory was prevalent around the turn of the century with the Thule Society and others. One imagines that the legends and their philosophical importance were understood very well by Otto Rahn. Consequently, it has been speculated that Rahn physically worked out these ritual practices and could literally melt away, particularly if he went through the meditation of controlling the demons, which required one to spend six months in total isolation in complete darkness, normally in a cave or room built for this purpose. This would have taken him completely out of circulation. All Bönpo lamas must go through this ritual.

The Nazis began to organise expeditions to Tibet when sufficient funds built up and these succeeded without interruption up to 1943. Standartenführer-SS Dr. Ernest Schafer of the Ahnenerbe was the driving force behind these expeditions. A biologist, Schafer made at least two journeys to Tibet on behalf of the SS: one was to East and Central Tibet in 1934-36, and another from April 1938 to August 1939. In 1931 he also accompanied Brooke Dolan (later an officer in the OSS) on an expedition to Tibet, Siberia and China. Dolan was Ilya Tolstoy's second-in-command when Bill Donovan of the OSS ordered a mission to Tibet between May 1942 and June 1943.

Dietrich Bronder published *Bevor Hitler Kam* in 1964. He wrote of the SS expedition to Tibet set up with the express purpose of establishing a radio link between the Third Reich and the lamas. The *Stanzas of Dyan* were used as the code for all messages between Berlin and Lhasa during the war. Rahn and Schafer knew each other. Otto and Gabriele learned Tibetan telepathy techniques from him, which they practised together seated on benches at each end of busy Berlin streets.

Legend has it that the King of the World, the Lama of Lamas, lives in this timeless place called Agharti or Asgard. Tradition tells that in the distant past the Master dwelt in the Occident on a mountain surrounded by huge forests when the flower was on the swastika (this has reminiscences of the Pyrenees-Montségur area). The Black Cycles chased the Master from the West and he came to Tibet. He erased the flower and now the swastika alone symbolises the central power of the gem of Heaven. What might these allusions mean?

During its programme of explorations the Ahnenerbe found at

Montserrat a "swastika stone."[1] The Montserrat stone features a grid of small squares flanked by Sig runes surmounted by two swastikas, one deosil (clockwise), the other Widdershins (anti-clockwise). Above the swastika is a mandala of twenty four overlapping crescents, rotating widdershins. A concentric circular band beyond the circle of crescents contains eleven small circles (reminiscent of the stone floor labyrinth design at Chartres Cathedral), each divided into six equal parts by "flower petals" made by dividing the circumference into six by stepping off the radius of the given circle, and then drawing an internal arc centred upon each of the circumferential points thus derived. Maybe in this description we have a possible explanation for the King of the World's dwelling place.

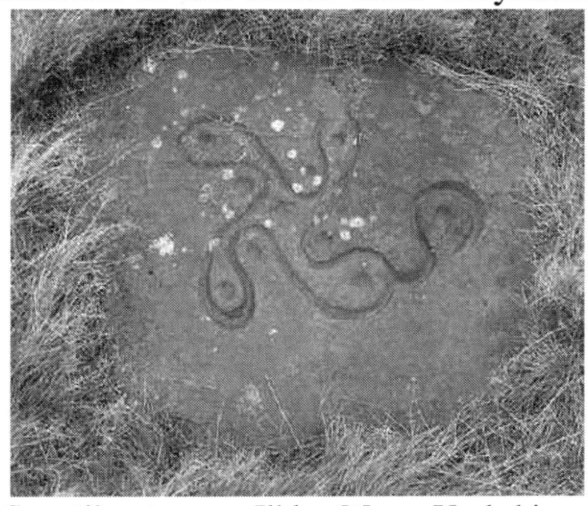
Swastika stone on Ilkley Moor, Yorkshire

Labyrinths have traditionally been associated with the function of a door or gateway to other times and places. The Chartres labyrinth, a design based upon eleven circles surrounded by more than one hundred petals and with a six-petalled flower at its centre, is rumoured to contain just such properties, as do each of the French Gothic cathedral labyrinths. If what is being depicted in the legend is a timeless realm accessible via a maze or labyrinth, passage through which requires a password or a code of some sort—a *dietrich*—then this begins to make abundant sense. Incidentally, the Benedictines are acknowledged as having had the ability to identify geomantic power sites on which to build their monasteries (including Montserrat).

Schafer took a specific interest in the Tibetans' sexual practices; for instance their public displays of masturbation but, generally, the expeditions were said to focus on geophysical, radiation and earth-magnetism research and anomalies. Schafer also succeeded in obtaining the Kangschur, the one hundred and eight volume sacred script of the Tibetans that needed nine packhorses to transport. These tablets were said to have later ended up in Russian hands. The expeditions included the anthropologist Dr. Bruno Beger who participated in the collection of one hundred and fifteen human skeletons at Auschwitz for controlled and scientifically managed decomposition experiments.

This Asgardian account of the origins of Tibet corresponds with

---

[1] Gale, Jack. *The Circle and the Square*. England: Capall Bann Publishing, 1997

a remarkable and truly bizarre event said by authors Preston Nicholls and Peter Moon to have taken place in Germany in 1923.[2] They describe an alleged event about a massive time travel experiment involving the Nazis in which key members of the Thule group are said to have collaborated with Aleister Crowley's Argentum Astrum (Order of the Silver Star), together creating a hybrid project called the Phisummum. This project and the purpose of the secret order behind it, the Order of the Black Sun, was time travel. The Black Sun stood for the centre of the galaxy. Moon and Nicholls make the incredible claim that in Project Phisummum the Order of the Black Sun wanted to retrieve the Holy Grail from a past century and put it into the hands of those grooming the Nephilim's Antichrist, Adolf Hitler. Sex magick was employed and the Spear of Longinus was supposedly used as a magical power source. A small but distorted time window was created and all involved began to feel the overwhelming power building up.

The authors go on to say that later in this year Dietrich Eckart, the leader of this ultra-satanic group, died and his successors made a botch of things, creating a time rift that rippled forward to Philadelphia on 12th August 1943 and to several other points in time. Students of "Metatronic" science name this wound in time the Kali Rift. If there is even the slightest substance to these frankly incredulous and extraordinary accounts could there have been some kind of extremely weird synchronicity, more than by similarity of name alone, between the 18th Century Philadelphus Society in France and the infamous WW2 Philadelphia experiment? [3]

Preston and Nicholls state that in 1939 the Ahnenerbe carried out its most ambitious experiment thus far—the harnessing of all natural and supernatural forces, drawing together Pythagorean metaphysical teachings, medieval black magic, and twentieth century technologies in an effort to create a unique, all-encompassing occult power.

The subject of earth energy grids and associated metaphysical sciences is huge. Frank Dorland, world-renowned biocrystallographer, wrote for example in his book *Holy Ice* about the Greek form of the Assyrian Goddess Ishtar, Astraea or Asteria. Asteria's daughter by Perses was Hecate. Legend tells that Asteria was a mistress of high

---

[2] Moon, Peter. *Black Sun*. New York: Sky Books, 1997

[3] The Philadelphia Experiment (also known as Project Rainbow) was an alleged naval military experiment at the Philadelphia Naval Shipyard in Philadelphia, Pennsylvania, in October 1943, in which the U.S. destroyer escort USS Eldridge was to be rendered invisible for a brief period of time. The U.S. navy denies that the event took place.

magic and that her principal task was in working with crystal energies because all the stars in her heaven were considered cosmic crystals. The story goes that at one time the earth was perfectly flat and regarded by the heavenly hosts as very precious. To protect it, Asteria magically fashioned a huge, hollow crystal dome to cover it. She cut holes in the dome to allow the clouds, the winds and the rains to pass through. To finish her creation Asteria hung millions of crystals by silver threads inside the heavenly dome and called them her stars. The Great She then created hollow crystal globes in which to carry the moon and the planets. She placed each one inside its crystal sphere for safekeeping and suspended them by crystal threads up among all her stars. Later, Asteria discovered that when the winds blew across the hollow crystal globes carrying the planets and the moon she would hear celestial harmonies like a great pipe organ in the sky. Asteria called this her "music of the spheres." With time the threads became black with oxidation and could no longer be seen.

Legend? In 1992 the annual Lunar and Planetary Science Conference held at Houston, Texas, reported that an analysis of studies carried out at the Infrared Telescope Facility at Mauna Kea in Hawaii indicated that molecular clouds contain a most unusual carbon atom bonded to a hydrogen atom and to three other carbon atoms. Further analysis showed that these blobs of gas and dust, which eventually give birth to stars, are full of floating micro-diamonds. Is it just an accident that ancient peoples believed that the twinkling stars in the heavens were crystals or did they have information from a time long lost in the distant past? *Indra's Net*, a verse from the Vedas (the Hindu Sacred Canons), is very appropriate:

There is an endless net of threads
Throughout the universe.
The horizontal threads are in space,
The vertical threads are in time.
At every crossing of the threads,
There is an individual,
And every individual is a crystal bead.
The great light of absolute being
Illuminates and penetrates
Every crystal bead, and also,
Every crystal bead reflects
Not only the light
From every other crystal in the net,
But also every reflection

Of every reflection
Throughout the universe.

The ancients, especially Pythagoras, believed that the physical universe was composed of geometrical figures, most interesting of which was the pentadodecahedron, identified as the "hull of the sphere." Plato refers in the Phaedo to the belief that the construction of the world was likened to the building of a ship by the use of geometric shapes.

Recent research does appear to indicate that the earth resembles a gigantic crystal with a rigid skeletal structure beneath its surface. The Russians ran this story in 1973 in Pravda and later Vyacheslav Marazov and Valery Makarov wrote a paper: *Is the Earth a Large Crystal*? Their theory is that the earth projects from within itself a dual geometrically regularised grid. The first grid layer consists of twelve pentagonal slabs over the surface of the earth, with the second formed by twenty equilateral triangles making up an icosohedron.

Marazov and Makarov maintain that by superimposing the two grids over the earth's surface a pattern of the earth's energy grid can be perceived. The lines tracing out the dual grid coincide with zones of active risings and depressions on the ocean floors, cave faults and mid-oceanic ridges like those of the Bermuda Triangle. There are twelve such areas. Also in these areas are regions of seismic and volcanic activity, while magnetic anomalies are found at the vertices of the polygons. The grid nodes are said to denote centres of great changes in atmospheric pressures; hurricanes take shape in these areas. Prevailing winds and ocean currents also fit into the network. The Russians' paper claims that if the grid was lined up on the surface of the globe so that all the many factors could be correlated the exact centre point is found to be Giza, the key being the "measure of Light."

Captain Bruce Cathie, a retired pilot and a pioneering researcher of earth energy science, believes that there exists on earth an all-encompassing grid whose interlocking lines correspond to the lines of flight of UFO appearances. The values of the grid reflect harmonic relationships with the acceleration and deceleration of light, gravity and the mass of the earth. His studies indicate that volcanic activity, atomic disruption (nuclear bomb blasts) and earthquakes are all connected to the grid structure.

The main plank of Cathie's work rests upon his observation that all major changes of physical state are caused by harmonic interactions of light, gravity and the mass of electrical and magnetic forces. The controlled manipulation of these resonant factors makes it possible to move mass from one point to another in space-time. Similarly, time can also be controlled by these manipulations of harmonic pulsations due to time's relationship to the speed of light.

The Germans were and are onto something very similar. Take, for example, Siegfried Wittman's 1952 book *Die Welt der geheimen Mächte* (*The World of the Secret Forces*). He and his study team concluded that the earth has upon its surface a grid system consisting of a checkerboard pattern consisting of positive and negative poles. The squared pattern has a centre pole surrounded by smaller poles within each section. The main pole is of diameter 2.54 metres (Cathie's harmonic), which concentrates energy through eight supporting poles. Four send pulses of energy skyward while the others send energy to the four points of the compass. The Germans' experiment seems to indicate that they have an awareness of the harmonic of the speed of light. Perhaps this is not surprising if they had access to work conducted by French mathematician Gaston de Mengel, whom we mentioned in Chapter 6. Let us remind ourselves of the content of the letter Gaston de Mengel sent to Otto Rahn in July 1937:

"*The axis, which is north east of Paris, works very well. But the axis is neither near Berlin nor Helsinki. I was able to calculate the origin of the forces from the average of the axis. It is in Murmansk (*Lapland*) approximately 35 degrees eastern length and 68 degrees northern breadth in the vicinity of Lowosereo (*Lovozero*) in Russia. I have also located the place of the big black centre. It is within the big triangle that is formed by Kobdo, Urumtschi and Bakul, near Sin-kinag in western Mongolia.*"

De Mengel's research was mainly concerned with pre-Christian Indian, Persian and Chinese documents, dealing with various religious matters. A treatise of de Mengel's on the symbolism of the trinity was published in 1932 in the bulletin of the Polaires, the same Theosophical-based sect that Otto Rahn had become embroiled with in the South of France. De Mengel's letter excited the elderly Weisthor who wrote to Himmler under "Strictly Confidential," bringing the Reichsführer's attention to this key passage.

At my request Bruce Cathie kindly analysed Gaston de Mengel's co-ordinates and reported to me his astonishing findings:

"It appears that the SS did have some knowledge of the grid and harmonic maths. The latitude and longitude you gave has connections with the harmonic 288 (twice the speed of light) and also the answer to one of the unified equations. They were getting close to the truth. Much is being kept hidden." (It is outside the scope of this present work to go

into any further detail on Bruce Cathie's astounding findings concerning earth energies. I encourage interested readers to explore them first hand.)

De Mengel's letter has many tantalising references that demand detailed analysis and interpretation. I am struck, for instance, by the remark about Paris. What immediately springs to mind is the Paris Meridian, which features so strongly in the geometry of Rennes-le-Château.

Lovozero lies northwest of the Ural Mounatins. The Pravda website of 30th April 2002 reports upon the findings by scientists at Bashkir State University in 1999 of a mysterious stone slab into which is etched a 3D relief map of the Ufa region, which is situated in the Republic of Bashkortostan between the Volga River and the Urals.[4] The scientists have concluded that the map proves the existence of an extremely ancient and highly developed civilisation, which pulls a rug from beneath all previous notions of the origins of human history. Tests indicate that the map was machined by precision tools and that it shows a view which could only have been plotted by aerial survey. It also shows precise details of massive civil engineering undertakings including irrigation and dams that would have required the removal of more than a "quadrillion"[5] cubic metres of earth to construct. The scientists believe that the map is only a fragment of a much larger one that would have shown the entire surface of the planet. It is more than possible that Gaston de Mengel was aware of the importance of these regions in terms of their significance in being the home of highly advanced, pre-cataclysmic civilisations whose secrets, like the planet wide earth energy mappings undertaken by the Atlantean priests of Ruta, await discovery.

Present day students of Grail geometry claim that in the antediluvian era there lay an island known as Ruta or Alta-Ru in what was then the Northern Hemisphere (later becoming the Southern Hemisphere, it is claimed, by virtue of an immediate and cataclysmic pole switch said to have taken place approximately eleven thousand years ago). The account records that among the inhabitants was a priesthood, which constructed a temple network in accordance with an energy pattern known as the Reshel Grid. The Reshel Grid system extended several thousand miles into an area that is now geographical Europe. Supporters of this theory claim that there are many hundreds of

---

[4] http://english.pravda.ru/main2002/04/30/28149.html

[5] It is not clear from the article which of the two definitions of a quadrillion the authors intended to apply. For interest see: http://en.wikipedia.org/wiki/Quadrillion

grids all over the earth, mirrors mirroring other mirrors. The Reshel energy poles are designated by Hebrew letters. Presently, we shall explore the context of the Reshel Grid and its key relationship with Edinburgh and Rosslyn Chapel.

The Black Sun-Centre motif also finds correspondences in the curious writings of Wilhelm Landig who in 1971 published *Kampf gegen Thule*—Battle against Thule, (later republished as *Götzen gegen Thule*—Godlets against Thule), in which we find some connecting links to alternative possibilities for Rahn's destiny.

Landig told researchers in 1975 that during WW2 he had held a leading position in the central Nazi archive in Berlin where information from all around the world came in for processing and archiving. Landig told his enquirer that his book was not a fictional novel but one based primarily on facts that his higher-ups had given him leave to write about and to publish. Landig claimed to know personally people who had been to the Nazi polar base and who were still in contact with it. New people were joining the base at intervals. For some reason Landig would not be drawn on the question of the base's food supply. The enquirer believed that Landig's reticence was meant to draw attention to the hollow earth theory of openings at the poles that lead to a warm and lush inner earth environment. Landig gave the impression of being very sincere in his beliefs; that he was perhaps more of a scientist than a writer of fiction.

Landig's story focuses upon two German airmen: Recke (brave warrior) and Reimer (rhymer or poet). Note the latter's similarity with the Rahn family name of Römer-Rahn. The book does mention Rahn. Towards the end of WW2 the airmen are despatched to a secret base in Arctic Canada called Point 103. The base boasts state of the art equipment and facilities provided by American supporters opposed to certain elements in the Reich government identified only as 666. Travel to and from the base is by V7 vertical take off UFO-style glass-domed aircraft equipped with rotating turbine blades, manufactured in German and Czech factories. After Germany surrenders to the allies Point 103 declares independence and substitutes its German markings with the symbol of the Black Sun. Reimer and Recke are rescued from a plane crash in Arctic waters by Gutmann (good man), a Waffen SS officer who becomes their guide and philosopher-mentor.

Later, a contingent from Point 103, including Reimer and Recke, is sent out into the world to forge contacts with supporters of the Thuleans. During their journey Recke and Reimer meet a man named Belisse near Montségur. Belisse is aligned with the Cathar tradition and to the guardianship of the Holy Grail. He immediately recognises the airmen as spiritual brothers (recall that the Pyrenean folklore group with which Rahn became acquainted was called the Seigneurs de Belisse).

The enemies of Landig's Thuleans are Israel's black magicians of ancient Semitic origin who have a long cherished goal to rule the North. We have already reviewed the disturbing account published by editor Jim Keith in which these ancient sorcerers make alliance with Bavarian occult factions in the ninth century, a merging of unholy power fuelled by mass human sacrifice.

Landig reveals that the Ark of the Covenant was an astral accumulator, a device designed to steal and conceal the life- or soul-force of the Aryans and filter it through something called the Hebraic Pole so as to pervert it and make it work solely for the Israeli sorcerers. Landig does not describe the exact nature of this Pole. These descriptions make uncomfortable synchronicity with the dramatic final scene of *Raiders of the Lost Ark* when René Belloq and Nazi personnel are incendiarised by the Light of God released from the Ark. A divine cloud immediately fills the night sky over the remote island. Robert Dassanowsky-Harris describes this mushroom cloud as the spectre of forthcoming global, atomic-age cataclysm.

At some point Reimer and Recke become separated but when the Thuleans arrive in Tibet they meet Recke and another German named Juncker (Antichrist) who tells them of a plan for a world empire ruled by a Yellow race, which firstly awaits the coming of a Great Khan from Agartha. A lama, Ngon kyi Padma Dab-yang, tells them that initially the Nazis had been helped by both the left and right-hand paths of Shambala and Agartha. Later, factions within the Reich abandoned this neutral position and sided with the absolute negative energies of Shambala, the Wheel of the Black Sun, whose source of power was Stalin. Consequently, the Tibetans destroyed the Reich, having lost years of patient work through the Nazis' defection to satanic powers.

The Black Sun motif conjures a baffling array of imagery. Central to the theme is the power inherent within geometry, patterns, labryinths and glyphs to provide a point of meditative focus by which mystics may journey to the inner worlds. In practiced hands these disciplines are said to offer the adept the means to bend Time and Space to his will but the consequences, as observers such as Moon, Nicholls and Sklarr warn their readers, can be disastrous. Rahn's friend, Gabriele Winckler, is herself an authority on the Black Sun, a fact at odds with the lightweight role official history accords her as simply being a young girl saddled by "Uncle" Himmler with looking after an old man with a drink problem.

No matter what corner Rahn turned during his time under Himmler's direct command the occult imperatives of the Reich were directly in his path. We can only hazard a guess as to the nature of things and events he might have witnessed, even participated in, that provoked him in despair to say he "had seen things…he had to see the boss."

Shortly afterwards Rahn disappeared from the face of the earth, as if sucked body and soul into the heart of the Black Sun and burned to nothing by its lightless fire.

Chapter TWENTY FOUR

Prometheus Bound

In addition to the metaphysical Black Sun allusions a more specific connection between these dark occult traditions and Rahn has emerged. Frau Winckler-Dechend has described the friendship between Otto Rahn and the Georgian aristocrat Grigol Robakidse, a charismatic man described as having a magical aura. Gabriele Winckler told me that Robakidse regarded every meal, especially those he shared with Rahn, as a cult and that he expected fellow diners to partake in a meal in the spirit of such ceremony. This is a strange comment about social dining, as if made to draw attention to another aspect of Robakidse's persona in a roundabout way. Gabriele provides a clue as to what this could be. Her mother mentioned that Robakidse was a member of the Schwannen—the Order of the Swan. He sometimes wore a conspicuous (and what must have been comical) ceremonial black wig as an emblem of his allegiance.

The Order of the Black Swan was inaugurated in the eleventh century and was also known as the Guardian Order of the Grail. The Order is in existence today but in a form reconstituted in 1982 as The Order of the Noble Companions of the Swan, consisting of Knights from various Orders of Chivalry. In 1986, it was incorporated as an independent, international Order of Chivalry and Knighthood. Interestingly, the days of significance to the Order include July 22nd, both the Election Day of Godfrey de Bouillon as King of Jerusalem and Mary Magdalene's feast day. Among the distinguished list of religious leaders who have bestowed apostolic blessings on the Order is His Beatitude Maximos V, Patriarch of Antioch. This is significant because it is from within the U.S. based Catholic Apostolic Church of Antioch that information has emerged purporting to add new levels of insight concerning the true agenda of Hitler and his backers. It is also significant that the Order's Arms have been registered with the Russian College of Heraldry, thereby providing a probable link with the Georgian Order of the Swan, which today appears dormant. The Antioch ministry is a little known but influential source for students of mystical ("new paradigm") Christianity, earth energies and associated esoteric history topics.

The source[1] reports that immediately after the Eckart-Crowley group caused the alleged time explosion in 1923 Dr. Karl Obermayer, a seriously worried scientist working with the group, seized the materials that had facilitated the time-travel experiments and went underground. According to these extraordinary accounts, Obermayer was determined to heal the rip in the fabric of time ("Earth's time grid") and to connect positively to the Grail Spirit via a time window to the Order of the Black Swan initiates of the eleventh century. The story claims that with the aid of Rudolph Steiner and Nikola Tesla Obermayer set up a project in the Urals under the auspices of his Prometheus Foundation: one more link to nearby Georgia and Robakidse. Note that this area links geographically with Gaston de Mengel's triangle coordinates and its black centre.

The account goes on to say that between 1923 and 1933 the Prometheus Foundation used its time-window technology to maintain this nine hundred year old link with the Swan initiates and create a controlling balance over the Nazi occultists' efforts to open a dimensional gateway to ultra-negative forces. The 1933 ascension of Adolf Hitler into power as the forces' human representative closed off this link with the Grail Guardians. Consequently, one of Hitler's first tasks was to form a special SS group to protect his timegate programme, the U.S. Montauk Project[2] equivalent for Germany but many times more powerful than the later American model. According to the Church source, however, the men Hitler chose were true Grail Blood knights and, at terrible personal risk, they worked successfully to sabotage Hitler's plan.

At the time of Otto Rahn's disappearance in 1939 he was working on the follow up to *Luzifers Hofgesind,* a work entitled *The Will of Prometheus: a Trip to Hell and Beyond*. Karl Obermayer and his fellows were bent on keeping the gates of hell closed, while at the same time Otto Rahn was writing a book whose title is suggestive of a journey, like Persephone's to Hades, but travelling deeper and further

---

[1] *Temple Doors* 1995-1999, also the *Koala* publication. (As at December 2007 the url http://www.spiritmythos.org/misc/archives/archive-zips.html is a redundant web address.)

[2] Allegedly a continuation of the Philadelphia Experiment—the story goes that in the 1950s researchers discussed military applications of the psychological effects of a magnetic field and that, subsequently, the Department of Defense, without Congressional approval, sanctioned the project using funds from a cache of Nazi gold recovered from a train by U.S. soldiers in France. (The 1978 movie *Brass Target* is a first rate fictionalised account of the Nazi gold train story.)

still into a hellish underworld. It is also at this time that Rahn tells Karl Wolff that he has such grave news that he can only convey them to Himmler orally. Weeks later Rahn disappears. It is stretching credibility to suggest that these various events and circumstances are not interlinked in some sinister fashion.

The researches of Vladimir Terziski, president of the American Academy of Dissident Sciences, cast a focus on these correspondences. Terziski is a Bulgarian born engineer and physicist who graduated Cum Laude from the Master of Science programme of Tokai University in Tokyo in 1980. He served as a solar energy researcher in the Bulgarian Academy of Sciences before emigrating to the U.S. in 1984. He is an international UFO and suppressed Nazi technology researcher speaking English, Japanese, Russian and German. He has some interesting things to say *à propos* the Tibetan line of enquiry. He claims that the Nazis experiments in mind-control, genetics and man-animal hybridisations were facilitated by their discovery and perfection of what Terziski refers to as a Teslan scalar-wave microscope, which helped the Germans unlock the human genome. Admiral Byrd's 1946 Antarctica force was said to have been subjected to a secret German Sonic Cannon, which had been tested in WW2 on Russian troops as they crossed the Elbe River. In this account Byrd's troops were paralysed and fled for their lives.

Terziski maintains that German occultists entered underground repositories below Tibet with the help of Ahrimanic and Luciferian secret societies in that country, where they gained access to ancient records from an early civilisation that had developed its own form of occult-technology. These are the supposed reptilian "greys" we read so much about among the proliferation of today's UFO conspiracy theories.

Dusty Sklar wrote in *Nazis and the Occult*: “Thule had an inner circle and an outer circle. Both were involved in raising their consciousness to an awareness of non-human intelligence in the universe and in trying to achieve means of communication with those intelligences.”

Students of “Metatronic” Science hold much the same views. They believe that Hitler is the most potent Antichrist incarnation in earth's ancient history and that he enlisted the Bönpo in late 1944 and early 1945 when he knew he was going to lose the war. They claim that Hitler asked the Bönpo priests to guide his soul and the souls of close confederates through the Sea of Souls by using the ceremonial Tibetan funeral service of Chod. In so doing, the story goes, they are said to have opened some form of channel through which they travelled to their next lives *en masse* and that in their wake they left open a timegate into which came the Greys associated with Roswell in 1947. The Kumir or "Greys" are thought by many to be just the tip of the iceberg. The account goes into more detail. Hitler's timegate project was sabotaged by the special SS group that he formed to protect the programme. They realized the terrible thing he had done and reversed the flow. However, the SS group was replaced by the Bönpo monks for the special job of passing on the transferring souls directly. The Bönpo group procedure would only involve the soul at its lower "Oritronic" level, not really the true soul or "Magna Soul," but a "low soul" that is useful in the outer or lower planes for transferring between incarnations and then is eventually dissolved. These two levels are found in Genesis in the so-called two lines of creation as man and woman: "zakar and nequebah" in the high soul range, and "esh and esha" in the lower.

I do not even begin to comprehend what is at the heart of these extraordinarily weird and bizarre accounts. I only know that what was happening in Germany between 1923 and 1945 is still a matter of the highest secrecy. I do believe that Otto Rahn and his confederates were a part of the small group that was dedicated to thwarting Hitler's occult battleplan.

In November 1938 Philéas Lebesgue published an article in the revue *l'Age Nouveau*, entitled *Sources Secrètes de l'Hitlerisme*. By this date Lebesgue had met Otto Rahn several times at the homes of both Maurice Magré and Antoinette Rives. In the light of Rahn's obvious credentials that place him at the forefront of neo-Templar esoteric philosophical thinking within his lifetime, it is astonishing that Rahn's name is not mentioned in the course of this article. This curious omission perhaps reveals more about Rahn's true affiliations than could be achieved by any number of accounts that explicitly address his timetable and activities in the Languedoc. Lebesgue could not make his point any clearer: "There was behind Hitler an order of chivalry, a secret order…the esoteric expression of Nazism…we neither know its name, its nature or its rules."

In *Emerald Cup-Ark of Gold: the Quest of Lt Col Otto Rahn* Howard Buechner echoed Lebesgue's remarks, writing that Rahn opposed the war for which Germany was obviously preparing in 1938, believing instead that Germany, Europe and, subsequently, other nations should be transformed under the auspices of a "New Order," which would adopt Cathar beliefs in the interests of world peace.

It is in a person's shadows that we will see their clearest

purpose. But it is not only a man's form that projects a shadow. His thoughts, words and actions also cast reflections in the form of code, cipher and symbol. Each of us constructs these internal clues, and in interpreting Otto Rahn's my hunch is that he was much more than he seemed but that all the same he was very vulnerable. This is not to say that Rahn had no sense of metaphysical heritage. His alignment with Joséphin Péladan's work suggests that Rahn belonged to an ancient Order, quite possibly of Rosicrucian base, to "reveal the mysteries and prepare for the coming kingdom of God." In this endeavour Rahn would surely have been one of a number. This presents us with a startling scenario.

Could there have been, as some observers have suggested, a seed of positive power buried deep within the Nazi regime that provided a balancing force to the mass insanity it unleashed? Universal law states that chaos and order exist side by side: that the one is in the other. There are no absolutes and there is no force, no matter how seemingly distant from the human values we cherish, that may exist in a vacuum.

Otto Rahn wrote: "is it accorded to me to become a Light-Bearer?" I believe that he did not direct the question to himself but to those who were drawn to his dreams and adventures.

In describing the Order, Lebesgue uses the term *par derrière*, which my Harrap dictionary translates in the sense of something going on behind a person's back or in an underhand way. It is important to bear this in mind. Lebesgue's article describes the destruction of the Druidic priesthood in Gaul by the Romans. However, the thread of order that had linked the Druids with all past, present and future esoteric orders was not severed by these actions. Simply, the Light went to sleep, awaiting an auspicious time to re-awaken. The task of maintaining the integrity of the Life-Force which permeates and gives validity to the physical experience fell, Lebesgue said, to the immortals: members of the invisible orders who since the beginnings of time have been the unseen inspiration for all wisdoms, philosophies and religions. Individuals who tap into the thread of order by virtue of their passion for life begin to understand that the chivalric ideal is descriptive of man's unceasing quest to re-unite consciously with that part which never dies—their Higher Self, the Life-Force within. To Lebesgue, it seemed evident that in the Germany of the day there existed a cadre of philosophers and metaphysicians who sought to regenerate the essence of positive quest.

The specific origin of the secret group, Lebesgue suggests, was the Teutonic Order, which was born in Jerusalem under the name of the Order of Our Lady of the Germans. But in describing this secret order Lebesgue did not once mention Otto Rahn, a man who had dedicated his life to a study behind Hitler's back (*par dèrriere*) of the histories of the ancient sects that had been the spiritual forefathers of the fraternity of Knights. In the article Lebesgue does refer, however, to Ram: the initiator of a mystical order established in India after the fall of Ceylon. The reference seems out of context but those reading Lebesgue's article and who knew of the Polaires controversy six years previously would have been aware of the piece in *La Dépêche* that named Otto Rahn incorrectly as Rams.

Bernadac's comments suggest that Lebesgue and Rahn knew each other fairly well; they were members of the intelligentsia belonging to Maurice Magré's circle. Lebesgue would not have wished to compromise Rahn by mentioning him overtly but, as is often the case, subconsciously he might have felt compelled to pepper his article with signposts suggestive of Rahn. Certainly, Lebesgue spares no mention of key elements of European heretical history that pop up frequently in Rahn's own writings. Lebesgue writes, for example, about the belief that England inherited the mantle of Templar tradition. In turn, Rahn also writes fondly of Englishman Lord Oldcastle, the 12th century lollard heretic and courtier to Lucifer/Apollo—the Light Bringer—and Oldcastle's "reincarnation" as John Falstaff in Shakespeare's Henry IV and Henry V. Lebesgue also dwells at length on Parsifal, the Cathars, the Fidèles d'Amour, Pythagoras, the Knight of the Mystical Way (of which Rahn's Knight of Berne represents a parallel archetype), the Dame of the Troubadours and other references that remind the informed reader of the like content of Rahn's published work.

Chapter TWENTY FIVE

Jehan's Last Steps

In 1934 the *Berliner Illustrirte Zeitung* published in Issue 48 an article by Otto Rahn entitled: *Jehan's Letzer Gang* (Jehan's Last Steps). The piece told the story of one Jehan Tessenre, a young family man moments away from his execution by Hugeunot troops in reprisal for the death of sixty-two of their brethren. They had been betrayed by Jehan to the townsfolk of Tarascon who lost no time in tossing them off the same high bridge on which he now stood to a painful death in the gorge below. A first casual reading of the story reveals nothing of obvious interest. In fact, the story is rather bland and on the face of it was something Rahn cobbled together to make a few marks and feed his growling stomach. But peer a little deeper into the text and a recognisable pattern emerges. It has clear Cathar correspondences but the story has also been observed to reflect elements of Bönpo ritualism and, in particular, with the Ceremony of Chod. As we have seen there are those who believe Hitler tried to undertake this extraordinary ritual in an effort to escape judgment in the next world. Here is a translation of *Jehan's Letzter Gang*, followed by an analysis:

A cloudless day in February, Tarascon. It's approximately 5pm on the sundial. The snowfields reflect the last rays of the winter sun so that passers-by are blinded; in fact they have to look to the west so as not to miss anything going on at this moment.

On the wooden bridge spanning the deep and wild gorge of the River Ariège there are two men. The elder, taller one is the executioner. The other one, Jehan Tessenre, is now to be transported from life to death. If one falls in the depths from the bridge he'll be dead. There is no rescue from the terrible currents of the waters that begin in the snowy mountains of Andorra.

But the judges didn't have in their minds a death in the water for the delinquent. Jehan is to be hanged at sunset. With the rope around his neck and his hands tied he stands over the gorge on a timber spar that forms a kind of seesaw. The end of the rope is tied to the bridge handrail. Currently, Jehan stands safely by the oblivion but as soon as the executioner will step off the other end of the timber Jehan's sense of balance will be lost and he'll fall. Yes, the judges made sure he cannot escape the punishment: if the rope tears he will die by drowning.

Frightened, Jehan looks into the depths then at the rope. He thinks that if it breaks there is a possible way out. I am a good swimmer. He can't believe that in a few seconds everything is going to come to an end. He doesn't want to die. He must not die. At home in the little house half a mile out of town next to the Lombrives Mountains there is his young wife and two young children.

Didn't he do his duty when he warned Tarascon of the planned attack by the Huguenots? It seemed to him as organised by Heaven when he woke in the middle of the night and realised there was a ray of light coming from the nearby Lombrives cave. He dressed and left the house. Under cover of broom bushes and blackberry hedges Jehan quickly climbed the steep mountain up to the cave, and had just arrived when the beam of light vanished into the depths. By a path known only to him he entered the cave and listened to the conspiracy: the sixty-two Huguenots waiting near the town intended to attack the castle and the gates that very same night, a plan that would have undoubtedly worked. Wasn't it his duty to warn the town of the danger?

He shall be killed. He's not frightened of death! But he has to live because of his children. Who will get bread for them? Who will accompany them through this hard life? And his poor wife is still very young! In all Tarascon there is no happier marriage than theirs. A groan escapes his breast. He knows that Marie will be too weak to work in the fields. There is little yield from them but it's enough for the two of them. What is going to happen to his helpless family? Desperately, he tries to pull on his bonds. No result, they won't move.

He's going to be hanged as a punishment for the death of the sixty-two conspirators. When they left the cave for the town they were surprised to be attacked from all sides by armed citizens and monks. None of them escaped. All of them were gagged and the next morning they were thrown from this bridge into the depths. The corpses were fished out of the waters of the Garonne. To take revenge for the death of these martyrs a large number of Huguenot troops arrived a couple of days later. Tarascon, to which he, Jehan, had fled, had to surrender soon after the enemy arrived. Now he had to pay for the sixty-two.

The sun gets paler and is about to depart from the sky. Her last mild beams fall on town and valley. Will he never see a sunrise again? If only the rope would tear! The executioner also looks to the mountains. Soon the moment when the sentence is to be carried out will come. The sun already touches the highest mountaintops.

Terrified, Jehan observes that the executioner slowly turns his head towards the town and waves his hand for the ringing of the poor-sinner bell. Then suddenly—even before Jehan can form the first word of the prayer with which he wanted to die—he feels himself falling. There's a loud noise in his ears. Darkness surrounds him. He sinks and sinks.

When he tries to scream ice-cold water penetrates his mouth. He opens his eyes wide. Green glassy light can be seen, becoming brighter and brighter. But however hard he tries Jehan can't separate his hands. Then a light surrounds him again. It is then that he realises where he is and what happened. The rope tore and he fell into the river!

The water surrounds him. He is chased by the current down into the valley. The evening sky is wide and colourful above him. Yes, the rope tore! He would like to cheer but already his mouth is full of water. Darkness begins to surround him again. He sinks and sinks.

He will be lost if he can't free his hands to swim. He can already feel a pain in his breast because he can't breathe. Again, he tries with all his might to free himself and his bonds, maybe stretched by the water, glide over his hands. He is free!

With three strong strokes he reaches the surface. He sucks in air deeply and relieves his aching lungs. The waters carry him as quick as a flash. He turns his head and looks back. The wooden bridge on which has was supposed to have died is already very far off in the distance. He can also see the people by the riverbank, witnesses of a failed execution. Yes, he can see them clearly. They run around, gesture wildly and point at him. He can also see the executioner still standing on the bridge. He also points to him carried away by the waves to freedom.

Jehan's power feels doubled, tripled. He safely manages to escape the currents that try to pull him into the depths. Oh, he is strong! Never before had he felt that strong. The waters can't harm him. For a long time he swims on. The dangerous currents are already behind him. There are fewer and fewer whirlpools and the water slows down.

He mustn't lose time. Time is precious because they will send hunters and horses after him. The best course of action will be to get to the riverbank and climb one of the gorge walls to reach the Catalonian border or the Roussillon. He has got friends there. They could help him. And once the Catholics rule again he will be able to return to his wife and children. By the way, once rescued he has to send a message to his family immediately so they don't believe he has been killed in the waves.

He reaches land. He stretches his limbs. He breathes in life deeply. He lifts his arms to the sky and gives thanks for the mercy. The first stars begin to flicker. He has to hurry if he doesn't want to be surprised by night while on the rock face. He quickly crosses the meadows, jumps over a road and assesses where the start of the climb would be most rewarding, and then starts to climb. It wouldn't be the first time in his life he would climb one of the almost vertical walls. Today, however, he has to be careful because it is getting dark already. His hands search skilfully for cracks in the rock face then he pulls up his body and supports himself with his feet.

He climbs and climbs. All of a sudden his hand grabs empty space. No matter how hard he tries he can't find a crack. With his other hand holding a ledge of rock he pulls himself up and continues on with his feet in a safe position. He wasn't wrong (to choose this ascent): a path interrupts the rock face and, running parallel to the oblivion, leads up to the top. He follows the path. Luckily, he doesn't have to climb any more. That's far too dangerous in the pitch black.

Nobody will think of him in the rocks that late at night. There is no danger of being caught. He climbs and climbs. Due to the darkness it seems there's no end to the upward path. Hours must have passed since he started following it. He peers into the depths searching for any light in the distance. Deep darkness is under him and surrounding him. Strange, one should see light somewhere. Jehan stops and listens. He can't hear a sound. No dog is barking. No night bird screams. Nothing! It is strange.

It's almost like an ominous fear that keeps him going. And again, he climbs and climbs. He can't see a hand before his eyes. I shouldn't go on so impetuously, he thinks. He stops again. It feels to him as if he could fly between heaven and earth. He uses both hands to feel around him. He feels something hard and is surprised to realise he touches a tree. How could he miss the fact that he's already reached the forest on top of the mountain! Now he can see clearly all the tree trunks in front of him and the treetops covering the flickering stars. It seems to become brighter and brighter around him. Soon the silvery moonlight penetrates the forest and is reflected by delicate cranberry bushes and ferns.

Now the path can easily be found. And who would not know it is easier to walk on the plateaux than in the depths of a gorge. With springy steps he goes on. He wanders and wanders all night through. His heart fills with happiness. His chest breathes more and more easily! He is free! No, it won't take long anymore and he'll sit with his wife and children again in front of the fire, and reminisce about the terrible day when both their father and husband should have been taken from them. Comfortable and calm, they will continue their lives. What happens in the towns and rural areas will never again intrude into their quiet lives. Their little world won't have anything in common any more with the big world out there.

Jehan smiles. Yes, that's what he'll do! Together with the memory of his rescue he will send his wife a piece of a bright cloth that she will wear instead of black. Then all of the town will know that Marie Tessenre doesn't have to mourn and that her husband is still alive. Yes, that's what he'll do. She always enjoyed dressing up, his Marie. He never did mind, after all she comes from the area around Lavalanet. There, women enjoyed dressing up more that anywhere else. It is a rich area. He almost didn't succeed in marrying Marie because of that. One who has no money is worth nothing. But since he, Jehan, is a smart and diligent fellow old Marius didn't mind giving him his daughter. It took, however, quite some time until his father-in-law finally agreed to it. Jehan smiled again. The wedding day arrived. On this Sunday in May Marie did not initially want to marry because she felt her wedding dress wasn't fashionable enough. There were lots of tears. With still-reddish eyes she would finally stand before the altar. Yes, she always enjoyed dressing up, his Marie. How her eyes will flicker and her mouth laugh when she has received a colourful cloth from her rescued husband. He has to think of that as soon as he's arrived.

But which way should he go? To Catalonia? Or towards Perpignan in Roussillon? That would be closer and less dangerous! Yes, he will go to Perpignan. He has faithful friends there and people are Catholic. He's unsure where he is at the moment but he feels he has to climb down into the valley. In the east the sky starts to change its colour and he has been wandering all through the night. According to his calculations the sun will rise in the next hour.

He doesn't have to look for the right way any more because the path becomes wider and leads downhill. One could think it is one of the roads leading to Roussillon and that is, thankfully, the direction he aims for. He continues to walk and is surprised that he doesn't feel tired at all. His energies derive from the happy knowledge that he escaped a certain death.

And he thinks again of his family. What did Antonin, his eldest—he'll soon be six—wish for recently? Ah, right, a trumpet. He shall get it. He will get two. Children are not careful with toys therefore it's better to think about a replacement immediately. Antonin is a fabulous chap. He looks like his father. He is, however, a little quiet and absent-minded just like his father. But more lively is his second son, Gaston. What will he get him for a present? That's hard to say. Maybe sweets. Once he is in Carcassonne he will find something.

Carcassonne? But he wanted to go to Perpignan? Jehan has to laugh at himself. First he thinks for ages about where he wanted to go and finally, when he comes to a decision, he forgets about it. A day like the one yesterday can make a man confused.

Is he really on the right track? It should be easy to determine that now, as it's bright daylight. He looks around. First, he looks to the top of the mountains because he knows all of them. He always liked the peaks. He had climbed the Lombrives Mountains on the wild Soudour to look down at the deep valley and up to Tarascon. He knows every house and every tree there. When he was a boy he stole apples off the trees from the Fournier farm (he's not afraid of heights).

And right away: there is the Fournier farm. And he is on one of the slopes of the Lombrives Mountains! At his feet is Tarascon! He can also see the wooden bridge where he would have found death. And there, very close, his house can be seen through the pines. He has walked in a circle!

Terrified, he wonders what he should do now. Shall he rush back to his house and tell his wife he lives? Shall he immediately run away and look for a way out far off? What shall he do? The questions penetrate his brain. Oh, no! He'll try to get to his house without being seen, stay there a moment and then return to the mountain heights. Everybody is still asleep and nobody would expect him at all to survive the waves. It's only a few steps to his farm. And he knows his wife is already awake: bluish smoke escapes the chimney and the bells of Saint John ring.

Jehan is already in the garden. He can't wait to hold his wife and children in his arms. The blood rushes through his veins in excitement. It hammers in his neck. It's almost painful. He tries to touch it to get some relief. Look at that: the torn piece of rope is still around his neck although he walked the whole night through. When he tries to slide the rope over his neck his hands won't move. He can't separate them! In this moment he feels a terrible blow…

…Just in that moment Jehan Tessenre fell from the wooden bridge into the depths. With a broken neck he hangs from the rope over the waters. The sunset is complete. The poor-sinner bell of Saint John rings.

Rahn's tale is mildly interesting but by no means does it fall into the category of a knuckle-biting potboiler. But that was not the intention. The story is a workmanlike effort whose sole purpose, at least in a commercial sense, was to earn Otto Rahn a little money at a time when earnings were scarce. But dig a little deeper into the text and we may identify distinctly observable metaphysical themes that offer fascinating elements for scrutiny.

Firstly, consider Jehan's grid-like or geometric passage from the execution bridge to his family home. Quickly, it dawns with awful clarity that he had come full circle but was his journey so completely one-dimensional? How could it be so? By the very nature of the extreme causal factor impelling him upon his journey, his execution, the young Languedocien is in a heightened new state of being, a product of a tale of death, of continuance, and of transition.

Some observers have recognised in the Jehan story a symbolic representation of what has been referred to as the spiritual earth bond, the time it takes for the life force to recognise its separation from its earthly anchor. Theorists put forward the synopsis that certain "ghosts" are spiritual beings that cannot make the connection from life to death and are incapable of making the transition until something happens to release them. In some cases the will is strong enough for them to remain in this limbo state until they complete an unfinished task and continue their journey to the Sea of Souls. It has always been said that the mind or the will is stronger than the material self; this is probably the key factor. By travelling on to the places mentioned in the story was Jehan indeed making the transition or, essentially earthbound by too strong an identification with love of family and life left behind, did he need to return home to realise that he must now make his final journey? Thinking of his family made him travel in a circle but arriving brought about the realisation or recognition of his death. Time has no meaning in this situation: all of life is as a fleeting second. There is no perspective in these uncharted spheres of higher consciousness. Rahn poses the unspoken question: how much do we take with us on our next journey and how much do we leave behind?

Let us also dwell awhile on the symbology and meaning of the noose imagery. In Rahn's exposition of the legend of the Knight of Berne we see that the hero finally attains his goal, to find the entrance to the Kingdom of Laurin, a portal protected by a seemingly impenetrable spider's web. In esoteric lore the web symbol relates to geomancy and sacred rites. There are numerous examples in legend asociated with web and spider mythology. For instance, these themes feature in the Northern tradition of the Web of Wyrd and the weaving of the Norns, returning us once more to Rahn's beloved tisserands-weavers theme. The Norns were occupied with activities of time, procreation and dissolution, archetypal forces cancelling each other out, a process epitomised by Jehan's circular journey.

Consider also the Spider Woman: a lunar deity who spins in both Time and Space, imagery echoed in the Eastern tradition of Kali to whom the noose is sacred. Ix Chel, ancient Mayan Lunar Goddess, was a deity of snares and ropes who received, somewhat like Morrigan, Goddess of Fallen Warriors in Celtic lore, the souls of the self-hung. For the Chibcu Indians the web is a boat in which to cross the lake of death. This allegory provides us with an even stronger link between Jehan's plunge into fast flowing waters and the Tibetan Ceremony of Chod for the deceased's passage through the Sea of Souls. Rahn was proud of his region's mythological associations with the grand god of the North, Oddhinn Alfaddir. Odin's steed, Sleipnir, has eight legs and Odin, himself, is also the gallows god and a conductor of the dead.

Marcus Williamson advances the astute insight that the Jehan story is rather like the Rosicrucian Chemical Wedding in the hidden message it is trying to convey. The use of symbols such as the tree (Tree of Life), black/darkness (first stage of the process), climbing/height/light (enlightenment), and death (of the conscious mind) are alchemical in nature, thereby describing an allegorical account symbolic of an initiatory experience rather than one explicitly pertaining to matters of time and space.

Ostensibly, Otto Rahn's association with Gaston de Mengel was related to the Frenchman's report on the coordinates relating to the curious "big black centre" but the relationship undoubtedly went further. De Mengel was an influential authority on alchemy, being the author of learned articles in the Journal of the Alchemical Society such as "*The evidence for authentic transmutation*" and "*The philosophical channels of alchemical tradition.*" We have seen in Chapter 20 how Rahn's writings highlight his own fascination and empathy with alchemical lore and history. In the story Jehan refers to his "second son, Gaston," asking what he would get him for a present, confident that once in Carcassonne he would find something. Carcassonne occupies an important place within the subject matter of Rahn's researches and scholarly endeavours. We have learned that it was to Carcassonne that the Visigoths brought a part of the Treasures of the Temple of Solomon in 410 A.D. We have also seen, furthermore, that a search in Carcassonne library will unearth numerous documents concerning masonic-alchemical rituals from the time of Chefdubien related to the mysterious "forbidden merchandise" later sought so brutally by the SS in Oradour-sur-Glane. All this is suggestive that in *Jehan's Letzter Gang* Otto Rahn was encoding certain key references to alchemic-Grail-treasure matters that would have made sense to the certain few in Rahn's circle who held the cipher keys (the "*dietrich*").

Before we move on I will pose one last point for reflection. Rahn has Jehan discovering he is close to the Fournier farm, that he is on the slopes of the Lombrives Mountains and that nearby is the place where he would have found death. Five years after the Jehan story was written Rahn exactly replicated these circumstances when he made his way to a farm in the mountains where he was supposed to make his death. But increasingly compelling factors suggest that Rechau farm in the Austrian Tyrol was a doorway to survival rather than a mausoleum for Otto Rahn. Within the lines of his Jehan story was Rahn, consciously or subconsciously, giving advance details of a time shortly to come when he would confront, and conquer, gathering circumstances that, left unchallenged, would culminate in untimely death by his own hand?

Chapter TWENTY SIX

Illumination

The classical esoteric schools of thought I have described are among the major developmental pathways whose origins can be traced back twenty five hundred years to Pythagoras' hilltop classroom at Crotona in the West and to the lands of his contemporaries, Masters Lao Tse and Buddha, in the East.

These wisest of men emphasised the importance of right thought, word and action. Their philosophies are rooted in the recognition and interpretation of unchanging archetypes: a golden fleece, a white rose, an emerald table, a Star of Isis, the fire of Prometheus. These symbols of light and of eternal life were the sources of comfort and inspiration that guided Otto Rahn's journey, especially during the closing years of the 1930s. For all his faults and foibles, Rahn demonstrated through his work the hope and determination of the alchemist who has little interest in clutching handfuls of gold to his chest, but who has every intention of transmuting his base character into an altogether higher quality of expression.

A common thread of order runs through each of these ancient expressions of spiritual belief. Each is an opportunity for the lone traveller to seek the God and Goddess by the light of the lantern within. In sharp distinction, Nazi cosmogeny derived its power from the very absence of Light, a Black Sun fed not by the quest of determined travellers but by terror and cruelty.

We can visualise the green-gloved monk acting as the central pillar for the swastika Sun-Wheel composed from his six suicided brethren. We can imagine standing on the summit of the legendary Mount Meru and having a 360-degree lighthouse view of the entire world. At a stretch we might perhaps conjure a picture of divine energy beings beaming down an axis of Light onto the plains of ancient Tibet. In each of these images the polar theme is the connecting thread.

Joscelyn Godwin writes at length in *Arktos* about the Spiritual Pole and the experience of mystical ascent to it. The mystic Persian theosophers did not situate their "Orient" towards the East but in the direction to the North. There is a darkness around this pole that corresponds to the shroud around one's individual spiritual centre.

Through self-discipline the initiate can make a pilgrimage to this Polar Orient that is not found on maps. The Pole is also a mountain, called in Iranian lore Mount Qaf, whose ascent, like Dante's climbing of the Mountain of Purgatory, represents the individual's progress through spiritual states. The Mountain of Qaf is the Sphere of Spheres surrounding the totality of the visible cosmos; an emerald rock is the keystone of this celestial vault, the pole.

Of course, the mountain is not a physical geographical entity because it is an allegory for individual spiritual ascent. It can be symbolized, therefore, by any place on the earth but there are earthly topographies that do have a power, which men and women may use in their quest for enlightenment. Montségur is a prime example. (Paramount Pictures's logo, the high mountain peak, serves as the opening insignia of Indiana Jones's filmic adventures, an irony made more cogent by the logo's girdle of stars that encircle the peak as if to emphasise the mountain's glittering appeal—the resting place of Grail treasures?)

Rahn likened the Quest for the Grail to the journey undertaken by students of the Brahminic and Cabbalistic mysteries. He described the Grail adventure as one in which the neophyte engages in a series of tests and trials in which each successful stage tears away a little more of the veil separating a person with a pure heart from free access to the divine kingdom within.

Rahn also likened Eschenbach's Montsalvat temple with the chakra structure of the human body. In Rahn's model the temple's inner sanctum corresponds to the heart chakra, where resides the Grail treasure, the mediating power linking the terrestrial to the Absolute. In the loftier parts of the temple, at the summit of the spinal column and hidden behind the royal veil, the seeker may find the celestial Grail: the impersonal Brahma beyond Reason where the Absolute reveals its secrets on the "blue peak of the great Mountain of Kaila."

Leni Riefenstahl's 1932 film *Das blaue Licht* (*The Blue Light*) tells the mythic story of a maiden who guards mysterious blue crystals in a mountain cavern. Those drawn to the area suffer untimely death, echoing the dreadful fate awaiting treasure-seekers pulled to the Schleigeiss Glacier in the Zillertal Pass. Like the brave Knight of Berne or Don Quixote, only one with love in his heart can retrieve the mountain goddess' treasures. Robert Dassanowsky-Harris has noted George Lucas' nod to Riefenstahl's zeppelin rally scene in *Triumph of the Will* in the 1977 *Star Wars* episode. Seeing that Lucas has story credits for all three Indiana Jones films, one might consider if Lucas was seeking to interpolate Grail metaphor ("the impossible dream") from Riefenstahl's work into the trilogy for esoteric, philosophical and historical emphasis.

The Cabbalist ascends to the heights by climbing the branches of the Sephiroth. In this context Répanse de Joie, the Queen-Guardian of the Grail, is a symbol of the dynamic female aspect of the Brahminic Shakti: the divine power that assists and guides the traveller towards illumination and self-knowledge. Maya is the mother of Buddha Gautama while Maia, the mother of Hermes, is the messenger of the gods.

There is an old legend that Rahn recounts in *Kreuzzug gegen den Gral* that is very apposite. He writes of an ancient lake of dark green waters surrounded by sheer cliff walls between Montségur and the peak of Thabor, Montségur's sister. It is the Lake of the Trouts or the Lake of Sins. It is situated between the mountain of Saint Bartholomew (opposite Montségur and known locally as Thabor) and the Pic de Soularac (Saint Bartholomew's twin summit). It is the lake where the druids threw gold, silver and precious stones in a time before Jesus. This treasure was said to be the fabled treasure of the Temple of Delphi. In 279 B.C. Brennus, the Celtic Chief, led two hundred thousand soldiers into Greece to raid the treasure. On the point of victory at Parnassus a series of natural calamities: lightning storms, falling rocks, hail stones and heavy snow assailed Brennus' troops, causing a mass slaying of the beseigers. The Oracle told the townsfolk of Delphi that Apollo would not allow them to suffer distress. However, some accounts say that the Celts were finally victorious and stole the treasure, bringing it to Toulouse (Tolosa) but because of the nature of its procurement the booty was cursed.

Subsequently, Celtic settlers in the Montségur area began dying in numbers of an inexplicable ailment. A man healthy in the morning could be dead by nightfall. Never before had such a malady struck in the mountains. The druids divined by the flight of the birds that the people would never get well unless the treasure was disposed of. They advised the mountain folk to throw away the Delphian spoils as gifts for the subterranean divinities, mistresses of life and death. On chariots drawn on stone wheels the mountain people brought their riches to the lake and plunged them in the fathomless depths. The druids then traced a magical circle around the pond. Immediately, all the fish perished and the waters, once green, became black. At this moment the people were cured of their terrible affliction. The legend says that all the gold and silver will belong to one who can break the magic circle. But, it warns, as soon as the finder touches these treasures they will succumb to the same malady as the old mountain folk.

Rahn writes also that a part of the Treasure of Solomon, the "Table of Solomon," was brought to Carcassonne by the Visigoths. Spanish romances say that this Table was hidden in the magical grotto of Hercules in the Pyrenees. The gold of Tolosa has echoes of La Toison d'Or: the Golden Fleece and the legend of Hercules. Hercules, after having skinned the cattle of Geryon, seduced the daughter of Bebryx, Pyreneus. He then abandoned her. Pyreneus, fearing the wrath of her father, fled but was met by wild beasts. In desperation Pyreneus called out to Hercules but he arrived too late. She was dead. His lamentations reverberate around the grottos and caverns to the echo of the name Pyreneus, such is how the range got its name. The name of Pyreneus will never perish because always the mountains will carry it. Rahn believed that Hercules found Lucifer's crown-piece. Eschenbach thought so, too.

In medieval times the Philosophers Stone was also called la Toison d'Or. Wolfram von Eschenbach had Parsifal looking for a stone, the Lapsit exillis (Lapis ex coelis), the "Desire of Paradise." For those on the path the joys of paradise are to be found in the stars, the grandeur of the firmament, transmuting nature's power within one's spirit-self and creating a state of grace and balance. This is the essence of alchemic endeavour.

The possession of the Golden Fleece hoisted the Argonauts towards the stars. Through his labours Hercules demonstrated that death is nothing to fear and is merely a stepping-stone to the threshold of the gods and immortal life. He also showed that Hell is a living nightmare suffered in proportion to the degree we make earthly life a trial of pain rather than a labour of love. Hercules prepared himself to become one with God, to take his place in the constellations between the Lyre, the Crown, and Castor and Pollux. The good ship "Argo," which had brought the precious relic across the sea, was transported to the Milky Way to join its sister stars in celebrating the infinite luminescence of God in the Heavens.

The Argonauts were Hyperboreans. The inhabitants of Crotona in the sixth century B.C. made out that Pythagoras was none other than Apollo reborn, arrived from Hyperborea to announce to mankind a new doctrine of hope and welcome. Later, Cicero saw that druidic doctrine, which included a belief in eternal life and the transmigration of souls, was Pythagorean in origin but a meld also of natural sciences and of Hindu and Babylonian traditions. The druids taught that the earth and all that grows and walks upon it is a creation of the God of Death, Dispater (the basis, too, of subsequent Cathar dogma). The immortal soul was obliged to migrate from existence to existence to purify itself eventually and to reconnect with its divine essence and enter the world of pure spirit. The druids' God was Belenus or Belis. This God was Apollon-Abelio, God and the Light. Dispater was the latinised name of the Prince of Darkness, Pluto, sovereign of pale souls and of the dead, guardian of all hidden treasures. The druids held earthly treasures to no account and it was on their order, as we have seen, that the gold of Tolosa was thrown into the lake.

In Parzifal the Grail is a stone. The human heart is often compared to stone when it is unfeeling. When a person's inner nature is at one with outer nature it is an emerald illumination, a Jade Pivot. From that moment on there is no going back. To borrow from the writings of Carlos Castenada, there is no return to Ixtlan once the question has been asked: who am I? It is then that the heart, whose chakra colour is green, transmutes from simple stone wrought from flesh and blood to an altogether higher quality of creation. It is that alchemical process which demarcates a major signpost along the mountain trail of the Grail Quest.

"Lucifer is nature, both external nature and one's inner nature," Rahn wrote in *Luzifers Hofgesind*. In this cosmogeny Lucifer is not one's god but a mediator, one who offers a model of right attitude of how to live and die in an exemplary fashion with nature as mother, guide and companion. It is the spirit of continuance expressed via the eternal cycle of nature and her seasons: conception, incubation, birth and nurture. But it is a journey we discover for ourselves. There is no route map to the higher senses. It is knowing that God is within, therefore obviating the need for priestly intermediaries to serve as a bridge between a God in the Heavens and humankind.

Miguel Serrano, Chilean writer, wrote *Adolf Hitler, el Ultimo Avatara* in 1984. He stressed the importance of Hyperborea. He tells how the solar race originated "from the Sun which lies on the other side of all suns. Our star is close by and appears to the Walkers of the Dawn to show them the way." The solar race "came down to live at the north pole, on the continent of Hyperborea." After a dramatic climate shift the "White Gods withdrew into the Interior Earth, although a few of them went to a trans-oceanic continent to the west where the Sun of the Golden Age had not yet set." This is the place "where the Black Sun of the South Pole rose at the point where Arcthus, Arthos, the Hyperborean bear became Antarctica…where Stonehenge, the

Observatory of the Sun, became…the star of Lucifer." The White Gods carried "a sword, a lance, a cauldron, together with the Soma plant. With them they also brought a stone which fell from the broken crown of Lucifer, the King of the White Gods, whom others have called Apollo, Abraxas, Siva, Quetzalcoatl." The Walkers of the Dawn, whose sign is the left-handed swastika, which begins the journey back to Hyperborea, the polar homeland, and the Morning Star, Venus, are "the followers of Lucifer, of the Morning Star." Once more we encounter a transcendental theme that is mindful of Jehan's fateful journey and its allegorical overtones.

Otto Rahn took each of these ancient wisdoms and belief systems and wove, like the Cathar-Tisserand spinners of old, their core metaphysical foci into his writings and public presentations. Moreover, he did not stop there. Rahn shared the view held by so many mystics before and since that the mystery schools from which emerged the major strands of spiritual development over the centuries were, themselves, outgrowths of a single source of universal wisdom whose power existed prior to the Fall as described in Genesis. Christopher Knight and Robert Lomas[1] relate the history of a document, the Ancient Charges, which appeared soon after Freemasonry had been brought to England by James I and his Scottish Court.

This document emphasises the achievement of the pre-Flood races and claims that all their knowledge: the seven sciences of Grammar, Rhetoric, Logic, Arithmetic, Geometry, Music and Alchemy, were all highly developed prior to the cataclysm, which many authorities claim struck the Earth many thousands of years ago. Moreover, these highly civilised peoples foresaw the disaster and preserved the knowledge of their sciences on two pillars—one resistant to fire made of marble, the other made of Laterus (a kind of brick) resistant to water. Descriptions of this far distant history are to be found on two documents. One is the Inigo Jones manuscript of 1607 that conveys the verbal traditions of the Origins of the Mason's Craft. The other is by J. Whytestones of 1610 in which we learn that one of the two pillars was found by the great, great grandson of Noah, Hermes Trismegistus, discovery of which led directly to the development of the highly evolved Egyptian civilisation. The other pillar was re-discovered by the Jews three thousand years ago during the construction of the Temple of Solomon.The rituals of the Ancient Scottish Rite indicate that the high priests of Jerusalem who survived the Roman sacking of 70 A.D. thereafter became the great families of Europe, then later

[1] Knight, Christopher; Lomax, Robert. *Uriel's Machine*. England: Arrow Books, 2000

became the founders of the Order of the Knights Templar in the early twelfth century.

Popular opinion has it that the nine founding members of the Order are said to have re-discovered the Treasures of the Temple of Solomon in Jerusalem, bringing them to France and entrusting custodianship of the artefacts to the Cathar elders.

One hundred and thirty years later the *tisserands* re-interred the treasures in the Sabarthès grottoes in March 1244 on the eve of the brethren's wholesale immolation at the hands of the Roman Church. Seven hundred years then passed before a "slender young man with a determined look and wearing a Boy Scout shirt and heavy Alpine climbing boots,"[2] nourished by his absolute belief in his philological and intuitive interpretations of key documents such as Eschenbach's *Parsifal*, entered the Cathar caverns and, as so many believe, unearthed Solomon's fabulous jewel case. One does not have to look far to identify the source for Spielberg and Lucas' Baden-Powellesque depiction of the young Indiana Jones, as played by River Phoenix in *Indiana Jones and the Last Crusade.* If Otto Rahn did indeed pull off the recovery then what became the next resting place for its fabulous contents?

It is interesting that Hyperborea derives from Bor (father of Odin). Bor is a contraction of bear, the polar Arktos. Arcturus (Arthur) is the "bear guard," which watches over the poles, signifying vigilance over the Earth's morphogenetic grid. The Ark of the Covenant contains the forces of creation and destruction, symbolised by Brahma and Shiva respectively.

We have already reflected upon the strong connections between Rahn's explorations and the plot of the first Indiana Jones movie. Bear in mind also that in the *Last Crusade* episode Jones and his beautiful heroine bluff their way into a German Schloss ("Castle Grunewalde"—could the writers have made a link to Rahn, Weisthor and the Berlin film studios any clearer?) in their quest to wrest Indie's father's Grail Diary from the Nazis. They make out to the bad guys in the Schloss that Indiana is a Scottish laird who has a castle of his own back home—a pointed reference to Rosslyn?

We begin to examine the possibility of a post-mortem connection between Otto Rahn and Scotland in the following chapter.

---

[2] Angebert ibid

Chapter TWENTY SEVEN

Arthur's Bosom

Rahn briefly visited Edinburgh in 1936 en route to Iceland. His ship docked at Leith and Rahn went off to visit Arthur's Seat, the highest of a series of ancient volcanic peaks, which take the form of a crouched lion. Rahn describes the visit in *Luzifers Hofgesind*; or rather, more tellingly, he does not describe the visit, devoting only a handful of lines to the sights. Instead, Rahn writes at length about the turn his thoughts took on finding himself on British soil. He states that for British heretics an Arthur-Arctus figure has a lot more meaning than an Abraham or a David.

Rahn then muses on the connection between John Falstaff in Henry IV and V and the Lollard heretic Lord John Oldcastle. He states that the 12th century English lollards firmly belonged to the Court of Lucifer; that they were light-bringers in a sea of Catholic repression. Rahn points out that Shakespeare then tries to muddy the connection he has portrayed by stating in the Epilogue to Henry IV Part 2 that "*Oldcastle died a martyr, and this (Falstaff) is not the man…My tongue is weary; when my legs are too, I will bid you goodnight: and so kneel down before you; but, indeed, to pray for the queen.*" Moreover, Doll Tearsheet, the landlady of the Eastcheap lodgings where Falstaff dies, states that he is not in hell but in Arthur's bosom. Why should she say this at all? And why should Otto Rahn be making these observations while enjoying Scottish soil and visiting Arthur's Seat?

There is no more powerful tale of Quest adventure than that of Camelot and Arthur's Knights' search for the Grail. But can Scotland possibly have any substantive claim to be the site for Arthur's Court? The Scottish heritage group, Magic Torch, certainly believes that the proposition has strong basis in fact. They point out that many scholars believe that Dumbarton Rock, ancient court for Rhydderch Hael, King of Strathclyde, may be the inspiration for the Arthurian legends of Camelot. Certainly, like Arthur, King Rhydderch was a King to the Britons and the Welsh histories portray him as a warrior King who wielded a magical sword. Interestingly, a number of pagan worship sites nearby are attributed to Lailoken, more commonly known as

Merlin.[1] Several medieval texts describe the protection that was given to Lailoken by King Rhydderch. He was allowed the freedom of the surrounding lands and forests. The epic "Scotichronicon" also details a meeting near Dumbarton of Saint Mungo and Merlin.

But the Clyde may not only be the setting for the adventures of Arthurian legend. It may also provide a clue as to the last resting place of Arthur. The Enchanted Isle of Avalon where King Arthur is said to lie sleeping is often referred to as the Isle of Apples. Not too far down river we find the island of Arran, which was originally called Emain Ablach. A literal translation of Emain Ablach is "the place of apples." Even more interesting is another translation of Arran: "the sleeping lord."

On the subject of Rahn's supposed suicide, it has been suggested that one can look at it in allegorical terms through the story of Galahad, Bors and Perceval entering the Grail chapel. Galahad is the one who does not close his eyes and when his companions open theirs' they see Galahad staring into space, dead. One cannot look God in the eye and live any longer in the physical world. Rahn is said to have died in the mountains. Like Galahad, had he seen too much? Recall that Rahn was a member of the Wandervogel that requires its members to quest in nature. These rituals can be very strange and demanding to undertake.

Five hundred years after Arthur entered his timeless sleep on Avalon the nine founder members of the Poor Knights of the Temple of Solomon travelled to the Holy Land upon another quest. Two hundred years later the Templar Order, polluted from within, was easy prey for King Philip and Pope Boniface and the Templar power was dissipated. But none of their staggering wealth was ever found.

It has been claimed that it was only a result of the extreme torture used by Philip of France in 1307 that word first emerged about what the Templars claimed was the true nature of the Arthur-Camelot experience. Under great duress the Templars said that Camelot was not a location one could walk or ride to but a dimensionsal area in which one travelled within an initiatory experience, as in the Mystery Schools of ancient times. Whether true or not, it provides a fascinating link between the Dream Dimension of Merlin and Arthur and the warrior monks' quest to locate and protect Solomon's treasures and the secrets of the Grail.

[1] In August 2007 the British Press reported on the findings of Scottish author, Adam Ardrey, who claims that Merlin was born in 450 A.D. in Cadzow (now Hamilton, Lanarkshire) and latetr lived at Ardery Street, just off the Dumbarton Road, in the Partick district of Glasgow.

In the last chapter we read of one strand of opinion that the Templars entrusted the Grail cache to the Cathars. Another popularly held belief is that the treasure was loaded aboard a fleet of ships and some of it taken to Scotland where, legend has it, the remnant Knights put themselves at the service of Robert the Bruce and the Grail was hidden in Rosslyn Chapel. This is an oft-told story but the members of the Magic Torch history group suggest that the truth is somewhat different.

The Greenock Telegraph of August 8th 2003 carried a story in connection with a parallel but separate research project I had been undertaking regarding the activities of U33, a Nazi submarine reported as being sunk by HMS Gleaner off the Isle of Arran in February 1940. The article linked the story with the Holy Grail and, extraordinarily, examined the theory that the submarine may have carried Nazi language specialist Otto Rahn, a person, the article emphasised, associated with the Third Reich's search for biblical artefacts. At the time of the U-Boat's mission, Rahn had been reported dead for eleven months. Why might any such discussion have been publicly aired in the west of Scotland in face of all the seemingly incontrovertible evidence that Rahn died by his own hand sixty four years earlier?

Records indicate that the Knights Templar owned a lot of the land around the Clyde, principally towns and sites associated with the ancient Celtic church. The village of Houston takes its name from Hu's Town, after Hugo de Pavinan, an 11th Century Templar Knight who built his castle there. One theory suggests that Hugo de Pavinan of Houston was in fact Hugh de Payens, founder and leader of the Knights Templar. Certainly, the similarities between the two names are striking and de Payens did visit Scotland around the time of Houston's foundation. It is in Houston that one can also find the remains of Saint Peter's Well, a medieval water source said to possess magical healing properties. There is a clear link here not only to the miraculous properties of the cup of the Holy Grail but also to the Knights Templar who venerate Saint Peter as their patron and protector.

It is also worth noting that the old Houston Mansion House was originally home to an Order of Cistercian Monks. The Cistercians were the forerunners for the Knights Templar and many of the codes subsequently adopted by the Knights were developed by the monks. Two of the original nine Templar Knights actually were Cistercian monks, which leads many scholars to believe that the two groups are simply the military and monastic arms of the same religious order. In latter years the two groups shared a kinship, linked by ties of blood and

›atronage. So close was this bond that any Templar who was expelled 'rom his order was required to seek sanctuary in a Cistercian monastery 'or personal rehabilitation.

It is said that the Renfrewshire villages of Houston, Kilbarchan ınd Kilmacolm form a "Golden Triangle," an equilateral triangle with he River Gryffe at the apex. At this site by the Gryffe can be found an ıncient yew grove over six hundred years old, thought to have once ›een used as a place of quiet contemplation for local noblemen. ›revious to this the site was associated with pagan worship and, indeed, he yew tree does have religious significance with druids, particularly in :onnection with prophecy.

This Golden Triangle is typical of the ancient geometry utilised ›y the Knights Templar and other pseudo-religious sects. It is likely hat Templar noblemen, knowing the site's previous ritual significance, ıdapted it for their own purposes. There are a number of other Templar :lues scattered throughout the district. Not far from Houston is the town ›f Johnstone and Saint John's Parish Church. Saint John is a hugely mportant saint for both Freemasons and the Knights Templar and, nterestingly, the town of Johnstone lies on almost exactly the same atitude of Roslin in Edinburgh; Roslin lies at *55 51.15* and Johnstone at he sacred number *55 50*. The line between these two latitudes was :nown as the "serpent rouge" or Roseline, an ancient meridian once ısed for telling the time. Similar lines can be found running through ıermetic churches across France, another country rich in Templar :onnections. Paisley Abbey also lies on this sacred latitude and, ›ignificantly, Hugo de Pavinan appears as a witness in the abbey's 'oundation charter. Templar churches are also said to have existed at ‹illallan, Chapeltown and Capelrig. Just outside of nearby Bishopton :an be found Rossland, another clear reference to the mystical roseline ınd another indicator of the scale of Templar activity within the area. Iowever, the most obvious remnants of the Knights Templar are to be 'ound in Inchinnan

Before the reformation Inchinnan's church belonged to the ‹nights Templar. Tradition states that it was built around 1100. Not ›nly does this tie in with the purported visit to Scotland of Templar eader Hugues de Payens, but it would also mean that the church at nchinnan predates Rosslyn Chapel. This church, latterly All Hallows Church of Scotland, was eventually demolished during the expansion of Glasgow Airport. Consequently, a number of Templar Knights are ıctually buried at the Renfrew end of Glasgow Airport runway. Entrance to this Templar Cemetery now requires the permission of airport security. A number of Templar tombstones were taken from the site and moved to Saint Conval's Church at Inchinnan where they can still be seen.

Another less obvious Templar connection to the Clyde was the wartime presence there of the Free French. This heroic order was established by Charles de Gaulle, who was according to Lincoln, Baigent and Leigh a member of one of the Knights Templar's modern successors: the Priory of Sion. The Free French Order of the Liberation deliberately borrowed organisational elements from medieval knights, a new chivalry serving a cause and a religious ideal—the freedom of France from the invading infidel. It is for this reason that de Gaulle adopted the Cross of Lorraine as the symbol of these new crusaders. The cross, commemorated locally upon Lyle Hill at Greenock, is also the cross of the Knights Templar.

Chapter TWENTY EIGHT

Wilhelm's Haven?

In the last chapter we reviewed compelling arguments that Rahn would have had good reason to make Scotland his sanctuary, having survived the enormous pressure on him from Himmler to take his own life. Now we will look at a raft of other, no less weighty reasons why the choice of Scotland as a bolthole and as a magnet for hidden treasures would have been hard to resist.

A few miles south of Edinburgh is one of the most curious "churches" in all of Christendom—Rosslyn Chapel, founded in 1446 by Sir William St. Clair. The Magic Torch historical group has provided strong arguments for western Scotland as the true place of concealment of the Grail Treaures but many more regard Rosslyn as the most likely spot. Rosslyn is known as the Grail in Stone.

Rosy Lyn=red tumbling stream and Rosslyn valley is red sandstone. A traditional Grail story has the grail hidden by a river that runs red. Compare the red running stream and red sandstone imagery with the account of Rahn's address to the Red Earth Society, and also to the review of *Luzifers Hofgesind* published in *Der Volkischer Beobachter*: "the book may be compared to a young brook which courses down the mountains, following by accident the slope in unpredictable jumps and zig-zag lines. Maybe it will not even rush to a stream because it will be a stream itself. Maybe a life's work prepares itself here."

Earlier we looked briefly at earth energy theories. Supporters of these theories refer to the chief pan-world energy grid as the Reshel system. They claim that the system is the "Chief Head Stone" referred to in Psalms 118:19-23, further claiming that Saint Columba knew of the system before the Templars, and that he re-installed it in the Hebrides and the Edinburgh area before the Sinclairs regenerated it. Bornholm, Rennes-le-Château and Montserrat are on the same grid line. The Reshel anchor of the Snowdon Heart and Anglesey Great Pyramid is the Ureaus, and Rosslyn is said to control the 28-mile radius Edinburgh matrix. Edinburgh, apparently, is the apex of all Alba-on (British) grids.

Reshel students say that the system was created by the priest-scientists of the island of Ruta in the north of Atlantis. Ruta is now the Faraday Seamounts on the Atlantic Ridge, even with Paris (reflect here on Gaston de Mengel's comment about north-east Paris being a major part of his discovered grid) and north of the Azores. The island's position is about 49N 29W, which is a line of latitude remarkably close to the 50th parallel. In a Nostradamus quatrain one reads: "*And afterwards, from the stem, what had been barren for so long, will burst into flower, and emerging from the 50th latitude, will renew the whole Christian Church.*"

The Reshel grid was also installed in the present Americas that cover this side of the globe from Western Europe to the Pacific and from North Dakota to the South Atlantic. The Clan Sinclair Templars understood these grids and "re-booted" the American grids in a 1398 expedition they are said to have made to Nova Scotia and to the U.S. East Coast, after having re-established them in Europe.

Students of earth energies and their invisible grid structures get very excited about the ancient geometry said to interlace most powerfully in and around the British Isles, its epicentre (or bosom) being Arthur's Seat. Rahn was evidently involved in the topic, at least peripherally, by virtue of his association with Gaston de Mengel. He was sufficiently immersed in the subject to ensure that if he visited just one place during his brief stopover in Scotland while en route to Iceland that it should be the volcanic mound famously known as Arthur's Seat.

In recent times the British grid is said to have been similarly re-booted in the form of the celebrated 1991 and 1997 Barbury Castle crop circles (located at Wroughton, near Swindon), which includes Avebury at its centre, Coventry as the *zayin* pole, and Glastonbury Tor as the *beyth* pole. Reshel geometry is claimed to have been utilised by the Templars for cathedral design, including Rosslyn. As if to cement the esoteric Hebraic aspect of the British energy grid system, the 1997 Barbury Castle crop circle's invisible makers constructed it in the form of the Kabbalistic Tree of Life.

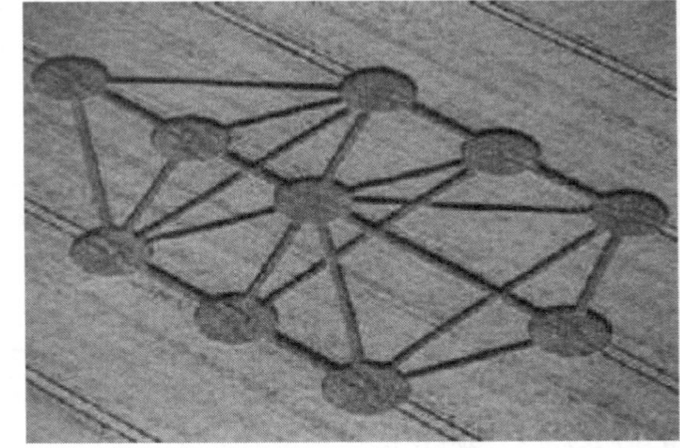

Barbury Crop Circle, Wiltshire, 1997

The Rosslyn grid contains an energy pole known as the Kaffa (Peter or Key). The Kaffa door opens directly to the Chapel's outside

Door of the Cavalier. Kaf in Hebrew means hollow stone and in Hebrew lore hollowness relates to divine essence, the No-thing. It also links with the concept of the hollow earth. When we consider the symbology here: ros/rose, chevalier/Knight, Hollow stone/inner earth, key/dietrich, it is only a small next step to Otto Rahn's exposition of the legend of the Knight of Berne and his Quest to find the Elfin Kingdom of Laurin in the Roses of Bozen. The brave Knight found the entrance to the enchanted realm to be hidden by an impenetrable spider's web, a symbol for crystal consciousness and an indication of the mystical gateway construct of our physical earth.

The Hebrew word "noun," meaning "eternally regenerating life," also figures in the Rosslyn grid interpretation and in ancient times was commonly drawn as a serpent. Recall that Otto Rahn made specific mention of treading on a viper in *Luzifers Hofgesind*. Add to this observation Rahn's vivid description of the Laurin legend, his communications with Gaston de Mengel, the fact that he visited Arthur's Seat in 1936, and I would be truly surprised if he (and de Mengel) were unaware of the Reshel dynamics.

It might also help to explain why Rudolf Hess flew to Scotland and why some people link his flight to some grand post-mortem scheme of Rahn's to retrieve the Grail from Rosslyn. In his book "*Sword and the Grail*"[1] Andrew Sinclair claimed that Walter Johannes Stein, the inspirational mentor of *Spear of Destiny* author Trevor Ravenscroft, was approached by Hitler through Rudolf Hess to find the Grail. There was evidently a strong belief in high Nazi circles that the Grail was concealed in Scotland. According to author Dale Pollock,[2] Philip Kaufman, one of the writers for *Raiders of the Lost Ark*, was inspired to develop the storyline having learned of Hitler's obsession to seize the Spear of Longinus.

We learned in earlier pages of the Vatican's belief that Hess travelled to Scotland to bring to Britain Germany's atom secrets. In his correspondence with me Bruce Cathie states that there is a clear connection between Gaston de Mengel's mysterious earth energy coordinates and how close the SS were getting in working out the "Grail" of quantum physics—the unified field equations.

The Clyde, Rosslyn, Edinburgh, Scotland—always these places swirl to the surface while reflecting upon the most likely destinations in

---

[1] Sinclair, Andrew. *Sword and the Grail: The Story of the Grail, the Templars and the True Discovery of America*. Edinburgh: Birlinn Limited, 2002

[2] Pollock, Dale; Photographic Illustrations *Skywalking - The Life and Films of George Lucas*. Harmony Books, 1983.

a survival scenario for Otto Rahn, determined to take control of his life and to outwit those who would prefer him to join millions of matryrs before him in ignominious final passage.

At one point I briefly considered a synchonicitous link between author Sax Rohmer (Arthur Henry Ward), the name Römer-Rahn (Rahn's niece, Ingerborgh, bearing this surname), and Sax Rohmer's Fu Manchu stories of evil Tibetan sorcerers. Imagine my surprise when I learned that Sax Rohmer, a member of the Hermetic Order of the Golden Dawn, wrote a foreward to a book called *The Devil's Mistress*, a powerful Scottish witchcraft tale written by a member of both the Theosophical Society and the Golden Dawn.[3] The focus of interest in the tale is King Arthur. Being a widely read fellow, it is not impossible that Rahn was aware of this work.

My researches have unearthed a number of key facts in conection with Scotland. The Thule Society made a trip to Edinburgh and Rosslyn in the thirties. There were a number of Germans in the party but it also included a big Spanish contingent (note that Canaris in particular was closer to Spain in terms of high level friendships than with any other European country). Rahn could also have been present.

The Thule Society placed particular belief in the old German hero Hermann (Arminius). Rudolf Hess identified Hermann particularly with Parsifal. Hermann can lead the traveller to the Green Land, the real Germany, beyond evil enchantment and the rush to materialism. This is achieved by a triumph of the imagination, a concept that does not translate well from the German and can be read as triumph of the will, which smacks of Hitlerism. Hermann is synonymous with the Knight of Berne in the legend of the Roses of Bozen, a tale which Rahn tells so passionately in *Luzifers Hofgesind*. French writer Pierre Mariel wrote that Rudolf Hess was a member of French mystical group Les Veilleurs (the Watchers), instigated by René Schwaller.

There has been strong German interest in Scotland for centuries. A particular Germanic tribe settled there before the Romans. In the 18th Century we have Templarism and Hanoverian interests versus Jacobites. Jacobite Freemasonry has its own arcanum of knowledge.

Von Hund kept a diary in which he recorded that he was initiated by one of the men closest to Charles Edward Stuart. He also alludes to a strange story about the Jacobite war. Germans were sent over to Scotland to dig a hole on the east coast near Aberdeen to find something that Von Hund had heard about from the Jacobites.

The trend has been that every few hundred years Germany has

---

[3] Brodie-Innes, John W. *The Devil's Mistress*. London: William Rider and Son, 1915

renewed its interest and links with Scotland, especially the Edinburgh area and Arthur's Seat. Rahn will have been aware of this close relation.

Stevenson wrote a book in the 1880s about old Northern monuments and their runic inscriptions. He concluded that there was evidence of a federation of visitors from Heligoland, Denmark, making its way to Shetland, the east coast of Scotland and to Ireland. Wherever you find runic inscriptions one finds evidence of the federation.

In February 1940 a party of visitors arrived from Heligoland to Scotland. On this occasion the travellers were borne by a submarine—U33. The true nature of U33's mission and its fate has been covered up for sixty-seven years but the conning tower hatchway is inching open. It is my belief that the Greenock local newspaper, The Telegraph, is not tilting at windmills and that the untold story of U33 concerns Anglo-German duplicity at the highest levels and, unsurprisingly, a treasure hunt.

We have encountered various instances in the context of Otto Rahn's life and times where geographical Scotland or Scottish themes have risen to the surface, mostly relating to the subject of documents or treasure of fabulous provenance. In Chapter 9 we read that among the influential eighteenth century French aristocrats who established Masonic lodges linked with a search for Merovingian and Visigothic treasures was Luc Siméon Auguste Dagobert. Dagobert was initiated into the Scottish Primitive Rite Branch by his uncle Hector, governor of a fort near Narbonne, a city that was host to many Masonic groups. Among these groups was the Philadelphus Lodge, established in 1779 and initially allied with a board of Scottish directors. This Lodge was steeped in Masonic-alchemic lore and one of its chief members, the Vicomte de Chefdebien, focused upon researches concerning the legend of the Golden Fleece. The grades of The Philadelphus Lodge included General of the Argonauts and Knight of the Argonauts.

Rahn is reported to have been acquainted with sensational singer and dancer Josephine Baker, the "Black Venus." Baker was active in the French Resistance. A commando mission organised by George Bergé, father of the French S.A.S, was named after her. In September 1941 Bergé, a great friend of British S.A.S. founder and Scottish laird David Stirling (shades once more of the Schloss scene in *Indiana Jones and the Last Crusade*), undertook training with the S.A.S. in Britain having won approval from de Gaulle. The French general was more than willing to give it because of his own lifelong friendship with Scotland. De Gaulle was proud that his forebears had fought in the Middle-Ages with the King of Scotland.

We have noted Rahn's admiration for the work of mystic Joséphin Péladan. In the last years of his life Péladan's secretary was Jesuit George Monti who, at the early age of twenty-two, became a high level Scottish Rite Mason. It is more than probable that Monti's occult associations combined with his attachments to the German film industry and his frequent visits to Berlin brought him into contact with Rahn. It is unlikely that their relations would have been warm considering the 1936 denouncement by the Grand Lodge of France that Monti was both a Jesuit informer trafficking in secret information and a fraudulent claimant to nobility.

The proof that Rahn came to Scotland after 1939, I freely admit, has not yet come to the fore. Nevertheless, I am confident of the gradual emergence of numerous points of synchronicity. Together these will encourage further study into the myriad associations between Rahn, the exigencies of his times, and the enigmas of history that make Scotland the esoteric, secret and veiled nation that it is today.

Chapter TWENTY NINE

Rudolf Hess' Scout?

I mentioned in an earlier chapter that in 1999 I came to Gullane on Scotland's south-east coast to give a talk about Otto Rahn to members of the Saunière Society. Imagine my surprise and consternation when I discovered that my visit had been preceded by press stories claiming that in addition to delivering the Rahn lecture I was going to be providing new information about Rudolf Hess' flight to Scotland in May 1941! Would that I had been so blessed with research riches that I could have satisfied my audience on that topic. I never did get to the bottom of who was responsible for that particular act of disinformation but whoever it was clearly wanted to satisfy a personal agenda. It was plain that someone wanted to promote a link between Otto Rahn and Rudolf Hess. On subsequent reflection it raised my suspicions that there are those in Scotland who know more about the Hess affair and, moreover, about an Otto Rahn connection than they are willing to bring into the public domain. Why one would wish to maintain this veil of secrecy after more than sixty years is open to question.

It has generally been accepted that Hitler knew nothing of his Deputy's plans and that he was surprised as anyone else when news broke about Hess' capture. For the record, readers might be interested to learn that a few years ago Stuart Russell, a British writer and historian who made Germany his home, interviewed Herbert Döhring, the administrator of the Führer's mountain retreat in Bavaria and one of a tiny circle in Nazi Germany whose members were most privy to Hitler's secrets. This man confirmed to Russell that in 1941 he had overheard Hitler talking in his study to a senior Luftwaffe officer, asking what needed to be done to ensure that a person could fly *out of* Germany undetected. Two weeks later Hess made his flight and the

Führer's servant was in no doubt that the flight and the discussion he had overheard a fortnight before were mutually connected. Karl Wolff said, too, that not only did Hitler agree to Hess' flight but pressed for it so that a consequent peace agreement with Britain would allow him the freedom to attack the Soviet Union.

If Hitler had been behind the plan he may well have wanted to do everything possible to ensure its success and Hess' safe arrival. Moreover, if Hitler had been inspired to spirit his Deputy out of Germany because of circumstances encouraged by astrology (Cecil Williamson's ploy) he may well have felt sufficiently coy to want to avoid at all costs any member of his immediate coterie discovering the bizarre facts. But just because Hitler might have felt compelled to send Hess to Britain based on irrational considerations it is by no means certain that Hess saw things in the same way. Let us consider for a moment that Hess might have been party to the deception (from the British standpoint). This is not so distant a topic for reflection as might at first seem the case. Bearing in mind the close relationship the Haushofer family enjoyed both with Hess and with the Duke of Hamilton and their common cause that a peace solution must be sought at the earliest opportunity, it is not unreasonable to posit that the Deputy Führer was in on the ground floor with the ruse, feigning innocence when Hitler tapped him on the shoulder and put to him the fantastical proposition.

It is likely, too, that any emotional attachment between Rudolf Hess and Scotland would have been heightened by virtue of his father Carl's sorry experience. It is a little known fact that Carl, working and living in England in 1890, married Elizabeth Mackie, a young woman of Scottish descent. The pair set up home in Devon. Carl worshipped Elizabeth and when she died at the age of thirty-five just twelve months later he returned, distraught, to Germany. Rudolf would surely have been aware of this all too brief time in his father's life when Hess Snr. had been so very happy with his Scottish bride.

I mention these facts specifically because according to Lynn Picknett and her research colleagues[1] there is evidence that Hess was escorted part of the way, his escort possibly consisting of Reinhard Heidrich and three other ME-109s, which accompanied the Deputy Führer over the Channel and the North Sea. Hess' captors also harboured few doubts that a second airman might have parachuted out of Hess' aeroplane elsewhere. Major Donald examined the wreckage of the ME-110 and was puzzled by the fact that only one person was

[1] Picknett, Prince and Prior ibid

reported to have bailed out.

Who might this second person have been and what might have became of him or her? Might Hess' passenger have been on board to undertake a completely separate mission than that to be carried out by the Deputy Führer? Frankly, the more I consider Hess' declared reason for making his trip—to meet with the Duke of Hamilton—the less convincing it becomes. Something just does not add up but it would all make more sense if Hess' action had been intended to conceal other, more critical, actions. Locating and retrieving the Grail, for example, would, I suggest, have been regarded by Hitler/Hess as a supremely important objective, to be carried out successfully, no matter the cost.

It has been said that both Otto Rahn and Rudolf Hess came to believe that the Grail was concealed at Rosslyn Chapel. Rosslyn Chapel has long been associated with the Grail. One of the most notable proponents of the story was Walter Johannes Stein, an influential figure in the 1930s and Churchill's adviser on the occult. According to Andrew Sinclair[2] "Stein was approached by Hitler through Rudolf Hess to help find the Grail…A belief that the Grail was, indeed, in Scotland may have been another inducement for the deluded Hess to fly there during the Second World War…An intimate of Hess and member of the secret Nazi Thule society, Hans Fuch, visited Rosslyn Chapel in May 1930 and signed the Visitors' Book and told members of the Edinburgh Theosophical Society that Hess identified with Parsifal (his nickname in Nazi circles) and believed Rosslyn was a Grail Chapel or *the* Grail Chapel."

In the opening lines of his chapter on Edinburgh in *Luzifers Hofgesind* Rahn associates the area with Arthur's Bosom, evident symbology for Camelot and the Round Table brethren of Grail Knights. Rosslyn Chapel lies just seven miles south of Edinburgh and can be said, therefore, to reside within its greater environs. Not too long ago Rosslyn Chapel was being overrun by fans of Dan Brown's global best-selling novel *The Da Vinci Code* whose core premise revives *The Holy Blood and the Holy Grail* claim that Jesus and Mary Magdalene married and produced offspring. Other writers have identified the Grail as being not a cup or chalice but Jesus' skull (the "Head of God") but similarly identifying Rosslyn as the hiding place for this more novel Grail artefact theory.

In *Spear of Destiny* Trevor Ravenscroft explained the importance Hitler attached to obtaining the Spear of Longinus and accruing to himself the magical powers the artefact is said to endow the

---

[2] Sinclair ibid

possessor. If Hitler thought along those lines imagine how much more power he believed he could gain by possessing the Grail—the ultimate talisman of authority. The opportunity to locate and bring it to Germany would have represented the crowning achievement in Hitler's esoteric gameplan. Nothing would have been left to chance. If Rahn was alive in May 1941 and under Hitler's protection then it is unthinkable that the Hessian scholar would not have been at the forefront of a mission to retrieve the Grail from Scotland and bring it to Germany. However, if Rahn had been alive at the time and wearing different colours (as an independent free agent with allegiance to no one or perhaps working in association with Canaris-MI6) he most certainly would have wished to thwart Hitler's efforts. Either way, and on balance I am inclined to favour the latter scenario, Otto Rahn would have been active in Scotland with pressing Grail business uppermost on his mind.

There are other strands to the Hess story which, seemingly much less connected to Grail mythography, do lead, inexorably, back to the grottoes of the Languedoc and to Rahn's quest to discover its treasures.

Britain's declared reason for involving itself in the war at all was to protect the sovereignty of Poland, Britain and France having made mutual defence pacts with Poland. However, Poland was attacked by two aggressors within seventeen days of each other—by Germany from the west and then by the Soviet Union from the east. Why then did Britain not attack the Soviets, too? A new Polish government in exile, headed by General Wladyslaw Sikorski, was moved from Paris to Scotland shortly after June 1940 where it remained for the duration of the war.

To the Poles, the Russians were the real and avowed enemy. They were open to a peace agreement with Germany from the outset of the war. However, there were many high level Britons who did not share Poland's position on wanting to kick the Russian aggressors speedily out of Poland and then to support a war between Germany and the Soviets. It was therefore the case that support in Britain for Poland and its sovereignty was polarised and this fact, too, is an important consideration in a review of Hess' flight to Scotland and its implications for a possible involvement by Otto Rahn in the affair. It is clear that the Hess debacle took place at a time when Polish interests and considerations were closely connected with British wartime policy but there is a much more specific link between the Hess flight and Poland.

Inexplicably, the very first person to interrogate Hess after his capture was a Pole by the name of Roman Battaglia. Early reports identified Battaglia as a clerk in the Polish Consulate in Glasgow. Foreign Office records have a note of the meeting, which the Pole conducted in German. Hess, naming himself as "Alfred Horn," said that he had flown from Augsburg and had an important message for the Duke of Hamilton, which was "in the highest interest of the British Air Force." This was a very brief summary for an interview that lasted for two hours. To this day there is a mystery as to why Battaglia arrived at the Home Guard H.Q. at Giffnock. The initial assumption was that he had been summoned by the police to serve as an interpreter during their own interrogation but Hess's own command of English was excellent. In a meeting nearly three weeks later between Battaglia and Lieutenant John Mair at Glasgow's Police H.Q. the Pole insisted that his name should not be publicised. Mair's report reveals that Battaglia had been posted to the Polish Consulate at Danzig between 1935 and 1937 where he had been trained in interrogation techniques for use on political suspects. Evidently, Battaglia was more than a lowly clerk and, in fact, he served later in the war as one of General Sikorski's intelligence officers. Clearly, anything could have been said between the two men during their two hours together, much of which was spent in a tense and difficult atmosphere.

Hamilton and Battaglia: two individuals in the Hess affair and seemingly unrelated in any way. But are they so mutually distinct, after all? One hundred and thirty miles from the Scottish border is Southport, Lancashire. The Rennes Group reports that a former member from the Southport area (who prefers to remain anonymous) accompanied his father many years ago on a visit to a family friend named Betty or Elizabeth Banks. "Betty Banks" said during the visit that in WW2 she was a member of the British SOE; that she became an inmate at Ravensbruck and escaped across Europe. When looking through some photos at Betty's house, the young man said he saw a paper with the words 'Prieuré de Sion.'

The Rennes Group looked into the Betty Banks story and discovered that the name had been given to her after she had escaped from Ravensbruck and been given refuge by British intelligence services to hide her identity. MI6 gave her a new place to live in Southport where Betty lived happily until a time in the 1950s when, she claimed, she was chased down the beach by German agents. It was rumoured that Betty's real nationality was Polish and it is a fact that there is a large Polish community in that part of Britain established, it is said, by Poles who escaped the war and among whom many were involved in intelligence work. The Rennes Group established that

"Betty" did undertake work for the SOE in connection with underground activities in France (as did, coincidentally, Cecil Williamson during the same period; they may even have known each other, even worked or planned work together).

Betty also spent time at the Duke of Argyll's Manor in Scotland for training work. Curiously, she had a painting done of herself in the style of a Shepherdess. This painting was bought by the Duke and today is in the Getty Museum in San Francisco. The painting recalls the work of Nicholas Poussin so closely associated with the mysteries of the treasures of Rennes-le-Château and the "forbidden merchandise" of Chefdubien. The reason why Otto Rahn came into the public eye at all was because of his steadfast belief that these artefacts were hidden in the Languedoc and his subsequent efforts over an eighteen month period to find them. Rahn's was a seminal quest shared by so many others, the architects of esoteric-political development in Europe among them such as Joséphin Péladan and the later founders of the Prieuré de Sion.

The Rudolf Hess—Betty Banks—SOE—Prieuré de Sion story provides further valuable and credible elements of synergy in determining the basis upon which Otto Rahn may have been active or influential in a covert British context post-1939. But that is not all. There is a further linkage to consider, namely the role of the Red Cross in the Hess affair. In making this assessment we should recall the ignominious activities undertaken by André François-Poncet, Gabriele's and Otto's pal from Molchow Castle, while he was Vice President, later President, of the Red Cross International Committee during the war.

The Duke of Hamilton's family home, Dungavel, where Rudolf Hess was heading for in his ME-110 in May 1941 served as a Red Cross centre, making it a neutral territory and an ideal place to host a "peace conference" or any other such clandestine meeting.

The Red Cross theme runs all the way through the Hess affair. Hess told his aunt Emma Rothaker that if all went well she would receive a message from the Red Cross. Albrecht Haushofer, stolidly anti-Hitler and an ardent peace supporter, met Carl Burckhardt, head of the Red Cross International Committee, a few days before Hess' flight and Burckhardt played a key role in co-ordinating the mission's arrangements, apparently with Hess' blessing. Albrecht was also a guest at Dungavel at the end of April 1938 and during the week that he was there he drew a map of Hitler's Greater Germany on an atlas. In September 1940 Hess wrote to Karl Haushofer and said "...possibly a mutual acquaintance (*Rahn*?), who had some business to attend to over there anyway (Scotland) might look him up (Duke of Hamilton) and make some communication to him using you or Albrecht as reference."

Clearly, it is by no means inconceivable that Otto Rahn had some part to play in Rudolf Hess' mission to Scotland. On the face of it Hess' crazy plan was ill-fated and ended in abject failure. But did it? If, as observers on the ground in the immediate aftermath of his crashlanding surmised, there was a second person in Hess' aircraft there is no way of ascertaining the success or otherwise of that other person's mission, one whose objectives may have been very different indeed from those Hess professed he wanted to undertake after his arrival in Scotland. It is wise to keep an open mind on the possibility of a Rahn participation in the affair until such a time that the lid on the unanswered questions of the Hess episode is flung open and those in the know come clean…if, indeed, that act of catharsis should ever come about.

Finally in passing, it is interesting to reflect on Churchill's visit in October 1944 to the Kremlin to meet with Stalin. Stalin quizzed Churchill about Hess and the British Prime Minister told the Russian leader that Hitler and Hess had been lovers. Stalin made a toast saying "to the British Secret Service which inveigled Hess into coming to England. He could not have landed without being given signals."[3] Harris and Trow also claim that Hess was carrying Hitler's peace proposals, which have not yet seen the light of day.

---

[3] Harris, John; Trow, M.S. *Hess: the British Conspiracy*. London: Andre Deutsch, 1999

Chapter THIRTY

Conclusions

The more I study Otto Rahn the less it seems I know him. And, of course, this is not surprising because the knowledge of a person is not derived from the aggregate of all they said and did but from observing the shadows they cast, rather like discerning patterns of probability in tealeaves.

All those who have stood out in history have been personally vulnerable by virtue of their exposure to the mass and critical opinion of their time, and by the inevitable pressure exerted by the power-seekers in the shadows around them who would most profit by their undoing. The clever ones have survived by creating their own shadows to conceal allies loyal to their unfulfilled dreams and ambitions.

We can appreciate the paradox in which Rahn has been mythologised as the purported discoverer of the Grail but at the same time we struggle to understand the paradigms that shaped and determined his actions. Yet despite the shroud that surrounded Rahn's activities between 1931 and 1939 the man from Michelstadt attained an aura of knowing that mesmerised the senior figures among the Nazi leadership.

Without doubt Rahn's was one of the brightest stars in Himmler's constellation of esoteric researchers in pre-war Germany. But what is most intriguing is how few observers glimpsed Rahn's star then or in the decades that followed. This fact, in itself, encourages speculation as to why a Hollywood scriptwriting team should base a movie character on an obscure German explorer of whom the world in 1981 knew less than zero. If the general public should be ignorant of Otto Rahn then why should not also the populist moviemakers of Hollywood?

What has been written about Otto Rahn in the last thirty years offers a myriad of contradictions. We have learned that Rahn was smart but impressionable. His close friend in the early thirties, Gabriele Winckler, can recall little of the charisma that imbues the vapour trail of Rahn's reputation today. They shared a few laughs and struck up with eccentric companions such as the Georgian mystic socialite Grigol

Robakidse but her recollection of the writer is largely undistinguished. On the face of it, Rahn's life was not wholly happy. To many of his peers he appeared socially unschooled and apt to embarrass himself in company. Certainly, Rahn was a walking contradiction. Howard Buechner portrays Rahn as an overgrown boyscout full of beans with the charming naïvete of a young Don Quixote. Christian Bernadac, on the other hand, paints Rahn as a fraud ("croc") and a swindler ("farfelu") who sold himself heart and soul to the Nazi cause. He even suggests that Rahn was the *éminence grise* who masterminded the supernatural ambitions of the Nazi elite even long after his reported death by suicide in March 1939.

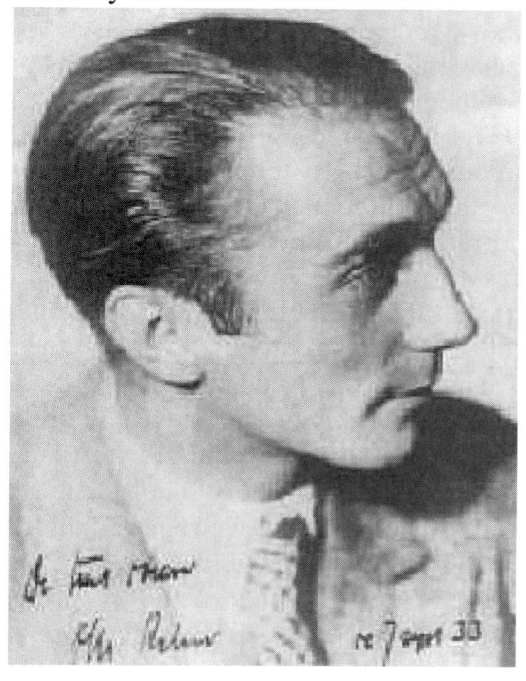

Whatever the truth, we will be hard-pressed to make judgement. Too much has been blurred and obfuscated both by the passage of time and by the will of those who perhaps even today have too much to lose by revelation. But let us remind ourselves that the stuff of legend is not born from the nondescript or from the mediocre. In Otto Rahn we glimpse a compelling brilliance that was powerful enough to cast a Pyrenean sized shadow into the latter two thirds of the twentieth century.

Nevertheless, we have reviewed sufficient indicators and evidence, which suggest that Otto Rahn was not what he seemed and that in all likelihood he was working, at extreme personal risk, with Canaris and other like-minded opponents of Hitler, including Britons such as Cecil Williamson in MI6, to subvert the Nazi creed. We have no knowledge as to what motives or circumstances might have led to Rahn either being picked out for an intelligence role and nurtured into this over time or that he actively sought a way to help limit Hitler's insane actions. Whatever the facts, it is my belief that Rahn's erudite and earnest personality endeared him to unidentified protectors who ensured his survival throughout the war years and beyond, but there is no proof to substantiate this belief. In the place of proof one, for now at least, can only look at Rahn's life, its tangents and byways, and reach for an intuitive grasp of the underlying agenda.

If we honestly believe that Otto Rahn died near Kufstein on the night of the 13th and 14th March 1939 then, of course, speculation on his survival is academic. However, I do not believe that Charon served as Rahn's ferryman that night or at any time in proximity to that date. We know that the Nazi leaders: Hitler, Himmler and Heydrich especially, were convinced of the existence of the Grail Treasures in the Pyrenees. Equally, several authors (Buechner and Angebert among them) are sure that these fabulous artefacts were located and subsequently removed from the Montségur area to a place of safekeeping in Germany. Buechner wrote: "Rahn spent three months in the mountains (Pyrenees) and either on this trip (1931) or on a somewhat shorter visit in 1937, he found something of great importance…(during the occupation of France) the results of Rahn's 'find' were removed to Germany by a special team of commandos, headed by Otto Skorzeny."[1] Regretfully, there is not a shred of evidence to back up Buechner's confident assertion.

The Languedoc is the source of innumerable legends concerning the hidden treasures. Legend, fable and myth invariably have their origins within a kernel of truth. It is as if the Ancients devised these timeless media to ensure that epochal events are never entirely forgotten for those who truly seek. We are never told the full story but, instead, we are provided with archetypal signs and symbols that we may come to interpret, provided we are patient and we remain faithful to the ideals of brave forbears, the Cathars laying down their lives in the thirteenth century Church-sponsored killing fields being a prime example.

In this present work we have increased our understanding of the high esteem in which Otto Rahn held the brethren of the medieval Cathar faith. To a degree, he was encouraged to develop these passions by virtue of his upbringing but his admiration of the Pure Ones was largely a result of his researches into the seminal work of Wolfram von Eschenbach's *Parsifal*. In these pages written more than six hundred years before, Rahn believed he had interpreted a code planted between the lines. Deciphered, Parsifal's journey of self-discovery convinced Rahn that the Grail treasure was cached by the remnant Cathar members on the eve of their execution at the foot of Montségur. More than that, the story revealed its exact whereabouts. In referring to key

[1] Buechner ibid

elements such as the altar, Hercules and the jewelcase of Solomon, Rahn was able to cross-match these signposts with actual locations within the Lombrives grottoes. This detective work was a magnificent academic tour de force requiring the highest degree of skill in a wide range of scholarly endeavours. No one had ever before put quite so many pieces of the Grail jigsaw together all at one time.

In 1931 (or earlier if one accepts Bernadac's account) Rahn embarked on his life's quest—to discover the Grail treasures hidden, he believed, by Cathar perfecti in the Ariège caverns seven hundred years earlier. We read that his efforts did not progress without encountering obstacles. Rahn quickly became acquainted with leading members of the French intelligentsia such as author Maurice Magré in whom Rahn found an immediate empathy in matters of Grail and Cathar folklore. Round-table shared opinions in the Bibliothèque Nationale led rapidly to action by Rahn on the ground.

Rahn's excavations were conducted over a wide area and his attachment to suspect German spies did not endear him to Montségur villagers who subjected Rahn to physical assaults. We see that Rahn attracted similarly rough treatment inside the grottoes when he was apparently caught faking cave drawings; hardly the actions of a principled researcher and academic. At the same time Rahn made the extraordinary decision to invest a large sum in the Hôtel-Restaurant des Marronniers with funds that seemed to materialise from nowhere and to disappear even faster, thereby leading him headlong into a bankruptcy scandal. The espionage claims forced Rahn to turn fugitive and make an ignominious departure under cover of darkness.

Shortly after his arrival in Ussat-les-Bains Rahn fell in with the Seigneurs de Belisse, the local elders who preserved a faith and belief in the old Cathar tradition. Indiana Jones' moral courage ensured his survival in the Canyon of the Crescent Moon, qualities which legitimately distinguish him as an honorary Seigneur—a true Son of the Moon and vassal of the Mother Goddess.

It was not long before Rahn was telling Ladame that he had made a most important discovery that would bring him worldwide prestige and great riches. However, this bold pronouncement was followed by complete silence on the matter, never to be raised again on record. Frustratingly, we are left to make up our own minds as to the truth and circumstances of this supposed find. If we choose to believe him we can be forgiven for concluding, albeit hesitantly, that Rahn's discovery was associated with the fabled Treasures of the Temple of Solomon, considering that Rahn's researches had focused upon

Wolfram von Eschenbach's Grail romances. Taking his claims at face value, Rahn clearly believed he had struck the motherlode. There were enough suspicious characters gathered around him to indicate that this was not only keenly anticipated but that news of it was to be reported in utmost secrecy to Germany with all due haste.

Whatever the truth behind Rahn's assertions, succeeding generations have been willing to accept that his Languedoc explorations yielded significant finds. Legends do not grow without good reason. They grow from the collective unconscious that, in turn, is fed by hints of success in impossible possibilities, especially successes achieved by the lone seeker battling against far greater odds of failure. The story of Otto Rahn is as enduring a twentieth century legend as any and one has only to type his name into a search engine such as Google to produce at the time of writing 226,000 references to the pre-WW2 writer and explorer. Rahn found something of great value or at least he was hard on its heels, otherwise our unconscious responses would not have registered his efforts so highly upon our inner scales of awareness.

A few facts and a few guesses, but what are the fundamentals we can piece together about the forces that drove Otto Rahn during his salad years? Karl Rittersbach tells the reader in the preface to *Kreuzzug gegen den Gral* that in addition to Rahn being a highly talented and passionate religious-historian he was above all a sensitive poet. Otto Rahn researched from the point of view of those oppressed under the brutal heel of the Inquisition. It is not hard to imagine how the Nazi chiefs, largely Catholic to a man, might have reacted to a young Protestant countryman (and possibly with Jewish blood on his mother's side) who devoted his considerable talents to highlighting the iniquities of a bygone age, which they were busy seeking to resurrect with such cruel fervour. Rahn did confide with friends in Fribourg in the first weeks of 1939: "I have been denounced," adding: "It is impossible for a tolerant man to live in this country. What has become of my homeland?" On the face of it, these are hardly the words of one who has allied with the evil forces taking root at the time.

From the outset, Rahn's beliefs and preferences seem to have placed him outside the pale of National Socialist thinking but without further proof one cannot be sure he was not playing a double bluff. On reflection, I consider it more likely that he was either in alliance with or, less likely, being used by those in the Third Reich who were secretly allied against Hitler.

Tantalisingly, we have no proof that Otto Rahn found anything of fabulous provenance. However, one should bear in mind the concluding remarks in Robert Dassanowsky-Harris's Starlog article. He points out that of all the captured Nazi documents held by U.S. National Archives there was just the one that had not been transferred to microfiche for public perusal. The document in question contains extracts from the records of Himmler's Ahnenerbe office that relate to the archaeological searches in the south of France in the 1930s and 1940s. There was no explanation as to why the U.S. authorities had not released this particular document.

The Perfecti priests of the Cathar order believed that they were the custodians of the true Christian heritage. Rahn not only agreed with them but was convinced that the tale of the traditional Grail artefact, the legendary cup or chalice, was a shroud to hide the second and real Grail—the Emerald Tablet of Hermes Trismegistus on which was inscribed the combined wisdom of the Ages, ultimate truth.

Otto Rahn studied these symbols with skill and patience. If anyone in the twentieth century could have discerned in them a signpost to the Grail Temple then it would have probably been he: the avid young scholar who arrived in the Ariège convinced he could succeed where so many before him had failed. Let us not forget that Rahn, despite his mood swings, was a very smart man. I am persuaded that he was clever enough to create a smokescreen of illhealth and accelerating emotional breakdown sufficient to convince his masters that he was physically and mentally unable to muster the resources to take flight successfully in the early months of 1939. I believe that he had assistance either from high-level members of the German Resistance movement or the British security services (or both) to help him go to ground and to keep his head down during the war years. I believe that there are those alive today who are aware of the deeper connections that Rahn created during his life but I also believe that no single person or group has all the answers to the mystery that was Otto Rahn. He took those to his grave...whenever he was placed there.

Professor James T. Hurtak claims to have examined Nazi documents on secret Nazi flying disc and Vril technologies and subsequently arrived at the opinion that the most important aspects of the Third Reich were that they literally opened a window to other worlds. In 1934 Himmler and Hitler are said to have met to discuss the Vril project to build a massive craft capable of travelling interdimensionally.[2]

In *Luzifers Hofgesind* Rahn quotes John the Evangelist: "re-assemble the pieces in order that nothing be lost." What might Rahn

---

Moon ibid

have been trying to say here? I have reflected upon the coincidence that Otto Rahn disappeared ten days after Eugenio Pacelli, "Hitler's Pope," was elected Pontiff. Had Rahn in the course of his investigations and scholarly researches discovered information about the Catholic Church that, laid out for the world to see, would have done enormous damage to its two thousand year old patriarchy?

May we conclude that Otto Rahn followed the waymarks to Laurin, found the impenetrable path, knocked upon the rose, sang the magic words, and took the Elfin Queen's milk-white hand as he crossed an immortal divide? When he caressed the bloom did he achieve the great prize sought by brothers of the Rosy Cross over the centuries, pulling the nails from the cross of the physical and walking free into eternity?

A thorough examination of what we know about Rahn combined with intelligent consideration of the grey areas ultimately encourages the observer to focus upon Britain as the principle contender for Otto Rahn's "after-life" bolthole.

Earlier we reviewed the activities of Frenchman George Monti, Scottish Rite Mason and representative of Aleister Crowley who, together with Gaston de Mengel, the bringer of mysterious map coordinates to the attention of Weisthor and Rahn, established the post-Péladan esoteric order: *Groupe Occidental d'Études Esotériques*, which Robert Richardson argues convincingly was the basis for the formation of the Prieuré de Sion. We have considered a wide array of facts and linkages in support of the proposition that Otto Rahn spent time in Scotland, a principle global earth-energy hotspot by virtue of Rosslyn Chapel, the "Grail in Stone," after his supposed death by the Cathar "white starvation" (Endura) in the mountains of the Tyrol in March 1939.

And what of the oft-quoted suggestion that Otto Rahn personified the very worst aspects of National Socialism; that he was no more than a fully fledged SS-adept? No, I do not believe such a conclusion corresponds with the facts and with an intelligent assessment of Rahn's life and work. All the evidence, signs and symbols steer one away from that grim conclusion.

Might he have been the polar opposite, a Grail Knight in Arthur's timeless service? In spirit, most likely, but that does not distinguish Rahn from countless men and women past and present who struggle against the tide of the mass conscious status quo in seeking the pathway within to enlightenment. In that regard each is equipped with the *dietrich* and where, I believe, we can derive inspiration from Otto

Rahn is to be able to understand that no matter how frightful, threatening and chaotic the world around us may appear there is always another way. A Grail Knight is never in a situation where (s)he has limitless possibilities but no options to exercise them. Rahn lived and worked among some of the most evil individuals who ever walked this earth and God knows what he saw or experienced that shook him to the core. Nevertheless, it is my firm belief that Rahn survived, beating seemingly impossible odds and living on.

Did Rahn earn a free pass to Laurin? Who can say? But I do believe Rahn had the personal power to open a threshold to freedom and the chance of a new life within a life, one in which his remaining years could afford him a degree of happiness and fulfilment that had eluded him in the pre-war years.

Maybe that is wishful thinking but, honestly, if we cannot exercise that gift then the doorway to Laurin will not reveal itself.

PART FOUR

Tale o' the Bank

Chapter THIRTY ONE

A Short Story

U-Boat 33

Kapitänleutnant (Ing) Fritz Schilling, First Officer and Chief Engineer of U-Boat 33, stamped his feet and blew into his cupped hands. The 5am temperature on the Wilhelmshaven dockside had given up trying to climb above freezing. Schilling could cope with the cold but the hangover was a less welcome companion. He couldn't complain. Bearing in mind the amount of beer and schnapps he'd consumed in the log cabin bar Dönitz had had built in the woods for the crew of U33, Schilling would have felt cheated had he woken from two hours sleep without a Tyrolean sized headache.

With just one hour from departure the provisioning of U33 was in full swing and the quayside was heaving with trucks stacked with boxes and crates of every shape, size and content. Over-revved engines and disgruntled curses rent the icy morning air. A surly driver, annoyed by the early hour, stepped down from an ancient truck, shoved a delivery note in Schilling's hand and gruffly pressed two men loafing nearby to lift crates down onto the dockside cobbles and carry them into the sub. Schilling barred access to the sub and in a few well chosen words offered the driver the choice between being tossed into the icy water or behaving himself and waiting his turn like everyone else. The driver was no fool, quickly recognising officer class in the well-built indignant man filling his field of vision. The contrite fellow brought new artistry to bowing and scraping as he backed off and climbed up into his truck.

A stroppy driver was the least of Schilling's worries. Von Dresky, U33's Kapitän, and he had been at loggerheads over the poor condition of the sub. Although U33 had had an extensive refit a little over two months previously, which included the fitting of a new diesel engine, the vessel did not, in Schilling's opinion, have a clean bill of health. Schilling did not make a fuss about normal day to day mechanical problems that elbow grease seasoned with a little ingenuity could usually solve. But in recent days a leak had been discovered in one of U33's torpedo hatches and despite Schilling's advice that U33 should not sail operationally until the problem had been properly fixed Dresky ordered a botched repair with rubber and a wooden wedge. The Kapitän said that U33 would put into Heligoland for a day or so to carry out minor repairs but under no circumstance would its departure be delayed further. Schilling was aghast. U33 was definitely not seaworthy and the Chief Engineer wanted his concerns put on record. Dresky had brushed them aside and Schilling had had to bite his tongue.

The history between them was already highly strained. During a mission three months earlier into the Bristol Channel Dresky had pointed a gun at his first officer's head to get him to carry out an order such was the contempt in which Dresky's authority and fitness to command was held among his senior officers. The standing joke among the members of the close-knit Kriegsmarine community was that men only followed Dresky out of a sense of morbid curiousity. Schilling wasn't at all curious about experiencing premature death; if a British destroyer's torpedo managed to find its quarry then so be it, that's the luck of the game. But why offer the sub on a plate to the enemy because it had holes in it and couldn't give them a run for their money? Dresky didn't see it like that. All that mattered was the rate of kill, the bloody statistics.

A shooting star traversed the high horizon and a shiver ran through Schilling's body like an electric charge. Jesus, what was that all about? He had no time to think about it before a black Mercedes swept onto the quayside, pulling up beside him. Dresky got out and opened one rear passenger door while the driver opened the other. Two men Schilling had never seen before dressed as Gefrieter (able seamen) stepped out and Dresky ushered them straightaway aboard the sub. The Kapitän saw the question on Schilling's lips but ignored him. His eyes just said: stow it, it's none of your business. Schilling shivered again. We're not expecting any more crew; we're up to full complement. And even if we were short handed those two men were patently not heads-down, arses-up working seamen. No, they had the bearing of seniority, politicians even. Spooks, maybe worse. Jesus Christ, that's all we need on this voyage.

Dresky had confided in his first officer that U33's next mission would be dangerous even by their daredevil standards. They would be travelling, Dresky had explained, into the upper reaches of the Firth of Clyde to the Boom defence area between Dunoon and Greenock to sink HMS Hood and as many other prizes as could be targeted. Shooting fish in a barrel, Dresky had called it. Fair enough, Schilling had thought, that's what we do (but let's fix the bloody boat first). But what were these guys doing on board? Where did they fit into the plan of operations? Even at that moment Schilling knew very well that they didn't; that their mission was far removed from U33's routine directive to inflict maximum damage to the enemy.

U33 slipped away from Wilhelmshaven. During the seven hour trip to Heligoland Schilling's men discovered another two holes in the torpedo tubes. U33 was in terrible shape. During the next thirty six hours while in harbour Schilling and his team worked frantically to fix a long list of repairs, but by the time Dresky announced they would be sailing in one hour there were still far too many holes and cracks in the structure for comfort. Schilling's dread now mixed with rising anger. Dresky wasn't being driven by operational imperatives but by Berlin! No wonder Dönitz had arranged a big, never-before-heard-of party with limitless booze and uninhibited girls. Small wonder that Hitler had visited Wilhelmshaven two days before departure to tell us all how brave and wonderful we were. They all knew we were going on a suicide mission. But he bet that the cloak and dagger goons now on board weren't expendable, put money on that.

Five minutes before departure, a slightly built figure draped in an overcoat two sizes too big and carrying a small briefcase was brought, no, hustled aboard by Dresky and directed quickly to his berth. Schilling saw but said nothing. The man's arrival merely accelerated his deepening sense of foreboding and malaise. Schilling had recognised the visibly nervous passenger. A lifelong passion for European history and Germanic legends in particular had led him two years earlier to attend a lecture at the premises of the Dietrich-Eckart Society in Dortmund. The speaker was young, fervent and eloquent. His name was Otto Rahn. He had made a name for himself as a seeker of ancient and fabulous artefacts: namely the biblical treasures of the Temple of Solomon, among them the Ark of the Covenant and the Grail Chalice. The fact that Rahn, a scholar and visionary and, seemingly, the antithesis of a professional fighting man was on board U33 made Schilling feel very nervous indeed. But what turned his nerves to a near faint was the fact that Rahn had committed suicide in March 1939. Dietrich-Eckart Society members had been abuzz with the news and had discussed it endlessly.

Let's see now: two big shots on board and a dead man. Nothing added up. The shiver clutching at his chest turned to dread. All at once, Schilling knew with absolute certainty that U33 was not going to make it home and neither were most, if not all, of the regular men on board.

Time passed largely uneventfully. Schilling, Dresky and the other forty crew members went about their business, exchanging few words. The two brass and the dead man kept to their berths. On the night of the 9th to 10th U33, travelling on the surface, passed through Fair Island Channel. A few hours later three aeroplanes were sighted, forcing U33 to submerge to periscope depth. Not long afterwards Petty Officer Paul Rausch spotted the first of two torpedoes speeding in U33's direction but quick action by Schilling turned the sub out of the line of fire before Dresky had been roused from sleep. No surface vessels had been seen and Schilling surmised that a British submarine must have been in the vicinity. No more indications of its presence were observed. On 11th February U33 bottomed for five hours from noon, removing four torpedoes and reloading with eight mines. After this she proceeded very quickly to the Firth of Clyde, arriving on the morning of Monday 12th February.

All that day U33 lay on the surface off Largs. In the early afternoon when Dresky raised the periscope to take a sweep of the surroundings the wife of the local chemist observed the movement and rang the police. She may as well have not bothered because, remarkably, no one came to investigate; not even the local bobby in his weathered rowing boat, let alone any of the armed vessels of the British fleet anchored just a few miles upriver in the Tail o' the Bank.

Schilling knew nothing of this and even if he had it was unlikely he could have grown any uneasier than at that moment. He knew U33 was now just a few hours from action. But what kind of action? The passengers weren't giving him any clues; they had barely left their berths since leaving harbour and not half a dozen words had been exchanged with him or with any other member of the crew. Nevertheless, Schilling's feeling of mortal dread had steadily deepened and now any reserves of calm he might have had even twelve hours before were draining out through the bilges. For a fleeting moment of melancholy Schilling wished he could pour himself out with them but, when all was said and done, what was he if not an officer in the German navy sworn to do his duty come what may. He would see this thing through but woe betide that bastard Dresky if he put U33 and its men at risk for any other reason than engaging with the enemy and blowing up a few British ships.

Night fell and Dresky ordered U33 to move slowly upriver. Ominously, the passengers were still on board. Dresky could have put them ashore to do their covert business at any time along the hundreds of miles of secluded Scottish coastline that the sub had shadowed. But here they were, unspeaking and arrogant (except Rahn who, although quiet, appeared abnormally subdued) biding their time, seemingly unconcerned that U33 was shortly to bring hell to the British. Their destination must, after all, be the inner harbour. But what did that mean for U33's operational priorities? Would Dresky launch an attack with brass on board? Schilling was aware of U-Boat missions undertaken in Irish waters where undercover agents, regarded quite rightly in Schilling's view by submarine commanders as second-class passengers, had had to wait until the conclusion of offensive action before disembarking. Fair enough, first things first. But U33 was sailing into a shark pool significantly more dangerous and short on escape options than in normal operational circumstances. Schilling's suspicions that his fellow crewmates and he were about to be sold down the river (in this case the Clyde) were growing apace.

At around eleven o'clock the U-boat surfaced seven hundred metres from the Boom defences stretching between the Cloch lighthouse and Dunoon. Dresky ordered a rating up on deck to hoist the Royal Navy White Ensign. Schilling was deeply equivocal about this action. On the one hand he was tempted to take comfort that the daring subterfuge, allowable in war provided that, prior to firing, the U-Boat ensign replaced the enemy flag or at least was raised above it, would if successful (and there was a bloody big if about that) give U33 safe passage into the Tail o' the Bank to wreak havoc. But, the No 2 reflected ruefully, the flag ruse would also allow the sub into the heavily protected inner harbour to indulge in complicitous action to disembark the passengers, perhaps without a shot being fired, a kick in the guts for the loyal servicemen aboard U33 who were ready to give their lives in defending the Fatherland but not in playing chaperone to dilettante peacemakers. The Chief Engineer hoped to God that that wasn't Dresky's gameplan. He fingered the small revolver he had stuffed into his trouser pocket; he was not afraid to use it, especially after Dresky had shoved a similar weapon in his face in the Bristol Channel the previous November. He'll bloody well pay for that if he puts a foot wrong in the next few hours, by God I'll do for him if that's his game.

Slowly, U33 made its way to the Boom. Schilling heard approaching footsteps. Behind him, decked in immaculate uniforms denoting senior officer status, stood Albrecht and Klinger. Albrecht was carrying a leather attaché case handcuffed to his wrist. Schilling saw on his finger a large, ornate ring. He hadn't seen one exactly like it before but it reminded him of the ring his father, a high-ranking Freemason, wore on ceremonial occasions. Klinger scratched his ear and Schilling noticed he was sporting an identical ring. Both men were composed, confident. Little wonder, they were going to a jolly Lodge meeting by all accounts. This is bad, very bad.

Klinger saw Schilling's gaze and understood his concern. He lips creased into a sinister smile and his eyes burned with a messianic light that was both compelling and chilling. Schilling recoiled. Von Dresky wasn't bringing hell to the British; he was chaperoning these spooks to a brass band reception on the bloody quayside! Not if I can help it, he won't. Schilling pulled out his revolver and pointed it at the two uniformed traitors. Without taking his eyes off the two men he addressed his captain. "Dresky, I won't allow you to risk the lives of the crew in the cause of treachery. I will shoot these men, and you, if I suspect you are even thinking about doing anything other than getting into the harbour, blowing up the Hood as Dönitz has ordered, and then getting us out of here. If during that time our friends here can somehow disembark and do their dirty work for God knows whom then so be it, no skin off my nose."

Dresky was a pragmatist. Schilling had over-reached himself, his attention would falter. U33 had reached the Boom. Out of the darkness came a lamp signal composed of short and long bursts. Dresky consulted his log and ordered the required response. A return signal verified all was well and good. Schilling retained his poise, the two men in his line of fire standing dispassionately, not for a moment taking their eyes off the resolute Chief Engineer. Dresky prepared for the raising of the Boom and passage into the Tail o' the Bank. But i wasn't to come. To his profound consternation, moments later the unseen lamp bearer asked for a second security signal. It was evident that something had gone badly wrong. This was not what Intelligence had reported. One successful exchange of signals should guarantee U33 safe passage into the harbour. That was the plan.

Schilling knew then that their only chance was to turnabout and run for it. He was about to forcibly press that course of action upon Dresky when his attention was momentarily diverted by the appearance of Otto Rahn on the bridge. It was enough. Klinger produced a gun of his own and fired at Schilling. The bullet passed through his shoulder and the force knocked him to the floor.

Albrecht commanded Dresky to respond to the second signal. This was a calamitous error of judgement and Dresky himself was only too aware of it. The least hopeless course of action would have been to bolt for it or, more sensibly, to surrender. But now, with a gun to his head, Dresky tried re-sending the response to the first signal, immediately confirming to the harbour watch that the enemy was knocking at its gates.

Within moments the harbour was ringing to the din of warning sirens and attack vessels were swiftly mobilised. In the testimony that a Greenock plumber would later give to an Admiralty enquiry he would describe how in the intense desire to join the chase after the intruder, a frigate moored in Garvel dock for fit-out raced out of the harbour dragging with it welding plants, burning cables, bottles, generators and gangplanks. People on the quayside chopped away with axes in a desperate attempt to cut free of the accelerating frigate. It was pandemonium.

On board U33 an icy and all consuming calm descended upon Dresky as the jaws of chaos threatened to snap shut upon the beleaguered vessel. He would answer his critics! He would show them what kind of character he was in the face of seeming hopeless diversity! To hell with Hitler, to hell with Dönitz; if all was lost then the British must lose something also. Dresky screamed a command to the engine room: "Full ahead, ram the Boom!!"

The sub careered forward and struck the Boom netting, tearing it but not making an opening it could pass through. Schilling, wounded but conscious, retrieved his weapon from where it lay under his outstretched leg. He shot Dresky who at the time of firing was suddenly thrown off balance by U33 rebounding off the Boom. Schilling's bullet, intended for Dresky's arm, entered his groin at close range. U33's Kapitän fell to the floor in agony clutching his spilling guts. Even while

Dresky was toppling to the bridge's metal decking Schilling turned and shot both Albrecht and Klinger, one in the head and one in the heart. Kill shots. Hunting with his father most weekends between boyhood and when he left home in his late teens to join the Kriegsmarine had made him an excellent marksman. Rahn looked on, wide eyed with fear but he wasn't a target for Schilling's determined rage. With a huge effort Schilling pulled himself to his feet and ordered the engine room to turn around and try to outrun the converging British attack ships.

It was a hopeless effort. U33 was outpaced and outnumbered by massive superior forces. Within an hour the sub was mortally wounded. Schilling gave the command to abandon ship, ordering those among the crew responsible for safeguarding the on-board Enigma machine to ditch the parts in the sea. Not all would be successful in this task.

Finally, U33 sank in shallow water between Wemyss Bay and Skelmorlie, just three miles from the Boom. Of the forty-two official crew of U33 twenty-five men died. Twenty-one bodies were recovered. The bodies of Albrecht and Klinger were also fished out of the sea and all twenty-three deceased were laid out in Greenock Town Hall hours after the attack. When the naval authorities saw the two bodies dressed in immaculate high ranking uniforms and wearing the ceremonial rings of 33rd degree Freemasons the cover up was immediately put into place.

Some time later the broken corpse of U33 was dragged from its resting place, towed 20 miles south-west and re-submerged off Arran's tiny satellite island of Pladda.

The cover up was concluded. News of the true story of U33 could never be told. Too many people occupying the loftiest circles in the British Establishment, and higher still, would be implicated.

The survivors were given dry clothes, fed and put under lock and key to await interrogation. One man among them, however, could not be allowed to mingle with the rank and file. He was brought under immediate escort to a safe house on the outskirts of Glasgow and ushered into an oak panelled drawing room. A thirty-year old man with a ready smile turned to greet him.

"Otto!"

"Cecil?"

"Otto, welcome, I'm so glad you made it, what a mess, heads will roll. Both Hitler and Himmler send their congratulations for your safe arrival. Come, there are some people eager to meet you."

Otto Rahn's stomach muscles tightened and he fingered the small piece of Sabarthés stone in his trouser pocket. But it wasn't the

Pyrenean grotto souvenir that gave him comfort but the tiny white petals in its hollow centre, the living symbol of the "Edelweiss Pirates," the rapidly growing youth movement in Germany opposed to Nazism.

Over the years Otto Rahn and his confederates had been a tremendous source of help and inspiration to the Edelweißpiraten and other like-minded courageous groups that dared to oppose Hitler. Canaris carried the Edelweiss, too. They all did. He wouldn't let the Admiral down. He wouldn't let any of them down.

The cup must not be seized. The door must not be opened…

Appendix

Papers and correspondence

A facsimile of the original publication of "Jehan's Letzer Gang"

Jehans letzter Gang

Review of Otto Rahn's presentation to the 'Rote Erte' Society, 1938

W. L. Z. - Rote Erde
Dortmund, 9. I. 1938

Otto Rahn las in Dortmund

Vortragsabend im Dietrich-Eckart-Haus

Otto Rahn, der junge Dichter und Forscher, las und sprach Freitag abend im Dietrich-Eckart-Verein vor einer außerordentlich zahlreichen und stark gefesselten Zuhörerschaft. Nach einführenden Worten des Kulturwartes des Dietrich-Eckart-Vereins, Kurt Eggers, der Rahn als Kameraden begrüßte und kurz das Luzifer-Problem, um das es Rahn geht, umriß, gestaltete Rahn mit eindringlicher und zwingender Sprache ein Luzifer-Bild, wie es erschütternder und größer nicht gedacht werden kann. Rahn las aus seinem neuesten Werk „Luzifers Hofgesind", das von seinen Reisen und Forschungen in Südfrankreich berichtet, wo er auf den Spuren des Grals und der Albigenser, der reinen und wahren Ketzer, und von neuen Blickpunkten aus ein fruchtbares Bild dieser damals auch in Deutschland verbreiteten antirömischen Bewegung zeichnete. Der Vortrag behandelte einen schwierigen Stoff und verlangte größte Disziplin und Aufmerksamkeit; es war ein gutes Zeichen für die Gemeinschaft von Vortragenden und Zuhörern, daß kein Wort verlorenging und das Bild Luzifers, den Rahn mit den Albigensern als Lichtbringer feierte, aufs stärkste zur Wirkung kam.

Zwei Teile des Abends lassen sich deutlich unterscheiden: der erste, in dem es Rahn um einen Forschungs- und Sagebericht des Gral- und Luzifer-Problems ging — hier schienen uns die besten Formulierungen und die wirklich packendste Gestaltungskraft zu liegen —, und ein zweiter, in dem der Vortragende an Hand konkreter Beispiele die Folgerungen aus seiner neuen Schau und Lehre zog und zu einer nicht nur interessanten, sondern auch weitgehend überzeugenden Umwertung historischer Erscheinungen, Persönlichkeiten und Sachverhalte kam. Auch die Klippe eines Nationalismus alter Prägung — eine Gefahr, die bei einer weniger echten und starken Naturbejahung und naturverbundenen Andeutung zweifellos gegeben wäre — vermied Rahn recht gut. In echter Spannung führte er immer wieder zu den Quellen und Ursprüngen echter Freiheitssehnsucht und wahrer Naturverbundenheit zurück.

Die Albigenser sind ausgerottet. 205 führende Anhänger Luzifers wurden in Südfrankreich nach einem großen Waffenkreuzzug im Namen christlicher Milde von Dominikanern auf einem riesigen Scheiterhaufen verbrannt. Mit Feuer und Schwert verfolgte man die Lehre Luzifers, des Lichtbringers, und ihre Anhänger. Die Albigenser sind tot, aber ihr Geist lebt und wirkt gerade in unseren Tagen in erneuter und verjüngter Begeisterung und Hingabe. Der Stellvertreter Christi konnte zwar Menschen verbrennen; aber er irrte, wenn er glaubte, mit ihnen auch den Geist, die Hingabe und die Sehnsucht zu verbrennen. Dieser Geist wurde gestern wieder lebendig, wirksam und sichtbar vor vielen Menschen in Otto Rahn, einem Nachfahren der alten Troubadours.

So setzte Rahn dem römisch gebundenen Geiste, dem Jenseitsglauben und der Höllenfurcht eine neue Grenze, verneinte Jahwe und die jüdische Lehre und bekannte sich zu Luzifers Hofgesind; in dessen Namen auch Kurt Eggers den Abend mit dem Gruß schloß: „Luzifer, dem Unrecht geschah, grüßt dich".

Der Abend war innerlich und äußerlich ein gleich großer Erfolg, der für die zukünftige Arbeit des Dietrich-Eckart-Vereins einen vielversprechenden Auftakt darstellte. Das Quartett des Konservatoriums umrahmte den Abend in ganz ausgezeichneter Weise und gab der Weisheit und dem Reichtum der Gedanken die künstlerische Fassung.

Dr. Wulf Heinrichsdorff

Neues Vortragsprogramm im Museum am Ostwall

Seit vier Jahren veranstaltet das Museum für Kunst und Kulturgeschichte in den Wintermonaten eine Reihe von Führungen und Vorträgen, die die reichen Kunstschätze der Sammlungen in allgemein verständlicher Form erläutern. Neben den Lichtbildern wird bei allen Veranstaltungen großer Wert auf die Vorführung der Originale gelegt. Diese Vorträge, die im Jahre 1934 in kleinem Rahmen begannen, haben sich zu einer ständigen Einrichtung entwickelt, die sich stets steigender Teilnahme erfreut. Um allen Interessenten die Veranstaltungen des Museums für Kunst und Kulturgeschichte, des Museums für Vor- und Frühgeschichte und des Dortmunder Museumsvereins zur Kenntnis zu bringen, ist soeben wieder ein von Künstlerhand entworfenes Programm erschienen, das in den Museen, im Verkehrsverein, in den Buchhandlungen und in den Kunstgewerbegeschäften zu haben ist.

Veranstaltungsring der HJ

Die Vorstellung der Reihe 5 findet am Montag,

Letters and notes between Otto Rahn and Nazi personnel (source: Berlin Document Centre)

1. 27th September 1935—Rahn to Weisthor—headed Strictly Confidential, concerning Rahn's future plans and visits to ancient European centres;

2. 24th April 1936—Himmler to Rahn concerning Himmler's genealogy (family Passaquai);

3. 27th August 1937—from Kassel to the Gau Law Court in Berlin re: Karl Mahler in Arolson and Rahn's incrimination in defamatory behaviour;

4. 28th August 1937—Secret—Rahn to Karl Wolff—Rahn attaches a handwritten oath abstaining from alcohol for two years and confirming that he will report to SS-Gruppenführer Eicke in Dachau on 1st September for punishment duty;

5. 1st December 1937—Rahn's Curriculum Vitae written while at Dachau;

6. 22nd January 1938—Rahn to Himmler concerning the proposed visit by Raymond Perrier over Christmas and New Year, and the proposal that Rahn and Perrier should work together on the Passaquai family tree research;

7. 11th April 1938—letter written by Rahn to Himmler about Himmler's family tree;

8. 28th April 1938—note written by Ullmann for Rahn's file about the Riedweg affair;

9. 9th June 1938—letter sent from Muggenbrunn by Rahn to Wolff concerning Riedweg and Alfred Schmid;

10. 9th June 1938—Rahn to Himmler concerning Rahn's workload and his current literary projects;

11. 9th June 1938—Rahn to Himmler asking for permission for Perrier to be shown around SS facilities, with Himmler's

handwritten note ("*Wie Söll das geschehen?*") asking how this should be handled;

12. 17th June 1938—Rahn to Himmler concerning his plan to marry 27 year old Asta Baeschlin née Holtz;

13. 27th June 1938—Himmler to Rahn, referring to letter of 17th and saying how pleased he is to learn of the wedding and inviting Rahn to bring his fiancée to Berlin;

14. 11th September 1938—Notice promoting Rahn to Obersturmführer (Otto Rahn's final rank in the SS);

15. 4th December 1938—Rahn to Alvenslebe, laying out the reasons why his marriage to Asta Baeschlin is not going ahead according to the original timetable. It includes Himmler's handwritten note inviting Rahn to inform him of the wedding costs to try to speed things up;

16. 28th February 1939—Rahn's handwritten note asking for immediate release from the SS;

17. 17th March 1939—Schmidt's official note of release of Rahn from the SS.

1

Otto Rahn
Tiergartenstrasse 8a
Berlin W 35

den 27. September 1935

An
SS Oberführer
K.M. Weisthor
Berlin - Grunewald

Streng vertraulich !

Lieber Herr Oberst,

Es ist Ihnen bekannt, dass ich die letzten Wochen hindurch lediglich meinen Arbeiten lebte und eine Kartothek angelegt habe. Ich habe Ihnen weiterhin zu wissen gegeben, dass ich auf ganz grosse Überraschungen gekommen bin. Da es sich um Erkenntnisse handelt, die jahrelange Arbeit meinerseits verlangt haben, war ich bislang Ihnen wie jedem gegenüber nur wenig mitteilsam. Ich möchte es vorerst auch bleiben und nur mit Ihnen über meine Funde Rücksprache nehmen. Ich bitte Sie aber, vor Erscheinen meines Buches "Monsalvat und Golgatha", dem Reichsführer SS ausgenommen, mit niemand über das zu sprechen, was ich Ihnen mündlich anvertrauen möchte.

Um meine Arbeiten zu einem erfolgreichen Ende zu führen, sehe ich mich gezwungen, einige Lokalitäten an Ort und Stelle zu prüfen. Können Sie mir die Möglichkeit verschaffen, für 10 - 14 Tage eine Reise in den Odenwald, den Westerwald und das Sauerland zu unternehmen, oder - das wäre mir das liebste ! - hätten Sie nicht Lust mit mir und evtl. Oberscharführer Folgmann vor Einsetzen der schlechten Jahreszeit diese Reise zu unternehmen ?

Zuerst müsste ich die Ruine Wildenberg bei Amorbach (vgl. Kunis : Die deutsche Gralsburg) aufsuchen. Es finden zur Zeit Ausgrabungen statt. Mit dem Ausgrabungsleiter stehe ich im Briefwechsel. Dann möchte ich die Lichtweishöhle bei Wiesbaden besichtigen. Von dort aus wäre die Sporckenburg leicht zu erreichen (Vgl. Hebborn, Westerwald S.91 : Ruine mit uralter Geschichte; der Sage nach soll Kaiser Nero hier geboren sein; sporck = krane = Wachholder). Von hier aus müsste die Fahrt gehen nach dem Druidenstein, dem "Steimel" (Steimel oder Steinmahl), dem Hellenborn, dem Hiddenstein, den grossartigen Steinanlagen der Dornburg (Thorburg), Rossbach (angeblicher Geburtsort Heinrichs von Ofterdingen), Hillsdorf (Sitz der deutschen Katharer, durch Konrad von Marburg zerstört), Wanbach (vom Wanen) und Asbach (Asen). (Hier wurde übrigens im Jahre 1830 eine prächtig erhaltene Goldmünze mit der griechischen Inschrift : Lysimachus Basileus - Lysimachus war Feldherr Alexanders d.Gr. gefunden). Von Asbach aus möchte ich dann Stellen aufsuchen, über die ich nur Ihnen und dem Reichsführer SS mündlich Auskunft geben würde.

Nach der Hochzeit Herrn von Lechners möchte ich fahren, da ich dann frei bin. Können Sie veranlassen, dass mir diese Reise, über die ich natürlich ausführlichen Bericht machen würde, ermöglicht wird. Oder wären Sie bereit, diese Reise mit mir zu unternehmen ?

Wie ich mit Herrn von Lechner ausgemacht habe, werde ich Sie heute abend um 8 Uhr aufsuchen.

Heil Hitler !
Ihr
Otto Rahn

In this letter, headed Strictly Confidential, Rahn reminds Weisthor that he had previously mentioned he had "discovered very big surprises." He had not brought them up since because he wanted to keep them under wraps a bit longer. Rahn tells Weisthor that he wants the old man to accompany him on these trips and he repeats this request further on in the letter.

2

Aktbeleg:

Zum Akt:

, den 4. 4.1936.

Tgb.Nr. A/ 4185/

4.

Lieber H a h n !

Sie schrieben mir unter dem 31.3., Sie wären in der Lage, mir bei meinen Forschungen betreffend die Familie Possaqui in Savoyen behilflich zu sein. Hierzu folgende Angaben:

Die am 12.12.1775 in Straubing geborene Maria Magdalena Ottilie Possaqui ist die Frau meines Urgrossvaters. Ihre Eltern sind Johann Michael Possaqui, tabernarius, geb. ... 1739 in Savoyen, gest. 18.9.1803 in Abensberg, verh. mit Maria Katharina Bartl (Barthel, Parthel) von Greifenberg. --

Dann ist zur gleichen Zeit in Abensberg ein Sebastian Albert Passaqui, Archigrammaticus=Stadtschreiber, verh. mit Maria Barbara de Michel à Francance erwähnt, deren Tochter die Namen Anna, Katharina Maria Magdalena hatte, geb. 17.1.1776 in Abensberg, gest. 3.4. 1861 in Abensberg. - Ob dieser zweite Passaqui mit dem ersten verwandt ist, weiss ich nicht - es ist jedoch anzunehmen.

Ein letzter Anhaltspunkt ist der, dass es auf einem Friedhof in Chambéry einen alten Grabstein

mit

continued

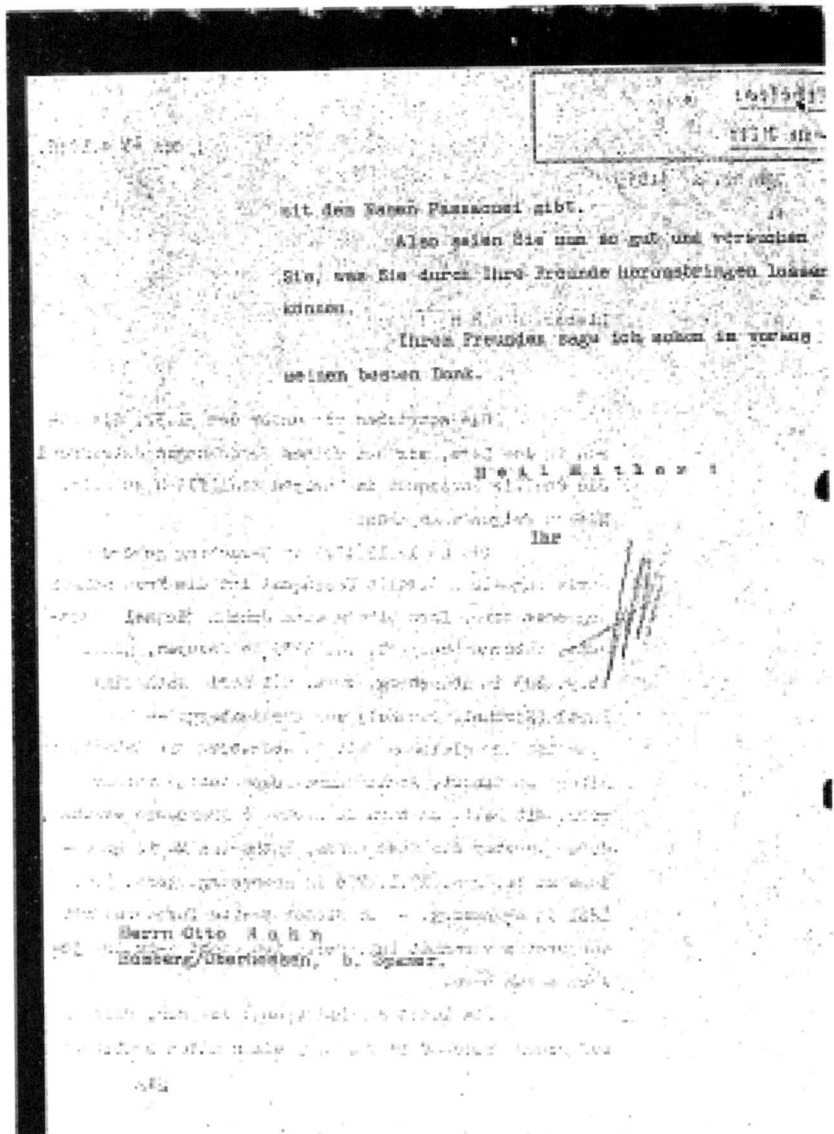

mit den Namen Passaquai gibt.

Also seien Sie nun so gut und versuchen Sie, was Sie durch Ihre Freunde herausbringen lassen können.

Ihren Freunden sage ich schon im voraus meinen besten Dank.

Heil Hitler!

Ihr

Herrn Otto Rahn
Homberg/Oberhessen, b. Spanier.

Himmler refers to Rahn's letter of 31st March when Rahn had said he might be able to help the investigations into the family Passaquai of Savoy. Maria Magdalena Ottilie Passaquai was Himmler's great grandmother.

3

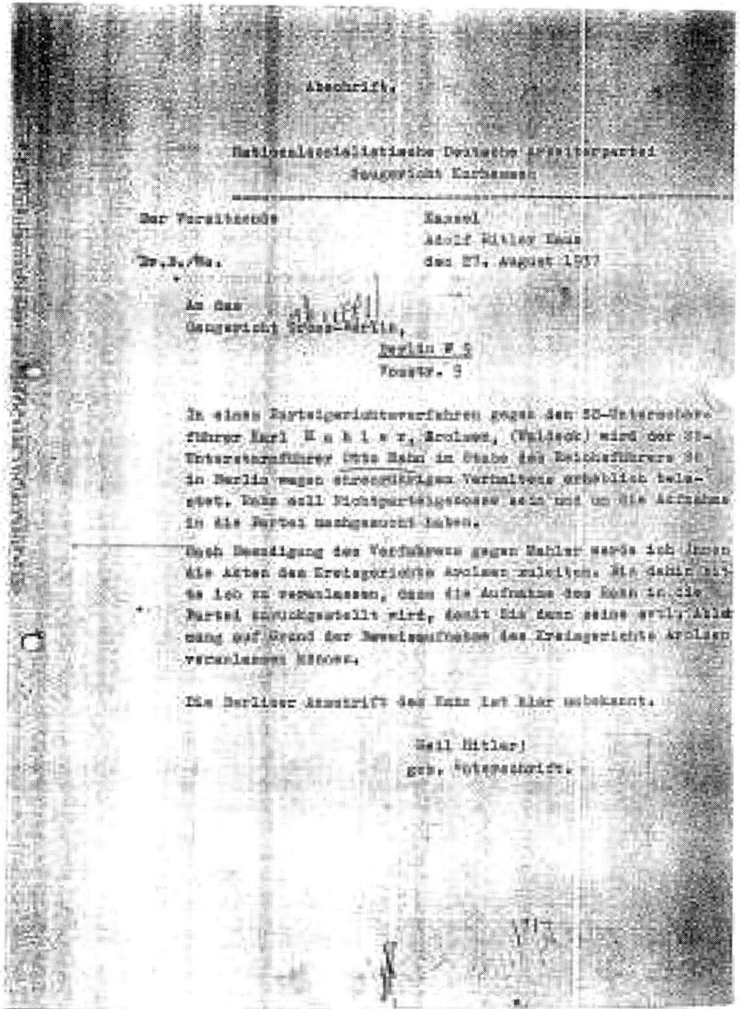

Abschrift.

Nationalsozialistische Deutsche Arbeiterpartei
Gaugericht Kurhessen

Der Vorsitzende | Kassel
Adolf Hitler Haus

Dr.B./Wa. | den 27. August 1937

An das
Gaugericht Gross-Berlin,
Berlin W 5
Vosstr. 9

In einem Parteigerichtsverfahren gegen den SS-Unterscharführer Karl M a h l e r, Arolsen, (Waldeck) wird der SS-Unterscharführer Otto Rahn im Stabe des Reichsführers SS in Berlin wegen ehrenrührigen Verhaltens erheblich belastet. Rahn soll Nichtparteigenosse sein und um die Aufnahme in die Partei nachgesucht haben.

Nach Beendigung des Verfahrens gegen Mahler werde ich Ihnen die Akten des Kreisgerichts Arolsen zuleiten. Bis dahin bitte ich zu veranlassen, dass die Aufnahme des Rahn in die Partei zurückgestellt wird, damit Sie dann seine evtl. Ablehnung auf Grund der Beweisaufnahme des Kreisgerichts Arolsen veranlassen können.

Die Berliner Anschrift des Rahn ist hier unbekannt.

Heil Hitler!
gez. Unterschrift.

The letter explains that in a Party court case against SS-Unterscharführer Karl Mahler, Arolsen (Waldeck), Otto Rahn, member of the Reichsführer's personal SS attachment, Berlin, is heavily implicated due to dishonourable conduct. It states that Rahn was not yet a member of the Party but had asked to join. Kassel goes on to ask that Rahn's Party membership should not be processed yet in case the evidence against him should prove to be incriminating.

4

A b s c h r i f t !

ᛋᛋ-Unt[illegible]
Otto R[illegible]
z.Zt.Homberg/Oberhessen

am 28.8.1937

An den
Reichsführer - ᛋᛋ
Chef des Persönlichen Stabes

B e r l i n SW 11

Prinz-Albrecht-Straße 8

Tgb.Nr. AR/4067 geheim! Scha/E -

Beiliegend lasse ich Ihnen eine handschriftliche ehrenwörtliche Erklärung zugehen, wonach ich mich verpflichte, zwei Jahre lang keinerlei Alkohol zu mir zu nehmen.

In den Vormittagsstunden des 1. September werde ich mich bei ᛋᛋ-Gruppenführer E i c k e im Konzentrationslager Dachau melden, um bei dem ᛋᛋ-Totenkopfverband "Oberbayern" in Dachau mindestens vier Monate lang aktiven Dienst zu leisten. Ich werde während meiner Abkommandierung zu den ᛋᛋ-Totenkopf-Verbänden im Dienst und außerhalb des Dienstes die Dienstgradabzeichen eines ᛋᛋ-Untersturmführers ablegen und die Abzeichen eines ᛋᛋ-Mannes tragen.

Ich werde mit aller Kraft versuchen, durch tadellose Pflichterfüllung und einwandfreie dienstliche Führung in Dachau mein ᛋᛋ-schädigendes Verhalten in Arolsen, das ich zutiefst bedauere, wenigstens teilweise wieder gutzumachen.

gez. Otto R a h n
ᛋᛋ-Untersturmführer.

1 Anlage.
F.d.R.d.A.
[signature]
ᛋᛋ-Obersturmführer.

Rahn refers Karl Wolff to his hand-written attachment in which he solemnly declares that he will abstain from alcohol for the next two years. In the morning hours of 1st September Rahn will report to Eicke in the concentration camp Dachau to join SS-Totenkopfverband "Oberbayern" for at least 4 months active service. During this time Rahn promises to remove his insignia of rank even when off-duty, and will only wear the signets of an SS soldier. He will endeavour with all his best efforts to partly compensate for his dishonourable behaviour at Arolsen.

5

OTTO RAHN

SS-Untersturmführer
im Persönlichen Stabe
des Reichsführers-SS

SS-Nr.: 276 208

z.Zt. SS-TV "Oberbayern"

D a c h a u bei München
am 1. Dezember 1937

L e b e n s l a u f

Ich wurde am 18. Februar 1904 als Sohn des Karl R a h n (jetzt Justizamtmann am Landgericht Mainz) und seiner Ehefrau Clara (geborene Hamburger) in Michelstadt (hessischer Odenwald) geboren. Ab 1910 besuchte ich das humanistische Gymnasium. Zuerst in Bingen am Rhein; dann in Giessen, wo ich 1922 die Reifeprüfung ablegte. An meine Schulzeit schloss sich ein Hochschulstudium an den Universitäten Giessen und Freiburg (Breisgau) unmittelbar an.

Nach fünf Semestern fasste ich den Entschluss, mich der schriftstellerischen Laufbahn zu widmen und änderte infolgedessen meinen Ausbildungsweg grundlegend. Ich stellte mein Studium, das bis dahin in erster Linie der Jurisprudenz gegolten hatte, völlig auf die Philologie ein und absolvierte nebenher eine regelrechte Ausbildung im Sortiments- und Verlagsbuchhandel. Dieser Zeit, die ich in Giessen, Berlin und Heidelberg (wo ich während zwei Semester immatrikuliert war) verlebte, folgte ab 1928 ein mehrjähriger Studienaufenthalt in der Schweiz und in Frankreich :

In Genf, wo ich die Gestalten Calvins, Rousseaus und Voltaires in den Mittelpunkt meiner Studien stellte, war ich, um meine materielle Lage zu verbessern und um meine Sprachkenntnisse zu vervollkommnen, als Sprachlehrer und Dolmetscher tätig. In Frankreich lebte ich in den Pyrenäen und dem Lande Languedoc. Hier oblag ich eingehenden Forschungen über die Westgotenfrage, den Minnesang und die albigensische Ketzerei. Dieser Aufenthalt wurde mehrmals durch Quellenstudien an der Pariser Nationalbibliothek unterbrochen. Eine ursprünglich als Doktorarbeit gedachte Abhandlung über das Ergebnis meiner Studien und Forschungen erweiterte ich schliesslich zu einem Buche, das ich im Jahr 1933 unter dem Titel "Kreuzzug gegen den Gral" in Deutschland der Öffentlichkeit übergab. Mit dem weit über die deutschen Grenzen gehenden Erfolg dieses Buches, dem eine französische Ausgabe unter dem Titel "La Croisade contre le Graal" folgte, hatte ich den Eingang ins deutsche und europäische Schrifttum gefunden.

Seit 1933 lebe ich, einen halbjährigen Studienaufenthalt in Italien ausgenommen, wieder in Deutschland. Ermutigt und gefördert von dem Reichsführer-SS, dessen Stab ich seit Mai 1935 angehöre, setzte ich meine Forschungen im gleichen Sinne fort und erweiterte sie auf den gesamten germanischen Raum. Einen Teil meiner Forschungsergebnisse legte ich in meinem vor einem halben Jahr erschienenen Buche "Luzifers Hofgesind" nieder, zu

continued

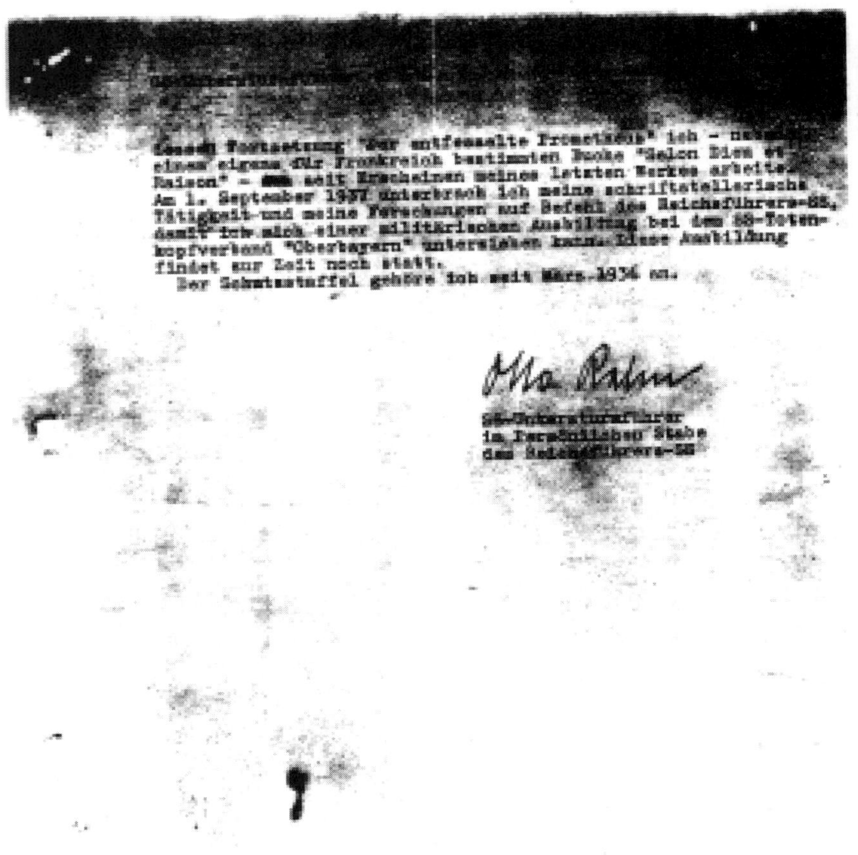

[illegible] Fortsetzung "Der entfesselte Prometheus" ich – neben
einem eigens für Frankreich bestimmten Buche "Selon Dieu et
Raison" – seit Erscheinen meines letzten Werkes arbeite.
Am 1. September 1937 unterbrach ich meine schriftstellerische
Tätigkeit und meine Forschungen auf Befehl des Reichsführers-SS,
damit ich mich einer militärischen Ausbildung bei dem SS-Totenkopfverband "Oberbayern" unterziehen kann. Diese Ausbildung
findet zur Zeit noch statt.
Der Schutzstaffel gehöre ich seit März 1934 an.

Otto Rahn

SS-Untersturmführer
im Persönlichen Stabe
des Reichsführers-SS

Rahn states that the publication of a French edition of *Kreuzzug gegen den Gral* led to his establishment in German and European literary circles. He confirms that since 1933 he had been living in Germany except for 6 months spent in Italy. He is intending to follow up *Luzifers Hofgesind* with a book translating in English as *The Will of Prometheus: a Trip to Hell and Beyond*, and will also produce a book for the French market—*According to God and to Right.*

6

SS-Untersturmführer
Otto R a h n

M ü n c h e n
Georgenstrasse 34
am 22. Januar 1938

An den
Reichsführer-SS und Chef der deutschen Polizei
Heinrich H i m m l e r
B e r l i n SW 11
Prinz-Albrecht-Strasse 8

Reichsführer !

Ich nehme Bezug auf das erste Schreiben, welches Sie persönlich seinerzeit bezüglich der Ahnenforschung Passaquay an mich gesandt hatten. Ihr Schreiben war vom 24. April 1936 datiert und trug folgende Tagebuchnummer : Tgb.Nr. A/ 4185
4

Nachdem verschiedene Versuche meinerseits, die Untersuchungen Passaquay weiterzutreiben, gescheitert waren, habe ich meinen Freund Raymond F e r r i e r (Nyon am Genfer See) für die Zeit von Weihnachten bis Anfang Januar zu mir eingeladen, um mit ihm alles durchzusprechen, was mir über die Frage Passaquay bekannt war, und um ihn zu bitten, in Savoyen an Ort und Stelle Erkundigungen einzuziehen. Durch meine Einladung konnte ich auch die Unkosten, die Herr Ferrier hatte und haben würde, gut machen.

Nunmehr liegt das vorläufige Resultat, das uns ein schönes Stück weitergebracht hat, vor. Ich habe die Unterlagen, die alles Passaquay-Material aus der in Frage kommenden Zeit (auch unbrauchbares) enthalten, übersetzt und lasse es beiliegend an Sie abgehen. Die Originale habe ich hier behalten, da ich ja im Begriffe stehe, zur Erholung in die Schweiz zu reisen. Von dort möchte ich das Gesamtmaterial und die notariell beurkundeten Dokumente mitbringen.

Sie finden zuerst einen Auszug aus dem Briefe meines Freundes Ferrier, dann einen Stammbaum Ihres Urgroßvaters Johann Michael Passaquay. Er ist, wie sie ersehen werden, nicht 1739 sondern 1736 geboren.

continued

Von den übrigen Unterlagen habe ich mit Rotstift das angestrichen, was für Ihren Stammbaum wichtig ist. An den anderen Stellen handelt es sich wohl um Seitenlinien.

Ich bin neugierig, was mein Freund Perrier nunmehr in Thorens noch ausfindig macht.

Wie ich Ihnen bereits schrieb, liegt die Wahrscheinlichkeit nahe, dass in Annecy und Turin noch allerlei zu finden ist. Sobald ich nur etwas mehr bei Kräften bin, werde ich diesbezügliche Schritte unternehmen. Ich trage mich ja mit der Absicht, meinen Erholungsurlaub, für dessen Bewilligung und Erleichterung ich Ihnen sehr danke, in der Schweiz zu verbringen.

Heil Hitler !

Ihr sehr ergebener

Otto Rahn

SS-Untersturmführer

4 Anlagen

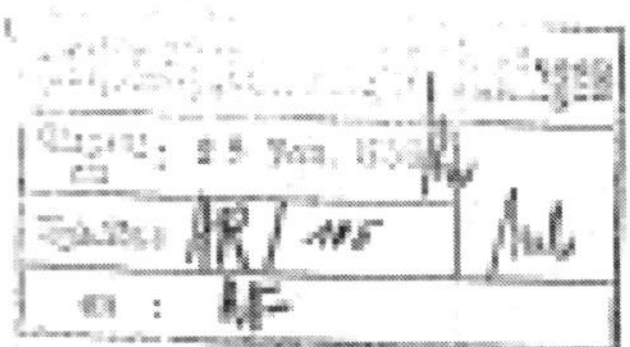

7

OTTO RAHN

Pension Schotzky
Werderstrasse 8
F r e i b u r g i.Br.
am 11. April 1938

An den
Reichsführer-SS
Chef des Persönlichen Stabes
B e r l i n SW 11

Ich bitte, dem Reichsführer-SS folgende Nachträge, die Ahnenreihe Passaquay betreffend, zur Kenntnis zu geben :
Claude P. (geboren 1606), der Vater des Maurice P. (1641 - 1691), war der Sohn des Collard P. und von dessen Ehefrau Autzon P. (geborene ?). Er ist am 26. Januar 1606 in der Pfarrei Thorens getauft worden. Sein Geburtsdatum ist nicht bekannt.
Durch die Pfarrei Thorens sind mir noch eine Reihe Daten (bis 1581) zugestellt worden, die zwar mit dem Namen Passaquay (vor 1600 : Passaquet) in Verbindung stehen, die jedoch keine Aufschlüsse über die Ahnenreihe des Reichsführers-SS geben können. Mit Ausnahme der beiden folgenden Daten, die allerdings nur eine Bestätigung von bereits bekannten Tatsachen geben :
22. Februar 1608 : Taufe des Guillaume P., Sohn des Collard P. und von dessen Ehefrau Autzon. (Guillaume ist also ein Bruder des Claude).
Ein Bruder des Maurice P., namens Claude, ist im Jahre 1686 zu la Roche gestorben.

Heil Hitler !

Otto Rahn

SS-Untersturmführer

Persönlicher Stab RF-SS Anlagen
Eingang: 1 2. Apr. 1938
Tgb. Nr.: AR/ 491

8

Berlin, den

Ulg/He.

Rahn

Aktennotiz.

Bei dem Besuch des SS-Untersturmführers Rahn am 25.4.1938 in meinem Büro sagte mir Rahn, er hätte gehört, daß Dr. Riedweg, der Sekretär von Altbundesrat Müsy ist, in die SS aufgenommen werden soll. Riedweg wolle zu diesem Zweck die deutsche Staatsangehörigkeit erwerben, will aber weiter gleichzeitig auch Schweizer Staatsangehöriger bleiben. Rahn hält nicht viel von Riedweg, da er mehr aus sich mache, als er in Wirklichkeit ist. Seine politische Stellung soll außerdem von keinerlei Bedeutung sein. Rahn glaubt, daß Riedweg nur deshalb in die SS will, um Karriere zu machen. Müsy ist dieser Schritt des Riedweg garnicht recht, zumal Riedweg Müsy vorher nicht davon unterrichtet hatte. Da Riedweg in der Schweiz offiziell bekannt gab, daß er am 1.5. in die SS aufgenommen würde, sah Müsy sich gezwungen, den Schluß seines Filmes gegen die Komintern zu ändern. Dieser Film wurde in Deutschland mit einem Kostenaufwand von 100.000 Franc gedreht. Der Schluß mußte, nach Aussagen Rahn's, entgegen der ursprünglichen Fassung ein sogenanntes demokratisches Gesicht bekommen, damit Müsy nicht der Vorwurf gemacht werden kann, der Film sei mit Geldern der SS gedreht worden. Rahn behauptet weiterhin, Riedweg soll noch vor ein paar Monaten für Pan-Europa eingetreten sein. Er rät daher unter keinen Umständen Riedweg irgendwie zu exponieren. Er glaubt, daß Riedweg sehr ehrgeizig und charakterlich nicht einwandfrei, obwohl er zu Rahn immer sehr nett und zuvorkommend war.

SS-Obersturmbannführer u. Stabsführer des Pers.Stabes RFSS.

The note also focuses on the former Member of Parliament Müsy and his unhappiness with his employee Dr. Franz Riedweg who did not have the courtesy to tell him before joining the SS. As a result, Müsy had to change the ending of a film he was making against the Komintern to give it a more democratic impact so that no one could accuse him of making a biased film supported by SS funds. This last minute change was expensive for Müsy.

9

Otto R a h n
SS-Untersturmführer

M u g g e n b r u n n
bei Todtnau / Schwarzwald
am 9. Juni 1938

An den
Reichsführer-SS
Chef des Persönlichen Stabes
B e r l i n SW 11

<u>Geheim !</u>

Unter Bezugnahme auf eine mündliche Unterredung wurde ich von dem Stabsführer des Persönlichen Stabes RFSS aufgefordert, über die Stellungnahme meiner schweizerischen Freunde und Bekannten zu Herrn <u>Dr. Franz R i e d w e g /Luzern</u> und seinem beabsichtigten Eintritt in die Schutzstaffel zu berichten.

Im Anbetracht der Tatsache, dass Herr Dr. Riedweg, den ich vor einer Reihe von Jahren durch den schweizerischen Professor Alfred Schmid/Berlin kennen gelernt habe, mir gegenüber korrekt und überaus entgegenkommend war, müsste ich eigentlich mich für befangen erklären.

Ich habe jedoch dem Chef des Persönlichen Stabes RFSS davon Kenntnis zu geben, dass meine (uns auch ideologisch nahe stehenden) schweizerischen Freunde und dass meine schweizerischen Bekannten (von denen ich einige durch Herrn Dr. R. selber kennen gelernt habe) mir ihre Verwunderung über die ihnen von anderer Seite bekannt gewordene Sachlage und auch ihre Bedenken nicht vorenthalten haben. Sie betrachten Herrn Dr. R.'s beabsichtigten Eintritt in die Schutzstaffel als einen Schritt, der lediglich aus Opportunismus und zur Beschleunigung einer in der Schweiz fast unmöglichen diplomatischen Karriere von ihm vorgenommen würde. Nachdem Herr Dr. R. (er ist Arzt) bereits auf andere Karten gesetzt habe (er soll, wie ich mehrfach vernahm, vor Jahren für Paneuropa geworben und dann, nach Coudenhove-Calergis Abstieg, die vermeintlich aussichtsreichere Karriere über Alt-Bundesrat Musy eingeschlagen haben), versuche er, obgleich er niemals Soldat gewesen sei, über "die mächtigsten Gruppen in dem

continued

wieder mächtig gewordenen Deutschland" zu arrivieren:
über die Schutzstaffel mittels eines Führerpostens; über
die Reichswehr mittels einer Heirat.

Was meine persönliche Meinung anbetrifft, so erkläre ich
mich aus den angegebenen Gründen für befangen und muss mich
einer Äusserung ebenso enthalten, wie ich es bezüglich einer
persönlichen Stellungnahme zu diesen schweizerischen Stimmen
tun muss. Es handelt sich aber, wie ich nicht unterlassen
darf zu betonen, um Urteile von mir freundschaftlich ver-
bundenen Menschen, die durchweg dem schweizerischen Offi-
zierskorps angehören, im öffentlichen Leben der Schweiz eine
nicht unwichtige Rolle spielen und von der schweizerischen
Presse des öfteren als "Nazis" angegriffen worden sind.

Abschliessend bitte ich sagen zu dürfen, dass - ganz
abgesehen von Herrn Dr. R.'s sehr engen Beziehungen zu
höchsten deutschen Stellen - noch kein Bericht mir so schwer
gefallen ist, wie dieser.

Heil Hitler!

SS-Untersturmführer

Persönlicher Stab RF SS

Eingang: 13. Jun. 1936

Rahn is following up Wolff's recent request that he should report about the statements of his Swiss friends concerning Dr. Franz Riedweg of Lucerne and his intended membership of the SS. Rahn says he and his friends believe that Riedweg is feathering his next and that his motives are driven by opportunism to give impetus to his diplomatic career. Rahn states that Riedweg is always changing horses and that he has built his career on the back of Müsy. Rahn stresses that he had never had so much emotional difficulty with any prior report as with this one about Riedweg because the Swiss had such influential German friends.

10

Otto R a h n
SS-Untersturmführer

M u g g e n b r u n n
bei Todtnau / Schwarzwald
am 9. Juni 1938

An den
Reichsführer-SS
Chef des Persönlichen Stabes
B e r l i n SW 11

Neben der Fortsetzung meines letzten Buches "Luzifers Hofgesind" (Titel der Fortsetzung : "Das Testament des Prometheus. Eine Reise zur Hölle und darüber hinaus") und neben der wissenschaftlichen Unterbauung dieses dann zweibändigen Werkes bearbeite ich zur Zeit einen gross angelegten Roman (Titel : "Sebastian"). Er soll, einmal abgeschlossen, ein Kunstwerk sein, in welchem ich die Quintessenz meiner Erkenntnisse und Thesen unter ausschliesslicher Bezugnahme und Nutzanwendung auf das heutige Leben niedergelegt habe, und wird meine bislang stärkste künstlerische und denkerische Leistung darstellen. Experten haben mir diese Gewissheit gegeben. Dieser Roman, welcher mich seit Jahren zutiefst beschäftigt, liegt in grossen Zügen und auch in abgeschlossenen Einzelkapiteln bereits vor. Es ist allerdings noch viel Kleinarbeit nötig, bis ich ihn in Druck geben kann.

Ich bitte den Reichsführer-SS um die Erlaubnis, diese Arbeiten (insgesamt etwa 2000 Manuskriptseiten) im Hochschwarzwald, wo ich in 1000 m Höhe ein absolut ruhiges Häuschen allein bewohne, weiter niederschreiben und druckfertig machen zu dürfen. So könnte ich gleichzeitig, ohne die Arbeit nochmals unterbrechen und von vorn anfangen zu müssen, meinen sehr labilen Gesundheitszustand festigen (immer wieder wechselt ein heftiger Bronchialkatarrh den anderen ab). - Ausserdem bedürfen meine jetzigen Arbeiten der uneingeschränkten Konzentration und Hingabe meinerseits noch mehr als die seitherigen. - Nicht zuletzt wäre ich endlich wieder im Stande, die von mir in der letzten Zeit gezwungenermassen stark vernachlässigten dienstlich-organisatorischen Pflichten zu erfüllen.

H e i l H i t l e r !

Otto Rahn
SS-Untersturmführer

11

Otto Rahn
SS-Untersturmführer

Muggenbrunn
bei Todtnau / Schwarzwald

am 9. Juni 1938

An den
Reichsführer-SS
Berlin SW 11

Tgb. Nr. AR/105
RF/Bra/V.

Reichsführer !

Es hat meinem Freunde Raymond Perrier, wie er mich unlängst wissen liess, eine aufrichtige Freude bereitet, dass er Ihnen mit seinen Nachforschungen über die savoyische Sippe Passaquay einen Dienst erweisen konnte.

Um Herrn Perrier für seine Bemühungen zu "entschädigen", hatte ich ihn letzten Dezember zum Skilaufen nach Oberbayern (Schliersee) eingeladen. Er war während drei Wochen mein Gast.

Sie möchten, wie ich Ihrem Brief entnehme, auch Ihrerseits meinem Freunde eine Freude bereiten und ihn gegebenenfalls kennen lernen. Ich weiss, dass Herr Perrier Ihnen ganz besonders dankbar wäre, wenn Sie ihn gelegentlich einen etwas tieferen Blick in die Schutzstaffel tun liessen, als ich es ihm bieten durfte.

Herr Perrier hat übrigens durch mich einige Führer des SS-Totenkopfverbandes "Oberbayern" kennen gelernt. Trotz der sprachlichen Schwierigkeiten war das Einvernehmen zuletzt so gut, dass ich auf diese Dachauer Kameraden stolz war.

Herr Perrier erwidert Ihre Grüsse aufs beste.

Heil Hitler !

Ihr ergebener

Otto Rahn

SS-Untersturmführer

RF. M. AR

Anlagen

[illegible] 15 Jun 1938

AR 4gilt

RF

12

Otto Rahn
SS-Unterscharführer

Ruggenbrunn
bei [illegible] / [illegible]

am 17. Juni 1936

An den
Reichsführer-SS und Chef der Deutschen Polizei
Heinrich Himmler
Prinz-Albrecht-Strasse 8
Berlin SW 11

Reichsführer!

Ich habe eine Lebensgefährtin gefunden.
Es ist mir eine Genugtuung, Ihnen die Versicherung geben zu können, dass ich auch in meiner Eigenschaft als SS-Führer auf die Frau meiner Wahl stolz sein darf.
Mit gleicher Post bitte ich den Chef des Persönlichen Stabes, SS-Gruppenführer Wolff, meiner Braut und mir Richtlinien bezüglich der von Ihnen angeordneten Formalitäten zu geben. – Meine siebenundzwanzigjährige Braut, Frau Asta Baeschlin geborene Halla, ist von Geburt Deutsche: ihr verstorbener Vater war Majoratsherr (auf Wojenthin bei Köslin) und deutscher Konsul in Genua; ihre Mutter ist eine geborene von Buengner. – Meine Braut, Mutter eines prächtigen blondhaarigen Sohnes von viereinhalb Jahren, war bislang mit einem Schweizer, ebenfalls aus bestem Hause, verheiratet, steht aber aus Gründen, die ich Ihnen auf Wunsch gern darlege, vor der (schuldlosen) Scheidung.
Ich bin mir bewusst, dass ich die Verlobung erst nach endgültiger Erledigung der Scheidungsklage, zu der ich keinen Anlass gegeben habe, und nach Erfüllung der von Ihnen, Reichsführer, vorgeschriebenen Formalitäten, die bei meiner Braut und bei mir keine Schwierigkeiten bieten, als vollzogen ansehen und bekanntgeben kann.

continued

Wenn irgend möglich, möchten meine Braut und ich an Weihnachten dieses Jahres verheiratet sein.
Meine Braut hat mich gebeten, Ihnen, Reichsführer, aufrichtig empfundene Grüsse zu vermitteln.

Heil Hitler!

Ihr sehr ergebener

Otto Rahn

SS-Untersturmführer

Rahn tells Himmler that he had found a female companion through life, 27 year old Frau Asta Baeschlin. She had a son four and a half years of age. She was divorced but the circumstances were not her fault.

13

RF/Pt.

, den 27. 6.1938

SS-Untersturmführer Rahn,
Muggenbrunn b.Todtnau /Schwzw.

Mein lieber R a h n !

Über Ihren Brief vom 17.6.1938 habe ich mich sehr gefreut.

Ich finde Ihren Entschluß, heiraten zu wollen, durchaus richtig und freue mich, daß Sie Ihre Lebensgefährtin gefunden haben. Wenn Sie einmal mit Ihrer Braut zusammen nach Berlin kommen, besuchen Sie mich doch beide.

Die Formalitäten zur Verlobung werden ja ziemlich rasch erledigt sein, sodaß von unserer Seite keinerlei Hindernisse bestehen und Sie im Laufe dieses Jahres heiraten können.

Ich würde mich sehr freuen, wenn Sie mir mitteilten, an welchem Problem bzw. Buch Sie jetzt gerade arbeiten. Schreiben Sie mir darüber doch gelegentlich.

H e i l   H i t l e r !

14

SS-Untersturmführer

Rahn, Otto

(SS-Nr. 276 208 - F.i.Pers.Stab RFSS)

SS-Obersturmführer

11.September 1938

gez.: H.Himmler

f.d.R.

SS-Gruppenführer

15

Otto R a h n
SS-Obersturmführer

Muggenbrunn/Schwarzwald

am 4. Dezember 1938

An
SS-Oberführer von A l v e n s l e b e n
Chefadjutant des Reichsführers-SS
Berlin SW 11

Tgb. Nr.: A/
v.A./Lo.

Oberführer !

Für Ihr so kameradschaftliches Schreiben vom 1. Dezember sage ich Ihnen vielen Dank !

Meine Heiratspläne, um die es in Ihrem Schreiben ja geht, sind nun einmal reichlich wirr geworden. In Anbetracht der Tatsache, dass meine Braut Schweizerin ist und in der Schweiz lebt (wir haben uns seit September nicht mehr gesehen), dass ich unerwarteterweise aktiven Dienst zu machen und obendrein unaufschiebbare Arbeiten (beispielsweise die im letzten Augenblick für Weihnachten gesicherte Neuauflage meines letzten Buches) zu erledigen hatte und noch zu erledigen habe, - das alles machte (abgesehen von den gesetzlichen Formalitäten, die ebenfalls ihre Zeit brauchen) ein "blitzartiges Heiraten", wie der Reichsführer-SS halb im Scherz und halb im Ernst sagte, leider nicht möglich. Hinzu kommt, dass meine Braut - lassen Sie mich, obgleich wir uns persönlich nicht kennen, ganz offen reden - entgegen dem Wunsche ihrer Eltern mich, der ich von der Hand in den Mund lebe, einem reichen Fürsten berühmten Namens vorgezogen hat und, um von den Eltern materiell unabhängig zu sein, in Zürich eine Anstellung als Buchhändlerin angenommen hat, dass sie also jetzt, vor Weihnachten, unabkömmlich ist. - Mit den Ersparnissen ihrer Tätigkeit möchte meine Braut, die zwar über ein im Schwarzwald gelegenes Landhaus und über sehr schönes Mobiliar aber vorläufig über keinerlei klingende Mitgift verfügt, mir, der ich alles andere als ein Krösus bin, bei den Kosten für die Hochzeit, für den Transport der Möbel nach Deutschland und für die Herrichtung ihres noch leerstehenden Landhauses behilflich sein. Ich selbst könnte das alles zur Zeit nicht allein bezahlen.

Im Anschluss an Ihren Brief habe ich heute mit meiner Braut telephoniert. Meine Braut wird über Weihnachten hierher kommen, damit wir alles besprechen können. Wollen Sie sich bitte mit einem endgültigen Bescheid bezüglich des neuen Hochzeitsdatums bis spätestens Anfang Januar gedulden, wollen Sie meine Braut und mich bei dem Reichsführer-SS in diesem Sinne entschuldigen und wollen Sie ihm für seine so aufrichtige Anteilnahme in unserem Namen herzlichst danken.

b.w.

16

An den
Reichsführer-SS
Chef des Persönlichen Stabes
Berlin SW 11
Prinz Albrecht Strasse 8

Gruppenführer!

Leider muss ich Sie bitten, bei dem Reichsführer-SS meine sofortige Entlassung aus der Schutzstaffel zu befürworten. Die Gründe, die mich zu diesem Entschluss und meine Bitte treiben, sind so schwerwiegender Natur, dass ich sie Ihnen nur mündlich darlegen kann. In diesem Sinne werde ich in diesen Tagen nach Berlin kommen und mich bei Ihnen melden.

Heil Hitler!

Otto Rahn

SS-Untersturmführer

17

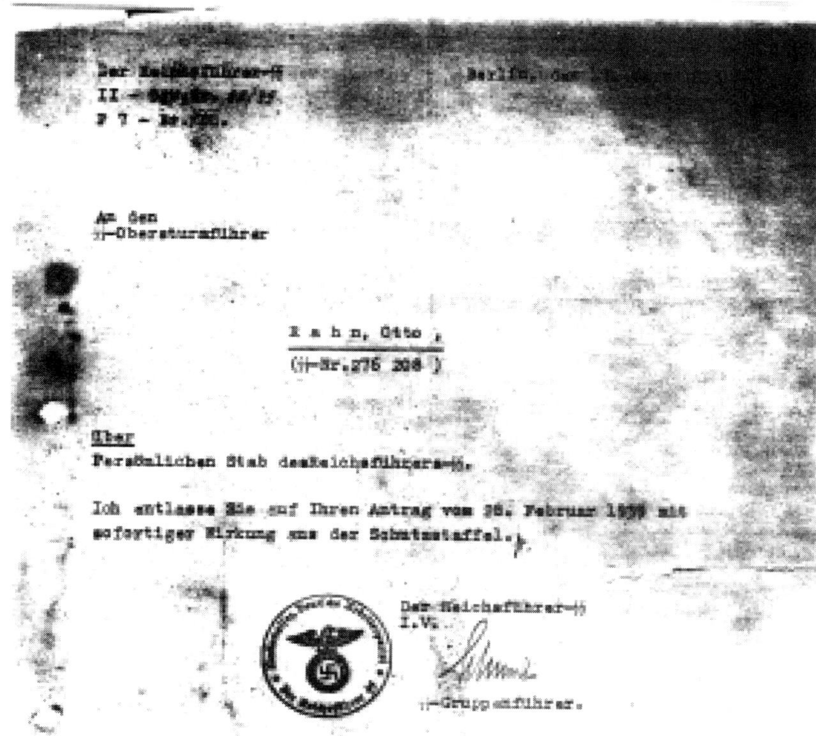

Der Reichsführer-SS
II – [illegible]
P 7 – Nr.[illegible].

Berlin, den [illegible]

An den
SS-Obersturmführer

R a h n, Otto,
(SS-Nr.276 208)

Über
Persönlichen Stab desReichsführers-SS.

Ich entlasse Sie auf Ihren Antrag vom 28. Februar 1939 mit sofortiger Wirkung aus der Schutzstaffel.

Der Reichsführer-SS
I.V.
SS-Gruppenführer.

BIBLIOGRAPHY

Aarons, Mark; Loftus, John, *Ratlines*, Heinemann, London, 1991
Angebert, Jean-Michel, *The Occult and the Third Reich*, Macmillan N.Y., 1971
Bach, Steve, *Marlene Dietrich: Life and Legend*, Harper Collins, 1993
Baring, Anne; Cashford, Jules, *The Myth of the Goddess*, BCA, 1991
Bernadac, Christian, *Le Mystère Otto Rahn*, France Empire, 1994
Brennan J. H., *The Occult Reich*, Signet, N.Y., 1974
Brissaud, André, *Canaris*, Grosset and Dunlop, N.Y., 1974
Buechner, Col. Howard, *Emerald Cup-Ark of Gold: the Quest of Lt. Col. Otto Rahn*, Thunderbird Press, 1991
Bulwer-Lytton, Sir Edward, *Vril: the Power of the Coming Race*, Kessinger Publishing LLC, USA (first published 1871)
Cathie, Bruce L., *The Energy Grid*, Adventures Unlimited Press, Illinois, 1990
Cathie, Bruce L., *The Harmonic Conquest of Space*, Adventures Unlimited Press, Illinois, 1998
Coogan, Kevin, *Dreamer of the Day*, Autonomedia, 1999
Cornwell, John, *Hitler's Pope*, Penguin, 1999
Dassanowsky-Harris, Robert, *The Real Indiana Jones*, Starlog Magazine, #152, March 1990
David-Neel, Alexandra, *Magic and Mystery in Tibet*, Abacus, 1977
Die Welt article, *The Double Rahn & the Holy Grail*, 12 May 1979
Dorland, Frank, *Holy Ice*, Glade Press Inc., USA, 1992
edited Cooke, Ivan, *The Return of Arthur Conan Doyle*, White Eagle, 1963
edited Keith, Jim, *Secret and Suppressed*, Feral House, 1993
edited Rosenthal, Bernice Glatzer, *The Occult in Russian and Soviet Culture*, Cornell University Press, 1997
Fauvre, Antoine, *The Golden Fleece and Alchemy*, State University N.Y. Press, 1993
Fitzgerald, Michael, *Storm Troopers of Satan*, Robert Hale, London, 1985
French, Peter J., *John Dee*, Routledge and Kegan Paul, London and Boston, 1972
Godwin, Joscelyn, *Arktos: the Polar Myth in Science, Symbolism and Nazi Survival*, Phanes Press, 1993
Goodrick-Clarke, Nicholas, *Hitler's Priestess*, N.Y. University Press, 1998
Goodrick-Clarke, Nicholas, *The Occult Roots of Nazism*, N.Y. University Press, 1985

Hall, Manly P., *The Secret Teachings of All Ages*, The Philosophical Research Society Inc, 1988

Haskin, Susan, *Mary Magdalene: Myth and Metaphor*, Harper Collins, 1993

Hastings, Max, *Das Reich*, Pan Books, 1981

Höhne, Heinz, *Canaris*, Secker and Warburg, 1979

Howard, Michael, *Occult Conspiracy*, Destiny Books, Vermont, 1989

Infield, Glenn B., *Skorzeny: Hitler's Commando*, Military Heritage Press, 1981

Jennings, Hargreave, *The Rosicrucians, their Rites and Mysteries*, Volumes 1 and 2, 3rd edition, John C. Nimmo, London, 1887

Jung, Emma; von Franz, Marie-Louise, *The Grail Legend,* Andrew Dyke's translation published 1971

Knight, Christopher; Lomas, Robert, *Uriel's Machine*, Arrow, 1999

Lamy, Michel, *Jules Verne, Initié et Initiateur*, Payot + Rivages, 1984

Lange, Hans-Jürgen, *Leben und Werk: Kreuzzug gegen den Gral / Luzifers Hofgesind*, Arun Verlag, 1995

Lange, Hans-Jürgen, *Otto Rahn und die Suche nach dem Gral*, Arun Verlag, 1999

Leasor, James, *Rudolf Hess: the Uninvited Envoy*, George Allen and Unwin Ltd, London, 1962

LePage, Victoria, *Shambhala*, Quest Books, 1996

McClelland, Alec, *The Lost World of Agarthi*, Souvenir Press, 1982

Moon, Peter, *The Black Sun*, Sky Books, 1997

Nicholls, Preston; Moon, Peter, *Montauk Project: Experiments in Time*, Sky Books, 1992

Nicholls, Preston; Moon, Peter *Montauk Revisited: Adventures in Synchronicity*, Sky Books, 1994

Nicholls, Preston; Moon, Peter *Montauk Project: Experiments in Consciousness*, Sky Books, 1995

Paris, Edmond, *The Secret History of the Jesuits*, Chick Publications, 1975

Patterson, William Patrick, *Voices in the Dark*, Arete, 2000

Pauwels, Louis; Bergier, Jacques, *The Dawn of Magic*, Anthony Gibb and Phillips, London, 1963

Pennick, Nigel, *Hitler's Secret Sciences*, Neville Spearman, 1981

Picknett, Lynn; Prince, Clive; Prior, Stephen, *Double Standards: the Rudolf Hess Cover Up*, Time Warner, 2001

Qualls-Corbett, Nancy, *The Sacred Prostitute*, Inner City Books, 1988

Rahn, Otto, *Kreuzzug gegen den Gral,* Urban Verlag Freiburg i/Breisgau, 1933

Rahn, Otto *Luzifers Hofgesind: Eine Reise zu den guten Gelstern Europas,* Schwarzhaupter Verlag, Leipzig, 1937
Ravenscroft, Trevor, *The Spear of Destiny*, Sphere Books Ltd, 1983
Ravenscroft, Trevor, *The Cup of Destiny*, Samuel Weiser, 1992
Reider, Frederic, *The Order of the S.S.*, Aztec Corporation Tucson, 1975
Rennes Observer
Research papers from the Berlin Bundesarchiv
Rux, Bruce, *Architects of the Underworld*, Frog Ltd, 1996
Sampietro, Luciano, *Nostradamus: the Final Prophecies*, Souvenir Press, 1999
Scholl, Inge, *The White Rose Munich 1942-1943*, Wesleyan University Press, 1970
Sebag-Montefiore, Hugh, *Enigma*, Phoenix, 2000
Shuster, Gerald, *Hitler and the Age of Horus*, Sphere Books, 1981
Sinclair, Andrew, *Discovery of the Grail*, Arrow, 1999
Sklar, Dee, *Nazis and the Occult*, Dorset Press, 1977
Tarrant, V.E., *The Red Orchestra*, Cassell plc, 1995
Thomas, Hugh, *The Unlikely Death of Heinrich Himmler*, Fourth Estate, London, 2002
Van Buren, Elizabeth, *Refuge of the Apocalypse: Doorway into Other Dimensions*, C. W. Daniel Co. Ltd., 1986
Von Lang, Jochen, *Top Nazi SS General Karl Wolff—the Man Between Himmler and Hitler*, Enigma Books, New York, 2005
Webb, James, *Occult Underground*, Open Court Publishing Co., 1974
Webb, James, *Occult Establishment*, Open Court Publishing Co., 1976
Wood, David, *Genisis: the First Book of Revelations*, Baton Press, 1985
Wood, David; Campbell, Ian, *Geneset: Target Earth*, Bellevue Books, 1994
Yates, Frances A., *The Rosicrucian Enlightenment*, Routledge and Kegan Paul, London and Boston, 1972

Get these fascinating books from your nearest bookstore or directly from: Adventures Unlimited Press

www.adventuresunlimitedpress.com

SECRETS OF THE MYSTERIOUS VALLEY

by Christopher O'Brien

No other region in North America features the variety and intensity of unusual phenomena found in the world's largest alpine valley, the San Luis Valley of Colorado and New Mexico. Since 1989, Christopher O'Brien has documented thousands of high-strange accounts that report UFOs, ghosts, crypto-creatures, cattle mutilations, skinwalkers and sorcerers, along with portal areas, secret underground bases and covert military activity. This mysterious region at the top of North America has a higher incidence of UFO reports than any other area of the continent and is the publicized birthplace of the "cattle mutilation" mystery. Hundreds of animals have been found strangely slain during waves of anomalous aerial craft sightings. Is the government directly involved? Are there underground bases here? Does the military fly exotic aerial craft in this valley that are radar-invisible below 18,000 feet? These and many other questions are addressed in this all-new, work by one of America's top paranormal investigators. Take a fantastic journey through one of the world's most enigmatic locales!

460 PAGES. 6X9 PAPERBACK. ILLUSTRATED. BIBLIOGRAPHY. $19.95. CODE: SOMV

LOST CITIES OF NORTH & CENTRAL AMERICA

by David Hatcher Childress

Down the back roads from coast to coast, maverick archaeologist and adventurer David Hatcher Childress goes deep into unknown America. With this incredible book, you will search for lost Mayan cities and books of gold, discover an ancient canal system in Arizona, climb gigantic pyramids in the Midwest, explore megalithic monuments in New England, and join the astonishing quest for lost cities throughout North America. From the war-torn jungles of Guatemala, Nicaragua and Honduras to the deserts, mountains and fields of Mexico, Canada, and the U.S.A., Childress takes the reader in search of sunken ruins, Viking forts, strange tunnel systems, living dinosaurs, early Chinese explorers, and fantastic lost treasure. Packed with both early and current maps, photos and illustrations.

590 PAGES. 6X9 PAPERBACK. ILLUSTRATED. FOOTNOTES. BIBLIOGRAPHY. INDEX. $16.95. CODE: NCA

LOST CITIES & ANCIENT MYSTERIES OF SOUTH AMERICA

by David Hatcher Childress

Rogue adventurer and maverick archaeologist David Hatcher Childress takes the reader on unforgettable journeys deep into deadly jungles, high up on windswept mountains and across scorching deserts in search of lost civilizations and ancient mysteries. Travel with David and explore stone cities high in mountain forests and hear fantastic tales of Inca treasure, living dinosaurs, and a mysterious tunnel system. Whether he is hopping freight trains, searching for secret cities, or just dealing with the daily problems of food, money, and romance, the author keeps the reader spellbound. Includes both early and current maps, photos, and illustrations, and plenty of advice for the explorer planning his or her own journey of discovery.

381 PAGES. 6X9 PAPERBACK. ILLUSTRATED. FOOTNOTES. BIBLIOGRAPHY. INDEX. $16.95. CODE: SAM

LOST CITIES & ANCIENT MYSTERIES OF AFRICA & ARABIA

by David Hatcher Childress

Childress continues his world-wide quest for lost cities and ancient mysteries. Join him as he discovers forbidden cities in the Empty Quarter of Arabia; "Atlantean" ruins in Egypt and the Kalahari desert; a mysterious, ancient empire in the Sahara; and more. This is the tale of an extraordinary life on the road: across war-torn countries, Childress searches for King Solomon's Mines, living dinosaurs, the Ark of the Covenant and the solutions to some of the fantastic mysteries of the past.

423 PAGES. 6x9 PAPERBACK. ILLUSTRATED. $14.95. CODE: AFA

LOST CITIES OF ATLANTIS, ANCIENT EUROPE & THE MEDITERRANEAN

by David Hatcher Childress

Childress takes the reader in search of sunken cities in the Mediterranean; across the Atlas Mountains in search of Atlantean ruins; to remote islands in search of megalithic ruins; to meet living legends and secret societies. From Ireland to Turkey, Morocco to Eastern Europe, and around the remote islands of the Mediterranean and Atlantic, Childress takes the reader on an astonishing quest for mankind's past. Ancient technology, cataclysms, megalithic construction, lost civilizations and devastating wars of the past are all explored in this book.

524 PAGES. 6x9 PAPERBACK. ILLUSTRATED. $16.95. CODE: MED

LOST CITIES OF CHINA, CENTRAL ASIA & INDIA

by David Hatcher Childress

Like a real life "Indiana Jones," maverick archaeologist David Childress takes the reader on an incredible adventure across some of the world's oldest and most remote countries in search of lost cities and ancient mysteries. Discover ancient cities in the Gobi Desert; hear fantastic tales of lost continents, vanished civilizations and secret societies bent on ruling the world; visit forgotten monasteries in forbidding snow-capped mountains with strange tunnels to mysterious subterranean cities! A unique combination of far-out exploration and practical travel advice, it will astound and delight the experienced traveler or the armchair voyager.

429 PAGES. 6x9 PAPERBACK. ILLUSTRATED. FOOTNOTES & BIBLIOGRAPHY. $14.95. CODE: CHI

LOST CITIES OF ANCIENT LEMURIA & THE PACIFIC

by David Hatcher Childress

Was there once a continent in the Pacific? Called Lemuria or Pacifica by geologists, Mu or Pan by the mystics, there is now ample mythological, geological and archaeological evidence to "prove" that an advanced and ancient civilization once lived in the central Pacific. Maverick archaeologist and explorer David Hatcher Childress combs the Indian Ocean, Australia and the Pacific in search of the surprising truth about mankind's past. Contains photos of the underwater city on Pohnpei; explanations on how the statues were levitated around Easter Island in a clockwise vortex movement; tales of disappearing islands; Egyptians in Australia; and more.

379 PAGES. 6x9 PAPERBACK. ILLUSTRATED. FOOTNOTES & BIBLIOGRAPHY. $14.95. CODE: LEM

A HITCHHIKER'S GUIDE TO ARMAGEDDON

by David Hatcher Childress

With wit and humor, popular Lost Cities author David Hatcher Childress takes us around the world and back in his trippy finalé to the Lost Cities series. He's off on an adventure in search of the apocalypse and end times. Childress hits the road from the fortress of Megiddo, the legendary citadel in northern Israel where Armageddon is prophesied to start. Hitchhiking around the world, Childress takes us from one adventure to another, to ancient cities in the deserts and the legends of worlds before our own. In the meantime, he becomes a cargo cult god on a remote island off New Guinea, gets dragged into the Kennedy Assassination by one of the "conspirators," investigates a strange power operating out of the Altai Mountains of Mongolia, and discovers how the Knights Templar and their off-shoots have driven the world toward an epic battle centered around Jerusalem and the Middle East.

320 Pages. 6x9 Paperback. Illustrated. Bibliography. Index. $16.95. code: HGA

TECHNOLOGY OF THE GODS

The Incredible Sciences of the Ancients

by David Hatcher Childress

Childress looks at the technology that was allegedly used in Atlantis and the theory that the Great Pyramid of Egypt was originally a gigantic power station. He examines tales of ancient flight and the technology that it involved; how the ancients used electricity; megalithic building techniques; the use of crystal lenses and the fire from the gods; evidence of various high tech weapons in the past, including atomic weapons; ancient metallurgy and heavy machinery; the role of modern inventors such as Nikola Tesla in bringing ancient technology back into modern use; impossible artifacts; and more.

356 Pages. 6x9 Paperback. Illustrated. Bibliography. $16.95. code: TGOD

VIMANA AIRCRAFT OF ANCIENT INDIA & ATLANTIS

by David Hatcher Childress, introduction by Ivan T. Sanderson

In this incredible volume on ancient India, authentic Indian texts such as the *Ramayana* and the *Mahabharata* are used to prove that ancient aircraft were in use more than four thousand years ago. Included in this book is the entire Fourth Century BC manuscript *Vimaanika Shastra* by the ancient author Maharishi Bharadwaaja. Also included are chapters on Atlantean technology, the incredible Rama Empire of India and the devastating wars that destroyed it.

334 Pages. 6x9 Paperback. Illustrated. $15.95. code: VAA

LOST CONTINENTS & THE HOLLOW EARTH

I Remember Lemuria and the Shaver Mystery

by David Hatcher Childress & Richard Shaver

Shaver's rare 1948 book *I Remember Lemuria* is reprinted in its entirety, and the book is packed with illustrations from Ray Palmer's *Amazing Stories* magazine of the 1940s. Palmer and Shaver told of tunnels running through the earth—tunnels inhabited by the Deros and Teros, humanoids from an ancient spacefaring race that had inhabited the earth, eventually going underground, hundreds of thousands of years ago. Childress discusses the famous hollow earth books and delves deep into whatever reality may be behind the stories of tunnels in the earth. Operation High Jump to Antarctica in 1947 and Admiral Byrd's bizarre statements, tunnel systems in South America and Tibet, the underground world of Agartha, the belief of UFOs coming from the South Pole, more.

344 Pages. 6x9 Paperback. Illustrated. $16.95. code: LCHE

ATLANTIS & THE POWER SYSTEM OF THE GODS

Mercury Vortex Generators & the Power System of Atlantis

by David Hatcher Childress and Bill Clendenon

Childress' fascinating analysis of Nikola Tesla's broadcast system in light of Edgar Cayce's "Terrible Crystal" and the obelisks of ancient Egypt and Ethiopia. Includes: Atlantis and its crystal power towers that broadcast energy; how these incredible power stations may still exist today; inventor Nikola Tesla's nearly identical system of power transmission; Mercury Proton Gyros and mercury vortex propulsion; more. Richly illustrated, and packed with evidence that Atlantis not only existed—it had a world-wide energy system more sophisticated than ours today.

246 PAGES. 6x9 PAPERBACK. ILLUSTRATED. $15.95. CODE: APSG

THE ANTI-GRAVITY HANDBOOK

edited by David Hatcher Childress, with Nikola Tesla, T.B. Paulicki, Bruce Cathie, Albert Einstein and others

The new expanded compilation of material on Anti-Gravity, Free Energy, Flying Saucer Propulsion, UFOs, Suppressed Technology, NASA Cover-ups and more. Highly illustrated with patents, technical illustrations and photos. This revised and expanded edition has more material, including photos of Area 51, Nevada, the government's secret testing facility. This classic on weird science is back in a new format!

230 PAGES. 7x10 PAPERBACK. ILLUSTRATED. $16.95. CODE: AGH

ANTI–GRAVITY & THE WORLD GRID

Is the earth surrounded by an intricate electromagnetic grid network offering free energy? This compilation of material on ley lines and world power points contains chapters on the geography, mathematics, and light harmonics of the earth grid. Learn the purpose of ley lines and ancient megalithic structures located on the grid. Discover how the grid made the Philadelphia Experiment possible. Explore the Coral Castle and many other mysteries, including acoustic levitation, Tesla Shields and scalar wave weaponry. Browse through the section on anti-gravity patents, and research resources.

274 PAGES. 7x10 PAPERBACK. ILLUSTRATED. $14.95. CODE: AGW

ANTI–GRAVITY & THE UNIFIED FIELD

edited by David Hatcher Childress

Is Einstein's Unified Field Theory the answer to all of our energy problems? Explored in this compilation of material is how gravity, electricity and magnetism manifest from a unified field around us. Why artificial gravity is possible; secrets of UFO propulsion; free energy; Nikola Tesla and anti-gravity airships of the 20s and 30s; flying saucers as superconducting whirls of plasma; anti-mass generators; vortex propulsion; suppressed technology; government cover-ups; gravitational pulse drive; spacecraft & more.

240 PAGES. 7x10 PAPERBACK. ILLUSTRATED. $14.95. CODE: AGU

MAPS OF THE ANCIENT SEA KINGS
Evidence of Advanced Civilization in the Ice Age
by Charles H. Hapgood

Charles Hapgood has found the evidence in the Piri Reis Map that shows Antarctica, the Hadji Ahmed map, the Oronteus Finaeus and other amazing maps. Hapgood concluded that these maps were made from more ancient maps from the various ancient archives around the world, now lost. Not only were these unknown people more advanced in mapmaking than any people prior to the 18th century, it appears they mapped all the continents. The Americas were mapped thousands of years before Columbus. Antarctica was mapped when its coasts were free of ice!

316 PAGES. 7X10 PAPERBACK. ILLUSTRATED. BIBLIOGRAPHY & INDEX. $19.95. CODE: MASK

PATH OF THE POLE
Cataclysmic Pole Shift Geology
by Charles H. Hapgood

Maps of the Ancient Sea Kings author Hapgood's classic book *Path of the Pole* is back in print! Hapgood researched Antarctica, ancient maps and the geological record to conclude that the Earth's crust has slipped on the inner core many times in the past, changing the position of the pole. *Path of the Pole* discusses the various "pole shifts" in Earth's past, giving evidence for each one, and moves on to possible future pole shifts.

356 PAGES. 6X9 PAPERBACK. ILLUSTRATED. $16.95. CODE: POP

SUNS OF GOD
Krishna, Buddha and Christ Unveiled
by Acharya S

Over the past several centuries, the Big Three spiritual leaders have been the Lords Christ, Krishna and Buddha, whose stories and teachings are so remarkably similar as to confound and amaze those who encounter them. As classically educated archaeologist, historian, mythologist and linguist Acharya S thoroughly reveals, these striking parallels exist not because these godmen were "historical" personages who "walked the earth" but because they are personifications of the central focus of the famous and scandalous "mysteries." These mysteries date back thousands of years and are found globally, reflecting an ancient tradition steeped in awe and intrigue. In unveiling the reasons for this highly significant development, the author presents an in-depth analysis that includes fascinating and original research based on evidence both modern and ancient—captivating information kept secret and hidden for ages.

428 PAGES. 6X9 PAPERBACK. ILLUSTRATED. BIBLIOGRAPHY. INDEX. $18.95. CODE: SUNG

THE LAND OF OSIRIS
An Introduction to Khemitology
by Stephen S. Mehler

Was there an advanced prehistoric civilization in ancient Egypt who built the great pyramids and carved the Great Sphinx? Did the pyramids serve as energy devices and not as tombs for kings? Mehler has uncovered an indigenous oral tradition that still exists in Egypt, and has been fortunate to have studied with a living master of this tradition, Abd'El Hakim Awyan. Mehler has also been given permission to present these teachings to the Western world, teachings that unfold a whole new understanding of ancient Egypt . Chapters include: Egyptology and Its Paradigms; Asgat Nefer—The Harmony of Water; Khemit and the Myth of Atlantis; The Extraterrestrial Question; more.

272 PAGES. 6X9 PAPERBACK. ILLUSTRATED. COLOR SECTION. BIBLIOGRAPHY. $18.00 CODE: LOOS

SECRETS OF THE HOLY LANCE

The Spear of Destiny in History & Legend

by Jerry E. Smith

Secrets of the Holy Lance traces the Spear from its possession by Constantine, Rome's first Christian Caesar, to Charlemagne's claim that with it he ruled the Holy Roman Empire by Divine Right, and on through two thousand years of kings and emperors, until it came within Hitler's grasp—and beyond! Did it rest for a while in Antarctic ice? Is it now hidden in Europe, awaiting the next person to claim its awesome power? Neither debunking nor worshiping, *Secrets of the Holy Lance* seeks to pierce the veil of myth and mystery around the Spear. Mere belief that it was infused with magic by virtue of its shedding the Savior's blood has made men kings. But what if it's more? What are "the powers it serves"?

312 pages. 6x9 paperback. Illustrated. Bibliography. $16.95. Code: SOHL

REICH OF THE BLACK SUN

Nazi Secret Weapons & the Cold War Allied Legend

by Joseph P. Farrell

Why were the Allies worried about an atom bomb attack by the Germans in 1944? Why did the Soviets threaten to use poison gas against the Germans? Why did Hitler in 1945 insist that holding Prague could win the war for the Third Reich? Why did US General George Patton's Third Army race for the Skoda works at Pilsen in Czechoslovakia instead of Berlin? Why did the US Army not test the uranium atom bomb it dropped on Hiroshima? Why did the Luftwaffe fly a non-stop round trip mission to within twenty miles of New York City in 1944? *Reich of the Black Sun* takes the reader on a scientific-historical journey in order to answer these questions. Arguing that Nazi Germany actually won the race for the atom bomb in late 1944,

352 pages. 6x9 paperback. Illustrated. Bibliography. $16.95. Code: ROBS

EDEN IN EGYPT

by Ralph Ellis

The story of Adam and Eve from the Book of Genesis is perhaps one of the best-known stories in circulation, even today, and yet nobody really knows where this tale came from or what it means. But even a cursory glance at the text will demonstrate the origins of this tale, for the river of Eden is described as having four branches. There is only one river in this part of the world that fits this description, and that is the Nile, with the four branches forming the Nile Delta. According to Ellis, Judaism was based upon the reign of the pharaoh Akhenaton, because the solitary Judaic god was known as Adhon while this pharaoh's solitary god was called Aton or Adjon. But what of the identities of Adam and Eve? Includes 16 page color section.

320 pages. 6x9 Paperback. Illustrated. Bibliography. Index. $20.00. Code: EIE

GUARDIANS OF THE HOLY GRAIL

by Mark Amaru Pinkham

This book presents this extremely ancient Holy Grail lineage from Asia and how the Knights Templar were initiated into it. It also reveals how the ancient Asian wisdom regarding the Holy Grail became the foundation for the Holy Grail legends of the west while also serving as the bedrock of the European Secret Societies, which included the Freemasons, Rosicrucians, and the Illuminati. Also: The Fisher Kings; The Middle Eastern mystery schools, such as the Assassins and Yezidhi; The ancient Holy Grail lineage from Sri Lanka and the Templar Knights' initiation into it; The head of John the Baptist and its importance to the Templars; The secret Templar initiation with grotesque Baphomet, the infamous Head of Wisdom; more.

248 pages. 6x9 Paperback. Illustrated. $16.95. Code: GOHG

THE FANTASTIC INVENTIONS OF NIKOLA TESLA

by Nikola Tesla with additional material by David Hatcher Childress

This book is a readable compendium of patents, diagrams, photos and explanations of the many incredible inventions of the originator of the modern era of electrification. In Tesla's own words are such topics as wireless transmission of power, death rays, and radio-controlled airships. In addition, rare material on a secret city built at a remote jungle site in South America by one of Tesla's students, Guglielmo Marconi. Marconi's secret group claims to have built flying saucers in the 1940s and to have gone to Mars in the early 1950s! Incredible photos of these Tesla craft are included. •His plan to transmit free electricity into the atmosphere. •How electrical devices would work using only small antennas. •Why unlimited power could be utilized anywhere on earth. •How radio and radar technology can be used as death-ray weapons in Star Wars.

342 PAGES. 6X9 PAPERBACK. ILLUSTRATED. $16.95. CODE: FINT

THE TESLA PAPERS

Nikola Tesla on Free Energy & Wireless Transmission of Power

by Nikola Tesla, edited by David Hatcher Childress

David Hatcher Childress takes us into the incredible world of Nikola Tesla and his amazing inventions. Tesla's fantastic vision of the future, including wireless power, anti-gravity, free energy and highly advanced solar power. Also included are some of the papers, patents and material collected on Tesla at the Colorado Springs Tesla Symposiums, including papers on: •The Secret History of Wireless Transmission •Tesla and the Magnifying Transmitter •Design and Construction of a Half-Wave Tesla Coil •Electrostatics: A Key to Free Energy •Progress in Zero-Point Energy Research •Electromagnetic Energy from Antennas to Atoms •Tesla's Particle Beam Technology •Fundamental Excitatory Modes of the Earth-Ionosphere Cavity

325 PAGES. 8X10 PAPERBACK. ILLUSTRATED. $16.95. CODE: TTP

LEY LINE & EARTH ENERGIES

An Extraordinary Journey into the Earth's Natural Energy System

by David Cowan & Chris Arnold

The mysterious standing stones, burial grounds and stone circles that lace Europe, the British Isles and other areas have intrigued scientists, writers, artists and travellers through the centuries. How do ley lines work? How did our ancestors use Earth energy to map their sacred sites and burial grounds? How do ghosts and poltergeists interact with Earth energy? How can Earth spirals and black spots affect our health? This exploration shows how natural forces affect our behavior, how they can be used to enhance our health and well being. A fascinating and visual book about subtle Earth energies and how they affect us and the world around them.

368 PAGES. 6X9 PAPERBACK. ILLUSTRATED. BIBLIOGRAPHY. INDEX. $18.95. CODE: LLEE

THE ORION PROPHECY

Egyptian and Mayan Prophecies on the Cataclysm of 2012

by Patrick Geryl and Gino Ratinckx

In the year 2012 the Earth awaits a super catastrophe: its magnetic field will reverse in one go. Phenomenal earthquakes and tidal waves will completely destroy our civilization. These dire predictions stem from the Mayans and Egyptians—descendants of the legendary Atlantis. The Atlanteans were able to exactly predict the previous world-wide flood in 9792 BC. They built tens of thousands of boats and escaped to South America and Egypt. In the year 2012 Venus, Orion and several others stars will take the same 'code-positions' as in 9792 BC!

324 PAGES. 6X9 PAPERBACK. ILLUSTRATED. $16.95. CODE: ORP

TAPPING THE ZERO POINT ENERGY

Free Energy & Anti-Gravity in Today's Physics

by Moray B. King

King explains how free energy and anti-gravity are possible. The theories of the zero point energy maintain there are tremendous fluctuations of electrical field energy imbedded within the fabric of space. This book tells how, in the 1930s, inventor T. Henry Moray could produce a fifty kilowatt "free energy" machine; how an electrified plasma vortex creates anti-gravity; how the Pons/Fleischmann "cold fusion" experiment could produce tremendous heat without fusion; and how certain experiments might produce a gravitational anomaly.

180 PAGES. 5x8 PAPERBACK. ILLUSTRATED. $12.95. CODE: TAP

QUEST FOR ZERO-POINT ENERGY

Engineering Principles for "Free Energy"

by Moray B. King

King expands, with diagrams, on how free energy and anti-gravity are possible. The theories of zero point energy maintain there are tremendous fluctuations of electrical field energy embedded within the fabric of space. King explains the following topics: Tapping the Zero-Point Energy as an Energy Source; Fundamentals of a Zero-Point Energy Technology; Vacuum Energy Vortices; The Super Tube; Charge Clusters: The Basis of Zero-Point Energy Inventions; Vortex Filaments, Torsion Fields and the Zero-Point Energy; Transforming the Planet with a Zero-Point Energy Experiment; Dual Vortex Forms: The Key to a Large Zero-Point Energy Coherence. Packed with diagrams, patents and photos. With power shortages now a daily reality in many parts of the world, this book offers a fresh approach very rarely mentioned in the mainstream media.

224 PAGES. 6x9 PAPERBACK. ILLUSTRATED. $14.95. CODE: QZPE

THE ENERGY GRID

Harmonic 695, The Pulse of the Universe

by Captain Bruce Cathie.

This is the breakthrough book that explores the incredible potential of the Energy Grid and the Earth's Unified Field all around us. Cathie's first book, *Harmonic 33*, was published in 1968 when he was a commercial pilot in New Zealand. Since then, Captain Bruce Cathie has been the premier investigator into the amazing potential of the infinite energy that surrounds our planet every microsecond. Cathie investigates the Harmonics of Light and how the Energy Grid is created. In this amazing book are chapters on UFO Propulsion, Nikola Tesla, Unified Equations, the Mysterious Aerials, Pythagoras & the Grid, Nuclear Detonation and the Grid, Maps of the Ancients, an Australian Stonehenge examined, more.

255 PAGES. 6x9 TRADEPAPER. ILLUSTRATED. $15.95. CODE: TEG

THE BRIDGE TO INFINITY

Harmonic 371244

by Captain Bruce Cathie

Cathie has popularized the concept that the earth is crisscrossed by an electromagnetic grid system that can be used for anti-gravity, free energy, levitation and more. The book includes a new analysis of the harmonic nature of reality, acoustic levitation, pyramid power, harmonic receiver towers and UFO propulsion. It concludes that today's scientists have at their command a fantastic store of knowledge with which to advance the welfare of the human race.

204 PAGES. 6x9 TRADEPAPER. ILLUSTRATED. $14.95. CODE: BTF

ORDER FORM

10% Discount When You Order 3 or More Items!

One Adventure Place
P.O. Box 74
Kempton, Illinois 60946
United States of America
Tel.: 815-253-6390 • Fax: 815-253-6300
Email: auphq@frontiernet.net
http://www.adventuresunlimitedpress.com

ORDERING INSTRUCTIONS

- ✓ Remit by USD$ Check, Money Order or Credit Card
- ✓ Visa, Master Card, Discover & AmEx Accepted
- ✓ Paypal Payments Can Be Made To: info@wexclub.com
- ✓ Prices May Change Without Notice
- ✓ 10% Discount for 3 or more Items

SHIPPING CHARGES

United States

- ✓ Postal Book Rate { $4.00 First Item / 50¢ Each Additional Item
- ✓ POSTAL BOOK RATE Cannot Be Tracked!
- ✓ Priority Mail { $5.00 First Item / $2.00 Each Additional Item
- ✓ UPS { $6.00 First Item / $1.50 Each Additional Item

NOTE: UPS Delivery Available to Mainland USA Only

Canada

- ✓ Postal Air Mail { $10.00 First Item / $2.50 Each Additional Item
- ✓ Personal Checks or Bank Drafts MUST BE US$ and Drawn on a US Bank
- ✓ Canadian Postal Money Orders OK
- ✓ Payment MUST BE US$

All Other Countries

- ✓ Sorry, No Surface Delivery!
- ✓ Postal Air Mail { $16.00 First Item / $6.00 Each Additional Item
- ✓ Checks and Money Orders MUST BE US$ and Drawn on a US Bank or branch.
- ✓ Paypal Payments Can Be Made in US$ To: info@wexclub.com

SPECIAL NOTES

- ✓ RETAILERS: Standard Discounts Available
- ✓ BACKORDERS: We Backorder all Out-of-Stock Items Unless Otherwise Requested
- ✓ PRO FORMA INVOICES: Available on Request

ORDER ONLINE AT: www.adventuresunlimitedpress.com

Please check: ☑

☐ This is my first order ☐ I have ordered before

Name

Address

City

State/Province | Postal Code

Country

Phone day | Evening

Fax | Email

Item Code	Item Description	Qty	Total

Please check: ☑

Subtotal ▶

Less Discount-10% for 3 or more items ▶

☐ Postal-Surface — Balance ▶

☐ Postal-Air Mail (Priority in USA) — Illinois Residents 6.25% Sales Tax ▶

Previous Credit ▶

☐ UPS (Mainland USA only) — Shipping ▶

Total (check/MO in USD$ only) ▶

☐ Visa/MasterCard/Discover/American Express

Card Number

Expiration Date

10% Discount When You Order 3 or More Items!